THE DICTIONARY OF BELIEFS

Richard Kennedy

THE
DICTIONARY
OF
BELIEFS

An illustrated guide to world religions and beliefs

WLE Ward Lock Educational

The appendices and some of the text entries have
been compiled by MARGARET HICKEY.
The line illustrations are by FIONA FORDYCE.

This book was designed and produced
by BLA Publishing Limited, Swan Court,
London Road, East Grinstead, Sussex, England

A member of the **Ling Kee Group**
LONDON · HONG KONG· TAIPEI· SINGAPORE· NEW YORK

British Library Cataloguing in Publication Data

Kennedy, Richard, 1984
    The dictionary of beliefs.
    1. Religion—Dictionaries   2.Ideology—
    Dictionaries
    I. Title
    306   BL31

ISBN 0-7062-4291-2

Colour origination by PLANWAY, London
Photoset by PRIMA GRAPHICS, Camberley, Surrey, England
Printed and bound in Italy by ARTI GRAFICHE V. BONA, Turin.

Contents

Acknowledgements

Picture credits

WE SHOULD LIKE TO THANK the following for their valuable assistance: Simon Blacker, Peter Cooke, Simon Jollands, Fatime Kasharvaz and the Reverend Martyn L. Hughes.

The following individuals and organizations were most helpful and we are grateful for their courtesy and co-operation:

Dr Hugh Baker, Miss H. J. Ballhatchet, The Buddhist Society, Christian Science Committees on Publication, The Council for Christians and Jews, Heraclio Fournier, The Hare Krishna Centre, The India Tourist Office, The Israel Government Tourist Office, The Japan Information Centre, The Japan National Tourist Organisation, Duncan MacPherson, The National Trust, Professor P. G. O'Neill, The Salvation Army Information Services, The United Africa Company, Francis Wacziarg & Aman Nath and The Watchtower Bible and Tract Society of Pennsylvania.

Note to the reader

WHEN THE GREAT 'Is God Dead?' debate was conducted in the 1960s, predictions were made that the world was moving towards a new godless era. It was felt that human beings would gradually shed the religious beliefs that had served their purpose in less sophisticated times: they were now no longer necessary. The reasons why many thinkers had come to these conclusions are numerous and varied. Some felt that our increasing scientific and technological knowledge had helped us to an understanding of the workings of the universe that was growing daily more comprehensive and that it was only a matter of time before we held the key to all the mysteries of existence. Others saw our need to believe in some power greater than ourselves as evidence of a psychological insecurity. Yet others felt that religion could be used as a valuable aid in promoting the highest and best human behaviour, but that it was a means towards a humanist end.

There were divers other angles of attack, but a considerable consensus of informed opinion seemed to favour the argument that the world was slowly outgrowing its childish and superstitious beliefs. This book does not set out to refute these ideas; its purpose is quite straightforward – it aims to inform – but the reader may be impressed by the vigour and the strength of the practice of religions worldwide, and, indeed, the resurgence of interest in religion that we are witnessing today.

The dictionary does not deal with religious belief only; there are entries on the major political doctrines and the most influential schools of philosophy, together with a small number of entries centred on beliefs relating to one's life-style.

Although it is not solely centred on religion, this work does concern itself principally with the religions of the world, both major and minor, and the elements which constitute them. The dogmas and doctrines of the different faiths and their organization and hierarchies are outlined briefly, the lives of the great leaders and founders of religions are recorded, and the nature of worship in individual faiths is explained. There are entries which inform the reader of the people involved in a religion, both the priests, ministers, monks and nuns as well as the mass of the faithful, and entries on the ceremonies and rituals performed by them. The book sets out to give as much essential information as possible in concise form.

It would be helpful at this stage to explain how to get the most from this book. Generally speaking, the dictionary format means that looking for information is simple: where something or someone is known by two different names, as, for example, the Jewish Feast of Weeks, known also as Shavouth, the main entry will be printed under the name which has wider currency, and the other name will be followed by an indication that the reader should refer to the main entry, thus, **Shavouth** *See:* **Weeks, Feast of**.

The words COMMON ERA, written as CE, and BEFORE COMMON ERA, BCE, have been chosen for use when a date is given, since this is generally considered acceptable to those for whom BC and AD have no religious significance. It should be recognised that very many people have a calendar and a system of dating which are not compatible with that based on the Gregorian calendar.

Where reference is made, in an entry, to something which is treated elsewhere in the book, and which may shed further light on the subject, it is printed in italics, to indicate that the reader should note the cross-reference. In addition, where it is felt that information on the subject could be amplified by reference to related entries, attention is drawn to these by the words: *See*, or *See also:*.

Where a word may be spelled in more than one way, for example, Hasidim or Chasidim, that which is more acceptable to members of the religion with which it is associated has been chosen to carry the entry, but the alternate spelling is listed, with a cross-reference to guide the reader. Where possible, variants arising from matters such as disputed spelling or pronunciation have been included.

It should be noted that, in the interests of conciseness, the entries referring to Jews do not, on the whole, distinguish between Orthodox, Reform, Conservative and Liberal and Progressive movements within Judaism. The reader will note that in certain respects there are significant differences between these groups.

At the end of the dictionary there is a section containing a number of appendices. These have been included to expand on the information already given and to introduce material which falls outside the scope of the dictionary *per se*.

The first section of the book deals with the more widespread living beliefs, but from a historical, anthropological and mythological point of view it has been thought proper to give at least an outline of gods, goddesses and worship of bygone ages, as well as an indication of beliefs held by millions of people living in rural and tribal societies.

Among the appendices is a calendar of the more important religious festivals and a map which charts the geographic distribution of the major faiths, together with a statistical analysis of their importance in demographic terms. Another valuable section contains chronological tables which give the reader a more panoramic view of the development of the different faiths. It becomes evident that certain periods of history witnessed a flaring-up of intense religious activity and the charts make it easy to compare the progress of events in one continent with those in another. It is fascinating to observe that Confucius, Mahavira, the founder of Jainism, and the Buddha, Siddhartha Gautama, were all contemporaries.

The appendices contain much more than is touched upon here, and they are explained more fully at the beginning of that section of the book. It is hoped that they, together with the dictionary itself, will be a valuable and fascinating source of reference to the reader. The subject is so vast and so complex, no claims are made to have dealt with any issue with the fullness it merits – rather, the reader should look to this book for knowledge but also for stimulation to research further.

It is a book designed to impart the maximum amount of information, presented dispassionately, in the most attractive way possible. The illustrations so lavishly used have each been chosen to complement the text – they add something to our knowledge and appreciation and reflect the diversity, colour and vitality of the different beliefs of the world.

a

Aaron A major figure in the *Torah*, or *Old Testament*, and Moses's brother. He was appointed head of a hereditary line of priests who established the *rituals* of Hebrew worship. In later years, only those men who could trace their descendants back to Aaron were regarded as legitimate priests.

abba An Aramaic word meaning 'father'. It is used three times in the *New Testament* in referring to God, notably by Jesus in prayer. More recently it has become the title for bishops of the *Coptic Church* and priests of the *Ethiopian Orthodox Church*.

abbess The spiritual and temporal head of a female religious house.

abbey A Christian monastery or convent, guided by an abbot or abbess, and often the church attached to a religious community.

Abraham was a prophet honoured by Jews, Christians and Muslims alike. The story of his readiness to sacrifice even his own son, if God so willed it, is to be found in the Torah, and in the Qur'an. The angel Gabriel appears just at the moment of sacrifice and offers a ram as a substitute.

abbot A title given to the superior in a monastery, or community, of monks in Buddhism, Taoism and Christianity. (The abbess is the female equivalent in a convent, or community, of nuns.) The abbot is the spiritual and administrative head within the monastery.

Abhidhamma (Pitaka) The third book of the Pali Canon of *Theravada* Buddhism. Also known as the Abhidarma (Pitaka). Its title means Higher Doctrine. Most teachings which originate from the Buddha himself are fairly short: the Buddha simply responded to problems, questions and situations as they arose. The Abhidhamma puts all this material in order and arranges these teachings systematically. It also examines and explains them with precise philosophical terms and ways of thinking.

Abraham One of the founding fathers, or patriarchs, of the Jewish, Christian and Muslim faiths. His life is recounted in the Book of Genesis and in various surahs of the Qur'an, and demonstrates the triumph of unquestioning faith in God. Abraham was even ready to sacrifice his son Isaac, or, in the Qur'an, Isma'il when God commanded that as a test of his loyalty. God's first *covenant* with the Hebrews was made with Abraham, who is said to have begun the custom of *circumcision*.

absolute When used as an adjective, it means that the thing or concept it describes is not caused by anything outside itself, but is the ultimate non-material basis from which all actual examples of the concept are derived. For example, 'absolute knowledge' is the sum total and basis of all examples of knowledge which a human being may have in his mind; absolute beauty is the cause and foundation of any particular examples of beauty in the world; 'absolute spirit or mind' is the sum total and basis of all spiritual and mental existence, from which all spiritual and mental existence derives. Absolute spirit or absolute being is the ultimate non-material basis of all existence whatever, especially of the highest form, that of spirit.

absolution The forgiveness of sins. Certain Christian denominations believe that if penitents confess, repent, and show a desire to reform in the future, then priests may grant them absolution in God's name.

absolutism A form of government in which one ruler has unlimited power over those he governs; a form of dictatorship.

Abu Bakr Traditionally believed to be one of the first converts to Islam. Abu Bakr was elected *caliph*, or deputy, in CE632 on Muhammad's death and spent the next two years trying to hold together the different groups within the converts to Islam. Tradition has it that, while caliph, he encouraged certain of the Sahabah, 'friends, attendants', of the prophet to commit his teachings to memory, and these people became known as Quarra's. At a later date the words were written down and now constitute the Qur'an.

abuna Head of the *Ethiopian Orthodox Church.*

Acts of the Apostles, The The fifth book of the New Testament, describing the history of the Christian Church from the *Ascension* of Christ into heaven until St Paul's final journey to Rome. It is a continuation of the Gospel according to St Luke and is attributed to the same author.

Adam According to the Qur'an, and the Book of Genesis, Adam was the first man God created; he was banished from the Garden of Eden, or *paradise*, for disobeying God. In Hebrew, the word 'adam' means 'man'.

Adamite A name given to several Christian *sects* who prayed and worshipped unclothed in order to remind themselves of the original innocence of Adam. The earliest known group of Adamites lived in the second century in Africa, and the movement also existed in twelfth-century Flanders. A third group, known as the Picards, was exterminated by the Hussites in 1421.

adhan The daily Muslim call to prayer: at dawn, midday, mid-afternoon, sunset, and after the fall of darkness. *See also*: **azan**.

Adi-Buddha 'First Buddha'. A term, used mainly in Nepal, which refers to the primordial source of all beings.

Adi-Buddhism A theistic form of Buddhism found in Nepal.

Adi Granth The sacred book of Sikhism compiled in the sixteenth century by Guru *Arjan* and placed in the Harmandir, or *Golden Temple*, at Amritsar. The word means 'First Granth' and distinguishes it from the 'Dasam Granth' of

Within the splendid Harmandir, or Golden Temple, at Amritsar in the Punjab, is to be found the sacred book of Sikhism, the Adi Granth. Also known as the Guru Granth Sahib, it is the sole authority for all Sikhs, for whom it is the very word of God.

Guru *Gobind Singh*, a collection of works of the *gurus* who came after Arjan. The book is seen as containing the same Divine Spirit which inspired Guru *Nanak*, the founder of the religion, and serves as a spiritual focus for the Sikh community. It is central to all Sikh rituals from birth to death. The line of human gurus, ending in Guru Gobind Singh, has been replaced by the Adi Granth and thus, since the death of Guru Gobind Singh, it is also known as the *Guru Granth Sahib*. Sikhs believe that wherever a congregation gathers to consult the teachings of the book, it provides the spiritual guidance they are seeking.

Adonai 'The Lord'. The word used by Jews in reading the *Torah*, whenever the letters YHWH occur. *See*: **Jehovah**.

advaita Hindu doctrine preached by *Shankara*, one of the three great interpreters of the *Vedanta*, which says that all reality is divine. Life and what we think of as 'the real world' are said to be merely an illusion, and only the '*Brahman atman*' reality is permanent and unchanging.

Advent Advent begins the Christian Church's year and lasts for four weeks until *Christmas*. It is a time when Christians celebrate the birth of Christ and prepare for his *Second Coming*.

Adventist A member of a Christian denomination which believes that the *Day of Judgement* is approaching. The Second Adventists prophesy exact dates for Christ's descent to earth, while the *Seventh-Day Adventists* do not.

aestheticism An attitude to life and art which places the search for beauty above all other considerations. The term was used especially in the latter half of the nineteenth century by the Pre-Raphaelites.

African Methodist Episcopal Church A missionary, black, Protestant church, which spread from its home base in the United States to the Caribbean during the last century. It had already established itself in Haiti by 1823, and later it spread to Guyana and Jamaica.

African Reform Coptic Church Set up by the Reverend Claudius Henry in Jamaica, as a centre for the Rastafarian religion.

afterlife Any form of conscious existence after the death of the physical body.

Aga Khan A hereditary title given to the leader of the *Ismailis*, a *Shi'ite* sect within Islam, numbering some quarter of a million followers at present. The Aga Khan is supposed by the faithful to be a descendant of *Ali* and therefore is the *Imam*.

agape A 'love feast' or communal evening meal of thanksgiving and fellowship which was held by the early Christians along with the *Eucharist*. Some Christian churches, such as the *Moravians*, still hold a similar meal, and other Christian groups have revived it recently.

Agni A Hindu deity of Aryan origins. He is the god of fire and it is through him that sacrificial offerings are made.

The sculpted figure of Agni, the Hindu god of fire, who personifies both its destructive aspects and the warmth and comfort it can offer mankind.

agnosticism Thomas Huxley first used the word 'agnostic' in 1869 to describe a person who believes that anything which cannot be proved scientifically is unknowable; the word literally means 'someone who does not know'. An agnostic is someone who does not know whether God exists or not, because there is not enough evidence to say for certain. He is unwilling to base his belief on faith alone. *See also*: **materialism, existentialism.**

Agnus Dei Agnus Dei means *Lamb of God*; symbolic title given to Christ by John the Baptist in the Book of Revelation of the *New Testament*.

ahimsa Non-violence. The doctrine is common to Jainism, Buddhism, and some Hindu sects; it includes refusing to harm any living creature. Killing animals for food is seen as violence and thus practitioners of ahimsa are vegetarians. Mahatma *Gandhi*, the Hindu leader, applied the doctrine to politics; he believed that peaceful non-cooperation was the only way in which India should struggle for independence from Britain. In Buddhism, ahimsa is an expression of unconditional love for other living beings.

Ahmadiyya A late nineteenth-century Islamic revivalist movement, led by Mizra Ghulam Ahmad, whose major book is called *Barahin-i*. Ahmad believed that he was the Messiah foretold by the Qur'an. He preached pacifism and the need for missionary work, and his followers continue to spread his teachings to the present day. They are particularly active in Africa, America, England and the Far East. They are considered *heretics* by orthodox Muslims and have been expelled from the international Islamic movement.

Ahmad Khan A nineteenth-century Muslim thinker who was conscious of the benefits science could bring to Islam.

Ahriman Ahriman, also called *Angra Mainyu*, is the destructive spirit of *Zoroastrianism*. Like *Satan* in Christianity he is the leader of a group of evil spirits; but unlike Satan he is the equal of the creator, *Ahura Mazda*. Ahriman is the force of corruption in the world, and he will be destroyed when men choose to live good lives and the kingdom of Ahura Mazda is established on earth.

Ahuna Vairya A Zoroastrian prayer, believed to have been composed by *Zoroaster* himself.

Ahura Mazda In Zoroastrianism, the creator of all that is good in the world. According to *Zoroaster*, Ahura Mazda (or *Ohrmazd*, as he is sometimes called) is the bringer of order, peace and beauty to earth and battles for men's souls with his sworn enemy, *Ahriman*.

Some version of the story of the fall from innocence of the first man and woman is common to several of the world's major religions. In this Muslim picture Ahriman, the sworn enemy of Ahura Mazda, seen in Zoroastrianism as the force of evil, is depicted tempting Mashya and Mashyoi with an apple. He is cunningly disguised as a holy old man.

Aisha (or Ayesha) Muhammad's favourite wife. Aisha opposed the authority of the fourth *caliph, Ali,* Muhammad's son-in-law, and fought against him at the Battle of Camel. According to Muslim tradition, the original full and correct version of the Qur'an was entrusted to her keeping.

Aiyanar Hindu deity, son of *Shiva* and *Vishnu* when the latter was in female form.

Akand Path The continuous reading of the Sikh sacred scripture, the *Guru Granth Sahib,* which takes place on important occasions such as marriages, funerals or on moving house.

Ala Queen of the underworld and spirit of the earth, worshipped by the Ibo of eastern Nigeria. Most families who follow the traditional religion have *shrines* or sculptures of Ala in their homes, where they can pray to her and make offerings to ensure rest for the dead and ask for help for the living.

Aladura Church A Christian church native to Africa; it was not founded by foreign *missionaries,* nor is it governed by any of the older churches which grew up in Europe. It emphasizes the importance of dreams and visions. 'Aladura' means prayer, and congregations often burst into joyful song and they spontaneously prophesy for the future.

al-Arkan The *five pillars* of Islamic religious practice: the repetition of the *creed*; the five acts of devotion and prayer each day; *almsgiving*; the fast during the sacred month of *Ramadan*; and the pilgrimage to Mecca.

al-Ashari A tenth-century Muslim theologian who argued that the Qur'an, as a written book, may have been created, but that, nevertheless, it still may be eternal. He opposed people who said that the use of reason alone could enable men to decide what was, and was not, true religion. al-Ashari argued that human reason cannot comprehend God. The Asharites insisted that God is omnipotent, or all-powerful: men's lives are predestined by God's divine plan to take the course they do, so men cannot decide for themselves what they will do. But God will still hold men responsible for their actions and will still punish and reward them on the *Day of Judgement*, depending on their behaviour.

alb A liturgical vestment made of white linen with openings at the neck and foot, gathered at the waist by a girdle. The alb is worn by Roman Catholic bishops, and priests when they celebrate Mass. In Eastern churches, the equivalent of the alb is called a *sticharion.*

In this clay representation of Ala, her elongated, leopard-spotted figure is flanked on the left by an incongruous European figure wearing a pith helmet and a collar and tie and who is, surprisingly, riding a motor cycle.

al-Din Afghani, Jamal A Muslim philospher of the nineteenth century who wanted to see a united Muslim world that based its social laws on the Qur'an. He believed that the practice of Islam could reverse the decline he thought was taking place in men's morals and should influence all aspects of day-to-day life.

al-Ghazzali, Muhammad An eleventh-century Muslim philosopher who began his career as a teacher of law and philosophy in Baghdad, where he achieved outstanding fame. At first he believed that by the use of reason God's existence could be proved, and religion would be shown to be a rational pursuit for human beings. His brother, Ahmad al-Ghazzali, was one of the most prominent *Sufis* of the time and it may have been by his influence that Muhammad al-Ghazzali became a wandering Sufi, seeking a direct experience of God through mysticism, although he did not abandon his scholarly work, and on the journey produced his most famous work, *The alchemy of happiness.*

al-Hallaj, Mansur A *Sufi* mystic killed in the tenth century for proclaiming 'I am the Truth', which people considered a heretical claim to divinity. After his death, he became the patron saint of a school of Persian Sufi mysticism.

Ali Born in CE600, Ali was the cousin and son-in-law of Muhammad and was elected fourth *caliph*, or leader of the Muslim believers, in 656. He was opposed by the Prophet's wife, *Aisha*, and the governor of Syria, who accused him of having plotted the death of the third caliph. This led to a civil war which continued until Ali was assassinated in 661. *Shi'ite* Muslims believe that the true caliphate passed to Ali's sons and later descendants. It now rests with the twelfth Imam, called the *hidden imam*, who will return as *Mahdi* at the end of time. Ali's shrine at Nejef has become a place of pilgrimage for his followers. *See also*: **Islam**, **Husain**.

Allah Allah in Arabic literally means '(Supreme) God'. According to the Qur'an, Allah is the same God who was proclaimed by *Moses* and Jesus prior to Muhammad. Islam, the Muslim faith, emphasizes that God speaks to man through his prophets and his last chosen was Muhammad, often called 'the Prophet'. It insists that man must, in turn, surrender to his all-powerful and merciful will. Muslims believe that nothing happens in this world unless God wants it to happen; therefore, they trust their lives to his justice and compassion. The phrase 'in sha'Allah' – 'if God wills' – is often used to stress that man cannot question God's decisions, but must accept them and be confident that God guides each indivi dual's steps through life. Allah can be described by ninety-nine *Beautiful Names* of which the most common are *al-Rahman*, the merciful, and *al-Rahim*, the compassionate. Whenever a Muslim performs a significant action, he does it 'in the name of Allah, the merciful, the compassionate'.

All Saints' Day Celebrated on 1 November, All Saints' Day (or All Hallows' Day) commemorates the known and unknown martyrs and saints of the Christian Church. The preceding night, 31 October, is *Hallowe'en*. Eastern churches observe this feast on the first Sunday after Whitsunday.

All Souls' Day Observed on 2 November, All Souls' Day is a time when many Christian denominations commemorate and pray for all the Christians who are believed to be in *purgatory*. Priests wear violet vestments and celebrate requiem masses on this day. Although the feast was abolished by the Church of England during the *Reformation*, it is still observed by many Anglicans and by other Protestant congregations.

almsgiving The donation of gifts, usually money, to the poor. Almsgiving is a widespread religious practice, found in Christianity, Judaism, Islam, Hinduism, Buddhism and Zoroastrianism. Its inspiration is usually compassion, love, or a desire for social justice. Christians give alms to purify the heart, to store up a 'treasure in heaven', and to make up for past sins, but the motive should be mercy and love.

In Islam, almsgiving, or *zakat*, is seen as the 'third pillar' of the faith, and is obligatory for all pious Muslims while *sadaquat* are alms which are given voluntarily. The *Shari'a*, the Muslim body of law, lays down specific amounts to be given; however, it is also stressed that how and why a gift is given is just as important as what is given. Zakat benefits the giver as well as the recipient.

In Buddhism, giving and generosity, or *dana*, are seen as very important indeed. In the *Theravada* it is one of the main spiritual practices of the layman. In the *Mahayana*, it is the basis of the *bodhisattva's* path. The highest gift of all is the gift of *dharma*, the teaching of how to progress to enlightenment, but money, material goods, education, fearlessness, and even one's life can all be given in the correct situation.

al-Rahman/al-Rahim Two of the ninety-nine *Beautiful Names* of God recognized by Islam. They mean 'the merciful' and 'the compassionate' and are used to ask for Allah's compassion, and in praise and gratitude.

altar In many religions the altar is the place where sacrifice is offered to the god or gods. Thus a Greek or Roman domestic altar was usually just a single stone on which a libation of wine was poured. In the Jewish temple in Jerusalem, the altar was a vast structure on which whole oxen could be killed. In Christian churches, the altar represents the table where Christ shared the *Last Supper* with his disciples.

Amar Das (1479–1574) From 1552 the third orthodox Sikh *guru*, Amar Das, was renowned for his devotion to the ideal of equality. He insisted that anyone who came to visit him ate a communal meal from a common dish, without observing the *caste* divisions which marked Indian society. The intention was to establish and improve the lot of all people, Sikhs and non-Sikhs.

Amaterasu Japanese sun goddess, the principal deity in *Shinto*. According to one version of the creation myths, the sun goddess was produced when *Izanagi* washed his left eye. Amaterasu represents fertility, growth and light, and her symbol is a mirror.

Amida Buddha (Amitabah). The Buddha of 'immeasurable light'. One of the five *Dhyani Buddhas* of *Mahayana* Buddhism, he is regarded as the ruler of the West, the Happy Land to which the setting sun carries the souls of the dying. *See*: **Pure Land Buddhism**.

Amidah 'Standing', the main prayer in Jewish religious services. Also known as Shemoneh Esray (eighteen benedictions) because the full form, not used on all occasions, originally contained eighteen benedictions; a nineteenth has been added in recent time to ask for God's blessing on Israel. This prayer is the only one recited at all Jewish services and in the *Talmud* it is known simply as Tefillah (prayer).

amrita 'Immortal'. In Hindu mythology, the nectar of life, produced when *Vishnu*, in an *avatar* as a tortoise, enabled the gods to churn the ocean; the amrita thus produced allowed the gods to win a battle against demons.

Amritsar The Sikh sacred town which contains the *Golden Temple*, built by Guru *Arjan* at the end of the sixteenth century. The name means 'pool of nectar', after the man-made lake which surrounds the temple.

Amshaspentans *Zoroastrian* Bounteous Immortals, these are both divine figures and personified aspects of *Ahura Mazda*. In later Zoroastrian belief, they are regarded as a type of angel.

These monks in Thailand are leaving the monastery in the morning, clad only in their saffron robes and carrying begging bowls, relying on the charity of others for all their needs. Almsgiving benefits those who give, by inspiring compassion and generosity, and those who receive, since it confers on them humility and faith.

Anabaptists A Protestant movement which emerged during the *Reformation* and based its beliefs on a literal (rather than interpretative) reading of the *New Testament*. The Anabaptists believed that religious ceremonies should not be performed unless the participants fully understood the purpose and meaning of the rituals. Thus they did not permit the baptism of infants. Adults were baptized, even rebaptized if they had been baptized as children. The name comes from a Greek word meaning 'second baptism'.

Anabaptists had different views, but generally they placed the greatest emphasis on personal communion with the Word of God, or Bible. Anabaptists sometimes refused to recognize the authority of the state, were often pacifists, and

The Anabaptist movement, formed in the Reformation period, rapidly became widespread among labourers and artisans particularly in Germany, Austria and the Low Countries. In England the fervour of its followers aroused a hostile reaction from moderate reformers, and this page from a tract of 1645 ridicules their ceremonies and the sects associated with Anabaptism.

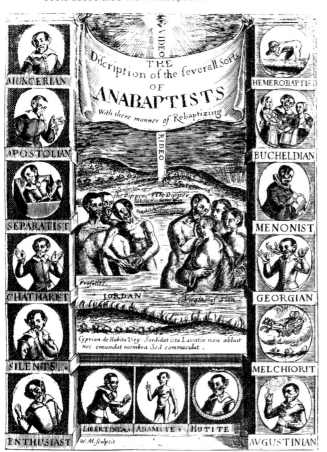

would take no oaths, since the Bible forbade it. Some Anabaptists concluded from their reading of the New Testament that the Second Coming of Christ would be soon, while others developed a communalist lifestyle. Such radical social ideas, combined with the violence of some Anabaptist groups, led to their widespread persecution in Europe. *See also*: **Baptist Churches**.

Analects Compiled after the death of *Confucius*, the Analects is held to be the most important of the four books which make up the body of Confucian thought and teaching.

Ananda One of the first and probably the greatest of Buddha's disciples, and his personal attendant for the last twenty years of his life. Through this link, Ananda heard a great many of the Buddha's teachings, and memorized them all. After the Buddha's death his disciples gathered together to recite the teachings they knew. Ananda's contribution was very important, and from this early gathering arose the core of the Buddhist scriptures.

anarchism Anarchists believe that any form of government is bound to interfere with individual liberty and should therefore be opposed. In place of government they wish to see a system of voluntary co-operation. They believe that such co-operation would naturally arise if governments and man-made laws did not exist, because man is naturally good: government and oppression create injustice and evil.

anatta In Buddhism, this is one of the three characteristics of ordinary existence, along with *anicca* and *dukkha*. It is the belief that there is no permanent, unchanging self, soul, or essence in any person or in any thing.

ancestor worship Ways of showing respect and reverence for ancestors after their death. Worshippers make offerings to the ancestors in order to obtain protection and guidance, and they believe that dreams are a form of communication between the living and the dead. The *soul* of the ancestor has to be helped on its way into the spiritual world through the ritual chasing away of evil spirits and through the provision of gifts for the journey. Ancestor spirits are supposed not only to provide assistance in avoiding any dangers which might be facing the family, but also to help members of a family to grow spiritually. On the other hand, failure to honour the ancestors in these ways will anger their spirits, which will seek revenge on the family by, for example, destroying their crops, sending diseases, or causing bad dreams.

Angad (1504–52) From 1539, the successor to *Nanak*, the founder of the Sikh religion, Guru Angad is best known for popularizing an alphabet called *Gurmukhi*. In the sixteenth century there was no written form of Punjabi and so it was difficult for the guru to communicate to the growing number of Punjabi disciples. His alphabet made it possible for him to guide this community through hymns, letters and meditational texts.

angel Angels are spiritual beings recognised by Islam, Zoroastrianism, Judaism and Christianity. They are seen as carrying out the divine will and acting as messengers to mankind. Muslims believe that angels are created out of light and, together with Christians, they distinguish a number of special angels known as *archangels*. Other orders exist such as *cherubim* and *seraphim*; and these are often depicted in religious paintings.

Angelus, The A Roman Catholic prayer concerning the *incarnation* of Christ, which is repeated in the morning, at noon and at sunset. In Roman Catholic countries the Angelus bell may be rung to announce the hour of this devotion.

Anglican Church, The *See:* **Church of England.**

Angra Mainyu *See:* **Ahriman.**

anicca In Buddhism, this is one of the three characteristics of ordinary existence, along with *anatta* and *dukkha*. It refers to the constant change and lack of permanence in the world.

animism The belief that spirits inhabit all natural objects, such as trees, animals, and rivers, and all natural forces, such as lightning. Accordingly, people can sacrifice to these objects and forces, or worship them.

Annunciation Many Christians celebrate the feast of the Annunciation to commemorate the day on which the Angel Gabriel announced to the *Virgin Mary* that she would conceive a son. It is also known as Lady Day.

Antichrist Literally, 'he who is against Christ'. This term is used to describe Christ's great opponent at the end of history, and the last false religious leader and teacher on earth who, it is believed, will be conquered and banished with Christ's *Second Coming*. The Book of Revelation of St John the Divine in the *New Testament* calls the Antichrist 'the beast', who uttered blasphemies against God.

During medieval times there was a well-established tradition of pious craftsmen and artists offering their work as an act of devotion. This depiction of the Annunciation is the work of Fra Angelico, a Dominican friar whose paintings are exclusively concerned with religious subjects. The serenity of the scene is countered by the woebegone figures of Adam and Eve, to the left of the canvas, who are being expelled from the Garden of Eden. Fra Angelico was concerned to remind observers that it was the fall from grace of the first man and woman that made it necessary for the Redeemer to be born.

anti-clericalism To be anti-clerical is to oppose the influence of the clergy, especially in politics. Anti-clericalism became important in nineteenth-century Europe and Latin America, where conservative Roman Catholic clergy used their influence to oppose social and political reforms, such as greater democracy or the redistribution of land. It was linked to the growth of *agnosticism* and *atheism*.

antipope The Roman Catholic Church claims to be able to trace back the line of *Popes* in an unbroken series to *St Peter*. Any rival who claims the title in opposition to the elected pope is known as an antipope.

anti-Semitism Discrimination against, or persecution of, Jews on the grounds of their origins or their religion. It reached its height under the Nazis when the so-called 'Final Solution' was implemented, which sent six million people to their deaths. *See also*: **Aryanism**.

Evidence of how apartheid affects everyday life.

For centuries Jews have been discriminated against and exploited, and have often been made the scapegoats in troubled times. This old engraving shows the panic and violence of a pogrom, an organized persecution and massacre of a Jewish community.

apartheid Derived from the Afrikaans word meaning 'apartness' or 'segregation', apartheid is the policy which has been applied in South Africa since 1948, which ensures that whites and non-whites are dealt with separately in social and economic terms, and, inasmuch as is possible, territorially. Repressive laws and strict censorship have had to be enforced to sustain these policies which have been widely condemned by both church and state leaders throughout the world.

Apocrypha A collection of Jewish texts excluded from the *Hebrew Bible* because scholars considered that they were not inspired by God. Thus Judaism sees the Apocrypha as instructive, but not scripture. The Greek translation of the Hebrew texts, however, did include these writings as holy scripture. The Roman Catholic Church follows this tradition, since Jerome's Latin Bible, the *Vulgate*, was based on the Greek translation. Modern Roman Catholic Bibles include in the *Old Testament* all but two of the works. Protestants, however, have generally accepted the Hebrew tradition; when they include the Apocrypha in the Bible, it is usually printed as a separate section. There exist also disputed texts in the New Testament known as Apocrypha.

The Apocrypha includes collections of proverbs, historical and apocalyptic texts, sermons and legends.

apologists Early Christian philosophers who wrote in defence of Christianity. Their writings were sent to the Roman emperors and other influential figures of their day. The apologists were educated men, aiming to explain their beliefs to the outside world rather than preaching to their own community of believers. They used philosophical ideas, such as those of *Plato*, current among non-Christians to explain the Christian faith in terms which outsiders could understand.

apostle One sent on a mission to preach the gospel. Most usually used of Jesus' twelve chosen Apostles who followed him during his three years of public life and who, after his death and *resurrection*, set out to spread the faith. The twelve administrative officials of the Mormon Church are also called apostles.

Apostles' Creed, The The oldest statement of faith of the Christian Church. It is almost certainly based on apostolic teaching, though not written by the Apostles themselves. It is used in the baptismal service in the Anglican Church.

archangel A chief or principal angel in Islam, Judaism and Christianity. The best known archangels are: Michael, God's warrior against *Satan*; Gabriel, God's messenger to man; and Raphael, who performs works of healing on Earth. All three of the archangels are mentioned by name in the Bible, and their feast days are observed with special devotion.

Ardas The Sikh prayer which forms a vital part of every service. It is also used on other occasions, such as at a housewarming or on starting a new business, since Sikhs believe that they should involve God in everything they do.

The Ardas is recited during every Sikh service. In the wedding ceremony it follows the singing of hymns which include the Lavan. Watched over by a picture of Guru Nanak. the men at this wedding who are not wearing turbans have covered their heads as a sign of respect.

Arhat, Arahat 'Worthy one'. In *Theravada* Buddhism, a monk who has broken the Ten Fetters of error and is thus about to achieve *Nirvana*.

Arjan (Dev) (1563–1606) The fifth Sikh *guru*, or holy man, and a great organizer as well as a poet. Arjan (Dev) built the famous *Golden Temple* known as the Harmandir, at Amritsar. He also compiled the first volume of Sikh scriptures, the *Adi Granth*. By the end of the sixteenth century, the Sikhs and the Muslims were becoming more and more opposed to each other and when Guru Arjan died in Muslim custody, he was proclaimed the first Sikh martyr.

Krishna, who is often depicted as blue-skinned, is engaged in discourse with the warrior-hero Prince Arjuna. The *Bhagavad Gita* relates how, on the plains of the Kurukshetra, Krishna became the Prince's charioteer. In this guise he imparted the wisdom that overcame Arjuna's reluctance to issue the order for battle against the Kuru family and gave him the strength to defeat the powers of evil that were ruling the world.

Arjuna An Indian prince, one of the two main characters in the great Hindu poem, the *Mahabharata*. In the *Bhagavad Gita*, which is part of the *Mahabharata*, he talks on the battlefield with his charioteer, who is the god *Krishna* in disguise. Arjuna is reluctant to fight because the enemy are his relatives. Krishna says he should carry out the duties of a warrior unquestioningly, since that is the task given to him by his *caste* and his *karma*.

Ark, Noah's According to the Book of Genesis in the *Torah*, or *Old Testament*, and various surahs in the Qur'an, God decided to destroy mankind, because of its wickedness, by flooding the world, but, because of their faith, he wished to save Noah, and his family. God commanded Noah to build an ark of cedar and to take at least two of every kind of animal aboard. The ark is said to have landed on Mount Ararat, in modern Turkey. *See also*: **Flood, The**.

Ark of the Covenant, The A sacred chest made of acacia wood in which the Israelites placed the *Tablets of the Law*. The Ark was an emblem of God's presence and only priests were allowed to touch it. Wherever the Israelites travelled, even on the battlefield, the Ark accompanied them. It is believed to have been lost.

The term 'Ark' is also used for the highly ornamented cupboard on the east wall of every *synagogue*, in which scrolls of the *Torah* are kept.

The *Ethiopian Orthodox Church* believes that the original Ark was not destroyed, and is now preserved in the Cathedral of Axum in Ethiopia. In every Ethiopian Orthodox church there is a copy of this Ark (known as a *tabot*) blessed by the *abuna* and used during *Mass*.

Armageddon According to the Book of Revelation in the *New Testament*, Armageddon is the place where the last and decisive battle between good and evil will occur. The word was probably suggested by Megiddo, the great fortified city which was the site of numerous major battles and invasions.

arti The sacred light or flame which is central to Hindu worship. The arti lamp contains a number of small wicks in ghee which are lit during the service and offered to the deities. The arti lamp is then passed around the congregation.

Aryanism The Aryans were an ancient people of central Asia who spoke a language called Aryan or Proto-Indo-European. Over hundreds of years their descendants spread through most of Europe, south-west Asia, and India, mixing and marrying with the earlier inhabitants of those areas. With them came their language, which changed and developed into many different languages, including English, French, Russian, Greek, and most Indian languages. These languages are often called Indo-European or Aryan languages and the cultures of peoples who have spoken them, especially in the ancient world, are often called Aryan.

Arya Samaj A Hindu reformist movement founded in the nineteenth century. It teaches strict observance of the *Vedas* and believes that the *caste* system should be based on merit rather than birth, and that child marriage and the untouchable caste should be abolished. The Arya Samaj works for reforms in education and has been responsible for setting up a network of schools and colleges. Its members reject the use of images and base their worship around devotion to the fire-god *Agni*; the central feature of their temples is thus a large fire and the principal ceremony is the havan or fire ceremony. They are intensely nationalistic and oppose all non-Hindu influence in India.

asanas The physical postures or positions practised in *yoga*.

Ascension Christians believe that Christ was taken up into heaven forty days after his resurrection. Having assembled his disciples and led them to Mount Olivet, Jesus told them to go out into the world and preach the gospel. Then he blessed them and was carried up into heaven on a cloud. The Ascension is commemorated in the Christian Church on the fortieth day after Easter Sunday which is known as Holy Thursday. In Islam, 'ascension' refers to Muhammad's ascent through the seven spheres in the company of *Gabriel*, until he reached the divine presence.

asceticism Ascetics believe that spiritual awareness, holiness, or salvation can only come through asceticism – conquering physical desires and resisting the temptations of the world. Some simply deny their physical needs; often they fast, practise *celibacy* and lead lives of solitary contemplation. Others also punish their bodies, subjecting themselves to extremes of heat and cold, wearing rags and walking barefoot, whipping themselves, and draping their limbs in chains. A life of asceticism can be practised either by an individual or by a community. Its ultimate goal is usually to make the practitioner more receptive to God, or to achieve *enlightenment*. *See also*: **yoga, Shi'ites, Sufism.**

The Brahmin priest *(left)* is wearing the sacred thread, showing he has been born twice. With him is a yogin, an ascetic who denies the flesh to concentrate on spiritual concerns. They are both seated before the fire, which is the god Agni.

A connection between the stars and human destiny has been believed in since the time of the Babylonians who mapped the constellation of the Zodiac. Each of the twelve astrological signs seen here has certain character traits associated with it which believers think will be found in people born under its influence.

ashavans A word used in *Zoroastrianism* for those people who have chosen to lead lives of righteousness (asha).

Ashkenazim Jews of Poland, Russia and Eastern Europe and their descendants. *See*: **Sephardim**.

ashram A house, or community dwelling place, where followers of a Hindu *guru* can live together, meditate and learn from him.

Ashvaghosha A Buddhist poet who lived in the first century BCE and wrote a work recounting the life of the Buddha up to the time of his *enlightenment*.

Ash Wednesday In Western Christianity, Ash Wednesday is the name of the first day of *Lent*, the forty-day period of fasting which precedes *Easter*. Nowadays, in some churches, ashes are used to mark crosses on the foreheads of the congregation. These ashes are obtained by burning the palms used on Palm Sunday. The priest applies them, using the words, 'Dust thou art and unto dust thou shalt return.' This signifies the beginning of the period of penance.

Assumption Observed on 15 August, this feast is celebrated in the Roman Catholic and Eastern Orthodox Churches. It commemorates the *resurrection* of the *Virgin Mary*, who was believed to be taken body and soul into heaven immediately after death. In the Orthodox Church it is known as the Dormition, or Falling Asleep of the Mother of God. The teaching behind this feast is that the Virgin Mary was given the privilege of receiving eternal life immediately after death. Protestants reject this doctrine.

astral plane According to *spiritualism* and *theosophy*, the astral plane is the soul's first resting place after death. Many, not only *psychics* or believers, claim that it is possible to leave the body and temporarily move to the astral plane.

astrology A belief that the position of the stars and planets at the time of one's birth affects one's character and destiny. In order to understand the individual and his or her future, professional astrologers draw up birth charts, which show the exact position of the planets in the zodiac at the time of birth.

asura In early Hindu mythology, the asuras were the elder brothers of the gods, or the gods themselves, but later they came to be regarded as inferior beings, and eventually as demons.

atheism Atheists deny the existence of God or gods, believing that human conduct should be shaped by personal morality and circumstances, not by a supposedly divine law. Atheism is different from *materialism* and *agnosticism*, since it does not merely doubt or ignore the existence of God but positively rejects it. *Humanism* and most expressions of *existentialism* are modern forms of atheism, because they stress that life has no universal meaning. They claim that individuals create their own purpose in life by their actions and decisions and are responsible only to themselves and their consciences.

atman In Hinduism, the soul or principle of life, whether that of the individual or the universal life force. In this latter sense it is very close in meaning to *Brahman*.

atonement An action which enables man to be 'at one' with God if he has been separated from God through sin. In Judaism this used to be achieved by animal sacrifice which overcame the evil effects of sin. Christianity believes that man cannot make atonement for his sins without God's grace or divine favour, because man is sinful and God is holy. Christians believe that this atonement is possible because of Jesus Christ.

Atonement, Day of *See*: **Yom Kippur**.

autocracy A form of government in which one person has unlimited power over others.

Avalokitesvara One of the most important *bodhisattvas*, or 'beings devoted to *enlightenment*', in *Mahayana* Buddhism. His name means 'the Lord who looks down (in compassion)', and he is the Bodhisattva of Compassion, a type of super-human representation of compassion. The *Dalai Lama* is believed to be an embodiment of Avalokitesvara. In China, Avalokitesvara became *Kuan Yin*, in Japan, *Kwannon*.

avatar In Sanskrit the word means 'someone who descends'. In Hindu mythology, the god *Vishnu*, the Preserver and Maintainer of the World, is said to descend to earth from time to time in human form as an avatar. On earth he reminds men of the true path to salvation, and destroys false doctrines and re-establishes order and the rule of law where anarchy and chaos reign. Nine of Vishnu's ten avatars are believed to have appeared, of whom *Rama* and *Krishna* are the most famous. The final avatar will be *Kalki*, who will destroy this present world, because it has become sunk in corruption. After this, Vishnu will rebuild the world.

Avesta The sacred book of Zoroastrianism. The Avesta is in three parts, the first of which is the *Yasna*. It contains the Zoroastrian liturgy and includes hymns called the *gathas*.

avidya Ignorance, in both Hinduism and Buddhism: one of the chief obstacles to man's spiritual development and one of the basic reasons why suffering exists. It is classed as one of the *Ten Fetters* in Buddhism. Its opposite is *vidya*, spiritual knowledge or insight; by gaining vidya we become free from all suffering.

ayatollah A title given to *Shi'ite* interpreters of Muslim law, (the *Shari'a*). Ayatollahs are very important men in the community and have a right to deliver legal opinions. Some have the right to pass laws based on their understanding of the sacred writings, which is known as the degree of *Ijtihad*. Because of this authority, certain ayatollahs of great importance and renown (such as Ayatollah Khomeini), are known as '*imam*'. This term, the highest title in Shi'ism, is normally reserved for descendants of *Ali* and such ayatollahs are often thought to be earthly mouth-pieces for the '*hidden imam*' who will return at the end of time, as the *Mahdi*. Otherwise, an ayatollah is called '*imam*' in its literal sense, 'leader', and in this sense the word is used even for an unknown *mullah* who leads a Friday prayer in a mosque.

Ayesha Another spelling of *Aisha*.

Ayida Wedo Haitian *voodoo* deity, associated with another deity, *Damballah Wedo*, the great serpent and creator of life. Ayida Wedo is usually portrayed in the shape of a rainbow.

azan From the Arabic 'adhan'. The Muslim call to prayer, made by the *muezzin* from beside the mosque or from the *minaret*.

The Dalai Lama, seen as the manifestation of Avalokitesvara, is the latest in a line of reincarnations since 1475.

b

Bab (1819–50) Sayyid Ali Mohammed of Shiraz in Persia. In 1844 he took the title of Bab, 'the gate' to the truth. *Shi'ite* Muslims believe that each age has its own *imam* or leader, and until the last great Imam appears on the earth it is only possible to communicate with him through a Bab. Sayyid Ali Mohammed said that his mission was to foretell the imminent coming of another, greater messenger. His followers multiplied, and the Persian authorities began to worry that a rebellion might take place. To prevent this they persecuted the Babis and executed the Bab himself.

Babel A city and a tower which, according to the Book of Genesis, were built by the descendants of *Noah* with the aim of reaching up to heaven. To punish their presumption God confounded them by making them speak in different tongues, whereas formerly all mankind had spoken the same language.

Babism An offshoot of Islam founded by the *Bab*, Sayyid Ali Mohammed of Shiraz. Babis believe that God is unknowable and reveals himself through prophets who, throughout history, have come down to earth to show men the path to spiritual enlightenment. As times change, so new prophets appear. Babis therefore differ from orthodox Muslims in that they do not believe *Muhammad* was the last prophet, but merely one of a succession which will continue as long as the universe exists.

Babis emphasize the mystic significance of numbers and their letter-equivalents in deciding what God is telling his people to do.

The Babis became divided on the death of the Bab. They split into two rival groups following Mirza Yahya and Baha'u'llah. In order to defuse the situation, both leaders were exiled. The followers of Baha'u'llah became the dominant group and remain, to the present day, members of a worldwide religion known as the *Baha'i faith*.

The beautiful white marble Shrine of the Bab, brightly lit against the evening sky, is situated in Haifa, Israel, where the World Centre of the Baha'i faith is established. The shrine was built on Mount Carmel, on the spot chosen by Baha'u'llah when he visited it towards the end of his life.

Babylon The country to which the Israelites were exiled in the sixth century BCE. Now a Rastafarian expression for their place of exile. Babylon is seen as the corrupt land of the white man, where blacks are exploited or reduced to slavery and seduced into Christianity, a 'white' religion worshipping the 'white man's god'. In general, any country apart from those in Africa, especially Ethiopia, is Babylon, and the police and other arms of the state are also described in this way. The *Old Testament* is fundamental to the Rastafarian *creed*, and they see their own situation as similar to that of the Israelites.

Badarayana He compiled a collection of short sayings known as the Brahma Sutras, in order to explain the teachings of the *Upanishads*.

Baha'i faith Also known as *Baha'ism*: the religion founded in the nineteenth century by *Baha'u'llah*, a follower of the *Bab*. In 1867, after the Bab's death, he claimed that he was the greater messenger foretold by the Bab. In a matter of months, the group which he led split from the Babists and started the Baha'i religion.

The most important principle of Baha'i belief is that the Bab and Baha'u'llah are, like Moses, Buddha, Muhammad and other great religious leaders, manifestations of the unknowable God. The religion's sacred literature (known as the *Kitab Akdas*, or 'Most Holy Book') therefore consists of the writings and teachings of both men, as well as their interpretation carried out by Abdul Baha, the eldest son of Baha'u'llah.

The Baha'i religion lays great stress on the unity of all men and all *creeds*. The duty of man is to love and serve his brothers, abolish prejudice within his own heart and that of society, and work towards a peaceful, united planet. Allegiance to one's country is not as important as loyalty to the world. However, everyone must respect the laws of their government. If a war should arise, the Baha'is should try to find a solution to international problems using non-violent means. The family is sacred and monastic *celibacy* is forbidden. Marriage is not compulsory, but is highly encouraged. Drugs and alcohol are forbidden, as is cruelty to animals. Men and women are equal in the eyes of God and should have the same rights and obligations in society.

The Baha'is do not follow set rituals or have a priesthood. The daily prayer is compulsory, and each year believers fast between 2 and 20 March. The worldwide leadership rests with the Universal House of Justice, composed of nine people, elected from the national assemblies.

Baha'u'llah The founder of the Baha'i faith. A follower of the *Bab* until the latter was executed, Baha'u'llah became the leader of a splinter group which broke away from the Babists and eventually outnumbered them. In 1867, he declared himself to be a manifestation of God, the latest of a succession of prophets sent to earth in order to guide. In 1852, he was banished to Baghdad by the Persian authorities, who feared that the phenomenal following he had gathered posed a threat to the stability of the regime. The Turks then sent him to Constantinople, and finally incarcerated him in Akka where he died in 1892. Akka has become a centre of pilgrimage for the Baha'is.

Bairam Two festivals of Islam: (1) The Lesser Bairam, also known as Id-ul-Fitr, follows the fast of *Ramadan* and lasts for three days. During this period Muslims hold receptions, send greetings cards, exchange presents and visits, and give alms to celebrate the end of the period of fasting. (2) Sacrifice Bairam, also known as Id-ul-Adha, is observed on the tenth to fourteenth days of the last month of the Muslim year. The faithful kill and eat an animal, normally one sheep per family, to commemorate the ransoming, with a ram, of *Ishmael*, the son of *Abraham*. The month in which it is celebrated is also the month of *Hajj*, the yearly pilgrimage to Mecca. The festival is, therefore, a way of sharing in the pilgrimage without going to Mecca. Near Mecca itself, the sacrifice is performed publicly, involving many animals.

These goats have been sacrificed after the Islamic fashion as an offering to Allah for the feast of Bairam.

Baisakhi A Sikh and Hindu festival marking the religious New Year in April. For Sikhs it particularly commemorates the formation of the *Khalsa*, a casteless brotherhood of believers committed to truth, service and self-sacrifice at Baisakhi 1699. The festival also reminds the faithful of the protest against the British which took place in 1919 at Jallianwala Bagh, during which very many people were killed by the British. The Amrit ceremony of initiation into the Khalsa is often held at this time.

Baker Eddy, Mary *See*: **Eddy, Mary Baker.**

bambino An Italian term applied, especially in the Roman Catholic Church, to an image of the infant Jesus.

baptism The Christian ritual through which someone becomes a member of the Church. Anglicans, the Eastern Churches, and the Roman Catholic Church consider baptism to be a *sacrament*. The ceremony usually takes place in very early childhood, although the Baptist Church, along with some other non-conformist churches, rejects child baptism and baptizes only adults, which it does by fully immersing them in water. In child baptism the child is given a Christian name, is sometimes anointed with oil and is sprinkled with water or immersed in it three times. Usually among those present are godparents, adults who promise to look after the child's spiritual and physical welfare until he or she grows up and can take responsibility for his or her own religious beliefs and conduct.

Water is the symbol of rebirth and cleansing. It is used to show that the child or adult is identifying with the death and resurrection of Christ, that he is receiving the new life which comes from making this declaration of faith, and that the taint of *original sin* has been washed away. The Amrit ceremony in Sikhism is sometimes referred to as baptism.

Dressed in an animal skin, John the Baptist, having returned from his retreat in the desert, is baptizing in the River Jordan. He said that he was preparing the way of the Lord, who was shortly to come to save mankind.

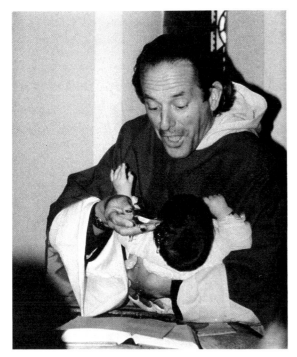

These pictures of baptism illustrate two interpretations of this sacrament. In many Christian churches, baptism, which brings a person into the Christian community, is carried out when a child is still very young, the parents and godparents acting as representatives. Baptists, however, reject infant baptism, believing that an adult must actively choose to embrace Christianity. The decision is then symbolized in a ceremony involving the total immersion of the new Christian.

Baptist churches Christian Protestant churches which reject the *baptism* of infants. They believe that only people who have, by their own decision, accepted the truth of Christian teaching are fit for baptism. The ceremony which involves total immersion, symbolizing the death of sin and rebirth into righteousness in imitation of Christ's death and *Resurrection*, is known as 'Believer's Baptism'.

Baptists emphasize the importance of the Bible as the Word of God and yardstick of religious faith and practice. Baptists were persecuted during the seventeenth century, but have now become a large and worldwide movement within the Christian religion.

baptistry The part of a church which contains the font, used for baptisms.

Barabbas According to the Christian *Gospels*, the criminal whom *Pontius Pilate* pardoned in place of Christ, in response to the demands of the crowd.

Bardo Thodol A Tibetan Buddhist book giving instructions to the newly dead. Bardo is believed to be the intermediate state between death and rebirth, whose conditions depend on the personality of the dead person.

Barmen Declaration A declaration drawn up in 1934 by a meeting of Protestant Church leaders, to voice Christian opposition to the policies and actions of Hitler's *Nazis. See*: **confessing church**.

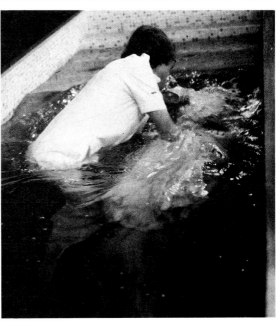

The Bar-Mitzvah ceremony marks the day a young Jewish boy becomes a man in the religious community, for which day he has been preparing under the guidance of the rabbi. For the first time he wears the tallith, or praying shawl, and the phylacteries, leather boxes containing biblical texts, that are worn on the left arm and on the forehead. So dressed, he reads publicly from the scrolls of the Torah and is blessed by the rabbi during his sermon.

Bar Mitzvah A Jewish ceremony which takes place on the *Sabbath* after a boy's thirteenth birthday. During this initiation rite the Bar Mitzvah boy reads publicly in Hebrew from the scroll of the *Torah* for the first time and accepts the commandments of his faith: the words 'Bar Mitzvah' actually mean 'Son of a Commandment'. From this moment onwards, he is seen as a responsible adult and as a member of the religious community. Girls can take part in a similar ceremony, known as *Bat Mitzvah*.

Baron Samedi Haitian *voodoo* god of the dead. Baron Samedi is said to rule and guard the dead and tradition describes him as a frightening figure, dressed in black, carrying a cane and looking like an undertaker.

basilica Any large Christian church which is rectangular, has a broad nave flanked by colonnaded aisles, and very often an apse at the east end.

Batala A god of the Yoruba people of Nigeria, identified with the Catholic *St Benedict*.

bathing As a ritual of purification, bathing is common to many religions. Believers wash away sins and evil and become pure and holy.

Bat Mitzvah At twelve years of age, all Jewish girls automatically come of age and are known as Bat Mitzvahs, or Daughters of the Commandment. In Reform and Liberal Judaism, this event may be marked by a ceremony similar to the *Bar Mitzvah* for boys.

beatification The first major stage in *canonization*, or the way to being declared a saint by the Roman Catholic Church. When a person who has died is beatified by the *Pope*, the title 'Blessed' can be put in front of his or her name. Catholics may pray to beatified people for help and to ask for their prayers.

Beatitudes This word is used to describe those sayings which Jesus used to begin the Sermon on the Mount; each of the sayings starts: 'Blessed (or happy) are the . . .' The Beatitudes are found in the Gospels of St Luke and St Matthew.

Beautiful Names *See*: **Amshaspentans**.

belief A concept, doctrine or philosophy in which one places one's trust. In a religious, political or philosophical context, to have a belief implies commitment to that belief and a resolution to act accordingly.

believer Someone who is convinced of the truth of his or her religion or faith.

Benares Now called Varanasi, a city in north-east India on the banks of the Ganges and the place of Hindu pilgrimage. Pilgrims immerse them-

Hindu pilgrims washing themselves in the Ganges at Benares – a symbolic act of purification, signifying a washing away of sin and evil.

selves in the river in order to cleanse themselves from their sins. One of the most sacred places in Hinduism and full of holy sites, especially along the banks of the Ganges.

Benedictines Known as the black monks because of the colour of their habits, or clothing, the Benedictines are the Christian nuns or monks who live according to the Rule of *St Benedict*. This Rule emphasizes: (1) stability: monks normally remain in one monastery until they die; (2) study (3) community prayer balanced with work and recreation; and (4) total obedience to the *abbot*, who is elected by the monks themselves, generally from among their number.

Benedict, St (480?–547) The founder of the worldwide *Benedictine order* of Christian monks and nuns, which was first established at Monte Cassino in Italy, where Benedict was abbot. Other orders of monks also follow this Rule, including the *Cistercians* and *Trappists*.

Benediction Generally the divine blessing at the end of any Christian service, especially the Mass. In the Anglican Church the Benediction is also said at the end of the morning and evening services. The Roman Catholic Church holds a service called the Benediction of the Blessed Sacrament where the consecrated bread is elevated and used to bless the worshippers.

Benedictus The song of Zacharia, thanking God for the miraculous birth of his son, *John the Baptist*, found in the Gospel of St Luke.

benefice Any holding of property by a churchman or church corporation. Bishoprics, deaneries, and rectories are all benefices.

Benjamin The youngest and favourite son of Jacob in the *Torah*, or *Old Testament*. Benjamin's descendants are said to have been a warlike tribe who were responsible for many of Israel's conquests.

Bethel Literally, 'house of God'. A town twelve miles north of Jerusalem, prominent throughout Hebrew history. It was at Bethel that *Abraham* pitched his tent and Jacob had his dream; here, too, the *Ark of the Covenant* was given a resting place. Ancient Bethel has disappeared but many Nonconformist chapels, mainly in England and Wales, are named after it.

Bethlehem A town five miles south-west of Jerusalem. Bethlehem was the birthplace of King David and of Jesus.

Bhagavad Gita Literally 'the Song of the Lord'. It is part of the Hindu epic known as the *Mahabharata*. The *Bhagavad Gita* is a dialogue between Prince *Arjuna* and his charioteer *Krishna*, the eighth *avatar* of *Vishnu*. Krishna outlines the path of devotion to God known as *bhakti*, emphasizes the need for men to perform the duties of their *caste* selflessly and to follow their karma, and finally reveals himself in splendour to Arjuna as God Himself.

Bhagavan An Indian title meaning 'Blessed One', 'Sublime One', or 'Lord'. Hindus often use it when talking of, or addressing, holy men or the god *Vishnu*.

Bhagwan Shri Rajneesh *See*: **Rajneesh, Bhagwan**

bhajan A Hindu or Sikh hymn sung at communal gatherings in praise of God, often accompanied by various musical instruments.

bhakti A Sanskrit word meaning '*devotion*'. In Hinduism it often means the path to union with God which stresses love and devotion rather than *ritual* and organization. According to the bhakti tradition people can come to know God through personal experience, and faith and communication with God through hymns and passionate personal prayers are more powerful than traditional rituals, sacrifices, or study. God is not seen as an abstract term, but as a beloved person. This way of devotion is outlined especially in the *Bhagavad Gita*, and bhakti is in general directed either to the hero of that book, *Krishna*, or to *Shiva* and his wife, *Mahadevi*.

In Buddhism, bhakti is the feeling of love that a person can develop towards anyone spiritually more advanced, such as a Buddha. It is usually connected with faith in that person.

One of the most important Upanishads in Hindu sacred literature, the *Bhagavad Gita*, deals with the spiritual guidance that Krishna, acting as his charioteer, imparts to Prince Arjuna on the battlefield. Krishna chooses the warrior because of his devotion, and urges him on in the battle to defeat evil forces.

bhikkhu The usual Pali term for a Buddhist monk, a member of the *Sangha*. The word (which means 'beggar') was used, before the Buddha, of Hindu religious mendicants. It is used in Buddhism to describe one who is totally reliant on the Sangha and on lay gifts for support: bhikkhus often go out each morning with alms bowls to receive gifts of food which are shared in the monastery. A bhikkhu owns only his robes, alms bowl, water strainer, needle and razor, and lives a celibate and ascetic life.

bhikshu The usual Sanskrit term for a Buddhist monk. *See* **bhikkhu.**

Bible A sacred book in two main parts. The first and longer part, known as the *Old Testament*, contains the sacred book of Judaism; the second part, or *New Testament*, forms, together with the Old Testament, the sacred book of Christianity. The first five books of the Hebrew Bible are known as the *Pentateuch*, or the Five Books of Moses, and in Hebrew are called the *Torah*. The Torah contains the Jewish law, including the *Ten Commandments* delivered by God to Moses and dietary and moral rules. The remainder of the Old Testament contains the writings of the Hebrew *prophets* and a collection of books known as the Writings, which includes Psalms, Proverbs, and other compositions.

The New Testament comprises the Gospels attributed to four of Jesus's disciples, the letters of St Paul and others, the *Acts of the Apostles*, which describe events during the thirty years after Christ's death, and the *Book of Revelation*, a vision of the future and the end of the world.

bimah A raised platform found in Jewish synagogues from which the *Torah* scroll is read.

bishop A senior *minister* in the Roman Catholic, Anglican, Orthodox, and other Christian churches. He has authority over an area called a *diocese* or bishopric, and can be elected or appointed.

'In the name of Allah – the merciful, the compassionate.

Bismallah In Islam, a call for *Allah*'s blessing. It heads all but one of the 'surahs', or chapters, in the Qur'an and is in daily use: 'In the name of Allah – the merciful, the compassionate'.

Black Mass A mockery or parody of the Christian *Mass* for the dead. In the West it is traditionally believed to be used by devil-worshippers. Its name arises because its 'priests' wear black vestments.

Black Power A black movement which grew up in America in the 1960s and which opposed the economic and political power of what they saw as an oppressive, racialist culture. Black Power believed that equality would never be given to the black people unless they struggled to take it, by force if necessary.

Black Stone The sacred stone situated in the *Ka'ba*, a rectangular stone building in the great mosque at Mecca. It is the centre of *Hajj*, or Islamic pilgrimage, and pilgrims come to kiss and touch it. Tradition states that it was sent to earth at the time of Adam, the first man, and that it was originally white, but went black over the years as man's sins increased in number.

The Black Stone is to be found in a corner of the sacred Ka'ba, an ancient structure, found in the courtyard of the Grand Mosque in the city of Mecca. All Muslims aspire to visit this centre of pilgrimage at least once in a lifetime, if not prevented by poverty or ill health.

bodhisattva A Sanskrit word meaning 'a being of *enlightenment*'. In *Mahayana* Buddhism, a bodhisattva is a being who seeks to gain enlightenment, not for his own sake alone, but, because of compassion, for all living beings. Thus, he can be an ordinary human being who wants to help others by becoming enlightened, or someone who is so advanced spiritually that he is practically a Buddha. Sometimes an aspect of enlightenment is personified as a bodhisattva: in other words, wisdom, compassion, and boundless energy are pictured as beautiful – usually young – men or women. The most famous of these is *Avalokitesvara*, the Bodhisattva of Compassion.

Bodhi-tree Also known as *Bo-tree*. The tree under which Siddhartha Gautama sat and meditated, and achieved *enlightenment*, thus becoming the Buddha.

(left) This splendid figure is Avalokitesvara, the Bodhisattva of Compassion. He is, according to Mahayana Buddhism, a being in an active state of Nirvana.

This monk is seated serenely below what is believed to be the very Bodhi-tree under which Siddhartha Gautama gained enlightenment and was, from that time on, known as the Buddha. In the branches may be seen prayer flags and in the background is the Maha Bodhi temple at Bodhgaya, in Bihar, India.

Blavatsky, Helena Along with Colonel H. S. Olcott, she founded the Theosophical Society in 1875. In her writings, she defended the practice of *spiritualism* and the reality of *occult* powers.

blessing An act or words used to consecrate an object or person, to confer well-being or to protect someone or something from evil.

Bodhgaya The place near Gaya in north-east India where Prince Siddhartha gained *enlightenment* and became the Buddha.

Bodhi Literally 'awakening'; the traditional Buddhist term for *enlightenment*, the goal of Buddhism.

Bodhi Day Mahayana festival to celebrate the enlightenment of Buddha, under the Bodhi-tree.

Bodhidharma In the sixth century CE, the Bodhidharma was the twenty-eighth Indian and first Chinese Patriarch of Ch'an Buddhism. According to legend he floated from India to China on a reed, bringing with him the Buddhist tradition which developed into Ch'an (or *Zen*, as it was called in Japan).

bolshevism *See*: **communism**.

Book of Mormon The sacred scripture of the Mormon faith, which was revealed to its founder, *Joseph Smith*, in a vision. The Book of Mormon describes the conflict between two branches of a family who emigrated to America from Jerusalem in 600BCE. Mormons believe that it is the final part of the *New Testament*.

Booths Also known as *Succoth*, or Tabernacles: a Jewish festival in October at the end of the harvest. It commemorates God's protection of his 'Chosen People' during their forty-year trek through the wilderness from Egypt towards the *Promised Land*. During this journey they lived in temporary tents, or 'booths'. For the seven-day-long festival, covered booths are erected in gardens, on balconies, and in *synagogues*, and these temporary dwellings become the Jewish home, or at least dining and prayer rooms. The booths are decorated with fruits and leaves. Verses from the *Torah* and pictures decorate the walls, and the booths are furnished with the households' finest possessions.

bot A Thai Buddhist hall used for worship and teaching; part of a religious enclosure known as the '*wat*'.

Bo-tree *See*: **Bodhi-tree**.

Brahma The Hindu god of creation. With *Vishnu* the preserver and *Shiva* the destroyer, he forms the triple deity known as the *Trimurti*.

Brahman Also known as Brahma; the absolute or the divine in Hinduism. Brahman is the impersonal Universal Spirit, who is in all the gods and in everything that exists. The '*atman*', or human soul, is regarded as being part of Brahman, and it is in Brahman that the 'atman' will eventually be absorbed after all its *reincarnations*.

Brahma, the triple-headed god, is the Creator in the Hindu trinity, Trimurti. The other two members are Vishnu, the Preserver and Shiva, the Destroyer. Kings and holy men are depicted in attendance upon him in this nineteenth-century fresco from Rajasthan, but Brahma is worshipped by comparatively few Hindus, most of them being devotees of Vishnu or Shiva.

Brahmin The priestly caste of Hinduism. Many Brahmins are not priests, but all are treated with great reverence. Brahmins are responsible for sacrifices and other ceremonies, and for the study and teaching of the *Veda* scriptures.

Brahmo Samaj Founded in 1828 by *Ram Mohan Roy*, this Hindu movement aimed to reform traditional practices in order to return to the supposed purity of early Hindu worship. To achieve this goal, its followers established a Church which rejected the use of images in favour of a more abstract, intellectual *monotheism*. They tried to remove emotional expressions of faith and to replace them with a more rational, sermon-based faith. The ideas of a transcendent god took over from that of the Hindu *pantheon*. They were heavily influenced by Christian ideas and Western ways of thinking. Polygamy, the caste system, and the burning of widows were widely condemned by them, and they supported social reforms such as the right of widows to remarry and the end of child marriages. By the late nineteenth century, the movement had split into several sects and was losing influence in India.

Brethren An *evangelical* Protestant movement founded in 1827, established mainly in Britain, and based in Plymouth; therefore also known as the *Plymouth Brethren*. The Brethren are divided into closed and open groups. The former do not have any contact with people outside the Church, even if they are relatives. Both groups aim to keep up high standards of *puritan* morality. The closed groups frown on all forms of worldly pleasure, including drinking alcohol, dancing, gambling, and cinema-going. Members are encouraged to wear modest clothing and lead simple lives.

There is no *ordained* ministry; ordinary laymen – but not women – lead services consisting of hymns, Bible readings, prayers, and a sermon, and take the *communion* service on Sundays. These practices are intended to lead to personal devotion to Christ.

breviary A *liturgical* book of instructions for reciting daily services in the Roman Catholic Church.

This strange scene shows a bride but no bridegroom. In fact, he is there, invisible, since a novice who is ready to take her final vows considers herself a bride of Christ, and dresses accordingly. This young woman is to enter the Carmelite order, and will, from thenceforth, wear a wedding ring as a token of her spiritual marriage to Jesus.

Bride of Christ A term used by St Paul in the *New Testament* to describe the Christian Church's relationship to Christ. Nuns are also known as brides of Christ, because on taking their vows, they dress in white and receive a wedding ring to symbolize their commitment to their vocation.

Brother God A Jamaican *Rastafarian* prophet, who set up a community known as the *Twelve Tribes of Israel* at a camp called Dread Heights. In the community the members are expected to support one another materially and spiritually; the community should be self-sufficient and independent of outside assistance. Education is regarded as very important.

Brownists The followers of Robert Browne, a sixteenth-century English *Puritan*, who believed that each congregation of worshippers should be free and self-governing, independent of any central Church authority or hierarchy. As the first separatists from the Church of England, the Brownists were called *Independents* and later adopted the name of *Congregationalists*.

Buddha, The Buddhism is centred upon the teachings of Siddhartha Gautama, who came to be known as the Buddha. In his early twenties Gautama, a prince born in a small town in the foothills of Nepal, left his palace in search of spiritual enlightenment. For six years he wandered the country, denying himself all material comforts and possessions. Whilst these travels brought him a deeper understanding of the suffering and pain of the world, he felt himself no closer to answering the questions that plagued his soul.

At this point Gautama abandoned his severe lifestyle, and turned his attention to the development of his mind through meditation. Legend has it that for many days and nights he sat in deep contemplation beneath a fig tree — the Bo-tree or Tree of Awakening — until he finally found the *enlightenment* he had been seeking for so long. He came to understand the inevitability of human suffering as well as the path to salvation. From this point on Siddhartha Gautama was known as the Buddha.

He sought out the five followers who had been with him in the years before his Bo-tree meditations, and preached to them his first sermon – the *dharma* – in the deer park at Sarnath. They became the first Buddhist disciples.

This colossal Amida Buddha dates from the thirteenth century and is to be found at Kamakura. Japan.

Onlookers display their grief at the death of the Buddha and his final entry into Nirvana. He is shown in an attitude of perfect peace and composure.

These Buddhist monks are taking part in a religious procession as a public display of their dedication to the Buddhist perception of truth and the path to enlightenment.

Buddhism Is not primarily concerned with the worship of any single figure – man or woman, demon or god. At the heart of the religion is a set of universal laws or dharma.

Buddhist teaching centres around the *Four Noble Truths*. The First Noble Truth maintains that all existence is suffering; the Second that the cause of suffering is desire; the Third that the extinction of desire puts an end to suffering and leads to enlightenment; the Fourth that the path to enlightenment, the Eightfold Path, is open to all men. The Eightfold Path consists of: (*i*) right knowledge (*ii*) right thought (*iii*) right speech (*iv*) right actions (*v*) right livelihood (*vi*) right effort (*vii*) right mindfulness (*viii*) right concentration. The path of the Buddha, whilst avoiding the empty pursuit of pleasure for its own sake, also rejects the hardships of asceticism. For this reason, its moderation, it is known as the *Middle Way*.

Although in different countries a number of distinct forms of Buddhist practice have evolved, the two most important are known as *Mahayana* – which means the 'great vehicle' – and *Theravada* – which means 'teaching of the elders'. The major strongholds of Buddhism today are Sri Lanka, south-east Asia and Japan, although over the last century there has been considerable interest in the religion in the West. *See also*: **Sangha, dharma**.

Bundahishn A part of the *Zoroastrian* sacred writings known as the *Pahlavi* texts. The Bundahishn describes the creation and structure of the world.

bushido The code of behaviour of the Samurai or Japanese warriors, inspired by *Zen* Buddhism, with influences from *Confucianism* and *Shinto*.

Butsu-Dan A Japanese *altar* to the Buddha, which is set up in the family home. The Butsu-Dan is the focus of offerings and chantings and also contains ancestral memorial tablets.

C

Cabbala *See*: **Kabbalah**.

cakras *See*: **chakras**.

caliph A successor to Muhammad, responsible for handing down Islam's entire teaching unchanged to the people of his own day. Caliphs were considered to be leaders of the believers, responsible for ensuring that the community lived according to the lessons of the Qur'an and were responsible for the social welfare of the Muslim community. After Muhammad's death the first four caliphs were venerated because of their closeness to the *Prophet*, and their example was added to the Muslim sunna for all to follow. When Islam split into its two main groups, the *Sunni* and the *Shiah*, only the former retained a caliphate; this office was abolished in 1924 by the Turkish ruler, Kemal Ataturk.

Calvin is noted for his insistence on the Reformation idea of predestination – the belief that God chooses his elect, those who will be saved from damnation.

Calvary The place near Jerusalem where Jesus was crucified. It is also known as Golgotha, the Hebrew word meaning 'skull', the name being derived from the shape of a rock to be found in the vicinity. The present Calvary Chapel stands on the site of the first chapel which was erected in the fifth century, and is part of the Church of the Holy Sepulchre, built on the traditional site of Christ's tomb.

Calvin, John (1509–64) A French theologian who played a leading part in the Protestant *Reformation* in France and Switzerland. He dominated the religious and political life of Geneva which, along with his *Institutes of the Christian Religion* (1536), became a model for the Protestant movement known as *Calvinism*.

Calvinism A type of Protestant Christianity which is based on the teachings of John *Calvin* and which spread through parts of western and central Europe in the sixteenth century. Later it became strong in America and South Africa.

Calvin taught that the Bible was the only true source of Christianity and that the Roman Catholic Church was perverting and changing the original gospel of Jesus. One of his best-known ideas was *predestination*, which says that human beings are fundamentally corrupt and deserve to be damned; but God in his mercy has chosen in advance some people whom he intends to save from hell. Faith and a good Christian life are signs of being chosen and this type of faith in God's merciful salvation separates the elect, or chosen, from the condemned.

Puritanism, which involves avoiding all wordly pleasures, grew out of Calvinism. It arises from the belief that man has a sinful nature which has to be tamed, not encouraged.

From the *New Testament* Calvin got ideas on how to change the structure of the Church. He decided to abolish bishops and priests and replace them with elders and ministers, who are *ordained* but still live the lives of laymen and, with the council of elders, decide on all church matters: this council later became known as the presbytery. Churches which have been reformed in this way are called *Presbyterian* and have spread all over the world.

Canaan The land through which the river Jordan flowed and to which a group of Semites moved south. Moses led the great *Exodus* of the Israelites out of the land of Egypt and into Canaan, the land 'flowing with milk and honey', which their God had promised them. Because of this it was known as 'The Promised Land'.

Candlemas The Christian festival which falls on 2 February. In the Roman Catholic, Anglican, and Eastern Churches the feast commemorates the presentation of Christ in the Temple in Jerusalem when he was about twelve years old. Following the tradition of the early Church, the Armenian Church still keeps the feast on 14 February, the fortieth day after the *Epiphany*.

The name 'Candlemas' refers to the candles carried in procession as the symbol of Jesus Christ, whom Christians see as 'the Light of the World'.

canonization In Roman Catholicism, the process of recognizing that a deceased person can be venerated as a saint. A body known as the Congregation of Rites is appointed by the *Pope* to examine all the cases put forward for canonization and, if the claim is acknowledged, then the person is first *beatified*. At this stage permission is given for limited veneration, usually only in the person's own country. After further enquiry, beatified Christians may be raised to the status of saints. In this enquiry it is important that *miracles* or answers to prayer can be shown to result from prayers to these Christians.

canon The collection of writings in a religion which is regarded as authoritative.

canticle A song or chant, or a liturgical hymn, usually with words drawn from the *Bible*.

cantor A translation of the Hebrew word, 'chazzan': the prayer leader and chief singer in Judaism, who leads the public worship in the synagogue.

Cao-Dai A modern Vietnamese religion founded about 1920. It combines ideas and traditions taken from Buddhism, Roman Catholicism, *Taoism*, and *ancestor worship*.

capitalism A society or ideology based upon the possession of capital or the use of capital for production. The Marxist interpretation sees it as an historical stage wherein one class, the bourgeoisie, owns the means of production, while a second class, the proletariat, possesses the capacity to work, and the latter is exploited by the property-owning classes. In the non-Marxist view the majority of the instruments of production and the objects of consumption are to be privately controlled, and state intervention is to be restrained.

Capuchins A *Franciscan* order of *friars*, which tries to follow *St Francis of Assisi*'s teachings on the virtues of poverty combined with living and preaching the *gospel*.

cardinal A member of the high council of ordained officials of the Roman Catholic Church, second only to an *Ecumenical Council* in authority. Cardinals are appointed by the Pope to advise him and to help him govern the Church. Whenever a *Pope* dies, they elect a new Pope in the secret sessions known as the *conclave*.

cargo cults Religious movements to be found in New Guinea and Melanesia, among people who have only recently had any contact with Western civilization. This brief contact has led them to imitate certain rituals which they have observed, in the hope that by doing so they will obtain 'cargo', material goods, for themselves. They believe that these rituals will bring about the arrival of a type of saviour who will distribute cargo to everyone.

Carmelites A Roman Catholic order of friars founded at Mount Carmel in the twelfth century. They are known as the white friars because their habits, or clothing, are brown with a mantle of white wool. The first Carmelites were *hermits* who followed a common rule, but later the hermits came together to share one set of buildings. In the sixteenth century *St John of the Cross* and St Teresa of Avila founded a reformed order of friars and nuns, known as the Discalced, or 'barefoot', Carmelites, who intended to live a stricter life than the original order.

carol A Christian song usually sung at Christmas and celebrating the birth of Jesus and other events related to the Nativity.

caste One of the hereditary divisions of Hindu society. The caste people belong to determines how they live, work and worship. Traditionally, Hindus only mix socially and marry within their own caste. In other words, each caste is a closed community within society. Hindus believe that *Brahma* the Creator established the system: each caste sprang out of a different part of the body of *Purusha*, the original man created by Brahma: the *Brahmins*, or priests, from his head; the Kshatriyas, or warriors, from his arms; the Vaishyas, or traders, from his thighs; and the Shudras, or servants and peasants, from his feet.

These are the four main caste groups, but they are subdivided so that in all there are over three thousand castes in India, including many *Untouchable* communities. These are even lower on the scale than Shudras, suffer persecution and are forced to do the hardest, dirtiest jobs. Contact with an Untouchable pollutes a high-caste Hindu, so that he must ritually purify himself. *See also*: **dharma** and **karma**.

These catacombs are to be found beneath the Appian Way in Rome.

catacomb Any series of corridors found in an underground burial place. The early Christians met and hid in catacombs, especially in Rome, in order to escape persecution.

Catechesis Instruction in the Christian faith, sometimes by means of a *Catechism*.

Catechism A book which contains Christian doctrines or instruction in the Christian faith, aimed at preparing an individual for *baptism* or *confirmation*. It is written as a dialogue between a teacher and pupil, the teacher asking questions about the faith, and the pupil answering. Until recently candidates for confirmation in some churches had to learn the catechism answers by heart.

Catechumen Someone who is preparing for Christian *baptism*.

cathedra A bishop's throne in a cathedral.

cathedral The main church in a bishop's *diocese*, containing the *cathedra*.

Catholicism See: **Roman Catholicism**.

Catholicos The title given to the head of the Armenian and Georgian *Orthodox Churches*.

Celestial Master *See*: **Chang Tao-ling**, **Cheng-i**.

celibacy A way of life in which a person gives up sexual intercourse entirely and usually the idea of marriage as well. According to most religions, celibacy should be voluntarily chosen and not imposed on anybody, but in practice it is often a necessary requirement for the priesthood. In *theistic* religions the usual reason for celibacy is to enable the person to devote most of his or her time to prayer, the search for God, and work for God. Some religions, such as Judaism, strongly discourage celibacy.

In Buddhism, celibacy is the absence even of the thought of sex. This is seen as a natural by-product when someone who meditates enters higher states of consciousness. Thus trying to practise celibacy is seen as a help towards entering these higher states of consciousness.

cemetery A place for the burial of the dead, especially ground not adjacent to a church.

censer Also known as a thurible: a container in which *incense* is burnt in churches.

In these two censers, fumes from the burning incense escape through perforations in the lids.

ceremony An action or series of actions which have been selected for special occasions such as weddings, funerals, and religious rites.

chakras Also spelled *cakras*: psychological centres in the human body. Several Hindu schools, including *yoga*, and Tantric Buddhism believe that the brain is not the only place in the body where consciousness is centred. These other places, or centres, where consciousness collects and functions are the chakras. From them secondary streams of mental and physical energy radiate out. They are also foci where bodily, mental, and even cosmic forces come together and change into one another.

Different systems have different locations and numbers of chakras, usually five to seven in all. The most common locations are: the base of the spine or the genitals; the navel; behind the lowermost breastbone; the throat; the crown of the head or between the eyebrows. Rising up the body, the chakras are centres of steadily more refined energy and consciousness.

Through practices known as *kundalini (yoga)*, Hindus use the chakras to liberate all the potential energy of the organism to achieve union with Braham. Tantric Buddhists use practices known as chandali to let energy rise up through the chakras to help towards *enlightenment*.

chalice A sacred vessel shaped like a goblet and usually made of metal, used to hold the wine in Christian churches at *Communion*.

Ch'an A Buddhist tradition that arose in China, better known under the Japanese word *Zen*.

Chang Lu An early Taoist figure who ruled an independent Taoist state in second-century CE China. Taoist priests administered this state under Chang Lu, who was the chief priest and administrator, and they were famous for their tolerance. The people of the state had to examine their conduct at regular intervals. Free food was offered to poor people at the free inns built for passing travellers. If someone committed a crime, he would not be punished until he had commited the same crime twice again. At a time when the authorities were quick to kill subjects who stepped out of line, this peaceful Taoist community usually sentenced its members to mending the roads or, in cases of serious crime, to being visited by the demons of disease.

Chang Lu's claim that he was capable of keeping the universal demons and spirits under control was the basis of his authority. His sect is commonly known as 'Taoism of the Five Pecks', as he taxed his followers five pecks of rice.

Chang Tao-ling. A prominent *Taoist* figure, father of the movement which led to the creation of separatist Taoist *sects*. Establishing himself in western China and claiming that he was a magician, Chang Tao-ling was visited by the great *Lao-tzu*; as a result he is said to have made a treaty with the universe which placed all the spirits and demons in the world under his influence. This pact enabled him to protect his followers from evil spirits by issuing them with the appropriate charms and amulets, and in the second and third centuries it became fashionable to guard oneself against harm in this way. Chang Tao-ling passed his power to his son, who in turn passed it on to his son, *Chang Lu*. The person who had this power naturally had great authority, and this authority was passed on from father to son, together with the power, and still remains with the Chang family. The present Celestial Master lives in Taiwan. The sect which Chang Tao-ling established is known as 'Five Bushels of Rice', since this was what he taxed his followers.

The origins of Taoist ritualistic ceremonies such as those being performed by the red-robed priests can be traced back to Chang Tao-ling who founded a Taoist church in the second century.

chant A simple liturgical song, in which a series of words or syllables is sung to a single tone. Chanting is often used to help meditation. Christians and Jews chant the psalms; Buddhists chant *mantras*, *sutras* and other texts.

Chanukah The Jewish *festival of lights* celebrated at the beginning of December. It commemorates the recapture and rededication of the Temple at Jerusalem in 164BCE, earlier conquered and turned over to the worship of Zeus by the Greeks.

Tradition states that when the Maccabees freed the Temple, they could only find one day's supply of oil left for the lamp which was supposed to burn without ever going out. Miraculously, when they lit the lamp it lasted for eight days. In memory of this episode, Jewish families light candles every night for eight nights during Chanukah. They light one candle on the first night, two on the second, and so on, placing them in an eight-branched candelabra known as a *menorah*. During the candle-lighting they sing a hymn celebrating how God has always come to the rescue of his people throughout history. During the festival Jews eat fried food, such as doughnuts, in memory of the single jar of oil; they also play a game of chance with a *dreidel*.

chapel A building or part of a building set aside for Christian worship. Inside a larger church or cathedral separate chapels with their own private altars are often found, dedicated to particular aspects of God or to a saint. The term is also applied to small Protestant meeting places, especially in the *Methodist*, *Baptist*, *Independent* and *Brethren* movements.

chaplain A clergyman attached to a chapel, or anyone serving as a rabbi, priest, or minister in an institution, such as a prison, hospital, school or university, or with the armed forces. The term is used also for a Christian priest who personally serves a bishop, a mayor, or a member of a royal family.

chaplet A string of beads, one-third the length of a full *rosary*.

Charismatic Movement A recent Christian movement within the Roman Catholic and Protestant Churches that emphasizes the role of the *Holy Spirit* in giving the believer an intense personal faith in God and in leading the individual through life as well as in guiding the Church itself. In the *Acts of the Apostles* in the *New Testament*, it is described how the gift of the Holy Spirit descended on the fiftieth day after the *Passover*. Some Christians, notably those *Pentecostalists* who belong to the Assemblies of God, in the United States, claim to have the same gift, including the ability to speak in tongues and the gift of prophecy as well as faith, love and inner peace.

Fifty days after the Passover, the disciples of Christ were assembled when the Holy Spirit descended on them in the form of a dove, granting to them the gift of tongues. Followers of the Charismatic Movement seek to be similarly imbued with the Holy Spirit.

Chasidim Also spelled *Hasidim*: ultra-conservative Orthodox Jews, who stand out from mainstream Jews because they refuse to wear modern western clothes and keep the type of clothing their ancestors wore in the *ghettos* of eastern Europe. They never wear ties, since the Chasidim say that they divide the heart from the brain, and both must serve God. But the Chasidim wear a gartel, or cord around the waist to divide man's higher and lower parts from one another. They also grow locks of hair to hang by their ears. In their worship they emphasize joy, intensity, and spontaneity. They tend to worship in a small gathering known as a 'stibl' rather than in the larger synagogue gathering, characteristic of mainstream Judaism. *See also*: **Chasidism**.

The young man with the earlocks is a Chasid. an Orthodox Jew who observes the strictest code of religious practice. Chasidism is a movement which began in the eighteenth century. stressing the importance of mysticism and emotion in one's response to God. Chasidim wear distinctive clothing. notably a black. wide-brimmed hat and a long. black coat which is worn in place of a jacket or overcoat. In certain areas of New York. a street scene such as this would not be surprising.

Chasidism Also spelled Hasidism: a Jewish *mystical* movement which began in Poland in the eighteenth century under the influence of a man known as the Baal Shem Tov, which means 'Master of the Good Name' (the name of God). This movement believed that intense emotion was an important part of devotion, and the members expressed their emotion in dancing, singing and ecstatic prayer to God, which created a sense of joy in their hearts. Most of their ideas were based on the *Kabbalah*. Each local group of *Chasidim*, as these were called, was led by a rebbe, or master, who had absolute authority over his followers, who regarded him as a mediator between them and God; he prayed to God for his followers, and God blessed the Chasidim through him. The ideas of the Chasidim led to conflict with the more traditional Jewish rabbis, who were suspicious of strong emotions in religion and believed that the best way to worship God and achieve salvation was to study the *Torah* and the *Talmud* and concentrate on obeying the laws contained in them. They suspected the Chasidim of not following the Jewish laws strictly enough in a traditional way. Gradually, however, the two sides became less hostile towards each other, and the Chasidim in general began to give the study of the Torah and Talmud a higher and more important place in their religious practice.

The colour of the chasuble indicates the nature of the feast of any particular day, black, for example, being used for mourning and violet for sorrow and repentance. Here, the priest is wearing white, a joyful colour.

chasuble A sleeveless outer vestment which Roman Catholic priests and some Anglican and Lutheran ministers wear over the *alb* while celebrating *Mass* or *Communion*. Orthodox priests wear a similar but stiffer garment which is shorter at the front and longer at the back.

chauvinism Originally, an excessive devotion to one's own country or people, accompanied by a lack of respect for the rights and qualities of other peoples and countries. Nowadays the meaning of the word is often extended to include excessive devotion to one's own religious beliefs or lack of respect for the other sex.

chela A Hindu term for the follower or student of a *guru*.

Cheng-i A *Taoist sect* which sprang up at the beginning of the twelfth century in southern China. The Cheng-i based their beliefs on a legend of the *Celestial Master*, whose all-powerful sword had been preserved through the ages. A group of magicians learnt how to make charms against rain, practised the ritual of *exorcism*, and acted as mediums after instruction in the art of magic by the Celestial Master. They did not live apart from the community but, unlike most Taoist monks, married and stayed among the people. Many of the sorcerers were decorated by the emperor for their services.

Chenresig The Tibetan Buddhist term for *Avalokitesvara*, the *Bodhisattva* of compassion.

cherubim In Judaism and Christianity the cherubim form the second order of angels, after the *archangels*. Traditionally they have six wings and are often painted as winged children.

Childermass *See*: **Holy Innocents' Day**.

Ching Ming Chinese festival of the Dead. A time for worshipping the ancestors at their tombs with offerings of food and paper goods.

Chinvat Bridge In the teachings of *Zoroaster*, the Chinvat Bridge is the place of man's judgement. According to the kind of lives people have lived, they either cross it with no difficulty, or slip and fall to eternal torment.

chit The Hindu word for consciousness, intellect or mind, which is regarded as part of *Brahman*, or the *Absolute*. Brahman is known as chit, *sat*, and *ananda*: consciousness, reality, and bliss.

Ch'iu Ch'ang ch'un *See*: **Chuan-chen**.

choir (1) A group of singers who are trained to sing together in a church or other religious building during services. (2) The chancel of a church; during services the choir sits in that area in many churches.

chorten The Tibetan Buddhist term for a *stupa*.

Chosen People *See*: **Judaism**.

chrism The holy oil used by Roman Catholics and the Orthodox Church, mainly in the *confirmation* ceremony; hence the Orthodox use of the term 'chrismation' for confirmation. Holy oil is also used in *extreme unction*.

Christ, Jesus Jesus Christ lived from about 4BCE until CE29. The traditions about his life and teachings are found in the books of the *New Testament* – particularly the Gospels. They were written by the early Christians who believed Jesus to be the Christ – the Messiah promised by God. (The title 'Christ' is the Greek translation of the Hebrew 'Messiah', meaning 'Anointed One'.) Many had hoped for a military Messiah but Jesus was, in fact, crucified by the Romans for political and religious reasons. It was his resurrection from the dead which his followers saw as the real victory of the Christ – and Christians worship Jesus Christ as their saviour from sin and death.

Jesus was born in Bethlehem near Jerusalem, and, according to tradition, his mother Mary was a virgin when he was conceived. Shepherds and wise men are said to have visited him at his birth, and *St Matthew's Gospel* states that he escaped Herod's Massacre of the Innocents by being taken to Egypt. He was brought up in Nazareth in Galilee by Mary and her husband Joseph, and at about the age of thirty was baptized by John the Baptist, his cousin. He gathered twelve *Apostles* around him and began a wandering ministry of preaching. His message was that the universal rule of God over the earth, the *Kingdom of God*, had already begun and he was its herald. By repenting of their sins, men could accept this kingdom into their hearts and live a new life of love towards God, their neighbours and their enemies.

Jesus taught that God was especially concerned to win the hearts of social outcasts; nobody was outside his all-embracing love. Jesus's teaching was conducted mainly in the form of parables, which attracted eager listeners; he is also recorded as having performed many miracles, especially of healing. He criticised many of the religious authorities of his day for hypocrisy, particularly in their love of outward show – for example, when praying. Instead, he gave his disciples a simple model prayer, the *Lord's Prayer*, or 'Our Father'. He valued humility and inwardness in religion, as well as

practical works of mercy, forgiveness and love. His liberal attitude towards keeping some of the Jewish laws such as the Sabbath Law, as well as his miracles and his claims to be able to forgive men's sins, brought him into conflict with the *Pharisees* – to whom he was otherwise quite close in his beliefs – and the *Sadducees*. He was arrested after his *Last Supper* with the disciples and tried on a charge of blasphemy. He was brought for trial before the Roman governor, *Pontius Pilate*, on a charge of treason and subversion. He was crucified as a common criminal, but three days later is said to have appeared alive to his disciples and to have met them over a period of forty days before his final *Ascension* into heaven.

A King, not of this world, but who claimed his kingdom was in heaven. His humility is shown by the choice he made to enter the holy city of Jerusalem riding on a donkey. Word spread among his followers who lined his path with palm leaves. So great was the crush that Zacchaeus climbed up into a tree to catch a glimpse of Jesus.

(opposite) One of the central events in the gospel stories is the Last Supper, when Jesus is believed to have instituted the sacrament of the Eucharist, using the bread and wine to represent his body and blood, which would be sacrificed the following day at his crucifixion. His twelve Apostles are seen gathered at table with Jesus, one of whom is to betray him. In this picture Roberti depicted Judas in black, looking away from the others.

Christadelphians Established by John Thomas in the United States in 1848, the Christadelphians claim to have revived the apostolic faith. The members believe, among other things, that the Bible contains no errors and that only faithful believers will have a life after death; all others will merely become extinct. They believe, therefore, that when Christ's *Second Coming* happens, he will only raise to everlasting life those who have earned their *resurrection*. Christadelphians reject the idea of a personal superhuman devil, the torments of hell, the doctrine of the *Trinity*, and the rite of infant *baptism*. Like the *Baptists*, they say that immersion of the adult believer is essential to salvation. They also believe that when Christ does return to earth he will establish his capital in Jerusalem and visibly rule the world from there.

Christadelphians have no regular ministers, are *pacifists*, and have a loose internal church organisation. Every member has a right to vote for, and change, the constitution of the Church.

Christendom A general term for all the different Christian Churches and their members, when thought of as forming one worldwide body of Christians. It is often used when people are describing the Christian Church and its members in contrast to the *secular* or the non-Christian world in matters of belief and way of life.

christening Another word for *baptism*, the *sacrament* by which a person becomes a member of the Christian Church.

Christianity One of the largest religions, with about 900 million members, this faith takes its name from its founder, Jesus Christ. (*See entry*).

Christians do not only follow the example and teachings of Jesus in their own lives, they also accept the theories about the real nature of Jesus which emerged in the early Church after the Resurrection – theories collectively known as *Christology* and summed up in the creeds. These theories suggest that Jesus was more than a real man, with a human body and mind: he was also the incarnation of God – God in human form, with two natures, one *divine* and one human. From such reflections there emerged the distinctive Christian idea of God himself, that he is one God in three persons – a *Trinity* of Father, Son and *Holy Spirit*, also known as the *Holy Ghost*. The Son became man in Jesus Christ. The Holy Spirit, who came down on the Apostles at the first *Pentecost* after the Resurrection, is the 'breath' or energy of God who enters men's hearts, inspires them to believe in Jesus, and gives them spiritual wisdom and strength to proclaim the Christian *Gospel* to all mankind. Christians also believe that it is the Holy Spirit who inspired the writing of the Bible, both *Old* and *New Testaments*, since it is he who reveals God to man; the Bible is therefore the main authority and source for all Christian doctrine.

At the end of the world, Christians believe, the second coming of Jesus will occur, when he will return to earth to judge the living and the dead. Those who are saved (faithful Christians and other good men) will be united with Jesus in heaven – according to some, after a purifying period in *purgatory*; the condemned, however, will be sent to hell. The atonement and sacrifice made by Jesus at his crucifixion is available to all men; if they have faith in Jesus as the living Son of God and desire union with him, their sins will be forgiven and they can become members of his Church. As regards the moral conduct of the Christians, the emphasis is on love, both of God, one's neighbour and one's enemy, as Jesus commanded.

Christians remember Jesus and celebrate his saving life, death and resurrection in their services in church; especially in *baptism*, when they are initiated into the church, in *confirmation* when they receive the Holy Spirit, and in the *Eucharist*, where they are united to the spiritual body of Jesus Christ. Many Christians also go to *confession*, to repent of their sins, which repentance allows the priest to absolve them from their sins, and they celebrate other *sacraments* when they can receive grace from God. Christians also pray privately, study the Bible and meditate on what Jesus has done for them. Their main festivals are Christmas, Easter and Pentecost and many days are used to honour the saints. Some Christians prepare for Easter by fasting during *Lent*.

Christianity has splintered over the centuries into many *denominations* and *sects* which vary widely in doctrine and practice; the chief divisions are Roman Catholicism, Eastern Orthodoxy and Protestantism.

Three of the best-known Christian symbols, the pilgrim's cockleshell, the dove to represent the Holy Spirit, and the fish, a secret sign used by the early Christians.

Christian Science Founded by *Mary Baker Eddy* in the nineteenth century in the United States, the Christian Science movement's doctrines are drawn from her book entitled *Science and Health* (1875). According to this work, sickness and suffering are mere illusions, which can be overcome by right thinking. The material world, evil and the *devil* have no real existence, even though the effects of evil – ill health, death, poverty and sin – may appear to exist. In order to free himself from these illusions, man must seek *salvation* through union with God. He must return to the practices and faith of the early Church and must employ the science of healing. Since God is spirit, he is not therefore a material being; man is made in the image of God, and so must also be just spirit; the physical material body and all its physical problems are therefore figments of man's imagination according to Christian Science.

Discovery of the truth – God – banishes all thought of 'evil' and all the apparent effects of 'evil'; those who practise Christian Science will be both healthy and happy. Christian Science denies *predestination* and believes that those who acknowledge the truth of God find heaven on earth. God is not the masculine God of the *Old Testament*, but a Father-Mother God, compassionate like a mother as well as strong like a father.

In the first fifty years after the movement was founded it spread rapidly from its centre at Boston, until there are now some 3,500 Christian Science churches worldwide. These churches are governed according to Mary Baker Eddy's *Manual of the Mother Church* under a Board of Directors based in Boston. The movement has no *ordained* clergy, and local churches are organised along democratic lines, with decisions being submitted to the membership as a whole. Church officials are elected and individuals are expected to work for their own salvations. Meetings are held on Wednesdays and Sundays and include readings from the Bible, testimonies of healing and selections from the book *Science and Health*. These meetings are compulsory for the members of the Church.

Christian Science does not acknowledge the need for a ceremony of *baptism*, since members believe that they are spiritually baptised by acknowledging the truth of their faith. All marriages and funerals are conducted by ordained clergy called in from other *denominations*. In health matters, members are only allowed to consult Christian Science practitioners, who have no other occupation and have undergone courses based on the Bible and *Science and Health*.

The movement sponsors four religious periodicals and the *Christian Science Monitor*, an international daily newspaper, which exists to remind members of their duty to the world as a whole.

Recently the number of Christian Scientists has been declining, as orthodox medicine and its cures have taken the place of healing.

Christmas The Christian festival which, in most Christian churches, falls on 25 December every year and celebrates the birth of Christ. The date was chosen by the Christian Church only in the fourth century CE, to replace the pagan Roman festival formerly held on that date. As the Roman festival celebrated the rebirth of the Invincible Sun during the depths of winter, the Church saw the celebration of the birth of the Son of God as a fitting substitute. Also, the eating and drinking which went on at the Roman festival could be taken over in part by the Christian feast.

Only Easter is as important a feast in the Christian calendar. Christmas is a time of rejoicing during which greetings cards are sent, friends and family give each other presents and carols are sung. It is also a season when Christians should be especially moved to perform charitable works and give *alms*.

Christology A branch of Christian *theology* which deals with the nature of Jesus Christ. It discusses theories about the relationship between Jesus and God. The mainstream Christology of the Church was defined at the Council of Chalcedon in CE451: it states that Jesus Christ is both perfect God and perfect man in one single being. According to this belief, he has been God eternally, as the second person of the *Trinity*, but at a certain moment in time he took on a human nature in the *incarnation* and was born as a man. After this Council, all other definitions of Christ's nature were regarded as heretical.

Chuan-chen A *Taoist* sect founded in 1280 by *Ch'iu Ch'ang ch'un*. It later set up its headquarters in Peking, on the invitation of the emperor. Its temple was known as the White Cloud and was run by a community of ascetic followers, who were vegetarians, celibate, hardworking and self-sufficient. The basis of the sect's teaching was personal peace, learnt through tranquillity and self-denial.

chun-tzu Someone who follows the path of *Confucian* virtue. The chun-tzu is a 'superior man', not only when it comes to leading a moral life, but also in having well-developed social graces. He has good manners, is well-read and is a good administrator. The traditional English meaning of the word 'gentleman', an educated man of leisure, has a similar meaning.

church A building which is used for Christian religious practices and worship.

Church (1) A collective term to describe the worldwide community of all Christian believers. (2) A particular *denomination*, or group, within the worldwide Christian Church.

churching of women Also known as Thanksgiving after Childbirth: a very ancient Christian rite, in which a woman who has just given birth comes to church to thank God for giving her a child. In the Anglican Church, the ceremony consists of the *Lord's Prayer*, a psalm and responses. In the Roman Catholic Church the woman is also sprinkled with water and blessed by a priest; a similar service is used in the Orthodox Churches.

Church of God of Prophecy A West Indian *Pentecostal* Church organised in Britain along national lines and at present growing in numbers. As Pentecostalists, its members believe that true believers in Jesus Christ are given the gift of tongues, and that the *Holy Spirit* (or Ghost) can possess them. They take a fundamentalist, or literal, view of the Bible, which is the centre of their doctrine. Rituals play a central part in services, and they too are drawn from the Bible. Thus, before *communion*, they often wash each other's feet, in imitation of Christ at the *Last Supper*, as a means of achieving *grace*. Personal testimonies, prayers and songs are encouraged, as well as congregational chants and singing. People are strictly divided into the damned and the saved and no one can be saved unless he or she has been *baptised* and accepts the *Trinity* and the role of Christ as saviour of the world. The *Second Coming* is imminent, but no date has yet been prophesied for it. The Church is a highly structured organisation, within which all offices and duties are open to men and women alike. *See also*: **Charismatic Movement**.

Church of Jesus Christ of Latter-day Saints An American religious sect founded by Joseph Smith (1805–44) upon the *revelations* contained in the Book of Mormon. He said it was delivered to him by the Angel Moroni, written upon gold plates in an unknown language, and provided

This statue of Jesus Christ is in the Mormon centre in Salt Lake City. Utah. which is the home of the Mormon faith. The principal temple is seen below with a golden statue on top of one of its lofty spires.

48

This Mormon church in Alberta, Canada, is evidence of how the sect has spread throughout North America.

with a pair of jewelled spectacles for its decipherment. After three years Moroni removed the plates. The book contains many novel interpretations of history, stating, for example, that the American Indians are the ten lost tribes of Israel. The Church was founded in 1830. The Mormons believe full *salvation* is only possible within this Church and that Jesus is a saviour who will found a new Jerusalem or *Zion* in America. It is thus a Millenarian sect.

The early Mormons went west and founded Salt Lake City in Utah. They practised polygamy and executed sinners. These practices were abolished when Utah became a state of the United States in 1896.

Today the Church is growing rapidly in numbers, owing to the tireless work of its missionaries. Among its distinctive customs is that of 'baptizing the dead', by holding a type of baptism service in order to include the dead relatives of Mormons within the Church. Great efforts are made to trace the family trees of Mormon believers so that such baptisms can take place. The Mormons practise a form of *Eucharist* using water instead of wine, since they are forbidden to use all drugs, including alcohol, tobacco and caffeine.

Church of Scotland *See*: **Presbyterianism**.

ciborium A covered cup used for holding the *consecrated* wafers of the *Eucharist* in Roman Catholic and some Anglican churches.

circumcision The cutting away of the foreskin on the penis. Circumcision is practised by the followers of Judaism and Islam. The ceremony usually takes place eight days after birth for Jews, and at a few years of age for Muslims; it is accompanied by great rejoicing and festivities.

The Cistercian order of monks was originally moved to build with austerity, but the increase in their numbers created a need for more extended structures. This led to graceful, sometimes spectacularly original buildings such as Fountains Abbey in Britain.

Cistercians A Roman Catholic order of monks founded at the end of the eleventh century. The order was noted for the strictness with which they interpreted their laws, the Rule of St Benedict, and for their devotion to poverty, physical work, and a simple lifestyle. Large numbers of uneducated laymen joined the monasteries and worked on their huge farms. In the eighteenth century, after a period of decline, a movement of reform started at the monastery of La Trappe in France, and the *Trappists*, as the reformed order was called, took refuge in North America and eventually separated from the Cistercians proper. Their habit, or garment, is white with a black cowl. There are also convents of Cistercian and Trappist nuns.

clergy A group or body of *ordained* people in a religion, who are set apart from the rest of the believers – the laity – by their ritual duties.

The cloisters were often positioned on the south side of the adjoining church to catch the sunlight, but the open arcades must have been cold and cheerless during the winter months.

cloister The square or rectangular covered way joined on to a church or monastery, which encloses an open court known as the cloister-garth. In monasteries the cloister usually forms part of the passage which links the church with the chapter house and other outlying buildings. The word 'cloister' is also used as a general term for a monastery.

collect A short prayer which comes before the reading of the *epistle* in the *Mass* of the Roman Catholic Church and the *Communion* service of the Anglican and Lutheran Churches. The collect varies at least each week and is also recited in the morning and evening offices of these Churches.

The word 'collect' has its origins in the Latin 'collecta', an assembly, and dates back to the time when people gathered together before going in procession elsewhere. The collect sums up the various things which the Church wishes people to pray for in that particular service.

Commandments *See*: **Ten Commandments**.

Commination The service which the Anglican Church substituted for the Roman Catholic distribution of ashes on *Ash Wednesday*. The main part of the service, to which its title refers, is the reading of a long list of sins in which God is said to curse the person who commits them.

Communion *See*: **Eucharist**.

communism This term is today normally applied only to that theory of communism which is inspired by the teachings of *Karl Marx* and Lenin and practised in, for example, the USSR and China. Other forms of communism, however, have also been conceived, but behind all forms is the notion that any kind of property should belong to the community as a whole and not to the individual. Equally, a person should not work for himself, herself, or any other person, but for the good of the community. Utopian communism maintains that all individuals have the right to food, housing and dignity at work, which should be provided by the state. All individuals are equal in the eyes of the state, and thus should be given equal opportunities in education and welfare. In return, everyone is expected to offer his or her labour, to the best of his or her ability, for the good of all. Modern systems of communism, such as bolshevism, argue that such a system must be imposed by a totalitarian state dominated by a single political party.

Marxist-Leninist thought was received and adapted by mainland China early this century, and forms the ideological basis of Chinese politics. This parade shows workers in Hangchow demonstrating their pride in communal achievement. These young men and women are clearly in a festive mood and it is interesting to note that here and there the ubiquitous dark Chinese jacket is giving way to a lighter, casual, knitted top.

International Worker's Day, 1st May, is celebrated by marchers and family groups in Moscow's Red Square. A giant banner showing Marx, Engels and Lenin can be seen in the background, and portraits of Soviet leaders are being carried by members of the crowd. There is an air of holiday and the children are carrying balloons.

compline The Roman Catholic, Anglican and Orthodox night service, first introduced in the fourth century. It is the last of the six or seven Canonical Hours, or daily official services of the Church. Often it is sung as an evening service on Sundays in Roman Catholic churches.

conclave The Roman Catholic assembly of *cardinals* who meet to elect a new *Pope* on the death of the previous Pope. Eighteen days after his death, the conclave is called in great secrecy in the *Vatican*, and the members are locked in until they have reached a decision. The majority needed is two-thirds of the members plus one. When this is reached, a new Pope has been elected; the voting papers are burnt, producing white smoke that informs the public of the success of the conclave. If a vote fails to reach this majority, however, the papers are dampened before burning and the black smoke produces signals that another vote will have to be taken.

Concord, Book of The collection of documents, compiled in the sixteenth century, which contains the doctrines of the *Lutheran Churches*. By the beginning of this century, one of these documents, the Augsburg Confession, had come to be regarded as more important than the others and Lutherans today recognize it as the most satisfactory summary of their beliefs.

confessing church A grouping of Protestants in Nazi Germany who refused to accept *Hitler*'s ideology. A group of representatives were responsible for the *Barmen Declaration* of 1934.

confession Known also as penance, in Christianity, the declaration of personal sins made to a priest. In Roman Catholicism, the penitents tells their sins to the confessor, expresses repentance and asks for *absolution*. The confessor then gives advice to the penitent, imposes a penance which is usually a prayer, and declares that God has forgiven the penitent's sins. Anything which a priest is told during confession has to remain a secret, even if the priest is under pain of death to reveal the information. This is known as 'seal of confession'. The Roman Catholic and Orthodox Churches consider confession as one of the seven *sacraments*.

confessional Any structure in a Roman Catholic or Anglican Church where a priest sits to hear confessions.

51

confirmation A religious service common to Roman Catholic, Eastern, Anglican, Lutheran and several other churches which confirms or completes the ceremony of *baptism*. In the first two churches mentioned, confirmation is regarded as one of the seven *sacraments*. The practice of infant baptism and confirmation is normal in the Eastern Churches. In all other Churches, however, the age for confirmation has been changed to early adolescence. Confirmation is believed to give the participant the gift of the *Holy Spirit*, who gives the person strength to live the Christian life.

In the Roman Catholic and Eastern Churches, the participant is anointed with holy oil, usually by a bishop in the Roman Catholic Church, but by a priest in the Eastern Churches. The holy oil is known as *chrism*, hence the Eastern name of Chrismation for confirmation. In the Anglican and other Protestant Churches, the bishop (in the Anglican Church) or minister (in the others) lays his hands on the person's head as a sign of God's blessing.

Many Jewish Reform synagogues hold a confirmation service which takes place several years after the Bar- or Bat-Mitzvah, preparation for which helps to involve the young person in learning more about Judaism.

conformist Anyone who conforms to, or acts in harmony with, the usages and practices of an *Established Church*, especially the *Church of England*. The term is used most often to differentiate it from other English Protestants, who are called *Nonconformists*.

Confucianism The traditional religion of China, also known as the 'school of the learned' (Jii-kiao) to distinguish it from *Taoism*, the 'school of the way'. It has tended, however, to merge with Taoism and Buddhism into a composite set of Chinese beliefs. It includes the traditional ideas found in the books edited by *Confucius*, as well as ideas drawn from his own books, such as the *Analects*, and from those of his disciples, such as the *Great Learning*. Confucius is therefore the transmitter of this religion, not its founder. Among the texts of Confucianism are the *I Ching* and the *Annals*.

In Confucianism there is no *pantheon* of gods, or priesthood, no *creed* and no official organisation. There is an idea of a *Supreme Being* known as 'Heaven' or T'ien.

The main characteristic of Chinese religion is the importance given to *ancestor-worship*. This involves making offerings of food and other gifts to the ancestors to keep them content in the next world. One main way of ensuring that the offerings reach the after-life, which is seen as a world in all essentials identical to this one, is to burn paper models of the gifts needed by the ancestors. The gifts are then recreated in solid form in the next world. Such ancestor-worship can reach a tremendous degree of complexity, since it is the duty of the present family to keep all their known ancestors content in the next world; therefore sufficient offerings must be provided to ensure this.

The *morality* encouraged by Confucianism tends to be drawn from the ideas of Confucius himself; the ideal virtues are those of harmony and moderation (the Middle Way) and filial piety, expressed in ancestor-worship.

Since mainland China became Communist in 1949, the practice of Confucianism has been widely discouraged, but it lives on to some extent in other Chinese communities, including that of Hong Kong.

Confucius The Latin form of the name K'ung Fu-Tzu, the Chinese scholar and philosopher. Confucius lived from about 551 to about 479BCE. Very little is known about his origins. He is variously said to have been a man of good family, a civil servant in the state of Lu, the head of an academy for local intelligent youth and eventually an extremely successful minister of public works and pastures, who was dropped from this post because of the machinations of jealous enemies. He is then said to have become a wandering teacher and finally editor and reviewer of the classic texts of Chinese religion. It is because of his work in editing and transmitting these traditional texts that the specifically Chinese form of religion is generally known as Confucianism, even though some of the same texts are the basis for *Taoism* as well.

A book composed by disciples of Confucius, the *Analects*, gives an impression of his main interests. Religion as such, the worship of a *pantheon* of gods, and ceremonies such as sacrifices seem to have had little appeal for him. He was more interested in morality; he believed that man should live a harmonious, balanced life, avoiding all extremes in emotion and behaviour. This he called the 'Middle Way'; it would produce, he hoped, the 'Supreme Man' who would be a calm, moderate, well-mannered person who respected his parents and ancestors, and who did his best to bring about peace in himself, in society and in the world. He accepted *ancestor-worship* as the traditional expression of the highest virtue, filial piety, but he thought such worship should be confined to one's own ancestors and not extended to those of other families. He also accepted worship of the Supreme Being, Heaven, although in describing this Supreme Being he often seems to identify it simply with nature itself.

After his death, the memory of Confucius was increasingly honoured. Emperors, the people and his own family all worshipped him and even put him on the same level as Heaven. Pilgrimages have been made for centuries to his burial place at K'iuh Fow.

congregation (1) An assembly of people who come together for the purposes of religious worship, especially in Christianity. (2) Certain orders of monks, nuns and priests are called 'congregations'. (3) Certain committees of cardinals, bishops and priests in the Roman Catholic Church are also called 'congregations'.

Congregationalism The present-day Protestant Church which follows the ideas of the seventeenth century English *Independents*, who in turn had grown out of the sixteenth-century Brownists. The Congregationalist Church believes that each local congregation is complete in itself as a church, and should govern itself as far as possible. Thus Congregationalists do not have Popes, bishops, or kings at their head, but simply follow what they regard as the teachings of Christ as recounted in the Bible. Each congregation chooses its own deacons and minister who dresses as he likes. He does not preach a set system of beliefs handed down by a central authority, but simply interprets the Bible.

In the seventeenth century, the newly formed movement was persecuted in England and many members fled to Holland and America. The Pilgrim Fathers who sailed to New England in the Mayflower in 1620 were Congregationalists.

The term Congregationalist has normally been used only in Britain, where most Congregational Churches have now been absorbed into the *United Reformed Church*, which came about through the union of the Presbyterian and Congregational Churches of England (and, in part, of Wales).

These dissenters from the established religion are departing from Delft in July 1620. on their way to Plymouth and thence across the Atlantic to the New World. Note the banner being carried. which reads 'Freedom of Worship'.

conscientious objector Anyone who refuses to take part in military training and service on grounds of conscience, that is, because he believes it is wrong to kill or attack another human being. Various Christian groups have criticised conscription and military service and refused to kill their fellow men. The most prominent among them are the *Quakers*, Mennonites, *Jehovah's Witnesses*, *Seventh Day Adventists* and the Church of the *Brethren*. Because of the teaching of *ahimsa*, or non-violence, many Buddhists and Hindus also refuse to do military service. Some conscientious objectors agree to do military service that does not involve fighting, such as medical or intelligence work; others are totally opposed to participating in any way. They believe problems may be solved without violence.

consecration An act which sets people or things apart for the service of God and thus makes them holy. In the Christian Church, the *rite* is usually performed by bishops, although the consecration of the bread and wine during *Mass* can be done by a priest as well. Priests, and especially monks and nuns who devote their entire lives to their religion, are often regarded as consecrated.

conservatism An attitude or political set of beliefs which wants to preserve established institutions and practices and opposes radical change. Conservatives believe that change must be gradual if it is to be worthwhile and not destructive.

Conservative Judaism A movement which stands halfway between the *Orthodox* and *Reform* schools of *Judaism*. Conservative Jews accept the traditional law but make allowance for modern conditions and leave room for a limited number of changes and varieties of belief. Unlike the Orthodox, Conservatives allow women to sit with men in the *synagogue* and do not only use Hebrew for prayers. In the main, however, their services and ceremonies are closer to Orthodox than to Reform practice.

Constantine I (CE280?–337) Known as 'the Great', this fourth-century Roman emperor is believed to have been converted to Christianity in CE312. In a dream Constantine is said to have seen a fiery cross with the words 'In this sign conquer'; afterwards, he issued the Edict of Milan, ordering the toleration of Christianity which had been banned previously. By CE313, Christians were no longer persecuted as a matter of policy within the empire, and when Constantine decided to move his capital to Byzantium

The early Christians were persecuted and hunted down in the first three centuries following Jesus' death, but in Constantine I they found a champion. From the conversion of the emperor. Christianity was safe to establish itself throughout the known world.

(now Istanbul), he dedicated the city to the Blessed Virgin and named it Constantinople, after himself. In CE325 Constantine presided over the Council of Nicaea, at which many of the chief doctrines of mainstream Christianity were decided and summarised in the *Nicene Creed*.

contemplation A spiritual activity which attempts to empty the mind of all thoughts except God, ultimate reality, or the Absolute. It is especially common in Sufi, Christian, Taoist and some forms of Hindu mysticism, and various methods are practised in the different religions to reach this state. The aim of most contemplation is to reach some sort of experience of, or union with, God or the Absolute. *See also*: **meditation**.

contrition A feeling of sorrow and remorse for having sinned. Roman Catholics distinguish between perfect contrition, inspired purely by sorrow for having offended God, and imperfect contrition which may be occasioned by fear of punishment.

convent Another word for a nunnery or a religious house for Christian women. Convents are governed by the same sorts of rules that govern monasteries and are often centres of active charity, education or nursing work.

convert Someone who has changed from one belief to another or has adopted a set of religious beliefs which they formerly rejected as false.

Coptic Church The Coptic churches are the national Christian churches of Egypt and Ethiopia. Together with the Armenian *Orthodox* and Syrian *'Jacobite' Churches*, they form the *Monophysite* group of churches, which split from the rest of Christianity after the Council of Chalcedon in 451. This Council decided that Jesus Christ had two natures at once, a *divine* nature and a human nature. He was thus at one and the same time fully God and fully man. The Monophysites reject this teaching, saying that Christ has only one nature, a combination of divine and human, in which the divinity is overwhelmingly more important.

Corpus Christi A festival of the Roman Catholic Church in honour of the *Eucharist*. An outdoor procession of the consecrated *Host* is frequently held on the following Sunday. The festival is not officially observed by Anglicans, although it has been revived during this century.

covenant Also known as a testament. Any form of bargain or agreement. In the Old Testament or *Torah* the term refers to God's agreements with his Chosen People, especially to God's promise to Moses to lead them from slavery in Egypt to the *Promised Land* if they kept the Ten Commandments and the rest of the *Torah*. This was itself a restatement of the promise given to Noah and Abraham in return for their faith in God. A further covenant was made with King *David*: God promised to ensure that the Hebrews would always have a king to rule them, provided they were faithful. The Old Testament prophets Jeremiah and Ezekiel also look forward to a new, future covenant after the exile in Babylon.

The Christian religion believes that this Jewish or 'Old' Covenant has been replaced by a 'New' Covenant between God and the Christian Church recorded in the *New Testament*.

Creation In theistic religions, the act by which God brought the universe into being. Hindus traditionally believe that the universe is an extension of God and is therefore part of him, and will return into him at the end of time. Judaism, Islam and Christianity believe that the universe is separate from God, but was brought into being by God out of nothing, a theory known as 'creatio ex nihil', that is, creation from nothing. According to the Bible, nothing existed before the universe was made, apart from God; then God willed the universe to be there. The act of creation took six days, and on the seventh day God rested; hence the origins of the Sabbath (Saturday), the day of rest.

creation myth Most religions contain in their *scriptures* a story of how the world and man came into existence. These stories are attempts to explain (*a*) that the existence of the universe is not an accident, but part of a design; and (*b*), in simple terms, how this design may have been carried out. Well-known creation myths are contained in the *Old Testament* for Christianity the *Torah* for Judaism, and the *Rig-Veda* for Hinduism.

creed A statement of religious beliefs accepted as correct by the Church or religion concerned.

cremation The disposal of a dead body by reducing it to ashes with fire. Cremation is forbidden by some faiths, including the Parsi and Baha'i faiths, but widely practised by Hindus, Buddhists, Sikhs and Christians.

In accordance with Hindu belief in reincarnation, the bodies of the dead are cremated, the quicker to free the spirit from its former embodiment. The likeness of a cow is also being burned as a sacrificial offering.

crib A representation of the manger in which the infant Jesus was laid at birth. It is usually to be found in churches and Christian homes over the Christmas period. *See also*: **bambino**.

cross The chief symbol of Christianity. It was on a cross that Jesus was executed by crucifixion and, according to Christianity, fulfilled his role as *Redeemer* of man and the world. The sign of the cross is made as an act of faith, a blessing, or a prayer. During the Crusades, the Crusaders took the cross as their emblem.

Calvinists tend not to use the cross as a sign of faith, although the Anglicans and Lutherans keep it as a reminder of the crucifixion and use it for ceremonies.

crucifix A model of a cross which bears an image of the crucified Christ.

crucifixion A form of capital punishment practised in the ancient world by Persians, Romans and Carthaginians. The condemned man was bound or nailed to the crossbeam and raised to hang from the cross until he died of exposure or asphyxiation. It was traditional to place a board above the man's head, giving his name and the reason for the punishment.

Christ was crucified on the orders of *Pontius Pilate*, the Roman governor of Judaea, in about CE28 or 29. Together with the *Resurrection*, the Crucifixion is the central event in the Christian religion.

crypt A vault under the main floor of a church which is used as a place of burial, and often as a chapel for smaller services. Many churches now use their crypts for youth clubs or as soup kitchens or shelters for the poor and homeless.

cult (1) The system of rituals and ceremonies performed in a religion. (2) A religious sect. (3) *Devotion* to and veneration of a particular saint or god within a religion: for example, the cult of the *Virgin Mary* within Christianity, or the cult of *Shiva* or *Krishna* in Hinduism.

cynicism A philosophy in ancient Greece. Cynics held that virtue was the only thing worth aiming for, and that it could only be achieved if one was completely free of worldly pleasures and needs. They were critical of *materialism* and ignored social conventions. Over the centuries, however, the word 'cynic' has aquired a very different meaning. It is now applied to people who suspect the motives behind virtue or apparently good and kind deeds: modern cynics believe that all behaviour is prompted by selfishness and tend to believe, therefore, that real goodness is impossible to achieve.

d

dagoba A *stupa* in Sri Lanka usually enclosing a Buddhist relic.

dakhma A *Parsi* structure also known as a 'tower of silence', where the dead are laid naked to be devoured by vultures and crows.

Dakhmas are built outside residential areas and sprang up as a result of the Parsi belief that earth and water are sacred and not to be polluted by the touch of death; fire is also sacred, therefore cremation is forbidden. In their view, the vulture was created to devour the dead.

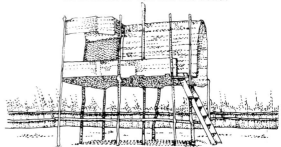

Upon the death of a Parsi, the body is taken by the mourners to a dakhma, or tower of silence, and is placed on the open platform. Shortly afterwards, vultures and crows gather round to devour it.

Dalai Lama The spiritual head of Tibetan Buddhism and, until 1959, the head of state in Tibet. Since then the present Dalai Lama, the fourteenth, has lived in exile, mostly in India.

Tibetan Buddhists believe that each Dalai Lama is the *reincarnation* of his predecessor and that all are manifestations of *Avalokitesvara*, the *bodhisattva* of compassion. The first Dalai Lama was acknowledged as such in the fifteenth century. *See also*: **lama**.

Damballah Wedo *Voodoo* deity known as the great serpent, associated with the birth and continuity of life: his followers dance in a weaving way to suggest the motion of the snake, and when possessed of his spirit, they climb trees and hiss in imitation of his all-knowing but unknowable words. Damballah is associated with water and is pictured as coiled around the world, kindly embracing the territory over which he has power.

damnation The opposite of *salvation*. Christians and Muslims hold that those who are not worthy to be united to God in heaven or paradise after the *Last Judgement* are condemned to live in an eternal state of punishment, often pictured as torture by fire. The place of their punishment is usually known as hell.

dana Willingness to give generously, a desired quality in every faithful Buddhist.

The word is also used for the 'giving ceremony' which can take place after a Buddhist marriage. The married couple go to a monastery where the monks or bhikkhus relate Buddha's teaching on marriage; the couple then give some food to the monks by putting it into their food bowls.

Daniel One of the books of the *Old Testament* or *Hebrew Bible*; it belongs to the section known as the *Writings*. The story it tells is set in the sixth century BCE, at the time of the exile of the Jews to Babylon; it was probably written, however, between 167 and 164 BCE during the persecution of the Jews by the Greeks, just before Judah Maccabaees revolted and led his people to freedom. The book is in two parts; the first tells how Daniel, as a slave in the court of King Nebuchadnezzar, overcame many near-disasters, including being thrown into a den of lions. The second part describes the end of the world, with the overthrow of all the enemies of the Jews at the coming of the *Messiah*, and the final establishment of the *Kingdom of God*.

Daruma A doll charm which is sold at New Year to Japanese children and looks like the *Zen Buddhist* master Daruma, or *Bodhidharma*. Although the dolls are Buddhist in origin, they are also sold at the entrance to *Shinto* shrines, where they are burnt for good luck in the coming year.

Darwinism The theory that plant and animal species are not immutable or created in a fixed form by *God* but evolve, or change through time, and that this evolution happens by a process of 'natural selection'. This last phrase was coined by Charles Darwin (1809–82), an English naturalist. In his book *The Origin of Species* (1859), he observed that the members of a species vary one from another. Some have characteristics which give them an advantage in surviving and breeding: these will have more offspring than others, or – as Darwin put it – nature 'selects' those best able to survive, what later thinkers called 'survival of the fittest'. Their characteristics are passed on to later generations and the less suitable characteristics die out. Thus the species changes, and out of one species evolves one or more new species.

In *The Origin of Species*, Darwin also amassed and organised the biological and geological evidence that evolution had taken place. These theories have become the foundation of modern biology, but they directly contradict a literal interpretation of the story of creation in the *Torah* and the Qu'ran. So Darwinism has always met bitter resistance from Christian, Jewish and Muslim fundamentalists who believe in the literal truth of the *scriptures*.

Dasam Granth The Last Granth: a collection of the writings of *Gobind Singh*, the tenth Sikh *guru*, compiled in 1734 by Bhai Mani Singh. In addition to the guru's poems and writings, the volume includes the work of several other poets. Sikhs do not use the book itself as frequently as the *Adi Granth*.

dastur A *Parsi* priest in charge of keeping lit the fires which are sacred to *Ahura Mazda* and which symbolize his purity and goodness. The Parsi priesthood is hereditary.

David A King of the Hebrews in the eleventh and tenth centuries BCE who made Jerusalem his capital and was renowned for his talents as warrior, poet, leader and musician. A number of psalms in the Old Testament, or Hebrew Bible, are said to have been composed by him.

David is the subject of many stories including an account of his legendary friendship with Jonathan, the son of Saul, who was King of Israel prior to David. Another story concerns a battle between the Israelites and the Philistines, where the two armies were represented by their respective champions, the Philistine champion being Goliath of Gath, a giant of a man, while David, an untried youth, put himself forward to represent his people. Goliath was armed with sword, spear and shield, but David took out a slingshot and killed him with a stone.

After David's death, his son, Solomon, became King and both Judaism and Christianity believed that the Messiah would be a descendant of the family of David. Jesus Christ is said by Christians to have fulfilled this prophecy; the Jews are still expecting the Messiah to come.

Day of Atonement *See*: **Yom Kippur**.

Day of Judgement *See*: **Judgement, Day of**.

deacon The lowest of the three major '*holy orders*' in the Roman Catholic, Anglican and Orthodox Churches.

In the Roman Catholic and Orthodox Churches the deacon is allowed to *preach* and *baptize* and assist at Mass. The Anglican Church permits deacons to perform all the duties of ordained priests except for the *consecration* of the Eucharist and the pronouncement of *absolution* and *benediction*. Among *Baptists*, *Congregationalists* and other *Nonconformists* the name is given to laymen who are elected to manage the affairs of the church.

These precious scrolls survived undiscovered inside earthenware jars for nearly two thousand years. Scholars were presented with the hidden documents of a Jewish sect, including Old Testament manuscripts which predate by a thousand years the earliest previously known.

Dead Sea Scrolls Parchment scrolls, dating mostly from the first century CE and preserved in the dry air of caves near to the Dead Sea in Israel until they were discovered by a shepherd in 1947. They consist of hymns, laws, teachings and interpretations of the *Hebrew Bible* and, above all, include the oldest existing texts of certain books of the *Old Testament*. The scrolls are thought to have been written by members of a Jewish sect known as the *Essenes*. The particular community which wrote the scrolls lived in a type of monastery at *Qumran*, which has been successfully excavated. The scrolls were hidden in the caves during the Roman persecution of the Jews after 135BCE. The Qumran community abandoned their home, leaving the scrolls behind.

dean An official in Christian churches. In the Roman Catholic Church the dean is a priest chosen by his bishop to supervise several parishes. In the Church of England, a dean is the priest in overall charge of a cathedral, or the main priest of a *chapel* attached to a university or college; he is in charge of other priests, who together make up a '*chapter*'. A rural dean acts as a spokesman for the clergy of the parishes in his deanery, or area.

deanery *See*: **dean**.

deism A system of belief which recognises the existence of a God but denies that he has revealed himself to the world by means of *scriptures*, *prophets*, etc. It is opposed to *theism*, which believes that God has revealed himself through prophets or scriptures to man and his other creatures, and it is opposed to *atheism*, which denies the existence of God.

deity Any *divine* being, especially: (1) Any god or goddess in a *polytheistic* religion. (2) God, or the Supreme Being, of a *monotheistic* religion.

democracy A political theory or system of government in which the people who live in any one country govern themselves or, at any rate, choose who is to govern them. They should also be able to change the government if it proves unsatisfactory. Most modern democracies are 'representative' democracies: the people elect representatives at will to an assembly, such as Parliament, or a legislature, which then controls the government.

denomination A group within, or branch of, a religion. The term is used especially to refer to any branch of the Christian Church that includes many local *congregations*.

dervish A member of a *Sufi* order who lives a semi-monastic life following the path of *mysticism*. Dervishes are respected for the physical feats which they are able to perform when in a state of ecstasy. These include swallowing red-hot coals and dancing on glass; they do this to demonstrate how total reliance on God enables his followers to do apparently impossible things, and frees them from any pain or bleeding during their performances. Reciting the names of God and dancing bring about states of ecstasy in dervishes.

despotism A despot is a tyrant who rules with absolute power, taking no notice of the needs or wishes of those whom he rules. Despotism is a term used to describe the rule of such an individual, who often ignores the law or changes it to suit his wishes.

determinism A philosophical theory which states that there is no such thing as *free will* and that man's actions and decisions are caused solely by forces and circumstances acting upon his will in a way that is outside his control; these may come from his psychological or mental make-up, the social conditions in which he lives, his physical needs, etc.

Deva (Sanskrit, 'a god') One of the good spirits in Hinduism, Buddhism and Jainism.

Devadatta A cousin and pupil of the Buddha, who broke away from the Sangha to form an order with more stringent rules.

Devaloka The world of a god. In Hinduism, any of the paradises, particularly the abode of *Indra*.

Devi *See*: **Mahadevi**.

Devil, The The force of evil in Christianity, Judaism and Islam. Also known as *Satan*, *Lucifer* and *Iblis*, he is traditionally supposed to command a host of lesser devils. At the *Last Judgement*, it is believed, he will finally be defeated and consigned to *hell* forever.

In general, any evil force opposed to a good God in any religion as, for example, *Ahriman* in *Zoroastrianism*.

In most of the major religions, the Devil is seen as an angel who fell from grace, but representations of him usually depict him as ugly in outward form as he is within. This woodcut, from the *Nuremburg Chronicles* of 1493, shows a horned devil on horseback, together with a witch.

devotion (1) Prayers or any other form of religious worship. (2) Religious enthusiasm or fervour. (3) Passionate love and reverence towards God, a god, or some other spiritual ideal or being.

dhamma The equivalent of *dharma* in *Pali*, an ancient Indian language used in Buddhism.

Dhammacakka Day Major Buddhist festival celebrating the Buddha's first sermon 'Setting in motion the Wheel of Truth (*dhamma*)'.

Dhammapada A Buddhist *scripture* of the Pali canon which urges men to pursue their own spiritual development now, and describes the true joys of spiritual life and *enlightenment* in comparison with our normal, passing pleasures.

dharma A word with many different meanings, found in several Indian languages. In Hinduism its most important meaning is that of '*caste* duties and obligations'. Each caste has its own particular dharma, covering both the jobs traditionally done by caste members and the religious duties they should perform. If a caste member does his dharma correctly he acquires good *karma*. This means that in his next life he will be born in a higher caste or on a higher plane of existence, nearer his final union with God. This teaching is emphasized in the *Bhagavad Gita*. Sometimes Hinduism itself is called 'the Eternal Dharma', which means 'the Eternal Way': this implies that if Hinduism is followed correctly, the Universe will remain in order, in harmony with itself and with God.

In Buddhism, the most important sense of dharma is the Teaching of the Buddha. Since the Buddha taught people how to gain *enlightenment*, dharma is often translated as the 'Way' or 'Path' to enlightenment, or simply as the 'Truth'. Buddhism describes quite a few different ways in which someone can become enlightened, but the Buddha also taught that anything which increases generosity, love and wisdom is dharma. Similarly, anything which increases greed, hatred or ignorance is not dharma. *See also*: **reincarnation**.

Dharmakaya *See*: **Trikaya**.

dhikr An Islamic meeting, at which dervishes chant prayers or passages from the Qu'ran rhythmically to glorify God and to bring on a state of ecstasy.

Dhyani Buddhas *See*: **Jina**.

diabolism The worship of the Devil or evil. As such it includes the worship of the Devil as the enemy of God and the spirit of evil. Many Christians describe witchcraft and other rites and religions they strongly dislike as diabolism.

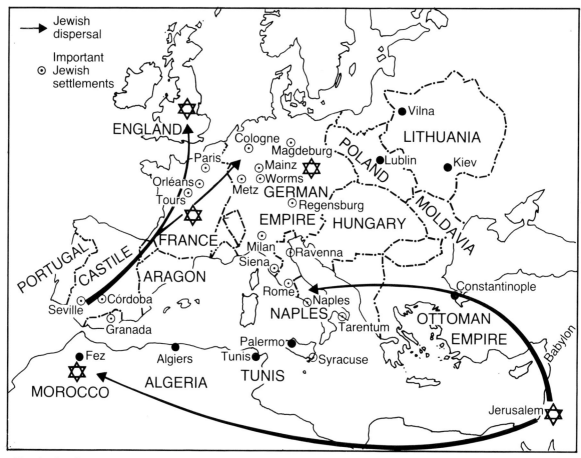

Jewish dispersal

⊙ Important Jewish settlements

ENGLAND
Cologne ⊙
Paris
Magdeburg ⊙ Mainz ✡
Orléans ⊙ ⊙ Worms
Tours
Metz GERMAN
FRANCE
EMPIRE
Milan ⊙
Siena ⊙ ⊙ Ravenna
PORTUGAL CASTILE
ARAGON
Córdoba Rome ⊙ Naples
Seville NAPLES
Granada Tarentum
Fez Palermo
Algiers Tunis Syracuse
MOROCCO ALGERIA TUNIS

LITHUANIA
Vilna
Lublin Kiev
POLAND
MOLDAVIA
HUNGARY
Constantinople
OTTOMAN EMPIRE
Babylon
Jerusalem ✡

After the first Roman conquest of Jerusalem under Vespasian, there was, sixty years later, a revolt of the Jews which was put down by Hadrian. From that time the Jews spread into every region of the Roman Empire, settling particularly in the Balkans, Asia Minor, North Africa and Spain. They were, in the early middle ages, put under the personal protection of the King but, around the time of the Crusades, they were increasingly subject to persecution. This persecution mounted, culminating in pogroms and the expulsion of the Jews from many European countries. Homeless, they escaped eastwards and banded together into communities in an effort to protect themselves.

Diaspora The dispersal of the Jewish people outside the land of Israel, which began with the Babylonian exile, and came to a head in CE70 after the Romans destroyed Jerusalem. The Jews spread mainly to the Middle East and North Africa and later to Russia, Poland, Germany, Britain and the United States.

dietary laws Any set of traditions in a religion which dictates what foods may be eaten or how they must be prepared. In *Orthodox Judaism* all food must be *kosher*, that is, it must be 'fit to eat'. For example, only the meat of animals that have cloven hooves and chew the cud is permissible in the human diet, and the mixing of meat and milk is prohibited. Birds of prey and certain fish cannot be consumed. Pork, shellfish and prawns are all forbidden.

Islam, influenced here by Judaism, also bans pork; in addition, it forbids alcohol. In both Judaism and Islam, proper (kosher or *halal*) killing is essential; for example, a cow must be slaughtered with one clean cut in the throat and drained of blood entirely. Some forms of Hinduism and the *Jain* religion ban meat products on the grounds of *ahimsa*, or non-violence, to living creatures. Orthodox Hindus will not eat beef, as the cow is a sacred animal to them.

Digambaras Literally, 'sky-clad'. A *Jain* sect whose monks practise total nudity. The sect is found mostly in Southern India.

diocese The district which is under the authority of a bishop in a Christian Church.

disciple Someone who follows the teachings of another person, especially of a religious leader. Christ's first followers are called disciples in the *New Testament*.

dispensation A relaxation of a rule in the Roman Catholic Church, usually granted by a bishop, in cases of hardship. For example, people who cannot fast on *Good Friday* for health reasons are automatically granted a dispensation to ignore the obligatory fast.

divine kingship A European political theory with its roots in the Hebrew Bible, or Old Testament, which sees God as the source of political authority, which he gives to kings and princes. They are responsible for their actions only to him, and not to the people they rule; rules do not need the agreement of their subjects. It is the duty of ordinary people to obey, because if they do not, then they are indirectly disobeying God. This divine office of king was believed to be inherited, usually from father to son. The theory had a strong influence on government and political thinkers, especially from the fifteenth to seventeenth centuries.

divine law Commandments or *revelations* from God or a god which set out a system of rules and prescriptions for people to follow in their life on earth.

Divine Light Mission Founded in 1960, the Divine Light Mission proclaims that the Perfect Master for the present age is Guru Maharaj Ji, the son of the founder. By 1973 more than six million members were hoping to receive his 'perfect guidance', by having the 'third eye', which lies within every human being, opened to the light by this Perfect Master. He is seen as a successor to Buddha, Jesus, Krishna and Muhammad. Premies, the followers of the Guru, may live in an *ashram* and dedicate themselves totally to serving the Mission, or may live in a premie house which has a less strict routine. They believe salvation is achieved by 'Knowledge' which comes to them through the cosmic energy given out by Guru Maharaj Ji.

Divine Principle The sacred writings of the *Unification Church*, founded by *Sun Myung Moon*. The book tries to combine elements of Christianity, Islam and Buddhism with *Taoist* notions of God, and preaches a unification of the religions of the world under a coming Messiah.

diviner Someone who is believed to be able to foretell the future by reading the signs of nature or studying certain objects such as stones and playing cards. Tarot-card readers and interpreters of the *I Ching*, the Chinese Book of Changes, are diviners. Some diviners just look for one particular substance, such as water, to which they believe their bodies have a special

With the aid of globe and compasses, this early diviner is drawing up an astrological chart.

sensitivity; they claim to be able to detect its presence by the vibrations in the 'divining rod', or forked stick, which they carry.

divinity A word meaning 'the essence of God', but also used in a number of other ways. The study of divinity is the study of *theology*, or the science of divine things, including the nature of God and his relations with man.

A divinity can also be the Divine Being, or a minor deity or god in a *polytheistic* religion.

Diwali Also spelled *Divali*. The New Year festival of the Hindus and Sikhs, held in October/November. The Hindus celebrate the return of the hero *Rama* from exile and his reunion with *Sita*, his consort. Bonfires are lit and images of the demon *Ravana* burnt. People also light lamps to welcome *Lakshmi*, the goddess of wealth, into their homes. The celebration is also known as the 'Festival of Lights'.

The Sikhs celebrate the laying of the foundation stone of the *Golden Temple* by Guru Ram Das by lighting up the sacred city of *Amritsar* and lighting their homes with lamps. Presents are also exchanged.

Diwan The morning service of worship in a Sikh *gurdwara*, especially the public service held, on the normal weekly holiday of the country (Sunday in the English-speaking world). The service consists of hymns, readings from the *Guru Granth Sahib* and ends with the Ardas prayer and the sharing of *karah Parshad*.

doctrine The principles, beliefs and teachings of a religion, ideology or philosophical system.

Dogen A pupil of *Eisei* who brought the teachings of *Ch'an* Buddhism in CE1227 from China to Japan, where it is called *Zen*. Dogen was the founder of the Soto school of Zen.

dogma Any body of doctrines which have been formally accepted and affirmed by a religious group, such as a sect or Church.

Dom A title given to Christian monks who are members of certain monastic orders, including the *Benedictine*, Carthusian and *Cistercian*.

dome A roof formed by a series of rounded arches or vaults set on a round or many-sided base. It is to be found in cathedrals, Greek Orthodox churches, synagogues and mosques.

Dome of the Rock Built on the site of the Temples of Solomon and Herod in Jerusalem, the Dome is a shrine over the rock from which tradition has it Muhammad ascended to heaven one night. *See also*: **Ascension**.

Dominicans A Roman Catholic order of friars and nuns founded in Toulouse in 1215 to fight the Cathar teachings, a widespread *heresy* at that time. The founder, St Dominic, stressed the use of the intellect in the service of God. The aim of the order is to teach truth, hence their motto: 'veritas' – truth. The order is divided into three branches: male preachers who spread teaching to others: enclosed nuns who live a life of prayer and contemplation; and *tertiaries*, some of whom live in the community, while others simply share in the work of the order.

Douay Bible An English translation of the Bible by Roman Catholic scholars working from the Latin *Vulgate* translation. The *New Testament* was published in Rheims in 1582 and the *Old Testament* was published in Douai in 1609–10.

dove In Christianity the dove is a symbol of the *Holy Spirit* (or *Ghost*) and of peace and hope.

The Dome of the Rock was built on the spot where Muhammad, having been taken from Mecca by the archangel Gabriel, met Abraham, Moses and Jesus, all of whom are recognized by Islam as being prophets of God. From the rock Muhammad ascended into heaven to receive Allah's message, which he then preached on his return to earth. Muslims travel on pilgrimage to Jerusalem to visit the shrine.

dreadlocks The uncut hair of male *Rastafarians*. Dreadlocks are so called because they are said to inspire dread in those who behold them. The locks help Rastafarians to identify with the warriors of the *Old Testament* and to remind them of the power of Samson's uncut hair and of his slaughter of the Philistines. Locks are a source of pride. They act as a symbol of unity and a badge of faith. They are also regarded as more natural than cut hair and therefore symbolise unity with nature and natural forces.

dreidel A four-sided top which has the Hebrew letters 'nun', 'gimel', 'he' and 'shin' inscribed on each side and is used in a children's game of chance traditionally played on the Jewish feast of *Chanukah*.

Druids The priestly order of the ancient Celts, who lived in Britain, Ireland and France, which was responsible for administration, teaching and ritual. Druids presided at ceremonies, including human and animal sacrifice. Other ceremonies involved oak and mistletoe. Druids were renowned for their ability in constructing calendars by observing the stars, planets and moon. Certain people today consider themselves to be Druids and hold ceremonies at British monuments such as Stonehenge on Midsummer's Day and on other occasions.

These distinctively dressed Muslims are Druzes, from Baalbek in Lebanon

Druzes An Islamic sect found in Syria, Israel and Lebanon. They await the return of Caliph Hakim of Egypt, whom they claim to have been the last divine manifestation, and who mysteriously disappeared. They are an offshoot of the *Ismailis*, a group of *Shi'a* Muslims. They have also tended to adopt certain teachings from Christianity, Judaism and other Middle Eastern religions.

Far from being priests of a primitive cult, the Druids in Britain were sophisticated to a high degree. At certain times, the sun's rays strike Stonehenge at angles of great precision, evidence of an advanced knowledge of astronomy.

dualism The basis of many philosophical systems, dualism is a doctrine which maintains that the world and man are both like a battle-ground where two equal and opposing forces are continually at war: the force of good and the force of evil, often pictured as light versus darkness. *Zoroastrianism* is a good example of a dualist religion; its two main gods are continually struggling to win absolute power over men and the world. *Gnosticism*, too, is a dualist religious system of this sort.

More generally, the word 'dualism' can be used of any theory which divides the world, or reality, into two opposing forces or realities, even if these are not the forces of good and evil. For example, in some Hindu philosophies, existence is divided into (*a*) what really exists, the Absolute , God or Brahman; and (*b*) what we think exists. In the philosophy of Descartes and many other thinkers, reality is divided into two main types of substance: on the one hand, body or material reality, on the other, soul or spiritual and mental reality.

dukkha The Buddhist belief that everything, however wonderful, leads to suffering. The first of the Buddha's Four Noble Truths is this insight. *See also*: **anatta** and **anicca**.

Dunkley, Archibald A colleague of *Marcus Garvey* in Jamaica who had the revelation that *Haile Selassie*, also known as *Ras Tafari*, then Emperor of Ethiopia, was the *messiah* of black people. With three men of the same conviction – *Robert Hinds*, *Leonard Howell* and *Joseph Hibbert* - Dunkley founded the *Rastafarian* faith.

Durga The consort or wife of the god *Shiva* in her warrior-like form. The goddess Durga is the object of great veneration in Hinduism, and even today, at her temple in Calcutta, animals are sacrificed to slake her thirst for blood.

Durga Puja The main Hindu festival, in honour of the goddess Durga. It is also known as 'Navaratri', meaning 'Nine nights', the length of the time it lasts. Another name for it is Dussehra. A many-sided image of the goddess is the centre of the festivities. People dance around this statue, clashing sticks together, and some may fall into trances or states of ecstasy. In India an image of the goddess is taken to a river at the end of the festival and ceremonially washed so that the goddess can make the earth productive for another year. The festival also celebrates the triumph of good over evil, of the hero *Rama* over the demon *Ravana*.

Dussehra *See*: **Durga Puja**.

e

Easter The Christian spring festival which commemorates the *resurrection* of Jesus Christ. Easter is a movable feast and was for a long time observed as a time for *baptism*, the distribution of alms, and the release of prisoners. Churches are decorated and in the Orthodox Church, bells are pealed, guns fired and sirens set off to mark the moment of resurrection.

Easter candle *See*: **paschal candle**.

Easter eggs Eggs at Easter symbolise new life, *resurrection* in Christianity. This symbol may come from old pagan rituals in Europe, celebrating the spring equinox which falls near Easter in the calendar. Christian families exchange coloured or chocolate eggs on Easter Sunday.

Eastern Orthodox Churches Also called Orthodox Churches: a family of self-governing Churches found mainly in eastern Europe, the Soviet Union and around the eastern Mediterranean. Each Church is led by a senior bishop usually known as a patriarch; among the patriarchs special honour is given to the Patriarch of Constantinople, who in some ways can be said to be the spiritual leader of this whole family of churches and as a result is known as the *ecumenical* Patriarch. The Eastern Orthodox and Roman Catholic churches formed one united church until 1054, when they split in two, largely because of the growing claims of the *Pope* to be the sole leader of all Christians everywhere, in addition to some differences over doctrines and customs.

Eblis *See*: **Iblis**.

ecclesiastic A priest, minister or other ordained person, especially in the Christian Church.

ecumenical Referring to the whole Christian Church, or to anything which promotes the unity of all Christians, such as the ecumenical movement.

In sumptuous robes these Greek and Armenian Orthodox Christians celebrate Easter, a central feast in the Christian calendar. Since the schism between the Orthodox Churches and the Roman Catholic Church, which took place in the eleventh century, the rites of these churches have evolved from the Byzantine tradition of Christianity, and much emphasis is put on the threefold nature of the godhead. The Orthodox communion recognises the four ancient patriarchates of Alexandria, Antioch, Jerusalem and Constantinople. The Patriarch, or bishop, of Constantinople is considered to be the spiritual leader for the churches, particularly those of Bulgaria, Cyprus, Greece, Romania and Russia, where the Orthodox faith is the major religion.

Ecumenical Council In theory, a meeting of all bishops of the entire Christian Church to decide points of Christian doctrine and morality. Nowadays the term is used in two ways: (1) in the Western and Eastern Orthodox Churches to describe the seven such councils of the Church held before the Orthodox and Roman Catholic Churches divided in 1054; (2) by Roman Catholics, to describe such meetings of all their bishops since 1054, presided over by the *Pope*.

ecumenical movement A movement which aims to achieve universal Christian unity. It encourages the formation of international organisations that include members of many different *denominations* to try to bring all the Churches closer together.

This portrait of Mary Baker Eddy still hangs on the wall of her Chestnut Hill house in New England.

Eddy, Mary Baker (1821–1910) The founder of *Christian Science*. Born into a *Calvinist* family, from an early age she suffered from continual ill-health. Eventually she came to the belief that a person's physical health was merely a reflection of his or her mental health. By studying the Bible she came to feel that Christ's healing powers could be recaptured in the present day and used to bring comfort to the sick. In 1875 she published *Science and Health*, which summed up her philosophy and the conclusions she had come to about the goodness and power of God. When she died, she left behind a flourishing Church.

Eden A garden which, according to the Book of Genesis in the *Pentateuch* and to the Qur'an, was planted by God for Adam and Eve, the first man and woman. After the serpent or *Iblis* had tempted them to eat the fruit of the Tree of Knowledge they fell from grace and thence from *Paradise*. Christians believe that their sin of disobedience is inherited by all mankind, in the form of *original sin*, and this accounts for human suffering and toil.

Eid-ul-fitr *See*: **Id-ul-Fitr**.

Eisei (1141–1215) The Japanese *Zen* master who, according to tradition, brought Zen Buddhism to Japan. One of his disciples was *Dogen*, who established the Soto school of Zen in Japan.

elder An official in the Presbyterian and Independent Churches. *Calvin* introduced the positions of minister and elder during the *Reformation* to replace priests and bishops. Elders have many tasks: they teach, take part in decisions affecting the government and administration of the Church, and often involve themselves in social work.

election To elect is to choose and, in Judaism and Christianity, the word 'election' refers to God's choice of the Hebrews as his chosen people through the covenant made first with *Abraham* and then with *Moses*. By the terms of this agreement, the Jews were to observe the *Torah* and to remain true to their faith, in exchange for God's protection and help. To this day, Judaism stresses that the covenant is still in force and has to be followed by Jews.

In Christianity 'election' also refers to God's choice of those people who will finally enter *heaven*.

Elijah This Jewish, Christian and Muslim *prophet* from the ninth century BCE has a name which means '*Yahweh* is God', and this is significant in that his role was to keep the people faithful to their God and to fight the forces which were threatening to turn the Hebrews to the false god, Baal. On Mount Carmel there took place a trial of power between Elijah, who was asserting that only Yahweh was to be worshipped, and the prophets of Baal and Asherah. When a mighty flash of lightning came down from the heavens on to Elijah's altar, the people were convinced, but throughout his lifetime he needed to be vigilant to prevent them from slipping into idolatry. At the end of his life Elijah passed from Bethel to Jericho and then, accompanied by his faithful follower, Elisha, parted the waters of the Jordan with his mantle. Suddenly a chariot of fire, drawn by horses of fire, appeared and he was swept up to heaven by a whirlwind.

Jews believe that Elijah takes such joy in every circumcision ceremony, and the entry of another child into God's Covenant, that he attends each ceremony. A chair is set out for him which is known as the 'Throne of Elijah'. Jews also believe that Elijah will return to herald the coming of the *Messiah*, and each year at *Pesach* a cup of wine is poured out for him.

élitism The belief that within any society a small body of people (an 'élite') will emerge or should be trained, who will be superior in knowledge, intelligence and ability to the majority of the population. Elitist theories state that a small body of this sort has the right and the duty to lead and rule the rest of the society. The political theories of the Greek philosopher Plato and the English philosopher Hobbes are élitist in character.

Elohim 'The Lord': a Hebrew title for God, used in the *Torah*, or *Old Testament*, in addition to *Yahweh*, the personal name of God.

emblem A sign, design or figure which is used to represent something else, such as a religion, institution or political party. The cross is the chief emblem of Christianity, the star of David and the *menorah* are emblems of Judaism, three swords enclosing a circle is the emblem of Sikhism.

A Jewish emblem *(left)*, the menorah, and *(right)* the symbol of Sikhism.

empiricism A philosophy which states that all true knowledge can only be based on experience gained through the use of the five senses.

End of the world The *Day of Judgement* of Christianity, Judaism, Zoroastrianism and Islam, when God comes to judge the living and the dead. The branch of theological study known as eschatology deals with death, the end of time and the implications of life after death. In Hinduism, Jainism and Buddhism, it means the completion of this world's cycle but not the end of life or worlds, because all is reborn or recreated.

enlightenment (1) In Buddhism, this is a translation of the Sanskrit word *Bodhi*, which literally means 'awakening'. It is one of the most common terms used for the goal of Buddhism, the state of being a Buddha. This goal is also called *Nirvana*, Buddhahood, liberation, the transcendental and the end of suffering, and in the later centuries is given more names, such as shunyata and the *Trikaya*. Nevertheless, the Buddha stated repeatedly that this condition of enlightenment could not be described in ordinary language: the unenlightened mind cannot grasp or understand what it means to be enlightened, to be a Buddha. Nonetheless, the Buddha did give some descriptions or indicators of enlightenment. Three such descriptions are: insight into the true nature of existence, of everything that exists, and of everything that happens; absolute wisdom, boundless compassion and unlimited energy; supreme bliss. (2) More generally, in any religion, realisation of the truth about God's or man's existence, can be called enlightenment. In some religions, such as forms of Hinduism, it can be achieved by one's own efforts; in others, such as Christianity, it can come only as the result of a revelation from God.

En Sof In the *Kabbalah*, God is often called by this name, which means 'the endless', the *Absolute*, whose nature is hidden from man and beyond his understanding.

epiclesis A short prayer within the longer prayer of *consecration* in the *Eucharist* service in the Orthodox Church. In the epiclesis the *Holy Spirit* is asked to come down from heaven on to the bread and wine, and to change them into the Body and Blood of Christ.

Epicureanism The school of thought founded in the fourth century BCE by Epicurus. According to its teachings, pleasure is the source of human happiness, and man must ignore the gods and concentrate on finding joy through the senses.

Epiphany From the Greek word for 'manifestation', a festival of the Christian Church celebrated on 6 January, when Christians remember the events in the early life of Jesus Christ. In the Roman Catholic and Protestant churches the services for this day concentrate on the visit of the *Magi*, or wise men, to Christ after his birth. In the Orthodox Church, however, it is Jesus's *baptism* by *John the Baptist* which is especially remembered; the feast is known to them as the *theophany* and on this day they hold baptisms and a special ritual of the Blessing of Water, which is often performed outdoors at a river or by the sea.

episcopal authority The authority which Roman Catholic, Orthodox and many Anglican Christians believe God has given to their bishops. They regard their bishops as successors to Christ's twelve apostles, with basically the same authority to teach the Christian faith, to interpret the meaning of the Bible for the believers and to perform the *sacraments*, especially those of *confirmation* and *ordination* (although they may share these tasks with others, such as priests, if they choose). Most Protestant churches reject this idea of the bishops' authority: they believe instead that all Christians have the right to interpret the teaching of the Bible for themselves and that God will guide each individual Christian to interpret the *scriptures* correctly.

Episcopal Church The name given to the Anglican Church in the United States, Canada and Scotland. It is given this name because, in contrast to most other Protestant churches, it is governed by bishops, who are known in Greek as 'episkopoi'.

epistle A letter. Epistles written by the Christian apostles are included in the *New Testament* and are read out during services.

esoteric Teachings within a religion or philosophy that are not made known to everyone, but only to an inner circle, are called 'esoteric'. Esoteric teachings are usually difficult to understand: that is why they are only revealed to the small number who are sincere enough, or have developed far enough spiritually, to really understand them.

Essenes Jewish *ascetics* who lived in communities similar to monasteries near the Dead Sea from 200BCE to CE200. In recent years many scholars have debated whether *John the Baptist* may have been an Essene and therefore whether Jesus may have come under their influence, but the controversy has not been resolved.

We do, however, know that as a group the Essenes practised ritual bathing, perhaps similar to *baptism*, as well as healing and *exorcism*, and that they studied alchemy and *divination*. The *Dead Sea Scrolls*, discovered in 1947, describe the rules and way of life of a Jewish sect thought to be the Essenes; they reveal a community that expected the end of the world in the near future, when they would be called upon to make war on God's enemies; afterwards they alone of the whole human race, including the Jews, would gain eternal life.

essentialism The belief that certain traditional concepts and ideals are crucial to society and should be taught methodically to everyone, regardless of individual ability or interest.

Established Church Any Christian *denomination* that enjoys a particularly privileged position within a country, such as the *Anglican Church* within England or the *Lutheran Church* in Denmark. Normally the monarch or president of the country will belong to this Church and will be, in theory, its head; the government of the country will support its principles, will listen to its comments on national affairs, and often will pay its clergy out of public taxes. The Church may, as in England, be more or less independent in running its own internal affairs, or it may, as in Denmark, be largely run by a government department. At one time the Established Church was the only one permitted to hold public services in its country, but now all denominations are allowed to operate freely in countries with an Established Church.

eternal *See*: everlasting.

ethics A branch of philosophy which deals with the values of human actions: whether they are good or bad, right or wrong, either in themselves or when viewed in terms of their effects and the motives which inspired them.

Ethiopianism The philosophy preached by *Marcus Garvey* in nineteenth-century Jamaica. He believed that the black man's spiritual home was in Africa. In this philosophy, the country of Ethiopia now represents the whole of Africa because the coronation of its emperor, Haile Selassie, in 1930 was seen as fulfilling a *prophecy* of Psalm 68 in the *Old Testament*. This says: 'Princes shall come out of Ethiopia, and Ethiopia stretch forth her hands unto God.' Garvey therefore saw Ethiopia as the spiritual centre and its emperor as spiritual leader for all Africa and for those of African origin. This led towards the creation of the *Rastafarian* religion.

Resplendent in their gorgeously decorated robes, these priests represent the Ethiopian Orthodox Church, which teaches the Christian message in the land that many Rastafarians see as their homeland.

Ethiopian Orthodox Church The branch of the *Coptic Church* which forms the national church of Ethiopia. Recently, many *Rastafarians* in Jamaica and elsewhere have joined this Church, since they see Ethiopia as their spiritual home, and regard the late Emperor Haile Selassie, who took a leading role in the Church, as their divine *Messiah*. Even though the Church rejects the Rastafarian doctrines about Haile Selassie, Rastafarians who have been baptised into the Church often hold these doctrines in combination with the Christian teachings of this Church.

ethnocentrism The belief in the superiority of one's own nation, group or culture, accompanied by a feeling of contempt for any others.

Eucharist From a Greek word meaning 'thanksgiving', this is an alternative term for the Christian service also known as the *Lord's Supper*, (*Holy*) *Communion* or *Mass*. This service is the most important act of worship in mainstream Christianity: together with baptism it is the only service which Jesus Christ directed his disciples to perform. At his Last Supper with his disciples before his crucifixion, he took bread and wine, blessed them and gave them to his disciples, saying that they were his body and blood, which he was about to sacrifice for them. He then told them to perform the same action in memory of him. Except for the *Quakers*, the *Salvation Army* and the *Jehovah's Witnesses*, all major Christian denominations throughout the world hold this service in some form, eating and drinking consecrated bread and wine to remember Christ's death and *resurrection*.

eugenics The branch of biology which tries to discover ways of ensuring that each generation of human beings will be genetically superior to the one before it. Some philosophers in the past were interested in the idea of producing a superior race of human beings; Plato, for example, wrote in favour of limiting human mating to certain men and women selected for their strength and intelligence. More recently, eugenics was studied by *Nazis* in their desire to ensure the dominance of the so-called 'Aryan' race of mankind.

Evangelicals Christians of any Protestant *denomination* who believe that a person does not become a Christian merely by being born into a Christian family or by being baptized; on the contrary, a conscious personal conversion and individual commitment is essential if someone is to be regarded as a true Christian. Evangelicals emphasize the central importance of the Bible in life and *worship*, and hold to the doctrine of 'justification by *faith* alone' first stated by *Luther*. According to Luther, men could only be saved through faith in the redeeming role of Christ, and not through their own actions. In their worship, Evangelicals lay great stress on the sermon, in which the preacher will explain a message of the Bible to the congregation.

evangelism Spreading the Christian gospel through the establishing of missions and the sending out of *missionaries*.

Eve According to the *Torah*, or *Old Testament*, Eve was the woman created by God to live with Adam, the first man, in the Garden of Eden. The story says she was made out of a rib from Adam's side. When Satan, disguised as a snake, tempted the couple to eat from the Tree of Knowledge, Eve gave way and ate the fruit of this tree. She bore Cain and Abel, Seth and other children, thus establishing the human race.

The fruit of the Tree of Knowledge is commonly taken to have been an apple.

evensong An Anglican service which is said or sung in the evening, similar to the Roman Catholic service of vespers.

everlasting (1) As an adjective: lasting for an unlimited period of time, lasting for ever. In many religions, God or life in heaven is said to be 'everlasting'. (2) As a noun: 'The Everlasting' is one of God's titles in Judaism and Christianity.

evil Any action contrary to the laws of the God or gods of a religion, or any serious infringement of the moral code of a society. In many religions, including Christianity, Judaism, Islam and those involving *dualism* (for example Zoroastrianism), evil is seen as coming from temptation by a devil, *Satan* or evil spirit. In other religions, such as Hinduism and Buddhism, evil may be seen to arise from desire or illusion (maya).

evolutionism *See:* **Darwinism.**

excommunication A procedure in the Christian Church, used much less often today than formerly, by which a member of the church is cut off from the rest of the Christian community and is denied certain privileges until he shows true repentance and performs the *penance* which is required from him. The main privilege he is denied is that of receiving *Holy Communion* at the *Mass* or *Eucharist*, hence the term 'excommunication'. In former times an excommunicated person would have been avoided by the church community until he became a penitent.

exile In Christianity and Judaism this usually refers to the exile of the Jews in the sixth century BCE from Judah, following the Babylonian invasion of that country. The Babylonians captured Jerusalem, destroyed King Solomon's Temple, and deported most of the Jews to Babylon. At the end of the century, King Cyrus of Persia conquered Babylon and allowed the Restoration, the return of the Jews to Judah.

existentialism A body of philosophical doctrine stemming from Soren Kierkegaard, a nineteenth-century Danish theologian. He insisted on the utter distinctness of God and man and the inexplicableness or 'absurdity' of relations between them. Most of those who developed his train of thought, however, have been atheists. The most famous name associated with it is that of Jean-Paul Sartre, the French philosopher and novelist. He contended that man is a self-creating being who is not initially endowed with a character but must create one by acts of will, existential 'leaps' and each individual is alone responsible for what he or she does. Once the individual has chosen for himself what he really is, he can commit himself to a way of life and moral values which follow from this decision.

Some Christian *theologians* have adopted existentialist ideas in an attempt to make Christianity more comprehensible to modern man; they say, for example, that to choose and commit oneself to do God's will is the only path to authentic existence.

Exodus The Hebrews' passage to freedom from slavery in Egypt, around 1200BCE, as related in the Book of Exodus in the *Torah*, or *Old Testament*. Led by *Moses*, they marched from Egypt on the night of the *Passover*; they crossed through the sea Yam Suph, or Reed Sea, now known as the Red Sea, whose waters miraculously parted to let them through and they were guided by God in the desert for forty years until they reached *Canaan*, their Promised Land. The term is also used for mass movements of people, such as the migration of the Mormons from Nauvoo to Salt Lake City.

exorcism The banishing of the Devil, demons or sin, through ritual and prayer. In many religions, objects, places and people can all be possessed by the devil or by evil spirits, and exorcism is used to force the evil spirit to abandon them.

expansionism A country's policy of expanding its territory, which involves its people spreading into and taking control over areas previously not occupied by that state. *See also*: **capitalism, communism, imperialism**.

extreme unction The anointing of the sick and dying: one of the seven sacraments of the Roman Catholic and Orthodox Churches. A priest rubs consecrated oil in the form of a cross on to the sick person, accompanying his action with prayer and the laying-on of hands. The sick person makes his or her confession, receives *absolution* and often takes *Communion*.

Ezrat Nashim The section of the Jewish *synagogue* used by women.

f

Fabianism A *socialist* society founded in Britain in 1884 which favours the gradual spread of socialism by peaceful and not revolutionary means.

faith To have faith usually means to believe in a system of religious teachings, *ethics* or scriptures without demanding proof of their truth. In Buddhism, faith must be verified by your experience as you grow spiritually. Faith is also used as another term for religion; for example, 'the Hindu faith'.

Fall, The According to the Book of Genesis in the *Old Testament*, or *Torah*, and to the Qur'an, God made Adam, the first man, and placed him in the Garden of *Eden*. He also made Eve, the first woman, and commanded them not to eat from the Tree of Knowledge of Good and Evil. But a serpent tempted them and they ate the tree's fruit, thus committing the first *sin*. God decreed that man's life should end in death from then on. This event, known as the Fall, Christians believe has affected all mankind.

Fall of Jerusalem The capture and destruction of the city and Temple of Jerusalem by the Romans in CE70.

faqir A *Sufi* word meaning 'deprived of worldly possessions', which applies to spiritual leaders and their initiated disciples; its Iranian equivalent is *dervish*'.

Farvadin The *Parsi* deity who presides over the spirits of the dead ancestors. During the festival of Farvardin, which lasts ten days, the dead are said to visit the homes of their descendants. To welcome them, worshippers attend special ceremonies for the dead on the hills in front of the *dakhmas*, or towers of silence.

fascism A type of extreme right-wing *ideology*, movement or system of government. Fascists believe in a strong, authoritarian state with a powerful army that it is willing to use to force other countries to give it more territories or special privileges. Fascists have no respect for individual liberty and oppose democracy, human rights and liberalism. Since they do not believe that all people are born equal, fascists organize society in a hierarchy. *Hitler* and Mussolini were both fascist dictators.

fasting To fast is to refrain from eating some or all food, and sometimes also from drinking, at certain times. *Ascetics* fast in order to reject the pleasures of the flesh and the world in favour of developing the powers of their soul and insight. Islam sets aside the month of *Ramadan* for obligatory fasting for all Muslims. Between sunrise and sunset they may not take any food or drink. *Jains*, both monks and laymen, stress the value of severe fasts. They believe it helps spiritual development by reducing the attachment to the body. Many Buddhist *bhikkhus* do not eat after mid-day. Judaism sets aside the *Day of Atonement* and *Fast of the Ninth Ab* as days of strict fasting and, together with Christianity, sees abstinence as a sign of repentance and mourning. Thus, on *Good Friday*, most Christians fast in order to remind themselves of the greater suffering which Christ endured by being crucified that day. *Ash Wednesday*, too, is traditionally respected as a day when fasting is observed, and in the Eastern Orthodox Church members are encouraged to give up meat, fish, eggs and animal products as well as alcohol and olive oil during the whole six-week period of *Lent*, the time of *penance* before Easter.

Fast of the Ninth Ab A Jewish fast which commemorates the destruction of the first and second temples in Jerusalem. The Fast of the Ninth Ab usually falls in late summer, and on that day Jews read elegies lamenting the suffering of their people and chant readings from the Book of Lamentations in the *Hebrew Bible*. The congregation prays that God will forgive their sins and accept their repentance, and in exchange will once again look upon his people with mercy and favour.

fatalism A philosophical viewpoint which states that everything we do is already decided by fate, that man has no *free will* and must merely play out the part he has been assigned in life, submitting to fate.

fate The notion of fate is usually tied up with the philosophy of *determinism* or the religious concept of *predestination*. Fate is a power or divine agency which decides how the future will turn out, and nothing that man does or fails to do can upset the pattern which has been laid down. Fate is therefore inescapable and unchangeable. For this reason, if we try to decide ourselves what to do, using what we think is our *free will*, this is an illusion in the eyes of the fatalist: the playing out of the role we have been assigned in advance.

Father In Christianity, the Father is the *Supreme Being*, the first person of the *Trinity*. The word is also used as a title for some of the earliest Christian writers and for Roman Catholic priests.

Fatiha The first surah, of one hundred and fourteen, of the Qur'an, which forms part of each of the five daily prayers of Islam, and is used as a prayer on many other occasions.

fellowship In the Christian faith, a community which is bound together by mutual love and lives according to a shared religious faith.

feminism A movement and doctrine that holds the belief that women are oppressed economically, politically, sexually and psychologically by the male sex and that demands equality for women in all respects. The feminist movement has grown in size and strength in the last twenty years, especially in Western Europe and North America.

Feng Shui 'Wind-water'. The Chinese term for geomancy, the art of selecting fortunate sites for buildings and graves.

festival of lights *See*: **Diwali, Chanukah**.

fetishism The belief that certain objects are extremely powerful since they embody or are inhabited by a spirit. Fetishes are worn to pro-

This South African witchdoctor is wearing fetishes which confer on him magical properties and ward off evil powers.

tect their wearer from evil influence and to give him or her magical powers. Fetishism is common among many so-called primitive peoples.

Fire sermon A *sermon* preached by the Buddha at Gaya. The audience consisted of fire-worshipping *ascetics*, to whom the Buddha explained that the only fire that truly burns is one stoked by lust and anger.

fire temples Temples which house the sacred fire of *Ahura Mazda*, the God of Light, lit by *Parsi* priests. The fire itself is a symbol of the purity and goodness of Ahura Mazda.

Five Ks The distinctive features of dress which mark out members of the Sikh brotherhood of the *Khalsa*. These are: the *kesh*, or uncut hair; the *kangha*, or comb, which holds the hair in place; the *kirpan*, or sword; short trousers, known as *kacch*; and a steel bracelet, the *kara*.

five pillars of Islam The five requirements of Islam which each Muslim must follow. These are: repeating the creed; praying five times a day, giving alms; fasting; and the pilgrimage to Mecca, which every Muslim should make once in his life, if not prevented by ill health or financial straits. *See also*: **al-Arkan**.

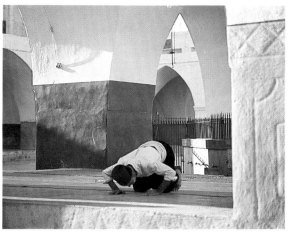

These Muslims *(above)*. each on his prayer-mat. are assembled in the courtyard of their mosque in Samarkand. in the USSR. to observe one of the five religious practices required by Islam. Salat. or prayer. is accompanied by a number of rak'as. or ritual movements. The barefoot believer *(left)* is prostrating himself in the direction of Mecca. saying. 'All glory to God the highest'. 'Subhana Rabiyal-a'a-la'. A Muslim has to pray two rak'as at sunrise. four at noon. four during the afternoon. three just before sunset and four more ninety minutes after sunset. The whole day is. therefore. punctuated by worship and devotion to Allah.

Five Precepts A set of guidelines for ethical behaviour in Buddhism. According to Buddhism, there are skilful actions and unskilful actions. The Buddha defined skilful acts as those arising from generosity, love and wisdom; unskilful ones arise from greed, hatred and delusion. Behaving skilfully helps you become happier and develop towards Enlightenment, therefore Buddhism has several sets of precepts which provide the Buddhist with everyday guidelines to behaving skilfully and avoiding unskilful action. Lay Buddhists try to follow one of these sets, the Five Precepts, which underlies all other sets: (1) abstaining from taking life. (2) abstaining from taking the not-given. (3) abstaining from sexual misconduct. (4) abstaining from false speech. (5) abstaining from taking drink or drugs that cloud the mind.

five relationships According to *Confucius* there are five relationships in life, and within each relationship the inferior should show deference and respect to the superior. In return, the superior should be kind and merciful.

These relationships are between: father and son; older brother and younger brother; husband and wife; elder and younger; and ruler and subject. If each relationship is conducted along these lines the whole fabric of society will benefit.

Flood, The According to the Book of Genesis in the *Torah*, or *Old Testament*, and to the story of Noah in the *Qur'an*, God determined to send a flood to destroy mankind for its wickedness, but spared *Noah* and his family on account of his righteousness. Genesis tells how, following God's instructions, Noah built an Ark into which he put his family and at least two of every species of creature on the earth, so that it might be repopulated when the waters finally subsided.

From one of the first books printed. Caxton's *Golden Legend*, comes this woodcut of the Flood and the Ark in which Noah escaped, together with his family and the animals of the earth.

font A receptacle or container found in Christian churches, often made of stone with an inlaid metal bowl. Fonts are usually in the *baptistry*, since they hold the baptismal water.

foreknowledge The power of seeing what the future holds before it happens. Many mystics and psychics claim to have foreknowledge. In Judaism, Christianity and Islam especially, God is believed to have infallible foreknowledge of the future, because of his *omniscience*.

Four Freedoms In 1941 President Roosevelt made a speech to the United States Congress in which he said that every citizen had a right to four freedoms: freedom of speech and worship and freedom from want and fear.

Four Noble Truths A basic formula in Buddhism, taught by the Buddha in one of his earliest talks. It is still taught throughout the Buddhist world. At its shortest, the formula runs: (1) the Truth of *dukkha*, or suffering; (2) the Truth of the origin of dukkha; (3) the Truth of the way leading to the end of dukkha. What this means is that: (1) all ordinary life and experience is ultimately suffering because all our pleasures and moments of happiness will eventually come to an end; (2) this suffering is rooted in *tanha*, craving and greed, strong desires for things that we do not actually need or which harm us; (3) when we stop craving then all suffering ends: one has gained *enlightenment*, the supreme happiness that never fades; (4) there are methods, paths or practices which we can use to become enlightened, such as the *Noble Eightfold Path*.

four rightly guided caliphs In Arabic, *Rashidun*: *Abu Bakr*, *'Umar*, *'Uthman*, and *Ali*, the first four *caliphs* who followed Muhammad. While the first three are acknowledged by the *Sunni* Muslims, the *Shi'ites* feel that they usurped the lawful right of succession to the Prophet, which should have passed to Ali.

four stages of life According to Hindu belief, each high-caste individual has four levels of growth to pass through in life. The first quarter of a person's life is marked by immaturity and is the time set aside for study. The next quarter is for marriage and working to support the family. This is followed by the third period, during which the individual is free to work for the good of society, since his family is able to take care of itself. Finally, in the fourth stage, the world is no longer important and each person must detach himself from its concerns, and give all his time to prayer, meditation and the search for union with God.

Franciscans Order of Roman Catholic and Anglican *friars* founded by *St Francis of Assisi* in the thirteenth century CE. The Franciscans, sometimes known as the Greyfriars, lead a simple life and serve the community by tending to the sick, and, following the example of their founder, they respect nature and the birds and creatures which he loved.

Francis of Assisi, St. *See*: **Franciscans**.

freedom The power to make choice without being restricted by external or internal pressures. Self-determination, the liberty to make of yourself what you wish to become, is closely linked to the notion of freedom, and extends beyond individual freedom to include the right of nations and groups to decide their own destiny. Oppression, dictatorship and *autocracy* all severely limit freedom, often in the name of stability and order, by restricting the choice, movements and actions of individuals and minorities.

Freemasons In medieval Europe, most crafts and trades were organized into guilds, a type of religious brotherhood and self-help society. Among them was the guild of masons, which gradually attracted non-masons into its branches in England. By the eighteenth century the movement had developed into a secret fraternal society with lodges, or branches, throughout Europe. Since then it has spread around the world. Freemasons have developed a secret code which enables members to recognize each other, and they pledge to help one another whenever called upon to do so. Elaborate rituals, secret signs and passwords help to bind the members together and give them a feeling of separateness from the rest of society. Members have to believe in God, whom they call the 'Architect of the Universe'. There has been a long history of hostility between traditional Christianity, especially Roman Catholicism and the Masons, partly because Freemasonry was supposedly linked with the French Revolution, but this hostility is diminishing today.

free will Man's ability to make a decision of his own about his future actions. Free will implies that we are all able to shape our lives by our own decisions and efforts. Belief in free will is the opposite of belief in fate or determinism. While most Muslims subscribe to the idea that people behave as they do by the will of Allah, there exists, for example, the school of Ikhtiyar, 'free will'. Its followers, Ikhtiyariyun, believe that while major events are determined by God, human beings are given certain possibilities to

This engraving of medieval stonemasons recalls the origins of the secret society whose members are known as freemasons.

choose, which is why bad deeds will be punished and good ones rewarded. The Christian religion in general accepts that man has free will, although some forms of it, such as *Calvinism*, do not believe that man can freely choose to attain salvation, since this is pure gift from God. Judaism accepts the idea of free will, as does Zoroastrianism.

friar A type of monk in the Roman Catholic and Anglican Churches who does not live permanently in one community, but is free to go from one community of his order to another. The title is usually reserved for members of the *Franciscan*, Augustinian, *Carmelite* and *Dominican* orders.

Fuji-yama

Shinto is the ancient religion of Japan whose chief deity is the sun-goddess, Amaterasu. Natural wonders, such as waterfalls, mountains and seas, are worshipped as kami, 'superior ones'. Mount Fuji-yama, the most sacred of these, is believed to be the home of Amaterasu, from whom the emperors of Japan are descended.

Fuji-yama The most sacred mountain of Japan, believed to be the home of a goddess who is the ancestor of the Japanese imperial family.

fundamentalism A movement in Protestantism which first became influential at the beginning of the twentieth century as a reply to Darwinism, the growth of science and modernism in general. It is the belief that the Bible is infallible since every word is the revealed word of God which cannot be doubted on scientific, archaeological or philosophical grounds. Strongest among Protestants of the United States, it is usually accompanied by a condemnation of Roman Catholicism and modern thought.

g

Gabriel In Judaism, Christianity and Islam, the *archangel* Gabriel is a messenger from God and part of the angelic hierarchy which attends his throne. Gabriel was sent to *Daniel* to explain the vision of the ram and goat and to pass on God's instructions. In the *New Testament*, Gabriel told the *Virgin Mary* that she would bear a son.

In Islam, Gabriel revealed the Qur'an to Muhammad, and guided the Prophet, on a winged horse called Buraq, from Mecca to Jerusalem and from there to the throne of God.

Galilee, Sea of Also known as the Lake of Tiberias: a lake in the northeast part of present-day Israel. The surrounding district of Galilee was the site of much of Jesus' ministry and several of his *miracles*.

Gandhi, Mohandas K. (1869–1948) Known as Mahatma Gandhi or simply 'the Mahatma' which means 'Great Soul', he was a Hindu spiritual and political leader and reformer. After having been trained as a lawyer he went to South Africa, where he strove to better the conditions of the non–whites and developed his doctrine of *ahimsa*, or non-violence. On his return to India, he vigorously attacked the way in which Hindu society mistreated the caste called the *Untouchables* and resolved to lead his country to independence. By preaching self-sufficiency and pride in oneself, he gathered a mass of followers and won India's independence from British rule by a policy of non-violent resistance. Greatly saddened by the split which occurred at the time of independence, whereby the northern, and largely Muslim, part of India became a separate nation, Pakistan, he nevertheless remained true to his pacifist beliefs. He died at the hands of an assassin.

Depicted with a human body, but with four arms rather than two, and the head of an elephant, Ganesha inspires much devotion in his followers, since he breaks through all obstacles which might stand in the way of his devotees' success and good fortune.

Ganesha The Hindu god of wisdom and good beginnings, the symbol of luck and riches. Ganesha is an elephant-headed god, particularly popular in western India.

Ganges The second river of Hinduism and a goddess, daughter of the Himalayas, the Ganges is said to have come from the toe of *Vishnu*, the Preserver. It was brought from heaven by the prayer of the sages, and its fall broken by *Shiva*, who caught it in his matted locks. Traditionally, Hindus bathe in its water to purify themselves and also scatter the ashes of the dead into it.

ganja Cannabis, the sacred herb of the *Rastafarians*, used in rituals and treated as a *sacrament*. According to Rastas, ganja promotes feelings of peace and love, brings on visions and unites the faithful against the suffering of the world in harmony and brotherhood. Ganja, though often used, is illegal in most countries in the world, and the Rastafarians see this as an attack on their faith and a form of religious persecution.

Garuda In Hindu mythology, the half-man/half-bird mount of Vishnu.

Garvey, Marcus (1887–1940) A black nationalist active in Jamaica in the period 1910–20. Garvey preached liberation of the black people from the injustices and oppression of Caribbean life through repatriation to Africa. He said that Africa was the true homeland to which all black people must return if they wanted to be free and happy and prophesied the crowning of a black king in Africa as a sign of deliverance. When *Ras Tafari* (*Haile Selassie*) was crowned Emperor of Ethiopia in 1930, the movement Garvey had founded began to grow rapidly, not only in his native Jamaica, but also in the United States, where he had lectured.

Garvey founded the United Negro Improvement Society and was also active in establishing the African Orthodox Church in New York.

gathas Seventeen hymns which form part of the *Avesta*, the Zoroastrian holy book.

Gautama (1) the family name of the Buddha. (2) Akshapada Gautama, an Indian philosopher who lived around 300BCE and taught the *Nyaya* system of Hinduism, which relies on logic and reasoning.

Gayatri A verse of the *Rig-Veda* addressed to the sun, regarded as particularly sacred by the Hindus. Its recital forms part of a ritual which every Brahmin must perform three times daily.

Gehenna Jewish term for *hell*, whose name derives from Gay Hinnom (valley of Hinnom), a place associated with *idolatry* and child sacrifice.

Gemara Part of the *Talmud* containing rabbinic commentary on the *Mishnah*.

genocide The deliberate and systematic murder of a specific racial or national group. *Hitler* committed genocide against the Jews in World War II.

gentile Anyone who is not a Jew.

genuflection The bending of one knee in front of an object or place of respect or worship. Roman Catholics normally genuflect in front of the tabernacle in a church.

Gethsemane The garden on the slope of the *Mount of Olives* in Jerusalem where Jesus was betrayed by Judas.

ghat In Hinduism, the broad steps which lead down to one of the sacred rivers, such as the Ganges. On the steps known as 'burning ghats', cremations take place.

Ghost, Holy *See*: **Holy Spirit**.

glossolalia Speaking in unknown languages. In the Christian Church, glossolalia is used to worship God and to communicate prophetic messages and visions. It is regarded as a gift of the *Holy Spirit* and is especially emphasized by *Pentecostalists*.

gnosticism A general term for the religious ideas of a number of mystical *sects* which arose in the early centuries CE, both within Christianity and Judaism (as *heresies*) and outside them. The most important ideas common to most of these sects were: (1) *dualism*: all matter is considered evil and is the creation of an evil god, the Demiurge. Spirit alone is good, since it flows forth or emanates from the good god or *Supreme Being*. (2) *élitism*: only those who possessed the secret mystical knowledge (or 'gnosis') revealed to members of the sect could hope for salvation. (3) *asceticism*: the means by which the spirit of the gnostic could be released from his body and achieve union with the Supreme Being.

Gobind Singh (1666–1708) The tenth and last Sikh guru, who founded the brotherhood known as the Khalsa, dedicated to truth and service. He replaced the old initiation ceremony of charn amrit by *khande-ka-amrit*, and added hymns composed by his father, the ninth guru, to the Adi Granth, the sacred book of the Sikhs. Guru Gobind Singh declared that after his own death there would be no more human gurus but that the Adi Granth, thereafter also known as the *Guru Granth Sahib*, would be the supreme guru, or guide to Sikh life and faith. His own poems and writings were later incorporated into the *Dasam Granth*.

god In general terms, a god, or goddess, is one of several superhuman creatures who is worshipped by mankind. Since the earliest times human beings have felt the need to venerate something beyond themselves and also to conceive of a structure which could offer some explanation for the mysterious workings of the universe. Both the ancient Greeks and the ancient Romans had rich and complex hierarchies of deities whom they worshipped and those names are familiar to us today, such as Zeus and Pallas Athene, Venus and Neptune.

Not all gods and goddesses are felt to be benevolent towards human beings and sacrifices may be made to placate them and calm their wrath. *Polytheist* religions, such as *Confucianism*, *Taoism*, *Shinto* and tribal religions are those which recognise several independent gods, often gods closely connected with natural phenomena, as well as ancestors. Hinduism is a combination of polytheism and *monotheism*, which fact,

Three ancient Greek gods, Zeus, Neptune and Pallas Athene in idealized human form.

although seemingly contradictory, may be explained by the tremendous breadth of belief and practice accommodated by Hindus. Original Buddhism may be classified as a non-theistic religion, since there do exist many gods and goddesses, but none are crucial to the Buddhist, who sets out on the *Noble Eightfold Path* to salvation guided only by right teaching and without divine aid. Zoroastrianism is a dualistic belief which teaches that there are two opposing forces in the universe, one god representing good and the other evil.

God The Supreme Being or Prime Mover in *monotheistic* religions such as Judaism, Christianity and Islam, which all acknowledge and worship one sole, loving God.

goddess *See:* **god.**

godly A godly person is someone who is pious and acts in a way which could please his god, by respecting the laws and duties of his faith.

Golden Temple Also known as the *Harmandir:* the central temple of Sikhism, built in the holy city of *Amritsar* in the sixteenth century by the fifth *guru, Arjan*. It is a place of pilgrimage for the faithful, and is a symbol of the Sikh religion.

good Action which is according to the laws of the God or gods of a religion, or which follows a given moral code. In some philosophies, for example, the philosophy of *Plato*, absolute good is said to exist as a sort of ideal *divine* being; in Christianity, Judaism and Islam, the good is often identified with God. God, or the good, is seen here as the force which enables appropriate beings to achieve goodness.

Good Friday The day on which Christians commemorate the crucifixion of Jesus Christ. On this day Christian churches are bare of decoration. Roman Catholic services consist of prayers and scripture readings before the veneration of the cross at three p.m., traditionally the time that Christ died. In the Eastern Orthodox Church, where Good Friday is known as Great Friday, there is a solemn re-enactment of Christ's burial procession.

Lutheran Churches usually hold a *Eucharist* service on this day, and many Protestant Churches hold joint services as a mark of Christian unity.

Unlike Simon of Cyrene, who was forced into helping Christ, these Christians are eager to carry the cross.

Gospel (1) Any of the four accounts of the life of Jesus, traditionally attributed to *Saints Matthew, Mark, Luke* and *John* and included in the Christian *New Testament.* (2) Literally, 'the good news': the message of Christianity. *Missionaries* are said to go out and 'preach the gospel'. (3) A reading from any of the four Gospels during the Christian *Eucharist* service.

grace (1) A form of thanksgiving said or sung before or after meals in most Christian countries. (2) Grace is the Christian term for the undeserved love of God given to mankind. Christians believe that men are not saved because they deserve to be saved, but because God's grace wills their salvation.

granthi The man or woman who reads the Sikh sacred book, the *Guru Granth Sahib*, during public worship.

Great Learning, The One of the four books of *Confucian* philosophy, designed to serve as a basis for the education of gentlemen and princes and compiled after Confucius's death. In classic Chinese education, this was the first text to be studied by schoolboys.

Guardian of the Cause *See*: **Hands of the Cause of God**.

Guardian of the Faith The title of Shoghi Effendi as head of the *Baha'i faith*. The will of *Baha'u'llah*'s son appointed him to this position when he was still only twenty-four and studying at Oxford University in England.

During his lifetime Shoghi Effendi preserved the Baha'i faith from divisions, translated Baha'i literature from Persian and Arabic into English, wrote the history of the faith, directed the policy and institutions of the Baha'i community, and lived a simple and exemplary life. His pronouncements on the interpretation of the Baha'i scriptures have formed a source of guidance to the Baha'i and are read in conjunction with the words of Baha'u'llah.

When Shoghi Effendi died in 1957, the Baha'i community did not appoint a second Guardian of the Faith, but decided that the *Universal House of Justice* should take over as the central institution of the Baha'i religion.

gunas In the *Samkhya* system of Hinduism, the gunas are the strands or bonding agents which give a structure to the natural world of matter, as opposed to the world of spirit. There are three gunas: *sattva*, a wise and happy one; an energetic and passionate guna known as *rajas*; and a brooding, moody one called *tamas*. The nature of the living world is determined by the way in which these three agents combine. The characteristics of an individual are due to the degree that any one of the three gunas predominates over the other two. If, for example, someone is intelligent and pure, sattva is shaping that person. If, however, he or she is dull and crude, then tamas is exerting an influence.

Guru Nanak, the founder of the Sikh religion, is depicted as a saintly old man, surrounded by his faithful disciples. Those who succeeded him as leader of the faith were also known as gurus, but the last guru, Gobind Singh, declared that after his death the sacred scripture would itself become the spiritual head of the Sikh faith.

gurdwara A Sikh community centre which is used for worship and meetings. The gurdwara contains a temple housing the *Guru Granth Sahib*, a communal kitchen and eating area, and accommodation for travellers who need shelter. Many Indian gurdwaras have built dispensaries where the sick come for treatment and medicine, financed by the local gurdwara committee.

Gurmukhi The alphabet popularized by the second Sikh guru, *Angad*, and still used today for written Punjabi.

Gurpurb A Sikh festival commemorating the birth or death of a Sikh *guru*. The most important are those which celebrate the birthdays of Guru *Nanak* and Guru *Gobind Singh* and the martyrdom of Guru *Arjan* and Guru *Tegh Bahadur*. During the commemoration, the *Guru Granth Sahib* is read and paraded through the streets, while people sing hymns and accompany the procession on foot. From time to time, the procession stops to allow speakers to address the crowd.

guru In Hinduism, a guru is a teacher or a guide who instructs his followers on how to find salvation. In the Sikh faith, the term refers to the first ten leaders of that religion and is also part of the name of the Sikh scripture, the *Guru Granth Sahib*, which has taken the place of human teachers in that faith as a source of guidance and inspiration. In *Tantric Buddhism*, a guru is a spiritual master, guide and true friend, who embodies the practice of the teachings he gives to his pupils.

Guru Granth Sahib Also known as the *Adi Granth*, the sacred book of the Sikhs. It is a collection of devotional poems and hymns by six Sikh *gurus* as well as Hindus and Muslims, compiled by Guru *Arjan* around 1600. Sikhs believe the book contains the same divine spirit that inspired Guru *Nanak*, the founder of their religion. Guru *Gobind Singh*, the last guru, named the book as his successor as head of the faith. It is central to rituals and life in the Sikh community.

The book is often carried in procession on special anniversaries and festivals. Weddings can only be conducted in its presence, most homes try to set aside a room where the book can be read and consulted, and every *gurdwara* contains a copy, set on a raised platform on cushions and covered by a canopy.

h

habit An outer garment, such as the cloak or dress of a monk, which is worn by specific religious orders.

Dominican

Carthusian

Franciscan

Hadith A collection of stories and sayings on the life and teachings of Muhammad, which forms the basis of a large body of Islamic law, known as the *Shari'a*. From the Hadith come many social and religious customs observed by Muslims.

Haggadah A collection of stories and hymns which are recited at the annual Jewish *Passover* meal, recounting the exodus of the *Chosen People* from captivity in Egypt.

hagiarchy (1) A country which is governed by holy men. (2) Government by holy men.

Haile Selassie *See*: Selassie, Haile.

Hajj The pilgrimage to Mecca, one of the *five pillars of Islam*. It is obligatory for all Muslims, at least once in a lifetime, as long as they are not prevented by ill-health or financial constraints, and takes place in the twelfth month of the Islamic year. Pilgrims go to the Great Mosque in Mecca and perform the ritual of making seven circuits around the *Ka'ba* before touching the sacred *Black Stone* and asking for forgiveness and guidance. They also have to visit several sacred sites in the region; at one of these, Mina, the sacrifice of *Id-ul-Adha* is performed, in memory of *Abraham*'s willingness to sacrifice his son, Ishmael, to God. On returning from their trip pilgrims are held in high honour by other Muslims, and can take the additional name Hajji, one who has made the hajj.

hakim A wise or learned Muslim and a term applied to philosophers and physicians.

Halakah The entire body of Jewish law. This is made up of the laws in the *Torah*, the oral law contained in the *Talmud*, and the interpretations of the Talmud developed over the centuries by the *rabbis*. They have had to decide how Jews of their own day should keep the law in conditions very different from those of the time when the Talmud and the Torah were composed.

Halal Halal is a term which denotes that Islamic ritual has been observed especially in relation to food, and, in this respect, is similar to the Jewish word 'kosher', meaning 'fit'. Halal butchers do not handle pork and follow traditional religious practices in preparing their meat. The animal which is about to be killed is turned to face Mecca, the butcher calls upon *Allah* before cutting its throat, and all the blood is allowed to drain from the carcass before it is cut up and sold. Muslims believe that eating blood is unclean, a stricture which is also shared by followers of other faiths, including the Jews.

Hallowe'en Also known as All Hallows. Hallowe'en is a pagan and Christian festival kept on 31 October, the eve of *All Saints' Day*, and has a long ancestry which goes back to the ancient Celts. Originally observed to signal the end of the summer and the eve of the Celtic New Year, it was also associated with the return of the dead to their homes and was supposed to be a good time for practising the art of *divination*.

According to tradition, demons, witches and ghosts are abroad on Hallowe'en; this belief is linked with the Celts' practice of protecting their crops and herds against evil supernatural powers, in the coming year. It is still widely believed that children born on this day have supernatural powers, and many people still put candles in hollowed-out turnips and pumpkins to ward off evil spirits. Children often go from house to house singing or reciting poetry in exchange for small gifts, and various party games are associated with the festivity.

On Hallowe'en, fires were traditionally lit to attract the souls of the dead. Hollowed-out pumpkins, eerily lit by candles, were supposed to scare away evil spirits, as shown in this nineteenth-century engraving.

halo A disc or circle of light, in pictures and other artistic representations that surrounds the head of a holy man or woman or a deity. Hindu paintings frequently extend the hair until it streams from either side of the head like a halo. Christian artists add circles of stars for the Virgin Mary, rays for saints and parts of the arms of a cross when depicting the halo surrounding the head of Christ.

Hands of the Cause of God A group of *Baha'is* originally chosen by the *Guardian of the Cause*, Shoghi Effendi, and entrusted with ensuring the spread of the Baha'i faith. From 1951 to 1957 thirty-two people were appointed to the inner circle of administration, but after the death of the Guardian they were freed from this role and urged to concentrate on spreading and guiding the faith throughout the world.

When the International Teaching Centre was founded in 1973, all the Hands of the Cause became members, along with three Counsellors, to link the various branches of the religion and the Universal House of Justice, the Baha'i central authority on matters of law.

The Hands of the Cause are not elected, but appointed by the Universal House of Justice.

Hanukah *See*: **Chanukah.**

Hanuman The Hindu monkey god, who, according to the *Ramayana*, led an army of monkeys against a host of demons and helped *Rama* to recover his wife, Sita, from the clutches of *Ravana*, the demon king of Lanka.

Hargobind, Guru The sixth Sikh *guru*, who protected the new religion against the armies of the Mogul Empire and formed the Sikhs into a clearly separate and united religious and social group.

The distinctive haloes of Jesus and his mother, Mary.

Harmandir *See*: **Golden Temple.**

Har Krishen, Guru The Eighth Sikh *guru*, who died at the age of eight.

Har Rai The seventh Sikh *guru*, who consolidated the achievements of his predecessor, *Guru Hargobind*.

Hasidim Another spelling of *Chasidim*.

Hasidism Another spelling of *Chasidism*.

Hassan-ibn-as-Sabbah Twelfth-century founder of the Assassins, who established a mountain stronghold in Iran. Alamut castle which, according to the Iranian historian of the time, Juwiyni, contained a large library, was conquered and burned by the Mongols who invaded Iran in the thirteenth century.

haumal Self-centredness or self-reliance: the characteristic of an unenlightened person in Sikhism.

Havan A ceremony practised by certain present-day Hindu sects, especially the *Arya Samaj*. It is based on the rituals for sacrifice found in the *Vedas*, although no actual sacrifice now takes place. A fire, sacred to the god *Agni*, is lit in the centre of the temple and is fed with wood, camphor, ghee (a sort of liquid butter) and sometimes with sweets, as prayers and hymns from the Vedas are recited by the priest and people. The revival of this ceremony is part of an attempt to return to a supposedly purer, more ancient form of Hinduism than the *bhakti*-dominated, image-using worship normally found in Hindu temples and homes today. The Havan is especially performed on occasions such as birthdays and weddings.

Havdalah A special Saturday evening ceremony which ends with the Jewish *Sabbath* and marks it off from the rest of the week. It includes blessings over wine, spices and flame and a main blessing which refers to the distinction between light and darkness, holy and profane, Israel and other peoples, the Sabbath and the rest of the week.

heaven A blissful state of existence beyond and above physical life in the material world, which followers of many religions believe is the destination of virtuous or godly people after death. Heaven is also considered to be the kingdom of God or the home of the gods.

Hebrew (1) A member of one of the *Semitic* tribes which eventually became the people of Israel, or Israelites, of the *Old Testament*, or *Torah*. (2) The language of the ancient people of Israel, or its descendant: the language of the present-day state of Israel.

Hebrew Bible The Jewish equivalent of the *Old Testament* in the Bible of Christianity. It contains the five books of the Law, known as the *Torah*, the histories and prophetic books, and the wisdom literature, psalms and later histories. The Hebrew Bible includes neither the *New Testament* nor the *Apocrypha*.

hedonism A view of life that regards the pursuit of leisure or happiness, of whatsoever sort, as the highest aim in life. Sometimes the term is used as a synonym for *utilitarianism*.

Hegel, Georg Wilhelm Friedrich (1770–1831) A German philosopher whose influential system of thought had a marked effect on *Karl Marx* and the Marxist doctrine of *historical materialism*.

Hegelianism A philosophical system which states that an assertable proposition, called the thesis, is necessarily always opposed by its opposite, the antithesis. The contradiction which arises between the two is finally reconciled on a higher level – the synthesis. This, according to Hegel, is how progress and change occur, for nothing ever remains static, but everything is in a constant state of flux and becoming.

Karl Marx added to and adapted this theory to fit the economic relations between the classes.

hegemony The leadership, dominating influence, or control which one state or group has over others. For example, one country may exercise hegemony over the others in a region, one part of a society may exercise it over another class. According to *Marx*, in every society other than a fully Communist one, one class – the ruling class – always exercises hegemony over the other classes, and its values and ideas shape the values and ideas of the other classes in all spheres of life. In general, according to this view, the ideas of individuals within any society will reflect the ideas of the ruling class.

hegumen The head of a monastery in the Eastern Orthodox Church, equivalent to a Western abbot.

hell The place or state of punishment of the wicked after death or the home of evil and condemned spirits. Originally people thought that hell was hidden at the centre of the earth. In Zorastrianism, Islam and Christianity, the dead are sent to hell on *Judgement Day*, while Hinduism teaches that hell is merely a stage in the soul's progress and does not last for ever. Similarly, in Buddhism, a person can be reborn in the heavens, or as a human, a titan, ghost or animal. Where rebirth takes place depends on the person's *karma*, his actions before that death. In the hells and in any other state, he will also die and again be reborn, in that or some other state. *Jainism* recognises five hells, where victims are tortured by demons until their souls have been exhausted and cleansed. Nigoda, the place below the hells, is the most difficult region to escape from and no one can be released once they have been sentenced there. Nigoda is reserved for the most serious offenders and offences. *See also*: **reincarnation, Gehenna, Jahannam.**

Hegel, the great German philosopher.

Henry, Claudius A Jamaican preacher and one of the founders of the African Reformed Church in New York.

heresy Any opinion or doctrine which contradicts or denies the accepted, orthodox teachings of any faith or religion. For example, in the first centuries of Christianity, both the *Monophysites* and *Aryans* understood the nature of Jesus Christ in a way that was unacceptable to the majority in the early Church. Therefore their views were condemned by the *Ecumenical Councils* of Chalcedon and Ephesus respectively. One could also argue that orthodoxy is just the doctrine and teaching that wins the strongest support in a religion, while heresy, or heterodoxy, is any differing view that is unacceptable to the dominant view. Sanctions against heresy vary widely from religion to religion; in Islam, death is still the official penalty, but in present-day Christianity, a normal punishment is *excommunication* – banning the *heretic* from receiving the *sacraments*.

heretic Anyone who believes in a heresy which opposes the orthodox doctrines of his own religion or faith.

hermit In many religions, such as Hinduism, Buddhism and Christianity, a person who removes himself or herself from ordinary life to live a life of solitary *contemplation*.

Herod the Great (73BCE?–4BCE) King of Judaea under the Romans. He tore down the Second Temple at Jerusalem and built the Third Temple, a magnificent place for state and religious gatherings served by twenty-four classes of priests. This structure lasted a mere ninety years before the Romans destroyed it, an event still commemorated in the Jewish calendar as a day of fasting, the *Fast of the Ninth Ab*. It is this Herod who is supposed to have massacred the *Holy Innocents*, all the male children under two years old in Bethlehem, after the *Magi* had told him that a new king of the Jews (Jesus) had been born there.

Herzl, Theodore Founder of the *Zionist* movement, which seeks to establish a national homeland for the Jewish people. Born in Budapest in 1860, Herzl grew up in a world where *anti-Semitism* was common and *pogroms* continued to devastate the Jewish populations of Eastern Europe. The Dreyfus Case, an example of anti-Jewish prejudice on the part of the French, soon persuaded Herzl that the idea of assimilation was a pipedream, for no country would ever truly accept Jews as its own citizens without noting their racial origins. In order to find peace, Jews would have to create their own state by using political means. Herzl wrote a book on this theme, *Der Judenstaat*, and approached several organizations and governments for support. Many like-minded Jewish organizations disa-with Herzl's view that it did not matter where the state was founded, since they believed that the Jews had the right to return to Israel and make their home in the land of their forefathers. Eventually, in 1897, Herzl founded the Zionist Congress and spent the remaining seven years of his life trying to unite the various factions for the common goal of a Jewish country.

Hexateuch The first six books of the *Old Testament* or *Hebrew Bible*, consisting of the *Pentateuch* with the addition of the Book of Joshua. Some scholars have seen the six books as together forming a unit: they take the history of the Hebrews further than the death of Moses (at the end of the Pentateuch), up to and including the take-over of *Canaan*, the Promised Land.

Hibbert, Joseph A *Freemason*, born in 1894, who founded the Ethiopian Mystic Movement in Jamaica after the coronation of Haile Selassie in 1930.

hidden imam Most *Shi'ite* Muslims believe that the twelfth Shi'ite *imam* has not died, but has concealed himself on earth, to reappear as the *Mahdi* or *Messiah* at the end of the world. The Seveners expect the return of the seventh imam.

Hiddur Mitzvah A general principle in Judaism which says that all duties (mitzvot) must be performed with beauty. Therefore only the finest materials may be used for the *Torah* scroll, its mantles, the plaques used to adorn it and the interior of the *synagogue*. Since God is the most valuable thing an individual has in life, only the most beautiful and precious possessions can be used in his service.

hierarchy Literally, 'rule by priests', the word was originally referred to an organized chain of command in which priests and the other officials of a religion are ranked according to their authority and responsibilities. Each level takes its orders from the level directly above it, and the laity, the ordinary members of the religion, are governed by the whole body of these officials, at least in their religious life. The word is also applied to the different levels of angels in Judaism and Christianity.

The idea of hierarchy has also been transferred to non-religious areas, so one can speak of a hierarchy in the Communist Party.

Hijra The migration of Muhammad from Mecca to Medina in CE622, after the Meccans had begun to persecute followers of the new religion of Islam. To commemorate this event, the Muslim calendar counts years 'after Hijra' (AH) and celebrates the New Year on the day of the Hijra.

Hillel A Jewish teacher who lived in the first century BCE. He was known for following the spirit and not the letter of the *Torah*. Some of Hillel's teachings on love and on the Law bear a striking resemblance to those of Jesus.

Hinayana Literally, 'small or lesser vehicle': the term coined by *Mahayana* Buddhists to describe *Theravada*. *See also*: **Theravada Buddhism**.

Hinds, Robert Following a revelation that *Haile Selassie* was the *Messiah* of the black people of the world, the Jamaican Robert Hinds joined with others of the same conviction to found the *Rastafarian faith* in Jamaica.

Hinduism The religion of the majority of Indians. It is difficult to define Hinduism, since it has no founder, no single creed or authoritative set of beliefs; even its sacred scriptures are widely diverse. Different Hindus worship different gods as the supreme being; rituals and festivals vary widely from one part of India to the other. Generally, however, Hinduism would appear on the surface to be a *polytheistic* religion with a vast pantheon of some three hundred million gods; it is also an extremely absorbent religion and can assimilate new concepts and divinities with ease, even from other religions. *Gandhi*, for example, regarded veneration for Jesus and his teachings as quite compatible with Hinduism. One feature, also, which is practically universal throughout Hinduism is that of the *caste* system: to be a Hindu one must belong to one of the four traditional castes or their sub-castes, since anyone who is not in a caste is, strictly speaking, *Untouchable*, and can have no part in the Hindu religion and ritual.

Western scholars claim Hinduism began when the *Aryan* warriors invaded the Indus Valley civilization of North India in about 1500BCE, submerging the religion and culture of the Valley-dwellers almost entirely for a time. The Aryan religion is expressed in the oldest Hindu scriptures, the *Vedas*; their gods were personifications of natural forces. Chief amongst these was *Indra*, the god of war and strength. *Agni*, god of fire, was also important and his fire rituals survive in the present-day Havan ceremony. The Aryans used no temples or images but these gradually came back into use as religious ideas re-emerged from the pre-Aryan Indus Valley civilization. Some of their ideas probably influenced the next set of Hindu scriptures, the Upanishads, which Western scholars believe was composed from 800BCE onwards, where concepts such as *karma*, *atman* ('soul'), *Brahman* (the supreme being or Absolute), samara (reincarnation) and *moksha* (final liberation into Brahman) are found for the first time.

The scriptures were explained in simpler form in the epics which Western scholars believe were written from the third century BCE onwards, the *Mahabharata* (including the *Bhagavad Gita*) and *Ramayana*. By this time the dominant gods in the Hindu pantheon were *Brahma*, *Vishnu* and *Shiva*, and Vishnu especially was thought to visit the earth in the form of human *avatars*. The avatars *Rama* and *Krishna* are the main heroes

This Hindu temple at Madura, built in CE1623, has a celebrated gopura, or gateway to a temple enclosure, and massive columns with life-sized figures attached.

Arjuna, the warrior prince, with his charioteer, the god Krishna, is seen on the plains of battle. The story of his dialogue with Krishna forms the central part of the *Bhagavad Gita. (below)* These children are enacting the story of Rama as part of the celebrations for the feast of Diwali. The god, Vishnu, in his incarnation as Rama, rescues Sita, his wife, who had been captured by the demon Ravana.

of the epics and Krishna especially became the focus for personal devotion and love for God as practised by the *bhakti* movement. The philosophical thinking of the Upanishads was developed and extended in the six systems of Hindu philosphy, the *Nyaya*, Baiseshika, Samkhya and Yoga schools.

Most Hindus today belong either to the *Shaivite* (Shiva-centred) or *Vaishnavite* (Vishnu- and especially Krishna-centred) sects, or venerate Durga, the mother goddess. Their daily *puja* is directed to these deities and the *Bhagavad Gita* is their favourite scripture. Some more intellectual Hindus practise meditation and yoga and end their lives as sannyasis. Almost all Hindus, however, visit temples on special days, celebrate the great feasts of *Divali, Holi* and *Durga Puja,* ensure that their sons undergo the *Sacred Thread Ceremony* if they belong to the Dvija castes and are cremated according to ancient custom – if possible, having their ashes cast into the river Ganges.

historical materialism A central concept in the philosophy of *Karl Marx*. He wrote that the material world is the real world. Man's material needs are his basic needs; hence, the production and exchange of material goods, like food, are the bases of all human relations. Production and exchange change, and this change determines how society changes. Marx concluded that in primitive societies men began by working together in co-operation. Then a minority gained control over the economic resources, and were able to live off the work of the majority, who became slaves.

As a result of progress, economic conditions changed, the balance of power in society changed and class struggle resulted in the overthrow of the slave-owners and the establishment of a new economic system: feudalism. Through a similar process feudalism was supplanted by *capitalism*. In capitalism, according to Marx, there is still class struggle between the minority who own the means of production, and the exploited workers who form the majority. Eventually workers will inevitably overthrow capitalism and establish socialism, in which they will own all the economic resources.

In Marx's view, the economic system is the real basis of society. All ideas, religion, laws, culture and institutions are just a 'superstructure' determined by the economic reality.

historicism A theory that says that the course of human history is determined by a series of laws and not by the actions of people. These laws cannot be altered and no human decisions or actions can prevent them from working.

Hitler, Adolf *See*: **National Socialist** (German Worker's) **Party**.

Hoa Hoa A sect influenced by Buddhism, which takes its name from the Vietnamese village where it began in 1939. Its founder, Huynh Phu So, claimed to be the reincarnation of various popular heroes and denied the need for temples of worship. In their place he set up teaching centres, where he spread a message of nationalism, obedience to one's parents and love of one's fellow men.

By the 1940s, he had gained a strong following and was seen as a threat by the French colonial authorities, who tried but failed to arrest him. Escaping to Saigon, Huynh Phu continued to draw support from the agricultural class in his native land, and in spite of his assassination in 1947, the movement has survived and developed over the last decades.

Holi *or* **Hollah Mohalla** The Hindu festival in March which commemorates the love of *Krishna* and *Radha*. People squirt coloured water and throw red powder over each other in the streets as a reminder of Krishna's love of amorous jokes and games. Bonfires are also lit, and women will walk with their young children around these fires, praying that their children will grow up strong and pious. This is inspired by a legend in which Krishna saved a young prince from being burnt alive by his father because of the prince's faith in Krishna.

Sikhs celebrate the festival too. For them it is the occasion of a three-day fair which features sporting competitions. The feast was first established by Guru *Gobind Singh*, as a substitute for the popular Hindu festival.

Holiness One of the titles of the *Pope* and the *Dalai Lama*.

The playful aspect of Krishna, perhaps the best-loved of the Hindu trinity, Trimurti, is seen here. Holi is celebrated annually in his honour.

holistic A holistic approach, in studying a subject or problem, does not merely examine parts of a subject or system in isolation, but believes that the 'whole' of the system contains the key to an understanding of its parts. It can be applied to philosophy, medicine and other subjects. Thus, man cannot be understood unless the whole of life is first examined, while the sickness of one organ or limb has to be seen in the context of the health of the whole body.

holy A person, place or thing is called holy if it is closely associated with or dedicated to the service of God or a god.

Holy Communion The Christian service of the *Eucharist*. More narrowly, the expression means the consecrated bread and wine which are eaten and drunk during the service.

Holy Days of Obligation Religious feast days on which Roman Catholics are expected to attend Mass and pay more attention to the spiritual than to the temporal side of life.

Holy Ghost *See:* **Holy Spirit**.

Holy Immortals *See:* **Amshaspentans**.

Holy Innocents' Day A Christian festival on 28 December commemorating the murder of all the male children in Bethlehem under the age of two. King *Herod* of Judaea had been told by the *Magi*, or wise men from the East, that a child, Jesus, who was to be the king of the Jews, had been born in the area. Herod determined to prevent the baby from growing up and becoming a threat to his rule, so he ordered the murder of all the young male children.

Holy Land The Christian name for Israel or Palestine, so-called because of its associations with Jesus Christ.

Holy of Holies The most sacred area of the Jewish Temple in Jerusalem where the *Ark of the Covenant* was kept, screened off from the rest of the inner *sanctuary* by a curtain. Only the High Priest was allowed to enter it, and then only once a year, on the *Day of Atonement*.

holy orders In the Roman Catholic and Orthodox Churches there are two grades of holy orders: the major orders and the minor orders. The former include bishops, priests and deacons. The latter includes door-keepers, readers (of the Bible during church services), exorcists and acolytes (who assist the priest during services). Men become members of the major orders through the *sacrament* of *ordination*, performed by a bishop. In the Roman Catholic Church a candidate must be a baptized and confirmed man. On being ordained or accepted into the clergy, he must obey the rule of *celibacy* and must recite daily the divine office, or special prayers said by ordained men. The *Church of England* does not regard ordination as a sacrament and has abolished the minor orders and rule of celibacy. It has, however, kept the major orders and requires everyone in holy orders to recite matins and evensong every day.

The Orthodox Churches do not demand celibacy, but will not allow a priest to remarry if his wife dies. Anyone who is unmarried at ordination must remain unmarried and become a monk; Orthodox bishops are chosen from among these monks. It is possible in all Churches for a priest to give up practising his orders and live as a layman once again, but he cannot undo his ordination and lose his holy order.

Holy Saturday The day before *Easter* Sunday in the *Holy Week* of Christianity.

Holy Sepulchre The tomb in which the body of Jesus lay between his burial and *resurrection*.

Holy Spirit Also known as the *Holy Ghost*: the third person in the *Holy Trinity* in Christianity. The Holy Spirit is often portrayed as a dove, fire or wind, and is regarded as the being who inspired the writing of the Bible. *Pentecost* commemorates the descent of the Holy Spirit.

Holy Trinity *See:* **Trinity**.

Holy Week In the Christian Church this is the last week of *Lent*, between *Palm Sunday* and *Easter*, when Christians contemplate Christ's sufferings and death on the cross. In many churches the services of these days re-enact in some ways the events in the life of Christ which led up to his crucifixion. For example, on Palm Sunday there is a procession in which people carry branches of palm, as did the people when Jesus entered Jerusalem on a donkey. On *Maundy Thursday*, an evening *Eucharist* is held to remember the *Last Supper* of Jesus and his disciples, during which the priest may wash the feet of several people in the church, imitating Christ washing his disciples' feet. On *Good Friday*, a wooden cross is carried through the church in procession and is venerated by the people.

homily A religious sermon, especially one preached during public services and addressed to the congregation.

The faithful carry palm branches in procession on Palm Sunday to commemorate the palms that were laid in his path as Jesus rode into Jerusalem on a donkey.

Honen (1133–1212) Also known as Honen Shonin, or Honem the Saint. The Japanese *bhikshu*, or Buddhist monk who founded the Jodo Shu or *Pure Land* school in 1175. Honen built especially on Chinese traditions of devotions to the ideal or symbolic Buddha Amitabha, known as *Amida* in Japan. *Pure Land Buddhism* declares that worship of or meditation on Amida brings rebirth in his Pure Land, *Sukhavati,* the easiest world in which to gain *enlightenment.* Honen's most famous pupil was Bhinran, founder of the Pure Land School.

Host The thin round wafers of unleavened bread used during most *Anglican* and *Lutheran* and all Roman Catholic services of the *Eucharist.*

Hougan A *Voodoo* priest.

Howell, Leonard A *Rastafarian* leader who set up the Ethiopian Salvation Society. He preached the six central ideas of the Rastafarian faith, most of which have been incorporated into the present belief that *Ras Tafari* is the true God and the black people will only find salvation by returning to Africa, their true homeland.

Hui neng The sixth and most important patriarch of Chinese Buddhism. As an illiterate and penniless boy he went to the fifth patriarch and impressed him with his insight and wisdom. Hui-neng was set to work in the patriarch's monastery; eight months later he was summond secretly to the patriarch at night, won complete *enlightenment* and was given the emblems that went with the position of patriarch. The fifth patriarch sent Hui-neng away to meditate and escape from enemies. After fifteen years he emerged from hiding to teach dharma and had a profound influence on the whole development of Ch'an. His most famous discourse is known as 'The Platform Sutra' or 'Sutra of Hui-neng'.

humanism A philosophy which says that man is the highest being there is, that he alone can create moral values and decide what is right and wrong. Man's aims should be to live as morally as he can, to develop his potential to the full and to serve his fellow men as well as possible before he dies. He should not follow any political or religious theory which would deny his freedom to make ethical decisions or to develop his potential. According to this view there is no life after death, so man's task must be to make life before death as valuable an experience as possible for himself and for others. Humanists generally reject the idea of a personal, active God.

Husain Son of *Ali* (Muhammad's son-in-law) and brother of Hasan. These two brothers were killed in CE680 at Karbala in Iraq. The *Shi'ah* sect in Islam regards Husain as the true successor to Ali, the fourth *caliph.* The yearly anniversary of the death of Husain and Hasan is kept in the tenth month of Muharram, and is the high point of the Shi'ites' religious calendar.

Hussein *See*: **Husain**.

Hutterites A Protestant *Anabaptist sect* that originated in central Europe in the sixteenth century. The Hutterites suffered harsh persecution and emigrated, eventually settling in western North America, along the Canadian-American border, where they lived in self-contained communities based largely on farming. They maintain an educational system centred on religion, a simple communal lifestyle, and a highly traditional style of dress.

hymn A song composed and performed in honour of God, a god, or any other being who is worshipped. Christians, Sikhs, Zoroastrians and Hindus, amongst others, include hymns in their services and meetings.

i

Iblis Name used in the Qur'an for the *Devil.* In the creation story, Iblis alone of the angels refused to bow down before Adam at Allah's command and was therefore cast out of Paradise to roam the world until the Day of Judgement.

Ibn-al-Arabi An Islamic philosopher and poet who was born in Spain in the twelfth century CE and who taught that God made himself known through man and the world.

Ibn Rushd A twelfth century Muslim philosopher who believed that Islam would be enriched if it incorporated ideas taken from ancient Greeks.

Ibrahim The Arabic name for *Abraham.*

I Ching *or* **Book of Changes** An ancient Chinese book of divination, containing a symbolic representation of the process of change. If a person wishes to ask a question about his or her future, he or she shuffles yarrow stalks or matches at random, forming hexagrams, or patterns of six lines. These lines may be complete (Yang) or broken (Yin). The sixty-four possible hexagrams have interpretations which give the answer to the question.

iconoclast An opponent of the use of images and pictures in religious worship. Iconoclasts believe that the use of such images can lead to *idolatry*, worshipping an idol or image instead of God or the quality it represents.

iconostasis *See*: **icon screen**.

icons Christian paintings of saints and the holy family, occasionally inlaid in mosaic but more often on a wooden base used as devotional images in the Eastern Orthodox Church. These can be found both in private homes and in public places and are venerated by the believers.

This icon of Christ Pantocrator, ruler of the universe, was painted in CE 1680 by Emmanuel Tzanes of Crete.

icon screen *or* **iconostasis** A screen found in Eastern Orthodox churches which separates the altar from the congregation. Only *ordained* clergy may go through the central door to the altar table, but the faithful are not cut off from the sight of the altar.

idealism (1) 'Practical' or 'moral' idealism is the notion that human beings are capable of perfection if they strive hard enough to achieve it. Idealists believe that, given enough time and effort, and that one has the right aims in life, things will turn out well in the end. (2) 'Philosophical' idealism is the notion that reality is not ultimately physical or material, but that behind the visible physical world lies the real world of thoughts, ideas and mind (those of human beings, of God, or of some *absolute* Mind), of which the visible world is a creation and expression.

ideology The body of doctrine, myths and symbols accepted by a group, especially a political or religious group. *Fascism*, *communism* and *socialism* are all ideologies.

idol An image that is worshipped. Often the worshippers believe that it contains the spirit of the deity it represents, as in so-called primitive religions. The term can also refer to anyone or anything honoured beyond reason.

idolatry In Judaism, Islam and Christianity, this means the worship of any god but the *Supreme Being*, or the love of anything which comes between the Supreme Being and man.

Id-ul-Adha The Islamic festival which takes place during the time of the *hajj*, or pilgrimage to Mecca. The pilgrims go to Mina, a town outside Mecca, where hundreds of sheep and goats are sacrificed. This commemorates *Abraham*'s willingness to sacrifice his son, *Ishmael* at God's command. Those not taking part in the hajj go to the mosque on this day for prayers, and on returning home sacrifice an animal in the same way, provided they can afford it; they eat as much of the meat as they need and give the rest to the poor.

This Muslim is marking the walls of his house with the blood of a sheep which he has slaughtered for the feast of Id-ul-Adha. Just as Abraham, in obedience to God, was about to sacrifice his son an angel appeared with an animal to be offered up in his place. The devout Muslim makes an annual sacrifice to mark this occasion.

Id-ul-Fitr The Islamic festival which takes place on the first day after the end of the month of Ramadan, the Muslim month of fasting. The feasting lasts for some days, during which friends are visited and greeting cards exchanged. Children are given money and dressed in new clothes during this period and the family as a whole gives to the poor the equivalent of the price of one meal for each of its members.

ihram The dress worn by Muslim pilgrims to Mecca, consisting of two white cotton cloths: one is wound around the waist, the other draped over the left shoulder. Women cover their head and whole body with the ihram. Since all must wear the same dress, any distinction between rich and poor is invisible, and the equality of all men before God is emphasized.

Ijma A ruling given by a *Sunni* teacher, based on the agreement of other Muslims, which allows Islamic laws to be adapted to fit changing circumstances.

Ijtihad A degree in religious knowledge. The *Shi'a* community denies that the interpretation of the law can be based on man-made decisions. In the absence, however, of the *hidden imam*, who is to reappear before the *Day of Judgement*, the Shi'ite leader of each age who occupies the position of Marja'i taqlid, (at present *Ayatollah Khomeini*), has the authority to lay down rulings for the faithful.

Ilm Special knowledge claimed by *Shi'ite imams* which gives them the right to exercise authority and make decisions binding on the community.

image (1) A likeness or representation of a person, animal or thing. (2) An idol.

imam The Islamic prayer leader in a mosque who delivers sermons on Fridays, the Islamic day for worship. The *Shi'ite* sect believe that each age produces a divinely inspired iman who has disappeared and whose reappearance as the *Mahdi* is awaited by the faithful. The title Marja'i taqlid is conferred upon the appointed imam.

imamis *See*: Twelvers.

Immaculate Conception The Roman Catholic doctrine which states that the Virgin Mary, the mother of Christ, was born without *original sin*. In 1854 the *Pope* declared that the Virgin Mary spent her life in obedience to God's will, untainted by original, or by any actual, sins committed during her life.

immersion Baptism by submersion of the whole body under water. Immersion is practised by the Baptists and other evangelical sects, as well as by the Eastern Orthodox Church.

immortality Endless life, even after death. Many religions offer a hope to believers that they will live for ever after death, either in the form of a spirit, or in some bodily form, as in *resurrection.*

immortals (1) *Taoist* beings said to live in the Realm of Great Purity. (2) A term used generally in any religion to refer to angels, spirits or deities.

imperialism The policy or practice of expanding one nation's territory at the expense of another. Imperialism can also refer to believing in such a policy, or supporting it. The feeling that one's country has the right to behave in this manner may stem from the simple desire for more living space, or from a desire to bring the benefits of one's own supposedly superior civilization to other peoples. The country to be taken over may be especially rich in natural resources, or expansion of territory in this way may help to keep the colonizing country equal in power to other strong nations. These, along with the sheer desire for prestige, are all reasons why certain nations adopt a policy of imperialism.

Inari shrines The common *Shinto* shrines found all over Japan, dedicated to the god of food. Anyone who wishes to succeed in business will visit them to pray for aid and guidance.

incantation The chanting of spells, words or charms in the hope of gaining magical powers. The word is usually used of so-called 'primitive' religions or cults such as *Voodoo*, but the *litanies* of Christianity could also be regarded as a type of incantation.

incarnation Any god who has assumed human form or a human nature is said to have been incarnated. The Hindu doctrine of the *avatar* is an example of incarnation. The doctrine of incarnation is also fundamental to the Christian religion, stating that God became man in Jesus Christ. Apart from *Unitarians*, all Christians accept this statement.

incense A sweet-smelling spicy substance burnt for its pleasant smell, especially in ceremonies in Hinduism, Buddhism, Christianity and other religions. To Christians it represents virtue, holiness, prayer and, at funerals, the communion of saints.

Independent Churches Christian Protestant churches which believe that each separate local congregation has a right to conduct its own affairs free from national or international supervision. They do not accept a rigid hierarchy or single figure of authority, such as the *Pope* in the Roman Catholic Church.

Independents *See*: **Independent Churches.**

Index A list drawn up by the Roman Catholic Church which specified books that Catholics were forbidden to own or read. The Index was first published in the sixteenth century and was abolished in 1966.

Indra Hindu god of war, rain and thunder. Indra was the chief god of the *Aryan* pantheon in whose honour the *Vedas* were composed. From the time of the invasion of the Indus valley by the Aryans onwards, Indra gradually became less important; his position was taken over by *Brahma*, the creator.

indulgence A release from the spiritual penalties payable by a sinner which is granted by the *Pope* and, occasionally, by Roman Catholic bishops. In the Middle Ages it was possible for the faithful to buy such pardon for their sins, and unscrupulous priests saw the selling of indulgences as an easy way of raising money.

Before receiving an indulgence, the individual had to show repentance, perform acts of charity and recite certain prayers. The abuse of indulgences spurred Martin *Luther* to make his criticisms which led to the *Reformation*.

infallibility To be infallible is to be unable to make a mistake. According to most *monotheistic* religions, God is infallible, and often the sacred scriptures, such as the Qur'an, are infallible as well. According to the Roman Catholic Church, the *Pope*, the head of the Church, is guided by God in certain major pronouncements on doctrine. When the Pope and bishops together make pronouncements on major matters of dogma or Church teaching, their authority and judgment are regarded as infallible. Both Roman Catholic and Eastern Orthodox Christians regard the pronouncements of *Ecumenical Councils* on doctrine as infallible. In *Shi'a* Islam, the *imam* is looked on as an infallible guide to the will of God for the age.

infidel A term used by Muslims and Christians to describe members of other religions, especially *polytheists*.

infinite As an adjective, it describes something which has no limits or boundaries, either in space or time. It goes on for ever and is everywhere. In the religious sense, the infinite is often used to signify God.

Innocents *See*: **Holy Innocents' Day.**

Inquisition An institution established by Pope Gregory IX in 1233 to persuade or force heretics to return to the Roman Catholic faith. The Church believed that non-believers and heretics

Believing that it was better for someone to perish than persist in a life of evil heresy, the Inquisitors were responsible for many deaths. The monks and priests were hopeful of a retraction from the heretic until the very moment of death.

would suffer for eternity in hellfire; therefore it was the Church's duty to make them realize the error of their thinking. The Inquisitors used argument and torture in their efforts to make heretics reveal others of the same views and to give up their views. Heretics were tried in Church courts, which could punish them with fines, life imprisonment, or even burning at the stake in extreme cases.

intercession When a Roman Catholic or Eastern Orthodox Christian prays to saints or angels he or she is asking them to intercede, or pray to God on that person's behalf. As the saints are believed to be already in heaven and very close to God, their prayers are especially effective. Any prayer offered by one person for the needs of another is also called an intercession.

interdict A Roman Catholic form of punishment imposed by the *Pope*, bishop or other *prelates* on countries or individuals. National and local interdicts mean that all public worship, administering of the *sacraments* and burial services are forbidden. Individuals are usually excommunicated.

International Auxiliary Language A language which, according to the *Baha'i*, should be taught worldwide in order that people of different nations may communicate more easily, in the hope that hostility between nations will be replaced by a sense of international brotherhood.

International Society for Krishna Conscious-ness Abbreviation: ISKCON A Hindu sect which is an offshoot of *Vaishnavism* and is heavily influenced by the teachings of Sri Chaitanya, a sixteenth-century Hindu sage. It expresses its intense love for Krishna as God through meditation, chanting, ecstasy, music and dance. Members of the sect are known for their *mantra* 'Hare Krishna', for wearing distinctive robes, and for handing out pamphlets as they go through the streets. The men shave their heads, except for a topknot. Devotees follow a life of *asceticism* with an emphasis on vegetarianism, teetotalism and chastity. The most important figure in recent years was A. C. Bhaktivedanta Swami Prabhupada, who brought the group to the West in the late 1960s.

International Teaching Centre The institution set up in 1973 to supervise *Baha'i* education all over the world. This body is made up of the *Hands of the Cause* and three Counsellors, and reports back to both the *Universal House of Justice* and various Continental Boards of Counsellors.

With the surge of interest in Eastern religions which swept the West in the 1960s, one sect, the followers of Krishna, won many converts. They have a distinctive style of dress and a habit of dancing and singing in the streets. The sect is noted for its great sense of mission to spread devotion to Krishna.

When Japan became unified in the Yamato period the Imperial family were raised to semi-divine status, and Ise Shrine, where the sun goddess Amaterasu is revered, had a close connection with the Imperial household.

Iqbal, Muhammad (1875–1938) An Indian Muslim poet, philosopher and political leader. Iqbal believed that Muslims should have a separate state within India and not co-exist with the Hindus.

Isa The Arabic term for Jesus.

Isaac The son of *Abraham* and one of the three *patriarchs*, the founders of Judaism, to whom God revealed himself and his teachings. According to the *Torah*, God commanded Abraham to offer Isaac as a sacrifice, but spared him at the last moment. *See also*: **Ishmael**.

Iscariot, Judas One of Jesus' twelve Apostles, who betrayed him to the soldiers in the garden of Gethsemane, by means of a kiss, which was a pre-arranged signal. After Jesus had been led away by the elders to his trial and crucifixion, Judas repented and gave back the thirty pieces of silver which had been given to him as a reward, and then, despairing, hanged himself.

Ise shrine The most important *Shinto* shrine, dedicated to the sun goddess *Amaterasu*. The shrine has always been associated with the Japanese imperial family, who claimed descent from the grandson of Amaterasu, and thus claimed divinity. During World War II, Ise was an important focus for Japanese nationalism. New prime ministers still inform the sun goddess that they have succeeded in forming a cabinet on taking office. Thus this shrine has both political and religious significance.

Ishmael The first son of *Abraham* and Hagar, an Egyptian. Muhammad claimed descent from him. Ishmael is said to be buried with his mother at Mecca. Whereas Jews and Christians believe that it was Isaac, his second son, whom Abraham was commanded to *sacrifice* to God, Muslims say that it was Ishmael; this event is celebrated at *Id-ul-Adha*. Muslims also believe that Ishmael helped Abraham to build the *Ka'ba*.

Ishvara Literally, 'Lord'. A title used of Krishna in the *Bhaghavad Gita*, but most frequently applied to Shiva.

Islam

Islam One of the most powerful religions in the world today, Islam has about six hundred million members. Islam was founded by the prophet *Muhammad* in the seventh century CE at Mecca in Saudi Arabia. In CE610 he received a vision of the angel Gabriel in a cave on Mount Hira near Mecca. The angel spoke to him then and on many subsequent occasions throughout his life, telling him to recite phrases which were later written down to form the Holy Qu'ran, the source of all Islamic doctrine. From these revelations Muhammad learnt that there was one God only, who could have no equals or partners, and that he himself had been chosen to be God's final prophet or messenger to mankind. The strictly *monotheistic* religion which he was to found was to be called Islam, which means 'peace' or 'submission (to God)'; and its followers would be known as Muslims. Such people alone would attain paradise after death; the rest would be condemned to hell on the Last Day. God's will is omnipotent and cannot be resisted without punishment. Islam would sum up and complete the message which God – or 'Allah' – had revealed to all the true prophets of Judaism and Christianity, such as Abraham, Moses and Jesus, but which had been distorted by the followers of those prophets when they recorded it in the *Torah* and Bible. Muhammad and his Muslim followers were to fight for the cause of Allah, to spread his message to the whole world, whether by actual physical fighting, or by preaching and teaching. This

This surah, al-Talag, is from the Mamluk Qur'an, copied in Mulaggag style in CE 1397.

'striving' or '*Jihad*' in the cause of Allah is a prime reason for the success of Islam up to the present day.

Opposition to his preaching in his home town of Mecca forced Muhammad to flee to Medina in CE622, a flight known as the *Hijra*, and this date is regarded as the beginning of Islam as a religion, the first year of the Islamic era, and the date for New Year's Day every year. By his death in CE632, Muhammad had spread Islam throughout Iraq and North Africa; nowadays Muslims can be found in practically every country.

All Muslim teaching and practice is based on the Qu'ran; but to complement the Qu'ran there are the collections known as the *Hadith* – sayings which record Muhammad's words and practice or *sunna*, by which he guided the early Muslim community. The laws of the Qu'ran and Hadith have also been developed and extended

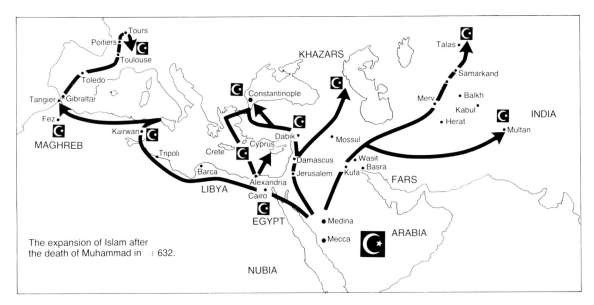

The expansion of Islam after the death of Muhammad in CE 632.

These Muslim tribesmen from Kandi, in Benin, Western Africa, are seen at worship on their prayer-mats, facing Mecca. Islam requires the faithful to observe Salat, or fixed prayer, five times a day.

in the *Shari'a* or body of Islamic law. The most important duties of a Muslim are summed up in the *five pillars of Islam*: (1) *Shahada* or statement of faith in one God and Muhammad his prophet, (2) *Salat* or fixed prayer five times a day, including the communal prayer in the *mosque* at noon on Fridays, (3) *Saum* or Siyam, fasting in the month of *Ramadan* until the feast of *Id-ul-Fitr*, (4) *zakat* or almsgiving, involving the sacrifice of one-fortieth of one's income to help the poor, and (5) *Hajj*, or pilgrimage to the *Ka'ba* in Mecca once in a lifetime, including the celebration of the feast of *Id-ul-Adha*, which takes place both in Mecca at this time and all over the Muslim world.

In the late seventh century CE a schism occurred within Islam which led to the formation of the minority *Shi'ite* sects, alongside the *Sunni* majority. From the eight century CE onwards, the *Sufi* mystical movement has also been influential. *See also*: **Wahhabis, Ahmadiyya, Baha'i.**

Islamic New Year *See*: **Hijra.**

Islamic socialism A movement which believes that the teachings of the Qur'an should be interpreted in a socialist way, and that the Islamic faith is a socialist faith.

The mosque is the focus of Islamic practice, and, having removed his shoes, a Muslim will enter it to pray, most particularly on Friday, the holy day of the week.

Ismailis A *Shi'a* Muslim sect, divided into two groups, the Nizaris and Musta'lis, who both believe in the return of the seventh imam as the *Mahdi*.

Israel *See*: Israelites.

Israelites Descendants of *Jacob* (who was also known as Israel), and thus of the Hebrews who entered the *Promised Land* with *Abraham*. These are the *Chosen People* of the *Torah*, or *Old Testament*, who were delivered from Egypt by Moses and are the ancestors of the modern Jews.

Isvara, Isha. A Sanskrit word meaning lord, master, Supreme Being. Used of Krishna in the *Bhagavad Gita*, but more frequently applied to Shiva.

Izanagi The Japanese god who fathered the islands and gods of Japan by a union with his sister *Izanami*.

Izanami In *Shintoism*, the sky-goddess, wife of *Izanagi*, who worked together with him to create the world of nature. They filled the natural world with *Kami* or spirits, which are the chief objects of devotion and worship for Shintoists. When Izanami finally died, she went down to the world of the dead and began to decay; she was shocked to find Izanagi following her even though she was rotting away, and so finally divorced him. *Also spelt*: Isanami.

Izumo The *Shinto* shrine where all the gods are said to return every year.

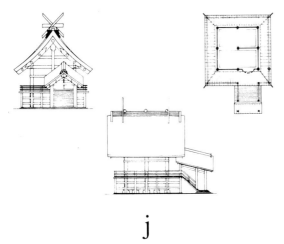

j

Jacob The third of the Jewish *patriarchs* and son of *Isaac*. He is also named Israel, which emphasizes his position as founding father of the twelve tribes of the *Chosen People* or Israelites, who are also called the Children of Israel.

Jacobite Church Also known as the Syrian Orthodox Church, this is one of the *Monophysite* Churches, and takes its name from its chief founder, Jacob Baradeus. Branches of the Church exist in Syria, Turkey, India and the United States.

Yu Huang, the Jade Emperor, is seen by Taoists as the chief member of the trinity of Three Pure Ones. He is the Supreme Master of the gods.

Jade Emperor The supreme *Taoist* god, who keeps an account of human actions and presides over life and death. In a bid to counter the tide of Buddhism sweeping China in the ninth century, the Taoists began to look for a god who would rival the popularity of the Buddha. The Emperor Chen Sung finally declared that he had received a revelation from heaven in the writing of *Lao-tzu* declaring the supremacy and greatness of the Jade Emperor, *Yu Huang*.

Jahannam The Islamic term for hell, the place of fire and brimstone.

Jaimini Believed to be the founder of the *Purva Mimamsa* school of Hindu thought. Jaimini stressed the need for following the *Vedas* in daily life but also taught that self-knowledge was the first step to knowledge of the world as a whole, and that right action was the road to the truth.

Jainism An Indian religion which arose between the ninth and sixth centuries BCE, partly as a reaction against the domination of Indian society and religion by the Hindu *Brahmin* caste. In this, as in some of its teachings, it resembles Buddhism. Its original founder was probably *Parsva*, in the ninth century BCE; although traditionally it is *Mahavira*, who lived in the sixth and fifth centuries BCE, who is credited with founding the religion. More probably, Mahavira took over and developed Parsva's ideas and founded the communities of Jaina monks who have always been the chief practitioners of the faith. Mahavira and Parsva are also believed to be the twenty-fourth and twenty-third of a line of *tirthankaras* or preachers of the Jaina religion.

The doctrines of Jainism can be found in its sacred scriptures, the Agarna, of which the most important are known as the Angas. The most characteristic features of Jainism probably arose in reaction to Brahmin Hinduism; its rejection of caste distinctions, for example, and of animal sacrifice. The rejection of animal sacrifice is a consequence of the Jains' strong belief in non-violence, *ahimsa*, an attitude which has in turn had an influence on Hindus such as *Gandhi* and on Buddhism. Since the laws of *karma* and *samsara* mean that a human soul can be reborn as an animal, even an insect, and since all forms of life have souls, even the smallest creature must not be harmed. Jains therefore will wear face-masks while walking and will brush the ground with a light broom in front of their feet to avoid harming any life that may be in their way. For the same reason, some Jaina monks avoid washing, so as not to kill parasites that live on their bodies.

Jainism is practised mainly by monks, who live a life of fasting and *asceticism*. They are supported by 'hearers' or laymen who take certain vows in the same manner as the monks. The five vows of the Jaina monk are non-violence, truthfulness, not stealing, avoidance of attachment to material things and chastity. They are bound to practise the 'Three Jewels' of right faith, right knowledge and right conduct. The aim of this severe life is to liberate the soul from *maya* or delusion and from all entrapment by worldly concerns. The philosophy which lies behind this aim is close to the Hindu system of *Samkhya*. Ahimsa and fasting will avoid the build-up of bad *karma*, and so will enable spiritual growth to take place. There is no supreme being in Jainism, although Jaina saints are venerated in temples.

In the first century CE the religion split into the *Svetambara* and *Digambara* sects and later in the eighteenth century the *Sthanakavasi* sect arose. The religion now has about two million members, mostly in Gujarat and Mysore.

Jallianwala Bagh The site of the Sikh Baisakhi fair in *Amritsar* where in 1919 about 379 Sikhs were killed when the British General Dyer ordered his men to fire upon a crowd in order to disperse it. At the time, India was striving for independence. The tragedy is one of the events commemorated at the festival of Baisakhi.

Janmashtami Hindu festival celebrating the birth of Lord Krishna. A model of Krishna is ceremonially swung at midnight amidst feasts and singing.

Janam Sakhis A collection of stories which tell the life of the first Sikh *guru*, Guru *Nanak*.

Janna An Arabic word meaning 'the garden'. The usual word for paradise or heaven in the Qur'an.

Japji A Sikh hymn, to be found at the beginning of the *Adi Granth*. The Japji is recited by Sikhs in their daily morning prayers and during the Amrit ceremony, and is an important part of public worship in the *gurdwara*.

Jashan A *Parsi* ritual which is performed on any number of different occasions: to ask for help, to thank God for saving his people, to celebrate an important event or to commemorate a special occasion.

Jehovah A name used for the God of the Israelites. In the *Torah*, the name of God is represented by the letters 'YHWH', known as the 'tetragrammaton'. This name is so holy, however, that Jews have never said it aloud, but always substitute another title; and when Hebrew is written down, no vowels need be indicated, so that over the course of time the correct pronunciation has been forgotten. Scholars have concluded that Yahweh is the probable pronunciation.

Written Hebrew does sometimes show what vowels to add. But when writers came to the word YHWH, they usually wrote the vowel signs for 'Adonai', meaning 'Lord', because this was what readers would say. If YHWH is combined with the vowels of Adonai, a word very close to Jehovah is formed.

The tetragrammaton, the four letters used in the Torah, because the name of God is too sacred for the human voice to speak.

Jehovah's Witnesses Their modern history dates back to the 1870s when *Charles Taze Russell* in Pittsburgh, Pennsylvania, joined other Bible students to consider the second coming of Jesus Christ and the establishment of God's Kingdom. From Bible chronology Russell pinpointed the autumn of 1914, and the Witnesses still preach the significance of this year as it relates to Bible prophecy and world events. Under the direction of Russell's successor, *Joseph Rutherford*, the organization expanded rapidly.

Witnesses are well known for their stand as conscientious objectors during the two world wars and in Nazi Germany they were, for this reason, among the first to be put into concentration camps in the early 1930s. Each Witness is a minister and as an active evangelist preaches from house to house as well as informally, offering Bible literature, particularly their journals, *The Watchtower* and *Awake!*, to encourage Bible study. The Witnesses also print and publish the *New World Translation of the Holy Scriptures* in eleven languages.

The faith of the Witnesses is based on the entire Bible as the inspired word of God. They worship the Creator, Jehovah, through Jesus Christ as the redeemer of the world. They view the earth as man's permanent home and believe that in the general resurrection, under the Kingdom government, the opportunity to live forever on earth will be extended to the human family. Only 144,000, the brides of Christ, will be taken to heaven to rule with him.

Jehovah's Witnesses seek to follow Christian principles in every aspect of life. They do not use tobacco. Only adults are baptized, after a period of comprehensive Bible study. In 1983, 6,767,707 people attended the Witnesses' annual memorial of the death of Jesus Christ.

jen A *Confucian* term for humanity or benevolence. According to Confucius, man's goal should be to achieve jen (true humanity) by transforming his life from one ruled by passions and emotions into one ruled instead by enlightened wisdom. To achieve this step, the individual must follow religious rituals and ethical paths which will develop spiritual awareness, harmony and self-transformation.

Jerusalem A holy city for Jews, Christians and Muslims alike. King *David* made it the capital of the Hebrew kingdom in the tenth century BCE. There three temples were built to house the *Shekinah*. Today the city remains a focus for the Jewish religion.

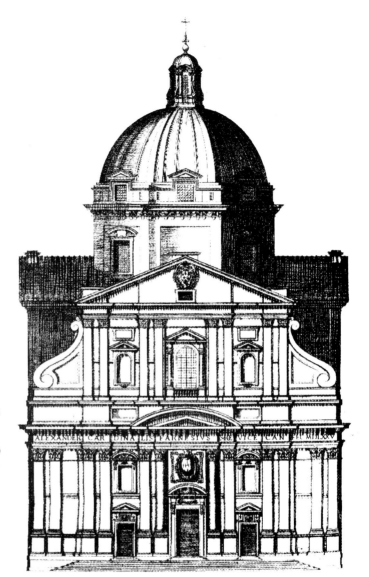

The splendour of the façade, and the grandiose scale of this mother-church of the Gesù of the Jesuit order, are not vainglorious, but were considered outward signs of divine perfection. The Jesuit General Oliva explained 'In our churches [we] try to reach up to the sublimity of God's eternal omnipotence with such appurtenances of glory as we can...achieve.'

(opposite) Jerusalem is thrice a holy city. Jews have considered it the centre of their world since David brought the ark of the covenant there, and Solomon caused a mighty temple to be built in which to place it. For Christians, it is the city where the passion, death and resurrection of Jesus took place, and is accordingly at the heart of the Christian universe. The Dome of the Rock is an outward sign of the significance Muslims attach to Jerusalem, since they believe it was from that rock that Muhammad ascended to heaven to receive Allah's message to mankind.

Christians associate Jerusalem with the life of Christ, for he was brought there to be sentenced and crucified and it was here, too, that the *resurrection* is said to have taken place.

Muslims have built a shrine there known as the Dome of the Rock. It commemorates Muhammad's 'Night Journey' on a winged horse led by the archangel Gabriel to the Temple of Jerusalem. There he met Abraham, Moses and Jesus and ascended into heaven into the presence of *Allah*, to receive the message he was to preach to the faithful.

Jesuits Officially known as the Society of Jesus. A Roman Catholic religious order founded by *St Ignatius Loyola*. He gathered a small group of men around him, and the group took vows of poverty, chastity and obedience to the *Pope*, as well as undertaking to do missionary work in the world. In 1540 the order was approved by the Pope and grew to thirteen thousand members within a century. They undertook missionary work in areas unfamiliar with Christianity and worked at countering the spread of the *Reformation*'s influence. To this end, the Jesuits travelled throughout the world.

The Jesuits are organized along military lines on the basis of Loyola's principles enshrined in his 'Spiritual Exercises'. The head of the order is called the General and is answerable only to the Pope. The order has a long history of being the intellectual spearhead of the Roman Catholic Church.

Jesus Christ *See*: **Christ, Jesus.**

Jesus Prayer A prayer used originally by Eastern Orthodox monks, which must contain the word 'Jesus' and can be up to twelve words long. By repeating the name and concentrating on it, monks believed that they could open themselves up to Jesus who would enter their hearts. The practise spread beyond the monasteries into homes, and it is now followed by most Orthodox believers.

Jew (1) A member of a Semitic people, descended from the ancient Israelites. By Jewish law, a child is a Jew if his or her mother is Jewish. (2) A believer in the religion of Judaism.

Jewish New Year In Hebrew, *Rosh Hashanah*, meaning 'the beginning of the year'. It is celebrated in September or October and begins the 'Ten Days of Return' which end on *Yom Kippur*. It recalls the act of creation and God's role as judge of all men and women. During morning service on New Year's Day a ram's horn, known as the *shofar*, is blown, to remind the faithful of their duties and of the worship due to God.

At home, the father of the household recites the *Kaddish*, or prayers of sanctification, before meals, and many of the dishes served are sweet, to symbolize the sweet year ahead. Traditionally, anyone who eats the head of a fish or a sheep is going to be lucky in the following twelve months.

Jihad An Islamic term for 'striving' to spread the faith. In the past, this often meant conquering non-believers and converting them, as well as simple missionary work. Nowadays jihad is carried on by Islamic education for Muslim children and by numerous Islamic publications in many languages.

Jimmu Tenno According to tradition, the first human Japanese emperor, enshrined at Kashiwabara, who is said to be descended from *Ninigi*, the storm god and grandson of *Amaterasu*, the sun goddess. As a result, the Japanese emperors have in the past claimed that they are descended from the gods, and that their judgements and decisions have divine blessing.

Jina Literally, 'a conqueror'. Also known as *tirthankara*: any of the twenty-four omniscient spiritual teachers who appear in each half of a 'time cycle' according to the *Jains*. The most recent Jina was *Mahavira*, the founder of Jainism. In modern times, the term is sometimes used for any person who has won infinite knowledge. Also known as Dhyani Buddha: any of the five most important *Sambhogakaya*

This is a statue of a Jina, of whom there have been twenty-four, according to Jain tradition.

Buddhas, who are symbolic, non-historic, ideal Buddhas in *Mahayana* Buddhism. They symbolize different aspects of enlightenment and wisdom and are often portrayed in a *mandala*, a symbolic diagram, picture or sculpture usually organized around a circle or square. All these Jinas are the subjects of *meditation* practices.

jinja A *Shinto* sanctuary used for prayer, ceremonial occasions and for making offerings.

jinn *or* **jinni** A spirit in the Islamic faith. Jinn are capable of being both good and bad: the Qur'an teaches that all jinni will be judged, and will attain future salvation or damnation. Before Islam started, the jinn were worshipped by the Arabs as gods.

jiva A soul. Jains believe space has an infinite number of jivas. These souls are trapped in a continuous round of rebirth in various 'bodies'. Liberation from this cycle can be achieved by absolute purification and by knowledge.

Jizo-sama A *bodhisattva* revered by Japanese Buddhists, who is commonly believed to care for children and infants who are stillborn or die in the womb, and women travellers.

Jodo (Shu) *See*: **Pure Land Buddhism.**

John of the Cross (1542–91) A Spanish mystic. He became a *Carmelite* monk and with St Teresa of Avila founded the ascetic Reformed Carmelites, also known as Discalced Carmelites because they either go barefoot or wear only open sandals. He was canonized by the Roman Catholic Church in 1726. He is one of the greatest mystical poets and writers of Christianity, and is chiefly remembered for his writings, which include, *The Dark Night of the Soul* and *The Spiritual Canticle*.

John, St *See*: **St John's Gospel.**

This Byzantine mosaic shows John the Baptist baptizing his cousin, Jesus, in the waters of the Jordan. The Holy Ghost is present in the form of a dove and the gospels relate that a voice from heaven was heard, saying 'Thou art my beloved Son; in thee I am well pleased'.

John the Baptist Christ's cousin and predecessor, he preached to the Jews that the Messiah was coming, and baptised in the River Jordan anyone who acknowledged his sins. At the beginning of his public life, Jesus travelled from Nazareth to be baptised by John.

John was subsequently imprisoned by King *Herod*, whom he had reproached for marrying Herodias, the wife of Herod's brother. At a feast one of the dancers greatly pleased the king, and he promised to give her whatever she wished: she asked for the head of John the Baptist on a platter, and so John was beheaded.

The Sabeans, who are mentioned in the Qur'an as 'People of the Book' along with Jews and Christians, were followers of John the Baptist; a small group of them, also known as Mandeans, still exists today.

Jonah The *Old Testament* or *Hebrew Bible* contains a story in which Jonah the prophet is swallowed by a sea monster. Jonah is sent to Nineveh in Assyria, to tell the people to repent of their sins and turn to God. God, therefore, is shown to be concerned for one of Israel's traditional enemies, as well as for the Chosen People. The story is also referred to in the Qur'an.

Joseph The husband of the *Virgin Mary*, to whom an angel appeared in a dream, telling him that Mary was to have a son, *Jesus*. He is not mentioned in the Bible after the incident where he accompanied Mary to Jerusalem when Christ was twelve years old.

Judah Ha-Nasi *or* **Judah the Prince** (135?–220?) A Jewish *rabbi* and scholar who was largely responsible for compiling the Jewish oral teachings known as the *Mishnah*. The Mishnah in turn formed the basis for the *Talmud*. His work helped to rebuild Judaism in Palestine following the last disastrous rebellion of Jews against Roman authority, which occurred before his birth.

This synagogue, in Tunisia, is the oldest in North Africa. After the destruction of the Temple of Jerusalem in CE70 and their subsequent exile by the Romans, Jews had no single spiritual home, and so the faith was preserved by observance of laws and customs within the family and within the synagogue, under the guidance of the rabbi.

Judaism The religion of the Jewish race, the descendants of the ancient Israelites and Hebrews. The Jews believe that they are a chosen people, specially elected by the one true God, *Yahweh*. To be a Jew is basically to be the child of a Jewish mother; conversion to Judaism is rare and difficult.

The Jews trace their origin as chosen people to the moment when God made a covenant with Abram, who was known as Abraham thereafter. Abraham was to stop worshipping idols and was to believe in only one God; in return, God would give him a mighty race of descendants and a *Promised Land*, Canaan, where this race could live for ever. As a sign of his willingness to keep this covenant, Abraham was to *circumcise* himself, his son and any sons he might have thereafter, and since that time all

Jewish boys have undergone cirumcision eight days after birth. This covenant with the Chosen People was renewed by God when he led the Jews out of slavery in Egypt (the *Exodus*), when he used *Moses* as his mouthpiece or prophet. He gave Moses the *Torah* or laws of the Jewish religion at Mount Sinai and allowed the Jews to settle in Canaan, provided they kept the Torah faithfully.

In the sixth century BCE the Jews were invaded and exiled to Babylon; this was interpreted by the Jewish prophets as a punishment for their disobedience to God. They were soon allowed to return, however, and to rebuild the Jerusalem Temple, which was the central focus of their worship, containing the altar of sacrifice. They also built synagogues, where they could hear the law read and interpreted. Further invasions by

Greeks and Romans followed, during which time Judah Maccabees led an uprising which is celebrated at *Hanukah*. The Jews began to hope for a new leader, sent by God, who would finally liberate them from their oppressors and rule them in peace in an eternal *kingdom of God*. This liberator, known as the *Messiah*, is still awaited by the Jews, as the Temple was destroyed a third time in CE70 and they were finally banished from their homeland by the Romans after CE135. Not until 1948 did the Promised Land, or part of it, come once again under Jewish control, following the rise of Zionism and the horrors of the Nazi holocaust in which six million exiled Jews were massacred.

The events of this largely tragic history form the main theme of the annual Jewish festivals – *Passover*, *Pentecost*, *Tabernacles* and *Chanukah*; repentance for their sins against God is expressed at *Rosh Hashanah* and on the Day of Atonement, *Yom Kippur*. Study of the laws given to Moses by God (the Torah), and the early *rabbis'* interpretations of these laws in the *Talmud*, play a very important part in the religion. Jews are meant to pray three times a day, in the synagogue if possible, and Saturday, the *Sabbath*, is a day given entirely to God, when no work is done. Once a male Jew is ready to take on these adult responsibilities, at thirteen years old, he takes part in a *Bar mitzvah* ceremony; girls in Reform Judaism have a corresponding Bat mitzvah. Faithfulness to God and the Torah will lead to heaven and eternal life, but Jews are not specific about what form life after death might take.

Since the nineteenth century Jews have been divided into various groups – the *Orthodox* majority, who retain all the old traditions, and modernizing groups such as *Conservative*, *Liberal* and *Reform Jews*.

Judgement, Day of *See*: **Judgement, Last**.

Judgement, Last Some religions, including Christianity and Islam, believe that at the end of time there will be a day on which God will judge all human beings on the basis of their conduct and faith during this life. Those in whose lives good has outweighed evil will be united with God: those who have preferred evil to good will be condemned to be separated from God for ever. This is the basic outline, though of course details vary from faith to faith. After the Last Judgement, the earth will disappear or be transformed into the *kingdom of God*, or heaven.

(below left) This Chasidic Jew, wearing the streimel, a flat fur hat worn on the Sabbath, is reading from the scriptures against the Western Wall in Jerusalem. *(right)* Inside the synagogue the Torah rolls are revealed in their splendour.

justification In the Christian religion, God's decision to put a sinner right with himself, to forgive his sins and count him fit to receive *salvation*; the concept occurs especially in the letters of *St Paul* in the *New Testament*.

k

Ka'ba The Islamic sanctuary in Mecca which contains the *Black Stone* and is said to have been built by *Abraham* and his son *Ishmael*. When Muslims pray, they must face towards the Kalba, and *Hajj* has the Ka'ba as its focal point.

Kabbalah Literally, 'the Tradition': a form of Jewish mysticism which developed in France and Spain. It was based on the esoteric teachings of a variety of groups. The Kabbalists believed that harmony had originally existed between God and his universe, only to be shattered by Adam and Eve in the Garden of *Eden*. The task of Israel was to restore the proper balance between the creator and his creatures by practising obedience, kindness and rituals designed to produce an ecstatic communication with God.

The most important book produced by this school is the *Zohar*, a commentary on the first five books of the Bible.

Kabir An Indian mystic and poet who was born a Hindu but brought up as a Muslim. His teachings attracted Muslims and Hindus alike; he was influenced both by the *bhakti*, or devotional, movement in Hinduism and by the *Sufis* in Islam. He stated that there was only one God, but that his name was unimportant. To worship the creator, men needed to bring love into their daily lives rather than to follow strict ritual and dogmatic teachings. He died in 1518.

The Sikh sacred book, the *Guru Granth Sahib*, includes many of Kabir's hymns, since he had a strong influence on the founder of Sikhism, Guru *Nanak*.

kacch Short trousers worn by members of the *Khalsa*, or Sikh brotherhood, originally for convenience in fighting, but now as a symbol of moral behaviour and self-control.

Kaddish A Jewish prayer glorifying God which is recited especially by those whose relatives have recently died. Although it is something referred to as the 'mourner's prayer', it does not mention the dead or death. Rather it reaffirms faith at a time when believers may be prone to despair.

kaftan A long black coat worn by *Chasidic* Jews, in place of a suit, jacket and overcoat. The kaftan is buttoned on the left, in keeping with the Chasidim's desire to distinguish their way of dressing from that of non-Jews. On the *Sabbath*, a silk kaftan is worn.

Kali Another name for *Mahadevi*, the consort of the Hindu god *Shiva*. Kali represents an active, sometimes violent side of the goddess. Kali is associated with death and destruction, but also with creation and fertility.

Kali-Yuga In Hinduism, the fourth and last *Yuga*, characterised by calamities, disease and impiety. Hindus believe that we are now living in the Kali-Yuga; at its end, this world will be dissolved, ready for creation of a new world and the beginning of a new cycle of Yugas. *See* **Kalki**.

Kalki The last *avatar* of *Vishnu*, the Hindu god who maintains the world. Hindus believe that Kalki, an embodiment of the god, will appear at the end of this world to destroy it to make way for the creation of a new world.

Kama, Kamadeva The Hindu god of love and desire, who caused *Shiva* to leave his asceticism and marry Parvati.

Kamadhenu 'Cow of wishes', in Hindu mythology. Produced during the churning of the ocean which also produced *amrita*, Kamadhenu is the cow which satisfies all desires. It is one of the reasons for the reverence with which Hindus regard the cow.

Kami *Shinto* spirits who help with fertility and growth. Tradition holds that the Japanese people are descended from the kami, who were in their turn created by the Shinto gods. Local *shrines* to worship the kami are found all over Japan. All the kami of Japan are said to gather at the *Izumo* shrine every year.

kamma The word '*karma*' in the *Pali* language. In this form it is used by *Theravada Buddhists*.

Kanada Reputedly the founder of the *Vaisheshika* system of Hindu philosophy.

kangha A comb which members of the *Khalsa*, or Sikh brotherhood, use to discipline their hair, symbolizing the need for controlling the mind as well as the body.

Kannon *See*: **Kuan Yin**.

Kanzeon *See*: **Kuan Yin**.

Kapila The reputed founder of the Hindu *Samkhya* school of thought.

kara A steel bracelet worn by members of the *Khalsa*, the Sikh brotherhood, symbolizing the oneness of God and the unity of man with God and other men.

karah parshad A mixture of flour, butter, sugar and water which is shared at the end of all ceremonies as a symbol of the brotherhood of all men, irrespective of caste.

Karbala A town in Iraq where *Husain*, the youngest son of Ali, died in a night battle in 680CE while attempting to establish himself as the rightful *caliph* in place of *Yazid*, the *Sunni* candidate. The battle lives on in *Shi'ite* memory and is re-enacted and mourned during the New Year festival of *Muharram*.

karma This Sanskrit word literally means 'action' or 'deed'. The idea come from Hinduism. It is the central teaching of much of Hindu belief. The actions we do will have an effect – a direct effect – on what happens to us later in this life, but, more importantly it affects the sort of rebirth we have. The *atman* is reborn time and time again, but its status in each rebirth is caused by the karma it has developed in its previous life. Karma arises, in Hindu thought, from any action.

In Buddhism, karma plays a similar role, except that there is no soul – the theory of *anatta*. Karma is caused, in Buddhist thought, by either skilful or unskilful actions. As there is no soul, what passes over at each rebirth is the effect or implication of these actions. The Buddha's Eightfold Path and Four Noble Truths show a way out of the karma cycle of action-effect. Through enlightenment, the wheel of Samsara can be broken.

In Hinduism, the intention is to accumulate good karma which reslts in better and higher rebirths until eventually union with Brahman, or *moksha*, release, is achieved.

Karo, Joseph The author of the *Shulchan Aruch*.

Kartikeya A Hindu god, particularly revered in southern India. He is portrayed with six heads and an aggressive appearance. Also known as Skanda, he is said to be the god of war.

Kashrut The Jewish code which states which foods are *kosher*; that is, the foods which may be eaten and how they are to be prepared.

kenosis A Greek word literally meaning 'emptying'. In Christianity it refers to Christ's voluntary humbling and giving up his divine characteristics to become man and suffer for mankind's sins.

kesh Uncut hair; according to the rule of the Sikh brotherhood of the *Khalsa*, members must let their hair grow to its full natural length as a mark of spirituality and respect for the laws of nature. In reference to hair, this also includes beards and moustaches.

keshdari A *Khalsa* Sikh who keeps his vows to the full.

ketubah The formal contract which is drawn up for a Jewish marriage, to ensure that the wife is provided for if her husband dies before her or divorces her.

Khadija The first wife of Muhammad. She encouraged Muhammad after his visions and during his early teachings.

Khalsa On *Baisakhi* in 1699 *Guru Gobind Singh* established the Khalsa as a militant brotherhood to defend the Sikh community against outside enemies and to create a spirit of comradeship to overcome internal rivalries. In the modern world, it has become a brotherhood of adult believers who pledge themselves to uphold the truth of their faith and to serve the community and each other. Both men and women can be admitted. Initiation is by the ceremony of *Khande-ka-amrit*; all male members take the surname Singh, meaning 'lion' and all female members the surname Kaur, meaning 'princess'. They all observe the *Five Ks* in their dress.

khanda A double-edged sword used by Sikhs to stir sugar into water for their initiation into the brotherhood known as the *Khalsa*.

khande-ka-amrit A Sikh initiation ceremony introduced by the last *guru*, *Gobind Singh*, which welcomes individuals into the *Khalsa*, or Sikh brotherhood. The first part of the ceremony consists of preparing a bowl of sugared water called amrit, or nectar, in the presence of five members of the Khalsa and the *Guru Granth Sahib*. Once the initiates have drunk the nectar five times and it has been thrown against their eyelids and sprinkled in their hair, they are instructed in their new duties and responsibilities, the chief being the wearing of the *Five Ks*.

Khordad Sal The festival observed by *Parsis* and *Zoroastrians* to commemorate the birth of Zoroaster and the day he received his revelation from *Ahura Mazda*.

khutbah An Islamic sermon preached by an *imam* at the time of the Friday noon prayer.

Kiddush A Jewish prayer of sanctification recited on the eve of *Sabbath* and certain festivals. It is recited over a cup of wine, which is the symbol of joy. The kiddush contains several fundamental Jewish teachings.

Kingdom Hall Any meeting place where the *Jehovah's Witnesses* hold religious services. Emphasis is placed on studying the Bible and each member of the congregation is considered a minister.

kingdom of God Jews believe that the time will come when the whole world will accept God's rule; they, as the *Chosen People*, have a mission to help bring this about by being witnesses to God's splendour and power and to the wisdom of his laws as written in the *Torah*. The actual arrival of the kingdom of God in its fullness will be heralded by the coming of the *Messiah* just before the end of the world, after which the earth will disappear and the resurrected souls will live for ever in heaven.

In Christianity, Christ declared that his coming down to earth was a concrete expression of the kingdom of God – or kingdom of heaven – at work in the world, preparing people to accept God's rule. The *Second Coming* will mark both the end of the world and the final establishment of God's eternal rule over the souls of all men in heaven; when this happens, the kingdom of God will have fully arrived.

kingdom of heaven *See*: **heaven.**

King James Version *or* **Bible** Also known as the Authorized Version. The English translation of the Bible ordered by King James I and published in 1611. It has exerted profound influence on Protestant Christianity in all English speaking countries and on the development of English literature.

kirpan A sword worn by members of the *Khalsa*, or Sikh brotherhood, symbolizing dignity, self-defence and the just use of power.

kirtans Hymns sung in praise of God with a musical accompaniment. This is a term used especially by *bhakti* tradition in Hinduism.

kiswa The black embroidered cloth which covers the *Ka'ba* sanctuary in Mecca. During the *Hajj*, or annual pilgrimage, the kiswa is divided by pilgrims into fragments which are taken home as souvenirs. It is donated each year by Egypt.

Kitab Akdas The *scriptures* of the *Baha'i* faith.

Kitchen God *See*: **Ssu-Ming-Shen.**

Knowledge of Good and Evil, Tree of According to the *Old Testament* or *Hebrew Bible*, the first man and woman, Adam and Eve, were banished from *Eden* as a result of eating fruit from the tree which God had forbidden them to eat.

Knowledge, Way of *See*: **Noble Eightfold Path.**

Knox, John (1505?–72) A Scottish Protestant theologian and historian and early figure of *Presbyterianism*. A royal chaplain to Edward VI of England, he fled when Catholic Mary came to the throne and joined *Calvin* in Switzerland. In 1559 he was called to Scotland by a group of Protestant nobles. There he preached against the Catholic regent of the country and helped overthrow the Roman Catholic Church. Knox helped to draw up the Calvinist Articles of Faith which became the basis of Scottish Protestantism. As a result of his influence, Scotland rejected the episcopalianism or Anglicanism of the Church of England in favour of Presbyterianism and Calvinist doctrines. The Church of Scotland today is the direct descendant of Knox's work.

koan In Chinese, kung-an. A phrase or question, in baffling or apparently nonsensical language, used by a *Zen* master to help a pupil achieve spiritual insight, *enlightenment* or *satori* as it is usually called in Zen. There are traditionally 1700 koans; one of the best known is the question, 'What is the sound of one hand clapping?' The koan cannot be solved by logical reasoning or by using the rational mind, no matter how clever or well-educated. It can only be solved by breaking through to a higher level of reality that goes beyond concepts and ordinary thinking.

Kobo-daishi (714–835) Also known as Kukai. The founder of *Shingon* Buddhism, or the Japanese form of the *Vajrayana*. He studied in China from which he brought the Vajrayana.

Kojiki *Records of Ancient Matters*, the oldest Japanese book, containing myths and histories of gods and men, creation, customs and ceremonies, which is the most important writing in *Shinto*.

Konko-Kyo A modern Japanese religion which is based on *Shinto* but rejects its many gods in favour of belief in one supreme God of the universe.

Koran *See*: **Qur'an.**

kosher Food permitted by the Jewish dietary laws is called 'kosher'. Similarly, the proper ways of preparing such food are also called 'kosher'.

Krishna In Hinduism, Krishna is one of the most popular gods, an *avatar* of *Vishnu* and a great lover. His name means 'black', which is his usual colour and he appears in the *Bhagavad Gita* as the teacher of Prince *Arjuna*. The *bhakti* movement of passionate personal devotion to God normally attaches itself to Krishna as its prime object of worship, and *monotheistic* or *polytheistic* Hindus often use Krishna as the name of God. Krishna's popularity owes a great deal to the many stories about his life which exist, and which portray him in a great variety of human situations. He is seen as a mischievous but lovable child and as the lover of the gopis or milkmaids, with whom he spent his youth, as well as the charioteer of Arjuna in the *Bhagavad Gita*.

Krishna, with infinite ease, is lifting up Mount Govardhana to protect the herdsmen and their cows from the rain, brought on by Indra, who was both war god and weather god.

Krishna Consciousness *See*: International Society for Krishna Consciousness.

Ks *See*: Five Ks.

kshyatriyas The Hindu 'warrior' *caste*, second to the *Brahmins* in rank.

Kshatriyas A *Mahayana* Buddhist *bodhisattva* who has the power to rescue souls from hell.

Kuan Ti The Chinese god of war and martial arts, originally the historic warrior Kuan Yu, who eventually became a figure of worship.

Kuan Yin A form of *Avalokitesvara*, the *bodhisattva* of compassion, found in Chinese Buddhism. Although Avalokitesvara is 'male', Kuan Yin is 'female'. She is the most popular figure in Chinese religion. There is also the Thousand Arm Kuan Yin or Kwannon, a symbol of her reaching out to all. In Japan she is called *Kannon*, *Kwannon* or *Kanzeon*.

This graceful figure is Kuan Yin, known in Japan as Kwannon, who is the well-loved bodhisattva of compassion, Avalokitesvara. In the Chinese pantheon she is the Goddess of Mercy.

Kukai *See*: **Kobo-daishi**.

kundalini The psychophysical force and energy, according to Hindu *yoga*, that lies dormant in the lowest *chakra*, or psychophysical centre, at the base of the spine. If this force is released, it can either destroy the *yogin* or bring him to *moksha*, spiritual liberation. Kundalini also refers to the arts and skills for using this energy for such liberation by releasing it in a controlled manner so it flows up the chakras. It is often pictured as a coiled snake which uncoils itself as it rises to the highest chakra. At this point the yogin has achieved liberation by uniting his mind with his creative and natural energies which are otherwise only used for reproduction or destruction. This union is often symbolized by the sexual union of the god *Shiva* with his *shakti*, or consort. The concept of kundalini is particularly associated with *Tantrism*.

Kurozomykyo A twentieth-century *Shinto* movement which has grown up around a priest named Kurozumi Munetada, emphasising the worship of the sun goddess *Amaterasu*.

kusti The sacred cord or thread worn by *Zoroastrians* or *Parsis*.

Kwannon *See*: **Kuan Yin**.

l

Ladino The language of the Spanish *Sephardim*, the Jews exiled from Spain around 1500 to live in Muslim countries and northern Europe. It is basically a form of Spanish with some Hebrew elements, written in the Hebrew alphabet.

Lady Day *See*: **Annunciation**.

Lailat-ul-Bara'h Muslim festival – the Night of Forgiveness. Falls a fortnight before the start of Ramadan and is a time for seeking and bestowing forgiveness.

Lailat-ul-Isra Wal Mi'raj Muslim festival celebrating Muhammad's night journey to Jerusalem on his miraculous horse. From the Rock in Jerusalem, Muhammad ascended to heaven, returning before dawn.

Lailat-ul Qadar Muslim festival – the Night of Power. It usually falls at the end of Ramadan and celebrates the giving of the Qur'an to Muhammad. Surah 97 commemorates this event.

Laillaha Illa Allah Part of the first of the *five pillars of Islam*, this phrase means 'There is no god but *Allah*'. It is part of the *adhan*, or call to prayer, which is heard in Islamic countries five times every day.

laity A Christian word for the ordinary members of a religion: those who are not clergymen or have not been ordained.

Lakshmi The goddess of wealth, beauty and good luck and the consort of the Hindu god *Vishnu*, Lakshmi sprang from the sea during the churning which produced *amrita*. On the festival of *Diwali*, people leave their doors open to invite her in for the coming new year.

lama A *Vajrayana* Buddhist from Tibet or Mongolia who is respected for his spiritual development or deep learning. The term is sometimes used to refer to a *bodhisattva* who deliberately chooses to be reborn time and time again to help other creatures towards enlightenment. The most famous is the *Dalai Lama*, the spiritual leader of Tibet, who is regarded as a manifestation of *Avalokitesvara*, the Bodhisattva of Compassion.

Lamaism The *Vajrayana* Buddhism of Tibet and Mongolia. Western scholars coined the word 'Lamaism' because of the importance of *lamas* in this tradition of Buddhism.

Lambeth Conference A gathering of the bishops of the Anglican Church which takes place approximately every ten years in England, the mother country of that Church.

Wearing their episcopal robes, the bishops of the Anglican communion, chief among whom is the Archbishop of Canterbury, meet to discuss matters of common interest.

Lamb of God (1) The prophet Isaiah first used the term to describe the 'suffering servant', who is either an individual, possibly Isaiah himself, or the nation, Israel. In the Book of Revelation, in the *New Testament*, the term is used to describe Christ who is seen as the victorious lamb of God who has overcome the powers of evil, and who reigns in glory in the heavenly kingdom. (2) A hymn to Christ used in the *Eucharist*, beginning with the words, 'O Lamb of God', or a liturgical response, often sung in the Latin form, 'Agnus Dei'. (3) The word 'Lamb' is used for the host in the Eucharist service in the Orthodox Church.

lament A formal expression of sorrow or mourning, especially one which is made in verse or song. Laments form part of the funeral rites in many religions.

Lammas (Day) A Roman Catholic festival celebrated on 1 August. Its name means loaf-mass, and it was originally a festival at which bread made with the first corn to be harvested was offered at Mass. It also commemorates the deliverance of *St Peter* described in *Acts of the Apostles* in the *New Testament*.

The guru ka langar, or communal kitchen, is to be found wherever Sikhs have established a gurdwara, a building in which they may worship. Food is freely distributed to all, regardless of caste, in accordance with the practice of Guru Nanak, the founder of the religion, who accepted all disciples, even the Untouchables.

langar The communal kitchen attached to a Sikh *gurdwara*. There, irrespective of caste, people share meals and passers-by and the needy can come to be fed. The langar is a reminder of Guru *Nanak*'s kitchen at Kartapur which was open to all, and is an essential part of the Sikh community.

Lankavatara Sutra A major *sutra*, or text, of *Mahayana* Buddhism. It represents enlightenment as the intuitive realization that the only reality is 'absolute mind'.

Lantern Festival An annual festival in Japan to welcome the souls of the dead, which are believed to return to their old houses, and a meal is provided for the returning spirits.

Lao-tzu *or* **Lao-tse** (604?–531?BCE) Traditionally a Chinese philosopher, founder of *Taoism* and author of the *Tao Te Ching*. His name means literally 'Old Master'. Lao-tzu may well be a mythical figure.

Last Judgement *See*: **Judgement, Last**.

Last Supper In Christian belief, the last meal which Jesus Christ shared with his disciples, on the evening before he was crucified. It was probably the normal Jewish *Passover* meal, with the difference that, at the end of the meal, Christ took bread and wine, blessed them, and broke the bread; then he gave them to the disciples to eat and drink. Saying 'This is my body, this is my blood of the new testament, which is shed for many for the remission of sins', he commanded the disciples to perform the same action in memory of him.

Almost all Christians have followed Christ's words since the earliest days of Christianity by taking bread and wine in memory of his death and *resurrection*, through which they believe they gain *salvation*. They do this in a service known in the different churches as the Breaking of Bread, *Eucharist*, *Mass*, Divine Liturgy or *Holy Communion*.

Latin The language spoken by the ancient Romans. Although no longer spoken as a living language, it is sometimes used in the services of the Roman Catholic Church.

Law, Tablets of the *See*: **Torah**.

layman A believer in any religion who is not a clergyman and has not been ordained.

Lazarus Either of two men in the *New Testament*. One, in the town of Bethany, was the brother of Martha and Mary who were disciples of Jesus. When news came that Lazarus had died, Jesus went straight to Bethany, and, although the body had been in the tomb for four days, he raised him from the dead. The other Lazarus is the beggar in the *parable* of the wealthy man at whose gate sat a poor man, feeding on the crumbs that fell from the rich man's table.

lectern The reading desk in a Christian church from which the Bible is read during public services. It is often shaped like an eagle with outstretched wings.

lectionary A book containing the sections of the Bible to be read at Christian services, especially the *Eucharist* and the Divine Office. It is used in many different denominations.

legend A story or collection of stories which has been handed down through generations and which has some basis in historical characters or events.

These children in Guatemala are dressed for a procession to commemorate the Last Supper of Christ and the Apostles, which takes place on Maundy Thursday during Holy Week.

Leninism The development of the theories of Karl *Marx* by V. I. Lenin (1870–1924), the leader of Russia's Bolshevik Revolution of 1917. As a revolutionary Marxist, Lenin maintained that although capitalism contains the seeds of its own downfall, this should not be a cause of complacency among the working class. He believed that every era has its 'revolutionary situations' which should be recognized and exploited by the workers. Power should be seized when circumstances seem most favourable to success.

Lenin developed the doctrine that *imperialism* is the last and highest stage of capitalism, and that his time was an imperialistic era. He argued that while the working class is the power base on which the revolution depends, such a mass movement requires the guidance of a vanguard – the Party.

The present-day *communism* of most Eastern European countries, including the Soviet Union, is known as Marxism-Leninism, the teachings of Marx as interpreted and developed by Lenin.

Lent In the Christian calendar *Ash Wednesday* marks the beginning of Lent, the period of forty days before *Easter* Sunday.

This period is traditionally seen as a time for reflection, prayer and penance, an occasion to concentrate on non-worldly concerns and to reject purely material values. The final week of Lent, *Holy Week*, witnesses an intensification of devotions and the liturgy commemorates the *Passion* and death of Christ.

lesson A passage from the Bible which is read during Christian services.

Levites One of the twelve tribes of Israel, descended from Levi, the third son of *Jacob* and Leah. The Levites acted as assistants to the priests in the Jerusalem Temple. When the Israelites travelled from Egypt to Canaan after the *Exodus*, the Levites took care of the *Tabernacle*.

Lhasa The capital of Tibet and religious centre of Tibetan Buddhism, Lhasa was the traditional residence of the *Dalai Lama*.

li In *Confucian* philosophy, li, ritual or reverence and respect for the correct forms of social behaviour, is necessary for any form of social harmony to exist. Confucius looked back to a time when people showed each other courtesy, and behaved according to their positions in society. He taught that men should learn to cooperate and work for the common good. If each family unit bases its relationships on li, then society as a whole will be peaceful and united in brotherly love. *See*: **five relationships**.

libation To 'make a libation' to the gods or ancestors is to pour a drink out in their honour, usually on to the ground.

liberalism A political belief favourable to changes and reforms which tend in the direction of democracy. Also a movement within modern Protestantism which stresses the need for a critical attitude towards authority and tradition and calls for the Church to adjust its beliefs in the light of scientific discoveries and the spiritual needs of its members. The movement is now gaining ground within the Roman Catholic Church.

Liberal Judaism A movement which emerged from the nineteenth-century rethinking of the role of Judaism in the modern world. Liberal synagogues exist alongside their Orthodox and Reform counterparts all over the world, but are particularly common in the United States. Liberal Jews believe that religion should adapt to changing circumstances and needs. Like the Reform movement, Liberal Jews do not observe all the regulations of the *Talmud*, for example about the Sabbath. They conduct services largely in the local language and do not separate men and women in their synagogues. And they interpret the *Torah* in the light of fresh evidence and contemporary research. Generally speaking, they go further than the Reform Jews in their attempt to adapt their religion to the modern world. Almost identical to Liberal Judaism is Progressive Judaism and the two movements have now been united.

liberation theology A contemporary Christian school of thought which believes that Christians should play a part in reforming society through political means, even through revolution if this is necessary in a situation of great injustice.

limbo According to some Christian traditions, limbo is the dwelling place of souls of children who have died without being *baptized* and of righteous people who died before Christ came.

lingam The erect phallus or male sex organ, a symbol of the Hindu god *Shiva*. It stands on a platform which is a stylized representation of the *yoni*, and libations of ghee (clarified butter) are poured on it.

Lion of Judah In the *Torah*, or Old Testament, Judah, one of the sons of Jacob, is referred to as a lion, and in the book of *Revelation*, in the New Testament, Jesus is referred to as the 'lion of Judah'. It is also one of the titles given to the late Ethiopian emperor, *Haile Selassie*. *Rastafarians* frequently use the lion symbol in their art and music.

litany A form of public prayer which consists of a series of short supplications and responses which can be sung or spoken; normally the clergy will recite the supplication and the congregation will reply.

literalism To take a literalistic approach is to accept the exact words of a text or document in their simplest, most obvious meaning, ignoring any symbolic or allegorical meaning they may have. As well, literalists will not accept that changing circumstances, scientific discoveries or the passing of time should affect how one reads or interprets a document or text. Fundamentalist Christians, for example, believe that every statement in the Bible, including the story of creation in seven days, must be taken at face value; they reject the idea that certain passages are merely trying to make points or give examples of how to act by using allegories or poetic imagery.

liturgy Public worship, the public service of God or a god, whence any prescribed form of worship in the Christian Church, especially any particular form of the *Eucharist* service. In the Eastern Orthodox Church, the Eucharist is known as the Divine Liturgy.

Lord's Prayer Also known as the *Paternoster* and the Our Father, it has always been a central part of Christian services. According to the *New Testament*, it was composed by Jesus and recited to his disciples as a model of how to pray.

Lord's Supper An ancient title for the *Eucharist*, the most important Christian rite. This name has gradually fallen from use in favour of the more common terms: Eucharist, Mass and Holy Communion. *Baptist Churches*, however, still frequently use this title.

lotus A water lily whose roots are embedded in mud and whose beautiful flower unfolds on the surface of the water. The lotus is an important symbol in Hinduism and Buddhism, with various meanings. In Buddhism its most important meaning is spiritual unfolding and development, but it can also represent the holy or pure, amitabha, meditation and enlightenment itself.

lotus position A *yoga* posture, also much used by Hindus and Buddhists in meditation. It involves sitting upright and crossing one's legs completely so that each foot rests on the thigh of the other leg.

Lotus Sutra In Sanskrit, the Saddharma-Pundarika-Sutra, which means the 'Sutra of the White Lotus of the Good or True Law'. This is an important scripture of *Mahayana* Buddhism, especially popular in China and Japan. In it, the Buddha preaches to thousands of humans, gods and spirits, teaching them that all three paths he has formerly taught are in reality just one, the path leading to becoming a supreme Buddha. Furthermore, this path is open to anyone.

love feast *See*: agape.

Loyola, St Ignatius (1491–1556) A Spanish nobleman who founded the Roman Catholic Order of *Jesuits* and wrote its basic manual, the *Spiritual Exercises* (1548).

Lucifer A Christian name for the *Devil* or *Satan* before he was banished from heaven. Christians believe that originally he was an angel of light, but he fell from God's *grace* because of his pride, which led him to try to make himself God's equal.

Luke, St *See*: gospel.

Lutheran Churches A group of national Protestant Churches that follow the ideas and practices of *Martin Luther*. More than other Churches, the Lutherans emphasize the doctrine that man receives *justification* by faith alone. Their particular beliefs are found in the *Book of Concord* 1577, especially the Augsburg Confession of 1530 and Luther's own Shorter Catechism.

In most traditionally Lutheran countries, the Church has a very close relationship with the state. The Lutheran Churches of Denmark, Finland, Norway, Sweden and Iceland are *Established Churches* and are controlled by a government ministry through the bishops; in Germany, where about half the population is Lutheran, the Church is governed by a group of clergy and laity known as the 'consistory'. The other main centre of Lutheranism is the mid-West of the United States, where churches were founded by immigrants from Germany and Scandinavia.

The Lutheran Churches regard baptism and the *Eucharist* as the only sacraments, although they still practise individual confession. Lutherans believe that the body and blood of Christ are received along with the bread and wine, a concept known as 'consubstantiation'. The structure of the Lutheran Mass is very similar to the Roman Catholic one, and it forms the normal Sunday morning service.

The Lutheran Churches, taken as a whole, make up the largest body of Protestant Christians.

Luther indicates that salvation comes through the blood of the Lamb, and consigns the Roman Catholic clergy into Hell.

Luther, Martin (1483–1546) The German leader of the Protestant *Reformation* and founder figure of Lutheran Christianity. The son of a miner, Martin Luther became a monk and theology professor. He was disturbed by what he perceived as abuses and corrupt practices in the Church at the time. He particularly criticized the selling of *indulgences* for personal gain by some clergy and preached against the corruption to be found among the hierarchy of the Church. He taught that Christians did not need intermediaries, such as priests, to enable them to worship God, since man and God could communicate with one another directly. Basing himself on *St Paul's epistles*, he taught the doctrine of *justification* by faith alone, which means that a man only gains *salvation* if he has faith in the *atonement* which Christ has made by his death. No amount of good works or devotion can compensate for lack of this faith, which alone separates the condemned from the saved and which is itself in the end a free gift given to those whom God has chosen.

This doctrine is the basis of Lutheran Christianity, which spread over much of Germany and Scandinavia, and later went to America. According to Luther, it was based on the Bible which he saw as the infallible Word of God.

Luther translated the Bible into contemporary German and wrote many hymns and religious and political tracts. He composed a number of commentaries on the Bible which are still respected today. He will, however, be best remembered in history as the man who after an intense experience of conversion pinned the *Ninety-Five Theses* criticizing the Church to the door of a church in Wittenberg in 1517. With this one gesture he began a period of reform and division which permanently changed the face of Western Christianity.

m

Maccabees, Judah The hero of the campaigns by the Jews against their Greek overlords in the second century BCE. Together with his brothers, the Maccabees, he led his people in their struggle for freedom. Judah Maccabees reoccupied Jerusalem with his forces in 164BCE, and had its Temple rededicated to God. This event is commemorated by the feast of *Chanukah*. He has been held up as a symbol of struggle for the Jewish faith ever since.

Madonna (1) The *Virgin Mary*, especially in Roman Catholic Christianity. (2) Any picture, statue or representation of the Virgin Mary.

Magdalene, St Mary Mary of Magdala: the first person to discover, after Jesus Christ's execution, that his tomb was empty and the first witness to his *resurrection*, according to the New Testament. The *gospels* say that Jesus cast out seven *demons* from her, and she became one of his close followers. She is sometimes identified with the prostitute who, in the Gospel according to St Luke, washes Jesus's feet with his tears, and also with Mary, the sister of Martha.

Magi The wise men from the East, according to Christian belief probably astrologers, who were led by a star to Bethlehem to worship the infant Jesus. They are said to have brought Jesus gifts of gold, frankincense and myrrh: gold for a king, frankincense for a holy child, myrrh for one who would die young. Before reaching Bethlehem, they had visited Jerusalem to inquire where the *Messiah*, the new 'King of the Jews', had been born. Traditionally this led King Herod to order the massacre of all infant boys around Bethlehem in an unsuccessful attempt to kill Jesus. This slaughter is commemorated by Christians on 28 December, *Holy Innocents' Day*.

magic The production of effects of phenomena supposedly with the help of *supernatural* beings or powers, or by using *occult* forces in nature or in human beings unrecognised by modern science. In the first case, the practitioner employs rituals to persuade supernatural forces such as gods, demons or spirits to produce these physical, mental or spiritual effects; in the second, the rituals harness the occult forces so that they can be directed as desired. Such forces may be intended for use to produce beneficial or harmful results.

Magnificat A Christian song which begins: 'My soul magnifies the Lord'. In Latin it starts: 'Magnificat'. The Christian Church has used it widely since the sixth century, and it is also known as the Song of the Blessed *Virgin Mary*, since it first appears in the New Testament, sung by her.

Caspar, Balthasar and Melchisedech, as they are traditionally known, paying homage to the infant Jesus. Their riches and finery are in sharp contrast to the humble stable.

Mahabharata A Hindu epic poem, which tells of the feud between two branches of an Indian royal family, and of the exploits of their cousin *Krishna*, an *avatar* of the god *Vishnu*. Its climax is the battle of Kurukshetra, where the Pandavas win victory with the help of Krishna, who serves as the charioteer of Prince *Arjuna*. Before the battle begins, however, Arjuna and Krishna begin a dialogue which is the *Bhagavad Gita*, the best-loved of all Hindu scriptures.

Mahadeva 'Great God', a title of *Shiva*.

Mahadevi 'Great goddess', the title of the consort of *Shiva* in her many forms. Mahadevi, or Devi, as she is also known, is the *Shakti*, or female energy of Shiva. She is known in her more active form as *Kali* or *Durga*, while in her more peaceful form she is Uma or *Parvati*. Mahadevi is also regarded as the great Mother, and is often the subject of special reverence and devotion.

Gandhi, most often known as Mahatma Gandhi.

mahatma A Sanskrit word meaning 'great soul'. It is used in India as a title of great respect; for example, Mohandas *Gandhi* was usually called Mahatma Gandhi.

Mahavira Twenty-fourth and most recent *tirthankara* of *Jainism*, also known as *Vardhamana*. He was born of a princely family in Northern India and died in about 468BCE, apparently from self-starvation. He organized a body of Jain monks to carry out his teaching and preach it throughout the country. He seems to have disliked the divisions in India society caused by the Hindu *caste* system, and in particular to have been unhappy about the influence of the priestly *Brahmin* caste. His monks had to take five vows: to do no violence (*ahimsa*), to remain chaste, to tell the truth, to form no attachment to material things, and not to steal.

Mahayana Literally, 'Great Vehicle': the branch of Buddhism that takes as its ideal the *bodhisattva,*, or being, who seeks *enlightenment* for the sake of all, and stresses what it sees as the spirit of the Buddha's teachings as well as his personal example and compassion. The Mahayana arose around 200BCE–CE100 in India. Its followers felt that the *Theravada* (sometimes referred to by the Mahayana as Hinayana, meaning 'Lesser Vehicle') was interpreting the Buddha's teachings too literally and narrowly. The Mahayana teaches that all living beings can attain enlightenment, whether monks or lay people, and sees the *Sangha* as the community of all who practise the Buddha's teachings.

Most forms of the Mahayana have more elaborate rituals than the Theravada and, in general, place more emphasis on transforming and developing the emotions. The highest emotion is compassion, which the Mahayana places on the same level as Absolute Wisdom: developing boundless compassion can be a road to enlightenment just as transcendental wisdom can be. Thus Mahayanists seek to become bodhisattvas and eventually full Buddhas.

The Mahayana recognises many texts as scripture, or the word of the Buddha,over and above the *Pali Canon*. The different Mahayana schools are distinguished partly by their preference for one or the other Mahayana scripture. They also emphasize different aspects of the Buddha's teaching, especially different methods of striving for enlightenment. For example, *Zen* stresses meditation, and *Pure Land Buddhism* devotion and faith. Other living forms of Mahayana include the *T'ien-t'ai* and *Vajrayana*.

Mahayana is the main form of Buddhism in Japan, Korea, China, Mongolia, Tibet and the Himalayas.

Mahdi 'He who is guided in the right path'. The Mahdi is the *Messiah*-figure expected by *Shi'a* Muslims. Their tradition says he will be a descendant of Muhammad and will be proclaimed Mahdi against his will at Mecca just before the end of the world and the Day of Judgment, or Last Day, to save all those who have been faithfully awaiting him. It is thought that he will turn out to be the 'hidden *imam*', who has been concealed on earth in a secret place until the time is ripe. Shi'ites themselves have differing opinions as to who the hidden imam is. Many believe that he was the twelfth imam, Adu el-Kasim: these are known as the 'Twelvers' and are the dominant sect in Iran. Other Shi'ites, such as the *Ismailis*, argue that it is the seventh and not the twelfth imam who has disappeared and they, in turn, wait for his reappearance.

Maimonides (1135–1204) A Jewish *rabbi* and philosopher, who wrote many books in which he attempted to reconcile the claims of faith and reason. He is noted for his bold argument and for the way in which he rejects much rabbinical tradition in favour of reasoning based on Aristotle's philosophy. At the time, this aroused a great deal of hostility although in retrospect he has come to be regarded as one of Judaism's greatest teachers. He formulated the *Thirteen Principles* of the Jewish faith, which Jews still recite in services and regard as an authoritative summary of their belief. Maimonides had a varied life, studying Aristotle, medicine and science, becoming Sultan Saladin's personal doctor, and lecturing at Cairo in philosophy.

Maitreya In *Pali* Metteya, in China known as Mi-lo-fo, and Japan as Miroku, Maitreya is the Buddha-to-come, important in all forms of Buddhism. *Theravada* Buddhists believe that after a time of religious and moral decline, a Buddha, Metteya, will arise and restore the truth. In *Mahayana* Buddhism the future Buddha is represented as fat and laughing, indicatiang prosperity and happiness.

mandala In Buddhism, mandalas are especially important in the *Vajrayana*. They are symmetrical diagrams, pictures, sculptures or even cities, usually circular or square and always built around a central point. A mandala is a symbolic representation of the universe, of reality, or of energies. Its structure represents the relationships between the various aspects of its theme. Mandalas are used in some *meditation* practices. Some schools of Hinduism also use mandalas.

manmukh In Sikhism, a person who is attached to his or her own desires or mind, rather than following the *guru*. Those who are manmukh are attached to the wrong things in this life through self-centredness and remain in the cycle of rebirth until they realize their error, and become aware of the presence of God within them. Then they can serve God and man and become gurmukh, or God-conscious. This is the only path to *mukti*, or liberation, according to Sikh teachings.

manna According to the *Torah*, the Israelites prayed to God to send them food in the desert during their *exodus* from Egypt. In answer to their prayer, God rained down manna, an edible substance, onto the ground during the night.

mantra In Hinduism, mantras are words or short phrases recited repeatedly during *meditation* in order to empty the mind of unnecessary concerns and to concentrate on liberation from *maya*, or illusion. Mantra *yoga* trains initiates to gain power from saying sacred words, and some yogins have been said to move objects merely by repeating the mantra. In some types of mantra yoga, the *guru* gives each initiate a secret mantra suitable only for him and which must not be divulged to others.

In Buddhism, especially the *Vajrayana*, a mantra is a syllable or group of syllables expressing and reflecting the essence of some transcendental quality, force or being, such as a Buddha, *bodhisattva*, or other aspect of enlightenment. Traditionally it is the sound given off by the enlightened mind or reality itself and is sometimes called 'the primordial cosmic sound'. The most famous mantra in both Hinduism and Buddhism is the syllable OM.

A square version of the rasa mandala, with multiple images of Krishna, as Gopinath-ji, dancing with the milkmaids.

Cardinal Stefaneschi commissioned Giotto to paint a great altarpiece for the high altar of Saint Peter's in Rome. The left-hand panel shows the martyrdom of Saint Peter, who was condemned to be crucified, as it was a customary Roman form of execution. As a mark of humility, however, Peter requested that he be crucified upside down, so that he should not suffer the same manner of death as his redeemer. Angels are preparing to receive the soul of the martyred Apostle, while mourners gather at the foot of the cross.

Manu The Father of the human race, according to Hindu mythology. He is the legendary author of the *Manusmriti*, or *Laws of Manu*. This book sets out the legendary origins of the various Hindu *castes* and describes in detail their rights and duties.

Mara Sanskrit: 'Killing'. Sometimes personified in Hinduism as a goddess of death, but primarily a Buddhist figure. While *Gautama* sat under the *Bodhi-tree*, Mara sent his daughters to tempt Gautama with sensual pleasure. When this failed, Mara attacked with an army of devils, who threatened Gautama but found themselves suddenly paralysed. Finally Mara hurled his terrible disk, which could cut a mountain in two, but this changed into a garland of flowers which hung above Gautama's head. Mara left, defeated, and that night Gautama achieved enlightenment and became the Buddha.

marabout A wandering Islamic holy man found particularly in North Africa, especially Morocco. Some of these holy men used to gather bands of dervish-like followers as they went from place to place, and their tombs are often revered by local Muslims.

Mardana A bard and musician who accompanied the founder of the Sikh faith, Guru *Nanak*, on his travels. Guru Nanak spread his teachings by setting his words to Mardana's music and, to commemorate this, present-day Sikh worship includes groups of musicians who accompany hymn singing on traditional Indian instruments during meetings.

Mardi Gras Literally, 'Fat Tuesday': a Roman Catholic festival held on Shrove Tuesday in Paris, New Orleans and Italy. The festival gets its name from the fat ox which is led in procession through the streets, followed by a triumphal car carrying a child, who bears the title 'king of the butchers'.

maror The horseradish or other bitter herb eaten at the *Seder* meal during the Jewish Passover. This symbolizes the bitter days of slavery spent by the Israelites in Egypt.

martyr Anyone who dies or is killed for his or her beliefs, especially for religious beliefs. The word literally means 'witness'; martyrs witness to their faith by dying for it. Judaism, Christianity, Shi'a Islam and Sikhism all revere and commemorate their martyrs on special days of the year.

Marx, Karl (1818–83) A German philosopher, revolutionary and economist. With his friend, Friedrich Engels, he wrote the influential pamphlet, *The Communist Manifesto* (1848). He is also the author of the massive work, *Das Kapital* (1867), which laid the foundations of Marxism and of modern *Communism*. In 1864 he helped found the First International, or International Working Men's Association. *See also*: **Leninism**.

Mary *See*: **Virgin Mary**.

Bishop Vangeke of the Roman Catholic Church giving communion to Vai'fa villagers in an open air Catholic Mass in Papua New Guinea. The Mass is at the heart of the Roman Catholic liturgy and the young girl believes that the consecrated host she is receiving is really and truly the body of Christ.

Mass The usual Roman Catholic term for the Christian service otherwise known as the *Eucharist* or *Holy Communion*. The Catholic theology underlying Mass contains two ideas with which Protestants in general do not agree. One is that the Mass is in some way a sacrifice, in which Christ renews the original voluntary sacrifice of his life to God for men's sins and makes it present for the worshippers; the other is that the bread and wine do really change when consecrated, to become the spiritual body and blood of Christ while still retaining their outward forms: this is known as *transubstantiation*.

materialism The belief or theory that physical matter is the only real substance in the universe, and that there is therefore no such thing as spirit, soul or God. Intellectual life, then, is nothing more than the result of mechanical combinations and interactions of matter. What is called mind, or soul, or intellect, is merely a product or effect of the brain and dies with the body; everything which happens in the world is the result of natural laws, and is not the work or plan of God or a god. Materialism is an *atheistic* philosophy, and is a fundamental doctrine of *Marxism. See also*: **idealism**.

matins The service of morning prayer in the Anglican Church; everyone in holy orders must recite it each day, publicly or privately. Originally the name was used to refer to the Roman Catholic *office* recited by monks at midnight or shortly after.

Matthew, St *See*: **gospel**.

matzah Also spelt: **matzoh**. Unleavened bread which is eaten for an eight-day period in Jewish homes over *Passover* as a reminder of the *exodus* of the Israelites from slavery in Egypt. On that occasion, the Israelites had no time to let their bread rise and so had to bake it without yeast on the day before they left for Canaan. The Feast of Unleavened Bread is an alternative title for Passover.

Maulawiya A *Sufi*-sect better known as the Whirling *dervishes*, founded by the poet Jalal al Din Rumi, who instructed his followers on how to dance in order to achieve ecstasy.

Maundy Thursday According to the Bible, this is the day when Jesus held the *Last Supper*, washed the feet of his disciples, and commanded them to do the same for each other as a sign of humility and the desire to serve. In the Roman Catholic Church, the priest frequently washes the feet of twelve members of the congregation during the evening Mass. The word 'maundy' comes from a Latin word meaning 'commandment': it reminds Christians that on this night Jesus also commanded his disciples to love one another, as he loved them – a 'new commandment' from God. In England on this day, money, known as maundy pennies, is given out at Westminster Abbey to as many old men and women as there are years in the sovereign's age.

Mawlud-al-Nabi An Islamic festival which celebrates Muhammad's birthday and is traditionally held on the twelfth day of the month of Rabi al-awwal.

maya Literally 'power', unreality. The Advaita *Vedanta* school of Hinduism and its founder *Shankara* taught that we do not perceive the world correctly as it really is: we see separate beings and individuals, but actually there is only one reality, *Brahman Atman*, the Absolute. Maya is the force that makes one see the world in this incorrect way, to see the One as Many.

The term can also refer to the false 'reality' produced by this force, or to illusion itself.

In *Mahayana* Buddhism, maya means 'the cause of illusion': it is the means by which we see the world incorrectly as permanent, substantial and satisfying. When, however, we recognize that the world is actually impermanent, changing, insubstantial and ultimately unsatisfactory, then maya becomes *Bodhi*, or *enlightenment*, itself.

Mecca The birthplace of Muhammad and most sacred city in Islam, located in present-day Saudi Arabia. One of the *five pillars of Islam* states that it is the duty of every Muslim to make a pilgrmage to Mecca, known as the *Hajj*, at least once in his life if he is able to do so. When saying prayers, Muslims turn to face the *Ka'ba* shrine which stands in the centre of the Great Mosque at Mecca.

Medina The second sacred city of Islam, some three hundred miles from Mecca. Muhammad, the founder of Islam, fled from his birthplace, Mecca, to Medina in CE622 because of opposition to his preaching. Here he and his followers formed the first Islamic state, prior to capturing Mecca. The Muslim calendar counts the years from this migration, and used AH – after *Hijra*, the migration – to indicate the starting point of the calendar. Muhammad is buried in Medina.

meditation Clearing the mind of all earthly concerns often through practical formulae such as set postures, rules of breathing or specific stages of thought, in order to allow the individual to concentrate his mind on God, the absolute or himself, in the hope that he will reach a higher stage of spiritual awareness.

medium In spiritualism, a medium is a person who links the worlds of the dead and the supernatural with the world of the living. Sometimes the medium is said to become possessed by the spirit of a dead person with whom contact is desired, or to become the agent of *occult* supernatural forces, as by being possessed by some god or demon. In some religions such possessed mediums are known as *shamans*.

Megillah The small hand-written scroll of the Book of Esther which is read in Jewish *synagogues* on the festival of Purim. The parchment itself is usually illustrated in the margins with designs and abstract motifs and is kept in an engraved wooden case.

mendicants Friars or monks who devote their lives to their religious duties and are entirely dependent on gifts or alms.

Mennonites A Protestant Christian denomination founded in Holland in the sixteenth century by Menno Simons. The Mennonites are an offshoot of the *Anabaptists*; they therefore baptize adult believers only, as do the Baptists. They believe that each individual should find salvation through studying the Bible and refraining from war, punishment, and taking oaths. Simons produced the *Fundamental Book of Christian Faith* (1539) and the movement spread through Germany to America and Russia.

Prevented from worshipping in their church, these Mennonites have gone out in a boat to pray in safety.

menorah A candlestick with seven branches which was first used in the *Temple of Jerusalem*. Similar candlesticks are now found in every Jewish *synagogue* and home, although traditionally the synagogue Menorah does not have seven branches, to avoid having an exact replica of the Temple light in the synagogue. A menorah is brought out at the *festival* of Chanukah – although this particular type has eight branches, with a ninth, smaller branch for the Shammash or helper candle, from which the others are lit – and the father of the family blesses and lights a fresh candle every night for eight nights to commemorate the miracle of the jar of oil. This jar contained oil enough for only one day but it kept the everlasting lamp in the Jerusalem Temple alight for eight days after the rededication of the Temple by *Judah Maccabees*.

Messiah In Judaism, the Messiah or *God's* anointed one, is taken to mean the person chosen by God to arrive on earth at the end of the world, to lead his people as their king, free them from all oppression and injustice, and bring the *kingdom of God* to earth. Some Jews maintain that the founding of the state of Israel in 1948 shows that the coming of the Messiah must be imminent, others are more cautious and make no such claims. Some members of *Reform Judaism* see the foundation of the Jewish State of Israel as equivalent to the arrival of the Messiah; they no longer expect an individual Messiah to come to earth. Christians believe that Jesus Christ is the Messiah, the king or saviour of the world, who had been prophesied in the *Old Testament* to be the redeemer of man and the world. Christians claim that Christ's *incarnation*, death on the cross and *resurrection* from the dead happened in fulfilment of those prophecies.

metaphysics The branch of philosophy dealing with 'first principles', that is, with questions such as: what is being, knowing, cause, space, time or reality?

mezuzah A small parchment scroll inscribed with two passages from the *Hebrew Bible*, enclosed in a box. One scroll is fixed on each doorpost of a Jewish home, except the bathroom

and the toilet. It is a symbol of the fact that God is present in the home and that the family who lives there is following God's laws.

Michael An *archangel* and warlike messenger of God, chief of all the angels of heaven. According to the *Old Testament* or *Hebrew Bible* he championed God's people against their enemies. This tradition continued into the *New Testament*, so in Christianity Michael is represented as fighting for the believer against the evils attacking him. In the Book of Revelation, Michael finally defeats the *Devil* and drives him down to hell at the end of the world before the kingdom of God finally conquers over evil. Michael is also mentioned in the Qur'an, where he is referred to as the 'Friend of the Jews.'

Saint Michael fighting with great intensity against the dragon, as is recounted in the Book of Revelation. The archangel is aided by other angels and the battle between good and evil is taking place high above a sunny, unsuspecting world.

Mid-Autumn Festival Chinese harvest moon festival, celebrated by observing the full moon, lantern processions and eating 'moon' cakes.

Middle Way The path taught by the Buddha which leads to enlightenment and the end of all suffering. It avoids the two extremes of asceticism and of sensuality.

mihrab A thin arched alcove or opening in the wall of a mosque which indicates the direction of Mecca and thus shows Muslims which way they should face in order to direct their prayers towards that sacred city.

millenarianism The belief that Jesus Christ, the twelfth Imam, Maitreya Buddha etc., will come to earth for a second time and will reign over the earth before the earth's disappearance and the kingdom of God arrives in all its glory. The name derives from the fact that Christians believe that Jesus will reign for a thousand years on his return, but the term has developed a wider usage.

Mimamsa *See*: **Purva Mimamsa**.

minaret The tower of an Islamic mosque from which the *muezzin* calls the faithful to prayer five times a day.

minbar Set of three steps in a mosque from which the *imam* preaches.

minister (1) A Protestant clergyman. (2) A Christian, whether ordained or not, who has been authorized to perform certain tasks within church services; for example, helping the priest at the *Mass*.

miracle Any event or set of events which are attributed to God, the gods, or another supernatural power because they cannot be explained in terms of natural laws or sciences.

miracle plays *or* **mystery plays** Medieval Christian dramas based on stories from the Bible or the lives of the saints. They were normally performed at *Easter*, *Corpus Christi* or on the eve of the saint's day. Several complete cycles of these plays exist in English, such as the Chester, Wakefield and York cycles, which cover the story of man's *redemption* from the *Creation* and *Fall* to the *Last Judgement*, with the life of Christ as the centrepiece.

Mi'raj *See*: **Night journey**.

Mirza Ghulam Ahmad Founder of the *Ahmadiyyah* sect in Islam, a sect which is no longer recognized as Muslim by the rest of the Islamic world. Ahmad lived from 1839-1908 and founded the sect in Lahore, India, although it is now centred in Rabuah, Pakistan. Ahmadija members regard Ahmad as the *Mahdi* who has returned to earth to purify and revive the Muslim faith.

Mishnah The Jewish oral law. According to *Orthodox* Jews, the written *Torah* was not the only law revealed by God to Moses, for he also revealed supplementary laws which were passed on by oral tradition until they were written down at the beginning of the third century CE.

These are called the Mishnah, the final edition of which was gathered together and edited by Rabbi *Judah Ha-Nasi* and Rabbi Akiba. There are six division in the Mishnah, covering such topics as farming, festivals, women and ritual cleanliness. Together with the Gemara, or 'completion', it forms the basis of the *Talmud*.

missal A book used in the Roman Catholic Church which contains the instructions, prayers and readings for the *Mass* for the whole year.

missionary Someone who teaches his or her religion or other faith to people in order to convert them to it. Missionaries often leave their own country in order to do this. Many are also involved in medical and educational work among the people with whom they live.

mitre The official headdress of a bishop of the Western Christian Churches, resembling a tall arched and pointed cap. It is made of stiffened cloth, often decorated with jewels; a bishop will have several mitres of different colours, for the different seasons of the Church's year.

Mitzvah 'Commandment'. Word used in Judaism for any religious duty.

mohel A specially trained Jew who carries out *circumcisions*.

moksha A Sanskrit term meaning 'liberation'. In Hinduism, it is liberation from the endless rounds of birth, death and rebirth, and from the illusory world we usually experience. It is the ultimate goal of most schools of Hindu thought and is defined in various ways. In some of the *Upanishads*, moksha is recognition that one's soul is identical with *Brahmin*, or the Absolute. The *Samkhya* philosophy sees it as an absolute isolation of the individual soul from all others and in this way it becomes similar to God in his eternal unity. The *bhakti*, or devotional, movements find moksha in union with *Vishnu* – usually in the form of *Krishna* – or with *Shiva*, and it can be achieved by personal devotion to the god and faithful performance of one's *dharmas*, or *caste* duty. Methods for achieving moksha also vary from one tradition to another. For example, the *yoga* tradition describes a path of ethics, physical postures and exercises, breath control, and meditation. Other systems recommend the accumulation of good *karma*.

The word is also used by Sikhs, generally in the form 'mukti', to describe final union with God and liberation from the otherwise endless cycle of death and rebirth. Moksha is also another Buddhist word for *enlightenment*, the goal of Buddhism.

monastery A religious house or group of buildings inhabited by *monks*. The buildings may include a chapel for services, a refectory or dining room and rooms where the monks sleep and study. The monastery may own farmland or workshops where monks work to support themselves.

This young Buddhist monk, wearing the colour of spirituality, is seated in the courtyard of his monastery in Thailand. Several of the major religions have communities of monks who come together to create a centre where spiritual concerns take priority.

mondo Literally, 'question and answer': a *Zen* dialogue, usually between a master and pupil. The pupil asks a question about Buddhism that has troubled him; the master avoids theory and answers in a way designed to reach the intuitive depths of the pupil's mind.

Sometimes the term can refer to verbal debate between two monks or two enlightened masters.

monk A member of a male religious order whose members live as a community in a monastery. Monks usually take religious *vows*, those of poverty, chastity and obedience being common, and they generally stay in one monastery for the whole of their lives. Monasticism exists in several religions, including Hinduism, Buddhism and Christianity.

125

Monophysitism The doctrine held to this day by the *Coptic Church* of Egypt, and the Syrian, Armenian and *Ethiopian Orthodox* Churches, which caused them to split off from the mainstream of the Christian religion after the *Ecumenical Council* of Chalcedon in CE451. This council decided that in the one person Jesus Christ there were two equal and complete natures: one divine, one human; Christ was therefore both divine and human equally. The *Monophysites* agreed that Christ was indeed both divine and human, but they argued that he had only one nature, basically a divine one. The word 'monophysitism' is derived from the Greek words 'monos', meaning 'one', and 'physis', meaning 'nature'.

Monophysite A person who believes in the doctrines of *Monophysitism*.

monotheism The belief or doctrine that there is only one god. Christianity, Islam and Judaism are examples of monotheism.

monstrance A receptacle used in the Roman Catholic Church in which the consecrated *Host* is presented for adoration and carried in procession; it is most frequently used in the *service* of *Benediction*.

morality A set of views on what behaviour is right and what is wrong, or what is good and what bad. Different religions, cultures and social classes have different moralities.

The word can also mean conformity to those accepted views on behaviour.

Moral Rearmament Abbreviation: MRA. A movement founded in 1938 by Frank Buchman that calls for an uncompromising, strict Christian morality of the most puritanical sort in public and personal lives as a means for improving the world. It stresses that improvement in sexual and religious conduct will eventually bring about an overall improvement in the general human condition.

morals Principles and ways of behaving based on views of what is right and what is wrong.

Moravians A Protestant Christian denomination which sprang from the Hussites of the Middle Ages. In 1722, a carpenter named Christian David led a number of families from Moravia in present-day Czechoslovakia to Saxony in Germany to escape persecution; there they settled on the estate of Count Zinzendorf. This event is the official foundation of the Moravian Church.

The Moravian Church is governed by elders and bishops and its theological beliefs are very close to those of the Lutherans. Before his death, Zinzendorf managed to secure exemption for members from military service and encouraged missionaries to travel throughout the world.

The Moravians' most distinctive custom is a regular meeting of the members of each local church, at which they hold an *agape*, or 'love feast', recalling the agape meal common in the early church after the *Eucharist. Holy Communion* often takes place and the brethren shake hands in a further gesture of fellowship.

(below left) Brethren of the Moravian Church in North America baptizing American Indians. *(right)* In accordance with Jesus' example, the women of the congregation are washing each other's feet.

Mormonism *See*: **Church of Jesus Christ of Latter Day Saints**.

Moses A key figure in the history of the Hebrews, Moses was the greatest of the prophets and is honoured by Christians and Muslims. Born in Egypt where the Jewish people were working as slaves, he was said to have been washed up on the riverbank in a basket and brought up by the daughter of Pharoah as her own son. He was forced to flee, however, to the Midian desert because he had killed an Egyptian soldier who was ill-treating a Hebrew slave. While he was in the desert, God manifested himself to Moses in the form of a burning bush and gave him orders to lead his people out of slavery and into the *Promised Land*. During this *Exodus*, Moses spent forty days and nights on Mount Sinai, where God gave him the *Ten Commandments* written on two stone tablets and made a covenant in which the special nature of God's relationship with the Hebrews was established. From this moment until Moses died just before reaching *Canaan*, the Promised Land, he fought to keep the Hebrews faithful to *Yahweh*, although they were often led into worshipping idols.

mosque An Islamic meeting place for prayer and worship. It normally has a special area set aside for women and an area where Muslims can wash themselves before entering. Inside there are no seats, just a lectern which has a copy of the Qur'an upon it, the *mihrab*, and a pulpit known as a minbar. The floor of the mosque is often covered with a carpet, since Muslims must pray on clean ground, and although there are no pictures, as these are entirely forbidden in Islam, the walls may have decorative patterns, often formed out of the Arabic text of the Qur'an.

Mother Goddess The earth mother and the symbol of fertility and nature, worshipped in numerous religions, including Hinduism, where she is known as *Mahadevi*.

Mothering Sunday The fourth Sunday of *Lent* in the Western Christian calendar. The term 'mothering' refers to three things: firstly, to the old *epistle* reading for the day, which talks of heaven as 'mother'; secondly, to a medieval practice on this Sunday by which the congregations of small, dependent churches and chapels visited their 'mother' or parish church, or the 'mother church' of the diocese, the cathedral; and thirdly, to the long-standing practice, in which people visit their mothers with presents on this day.

Mount Hira The place near Mecca where, in a cave, in CE610, Muhammad received a vision of the angel *Gabriel*. What the angel communicated to him there was eventually written down and became the text of the Holy Qur'an.

Mount of Olives A hill in Jerusalem where Christians believe Jesus went with his disciples after the *Last Supper*, in order to pray and rest before his trial and crucifixion. On the hill is a garden known as *Gethsemane*, and it was to this garden that *Judas Iscariot* is said to have led the chief priests and guards from the Jerusalem Temple to arrest Jesus and take him to be tried.

Mount Sinai A mountain somewhere on the Sinai Peninsula of eastern Egypt, where, traditionally, Moses, the leader of the Hebrews, received the *Ten Commandments* and the remainder of the *Torah* from God.

mourner Anyone who feels or shows sadness, whether over the death of an individual, for a lost cause, or for any other reason.

mudra Literally 'sign, token'. A symbolic gesture or hand position. Hindu dancers use mudras in ritual dances, some of which represent or take after the dances of the god *Shiva*, who is also called Lord of the Dance.

In Buddhism, a mudra expresses and strengthens an inner attitude such as fearlessness or generosity.

muezzin The man who calls Muslims to prayer from the *minaret* of the mosque five times a day. The call he chants is the *adhan*, and summons all to pray to *Allah*, who is great. It also includes the *Shahadah*, or statement of faith, 'There is no God but Allah and Muhammad is his prophet'.

Five times a day, from the sunrise until after sunset, the muezzin calls the faithful to prayer.

mufti An Islamic consultant to religious courts on points of Muslim law; he is therefore an expert on the *Shari'a*, the Muslim law.

Muhammad Also spelled Muhammed, Mohammed (570?–632). The founder of Islam and, according to Muslims, the final and greatest prophet of Allah, or God. Muhammad was born into the Arab tribe of the Quraysh in Mecca, now in Saudi Arabia. His father had died before he was born and he was brought up by an uncle. He became a trader and married a rich widow, Khadija. Then he began to have visions and hear the voice of the archangel Gabriel. He eventually realized that these were true *revelations* from the one and only God, and that he was God's prophet.

Until his death Muhammad continued receiving revelations and had them written down. They form the Qur'an, the sacred scripture of Islam, and set forth the Islamic belief in Allah as the one and only Supreme God. Muhammad met resistance to his role as Prophet in Mecca, and moved to *Medina* in a journey known as the *Hijra* (622), where he gained many converts. From this power base he gradually widened his spheres of influence, converting desert tribes by persuasion and force. During this period the religion of Islam developed, and after most of the Arab peninsula was under his control he finally conquered Mecca in 630.

Muharram The Islamic new year festival, observed during the first days of the first month. *Shi'ite* Muslims commemorate the death of *Husain* in the battle of *Karbala*. At the end of ten days, the Shi'ites perform a play which presents the events of the battle and looks forward to the *Last Judgement*, when Hussain will intercede for the *salvation* of faithful Shi'ites.

mukti *See*: **moksha**.

mullah A respected Muslim teacher or scholar who interprets the law of Islam for ordinary Muslims.

munmukh *See*: **manmukh**.

Muslim (1) As a noun, a follower of the religion of Islam; literally, 'one who submits' to God. (2) As an adjective, 'Muslim' refers to Islam: thus we speak of Muslim teachings or Muslim law.

Mutazilites A sect within Islam which appeared in the eighth century CE and eventually merged with the *Shi'ite* body of Iran. It emphasized man's free will and personal responsibility for his actions more strongly than orthodox Islam, which tends towards *determinism* in making the will of *Allah* responsible for all that happens.

mystic A person who dedicates himself to achieving a union with or direct, intuitive experience of God, the divine, the spiritual, the transcendental or some ultimate reality beyond the world of appearances. Mystics appear in many religions and use several practices in their efforts. Many Christian mystics have relied on prayer, asceticism and contemplation. Buddhist mystics reject asceticism and prayer, concentrating on meditation and solitude.

myth A story about gods, God, or other supernatural beings that attempts to explain how the universe, the earth, living creatures, rituals, customs and the like came into being. *See also*: **bhakti, Sufism, Kabbalah**.

n

Nabi Arabic: 'prophet'. Twenty-eight *prophets* are named in the Qur'an, including Moses, Abraham, and Jesus. Muhammad is seen by Muslims as the last and greatest of the prophets.

Nam Literally, 'name'. The 'name' of God, in the Sikh religion. Nam is God active and manifesting himself. Sikhs call God the 'true name', Sat Nam, who reveals his true nature to those who repeat and meditate on his name and follow a life of discipline. People who are initiated into the *Khalsa*, or Sikh brotherhood, *vow* to devote their lives to serving this true name.

naman Mark worn on the forehead by *Vaishnavites*, consisting of three vertical lines.

This devotee of Vishnu is wearing the naman.

Nam Japo Repetition of the Sikh name for God, *Nam*; such repetition takes place during prayers and meetings. By repeating his name, people learn to think of their duty to serve God and man and lose *haumai*, the negative, self-centred view of life. The practice of Nam Japo is similar to the Hindu use of *mantras* during meditation.

Nanak (1469–1539) The first Sikh *guru* and founder of the Sikh religion. Guru Nanak was born in the Punjab into a Hindu family. He came under the influence of *Kabir*, of *Sufi* mystics, and of the Hindu *bhakti* movement, and Sikhs believe that at the age of thirty he gained an experience of enlightenment when he was taken to the court of God, given *amrita*, or nectar, to drink, given the true name of God, and blessed by God. He realized that Hindus and Muslims were equal before God and that both religions had a partial grasp of the truth. He believed that Islam and Hinduism had become submerged in their rituals and traditions and no longer concentrated on showing their followers how to live a life at peace with God.

From that period onwards, he travelled, preaching God's name. In 1521 he settled in Kartapur with his followers, the beginnings of the Sikh community. By 1539 he had collected many followers and realized that he had to appoint a successor. By the time Guru *Angad*, the second guru, came to head the Sikh community the movement had spread throughout India.

Guru Nanak is best remembered for the hymns he composed and which his successors brought together in the *Guru Granth Sahib*; his character is portrayed in a collection of stories based on his life and teachings and known as the 'Janam Sakhis'. Sikhs believe that his spirit lives on in the Guru Granth Sahib, the 'living Guru' for today, and in the brotherhood of the *Khalsa*.

Nandi The white bull in Hindu mythology who is the chief personal attendant of *Shiva*.

Nataraja 'Lord of the Dance', a title of *Shiva*, who is often depicted doing a world-shattering dance, balancing symbols of creation and destruction.

nationalist A person devoted to his own country, nation or people. Nationalism is frequently associated with struggles for independence.

National Socialist (German Workers') Party Also known as *Nazi* Party. An extreme right-wing German political party founded after World War I and quickly taken over by Adolf *Hitler*. It denounced Jews, communism, democracy and the treaty imposed on Germany after its defeat in the war. Nazis preached that the so-called German 'race' was superior to all other 'races' and demanded the rearmament of Germany so that it could expand its territories.

Hitler led the party to power in 1933 and suppressed all opposition. The new regime persecuted Jews, gypsies, Slavs, Jehovah's Witnesses, homosexuals, handicapped people and many others. Eventually it set into operation the *Final Solution* to clear Germany and German-controlled countries of such 'undesirable' stock. This 'solution' was simply mass murder, primarily an attempt to wipe out the Jewish people; by the time Hitler was defeated, the Nazis had murdered over six million people, mostly Jews from eastern Europe. This *genocide* is often called the 'Holocaust'. When the Allies defeated Germany, the National Socialist Party was banned and many of those who had promoted its policies were tried and convicted of committing crimes against humanity.

Guru Nanak with his faithful companion, the musician Mardana. The Guru spread his teaching by setting his words to Mardana's music.

nativity The day of birth. Nativity stories exist in several religions. In Buddhism the conception and birth of *Gautama* are related, while Hinduism has the story surrounding the birth of *Krishna*. There are several nativity festivals in the Christian calendar. The most famous is Christmas Day, the nativity of Christ, which has been celebrated since the fourth century CE. The nativity of the *Virgin Mary*, a Roman Catholic and Eastern Orthodox festival, is kept on 8 September, and that of *St John the Baptist* on 24 June.

naturalism A theory which states that science is sufficient to account for all phenomena and that the whole of human experience can be explained by the laws of natural science. Naturalism denies the existence of any reality outside or greater than ordinary material nature. According to this view of life, religious ideas can be explained by studying man's natural mental processes and the development of human societies; any notion of *revelation* is discarded. The supernatural and spiritual are excluded from this picture of the world since they cannot be shown to exist by scientific observation or experiment.

Naw Ruz Ancient Persian (Zoroastrian) New Year Festival. Still celebrated by many Muslims, but particularly celebrated by Baha'is. It is customary to fast for nineteen days before Naw Ruz.

Nazareth A town in north Israel where Jesus Christ spent his childhood.

Nazarene An appellation given to Jesus Christ, because he spent his early years in *Nazareth*. Also a name for Christians in the Qur'an.

Nazi A member of the *National Socialist Party*.

Nazirites, Nazirim People belonging to the religion of Judaism who have taken a vow not to drink alcohol, not to cut their hair and not to contaminate themselves by touching a corpse. The vow was much more common in ancient times (Samson and John the Baptist are famous examples) but it is still sometimes taken today; it is one of the very few examples of *asceticism* in the Jewish religion. It is normally a temporary vow, taken for a specific period of time.

Nebuchadnezzar The name of three kings of Babylon, the most famous of whom, Nebuchadnezzar II, reigned from 604-561BCE. He invaded Judah three times and carried away many Jews into captivity in Babylon, thus beginning the period of Jewish history known as the 'Exile'. When his soldiers captured the city of Jerusalem, they burnt down the Temple of Solomon; the *Ark of the Covenant*, which was housed in it, disappeared at that time.

ner tamid The oil lamp which burns day and night in front of the ark in Jewish *synagogues*, a symbol of the continual presence of God.

Nestorianism A doctrine about Christ's nature stated by Nestorius, a *patriarch* of Constantinople from 420 to 431CE, but considered *heretical* by most Christians. Nestorius tried to define just how Jesus Christ could be at one and the same time God and man; he stated that there were in the one person Jesus Christ two natures, one divine, one human. His opponents, however, who were in the majority, attacked his theory for not stating strongly enough that these two natures were truly united together; it was as if the two natures coexisted side-by-side in Christ but retained their own identities and were not able to affect or interpenetrate each other. In particular, what annoyed his opponents was Nestorius's refusal to grant the *Virgin Mary* the Greek title 'theotokos', or 'God-bearer'; Mary could only be the mother of the human nature, he said, not of the divine. The Church called an *Ecumenical Council* at Ephesus in CE431 to discuss the problem; Nestorius was denounced and the title 'theotokos' was formally reaffirmed to be a true description of Mary; as a result of this judgement, Nestorius was banished to Egypt, where he died in 435. His followers split off from the mainstream body of the Church; though once very powerful in Persia and China, the Nestorian Churches today are small and much troubled by persecution. One branch exists in Iraq and is widely known as the Assyrian Church, another, in South India, as the Malabar Church.

New Testament The second part of the Bible, the holy book of Christianity. The New Testament contains stories about Jesus and teachings associated with him in the four Gospels; the founding of the early Christian Church by his disciples, in the *Acts of the Apostles*; letters or epistles from early Christian leaders, including St Paul, to the Christian communities they founded, on matters of *doctrine* and morality and an *apocalyptic* vision of the end of the world and the *Last Judgement*, known as the Revelation of John.

The *Old Testament* prophets promised the Israelites that a saviour or *Messiah* would come to earth and prepare the way for the founding of the kingdom of God. In the New Testament, Jesus Christ is said to have fulfilled these Messianic prophecies through his teachings, examples, crucifixion and resurrection.

New Year, Chinese The major Chinese festival. Immediately prior to New Year, paper models of the Kitchen god and god of Wealth are burnt to return them to heaven where they report on the family's behaviour. On New Year it is customary to eat only vegetarian food – to show respect for the animals after whom Chinese years are named. New Year is also everyone's birthday.

This god of wealth is wearing a hat which bears an inscription promising riches to anyone who beholds him. He is dressed in white, the Chinese colour of mourning.

New Year, Islamic *See*: **Hijra**.
New Year, Jewish *See*: **Rosh Hashanah**.
Nibbana The *Pali* form of the Sanskrit word '*Nirvana*', meaning the state of enlightenment. Nibbana is the most common *Theravada* term for the common Buddhist goal of enlightenment.

Nicaea, (Ecumenical) Council of A general assembly of Christian bishops called by the Emperor Constantine in June 325 to deal with the Arian controversy and to establish the correct day for observing the feast of *Easter*. The Greek theologian Arius stated that Christ was not eternally one with God and part of the *Trinity*, but was merely a semi-divine being created by God to carry out a specific task, that of teaching and saving mankind. The council condemned Arius and exiled him and his followers. At the same time, the council drew up the first version of what has come to be called the *Nicene Creed*, a statement of Christian faith which is recited during the *Eucharist* in the Roman Catholic, Anglican and Eastern Orthodox Churches.

Nicene Creed *See*: **Nicaea, Council of.**

Nichiren (1222–82) The Japanese Buddhist who founded the Nichiren sect. He was a monk in a Tendai monastery when he became convinced that only the *Lotus Sutra* revealed true *dharma*, or the real teachings of the Buddha. Nichiren strongly opposed all other beliefs, especially the more orthodox forms of Buddhism, and urged the government to impose his teachings on Japan and to suppress all other beliefs. As a result he was persecuted himself, but he still gathered followers, founding a sect which continues to flourish today. The Nichiren sect emphasizes the Lotus Sutra and chants its praises repeatedly.

Night journey Also known as *Mi'raj*, this refers to the night that Muhammad, the prophet of Islam, was taken from Mecca to the temple in Jerusalem, guided by the *archangel Gabriel*, riding a winged horse called Buraq. Here he met Abraham, Moses and Jesus and ascended into heaven to be received by Allah, or God. When he returned to earth he was filled with Allah's message which he preached to his followers.

nihilist (1) A person who rejects all established laws, authority and institutions and the social system in which he lives. Usually a nihilist is also an extreme revolutionary who seeks to destroy all these institutions and believes in destruction for its own sake. (2) A very sceptical person who rejects all traditional values, morality and religions and denies that there is any purpose to life.

Nihon Shoki A *Shinto* sacred text, written on the basis of oral tradition in the eighth century, which gives the traditional Japanese account of the Creation.

nineteen day feast The *Baha'i* meeting which falls on the first day of each of the nineteen months in the Baha'i calendar. These assemblies are only open to registered members of the faith; children who have reached the age of fifteen and not yet declared their belief as a Baha'i are also not permitted to attend, even if they go to all the other religious meetings.

During the nineteen day feasts, the *Spiritual Assembly* lets the local community know of its plans and progress in local matters. The feast is divided into three parts: the devotional, during which prayers are said; the consultation period, when committees make reports, read out their conclusions, and assess the state of the community finances; and the refreshment period, during which food or drink is consumed.

Ninety-Five Theses Ninety-five criticisms of abuses in the Roman Catholic Church written by *Martin Luther* and nailed by him to the door of the church in Wittenberg, Germany. The sale of *indulgences* was one of his main targets, but he also publicized his views on reforming the structure of the Church, on the role of the clergy, and on the Church's doctrines. This sparked off a controversy which grew into the *Protestant Reformation.*

Ninigi The grandson of *Amaterasu*, the sun goddess, according to *Shinto*. Ninigi was sent to earth to rule the islands of Japan. *Jimmu Tenno*, the legendary emperor of Japan around 660BCE, claimed descent from Ninigi and thus gave birth to the myth that Japanese rulers were divine beings.

Nirmana-Kaya *See*: **Trikaya.**

Nirodha Literally, 'cessation' or 'ending'. Nirodha is another term for the goal of Buddhism, *enlightenment*. It stresses that enlightenment is the end of all pain, suffering and unsatisfactoriness. As such, it is also the third of the *Four Noble Truths*: When craving ends, so ends all suffering.

Nirvana A Sanskrit word meaning 'extinction'. Nirvana is a common term for *enlightenment*, the goal of Buddhism. It stresses the nature of enlightenment as the cessation of the 'conditioned' ordinary worldly existence as most people experience it and as the experience of the 'unconditioned', of true reality. It is probably the most common term for enlightenment among *Theravada* Buddhists, especially in its Pali form *Nibbana*.

In a state of perfect enlightenment, the statue of the Buddha is reposing in a flower-strewn shrine.

niyama Self-purification by discipline, in Hindu *yoga*. Niyama is the second of the eight branches or stages of yoga and consists of rules of conduct often listed under the headings: purity of body, thought, word, diet and dwelling; contentment; ardour or conscious effort; self-education and study and dedication to God.

Noah The hero of the Hebrew flood story recounted in the Book of Genesis in the *Torah*, or Old Testament, and in the Qur'an. For an account of the flood story *see*: **Ark, Noah's**.

Noble Eightfold Path The fourth of the Four Noble Truths of Buddhism. The path to be taken by the man in search of *enlightenment* and nirvana is marked out by eight instructions. The overall aim of the path is to keep man in the Middle Way between too much self-indulgence and the opposite extreme of over-severe *asceticism*. The Buddha discovered this Middle Way after a period in which he tried asceticism and found it brought him no nearer his goal.

The eight instructions are that man should cultivate right understanding, right motives, right speech (for example, not lying), right conduct, right means of livelihood, right effort (directing one's will towards spiritual growth), right mind control and right meditation or serenity. Following this path should rid the Buddhist of unhealthy sensual desires and should cultivate compassion and love for all creation in his daily life. This will lead him to liberation and from the wheel of rebirth and will bring him to Nirvana.

nominalism A philosophical theory from the Middle Ages that general or abstract words do not correspond to anything which actually objectively exists. In all cases the individual alone can be said to have real existence; words for universal qualities, like manhood, are simply vocal noises. This theory is opposed to 'realism': realists believe that universal qualities do, in some way, have real existence; the problem is still hotly debated today in philosophical circles.

Nonconformist Any English Protestant who is not a member of the established *Church of England. See also*: **Independents, Presbyterianism**.

nones The *service* in the divine office of Roman Catholic and Eastern Orthodox Churches which takes place at the ninth hour of the day, 3 p.m.

nun A woman who belongs to a religious community; the female counterpart of a monk. Nuns are marked out from the world outside their community by the dress they wear and by their *vows*, often of poverty, chastity and obedience.

Nunc Dimittis The Latin name for the Song of Simeon, from the Gospel according to Saint Luke in the *New Testament*. It is a hymn in which the aged Simeon gives thanks to God for having allowed him to see the infant Jesus and a request that he may now die in peace.

Nyabingi Originally a protest cult, active in East Africa from 1890-1920. Recently ceremonial *Rastafarian* meetings have been called Nyabingis.

Nyaya A system of Hinduism that believes that *salvation* can only be achieved through clear and logical thinking, since *reincarnation* and suffering are caused by ignorance. Founded around 300BCE by Akshapada *Gautama*, the Nyaya teaches that true knowledge and understanding is based on four logical steps: (1) perceiving what happens; (2) coming to conclusions on the basis of what we have seen; (3) seeing parallels between events or things; and, (4) testimony, or what others tell us.

O

oblate A Christian layman attached to a particular religious order and devoted to special religious work or to a particular *rule* of prayer and life. He may live in a monastery without taking monastic *vows*, or he may live in the outside world but attend the monstery regularly for prayer, *retreats* and spiritual guidance.

oblation (1) The offering to God of the bread and wine in the Christian rite of the *Eucharist*. (2) Any offering to God or the gods, or an offering for religious or charitable use.

occult The occult consists of all magical, supernatural, supernormal and mystical events and practices. These practices or arts are often only revealed through initiation or after special training. Alchemy, *divination*, *witchcraft*, satanism, astrology and sometimes even *meditation* are considered occult practices.

offertory (1)The preparation and preliminary offering of the bread and wine to God in a Christian *Eucharist* service, before they are consecrated, to represent to be the body and blood of Christ. (2) That part of Christian Service during which the congregation makes its offerings, normally money, to the Church.

Ohrmazd Another name for *Ahura Mazda*.

Old Believer A member of any of several Christian sects founded in the seventeenth century in Russia. They refused to accept certain reforms in ritual and worship in the Russian Orthodox Church, and broke away from it.

Old Catholics A Christian denomination that split off after 1870 from the Roman Catholic Church, because the *Ecumenical Council* known as 'Vatican I' had declared that *papal infallibility* was a *dogma* of the Church. Old Catholics keep most of the doctrines and rituals of the Roman Catholic Church, but have their own bishops and priests, who are allowed to marry. They do not accept the authority of the Pope or other Roman Catholic bishops, whom they believe to have departed from the true Catholic faith. Today they are mostly to be found in Holland.

Old Testament The first part of the Christian Bible, which does not include the life of Christ. The Old Testament tells the history of the Jews and their relationship with the God who revealed himself to them, and who made a *covenant*, or 'Testament', with them. The Old Testament contains thirty-nine books, although sometimes the seven books of the *Apocrypha* are included as well. In Judaism, the books which Christians call the Old Testament are divided into three types: the books of the Law, those of the prophets, and the rest, i.e. the *Torah*, including historical books and collections of proverbs and poetry, known together as the *Writings*. *See also*: **New Testament**.

Om The most sacred word of Hindus, placed at the beginning and end of books and uttered before prayers. Composed of three sounds, it is said to represent *Trimurti*.

omens Signs which are believed to signal good or bad events to come. The practices of *magic* and *divination* rely heavily on the interpretation of omens.

Omer The period of forty-nine days between the second night of *Passover* and the Jewish festival of Pentecost; the counting-off of these days is known as the 'counting of the Omer'. In the days before the invention of written calendars, such counting was necessary if Pentecost was to be celebrated on the correct day. On the day of Pentecost itself, the Omer, or sheaf of newly-harvested barley, was brought to the Temple in Jerusalem to be offered to God. The period is kept as a time of mourning, except for certain feast days. The thirty-third day is 'Lag b'omer', popular for weddings; the twentieth is Israel Independence Day; on the twelfth day the Holocaust Remembrance Day is held to remember all those six million Jews who were murdered by the *Nazis*.

Om mani padme hum 'Hail, the jewel in the lotus, hail.' A phrase often used by Tibetan Buddhists on *prayer-wheels* and spoken when using prayer-beads. Some interpretations say that the jewel is the Buddhist doctrine, the lotus, the Buddhist scriptures or reality.

omnipotence Unlimited power: one of the attributes of God in many *theistic* religions. *See also*: **omniscience**.

omniscience The ability to know everything, to have complete, infallible and infinite knowledge: one of the attributes of God in many *theistic* religions. *See also*: **omnipotence**.

ontological argument A philosophical proof for the existence of God first used in Europe in the Middle Ages by St Anselm and later by Descartes and Leibniz. Their argument runs as follows: everyone can have the idea of a most perfect being (that is, God) in his or her mind; something that exists in reality as well as in the mind is more perfect than something that only exists in the mind. It follows that the most perfect being, God, must exist in reality, otherwise the idea we all have in our minds would not be that of a most perfect being. The argument has attracted many people, and is still being debated today, despite the heavy criticism levelled against it by Immanuel Kant and other philosophers.

ontology The branch of *metaphysics* which studies the nature of existence or being as a whole. It tries to answer the questions: 'What can be said to exist?' and 'What is existence?'

Oomotokyo 'The teaching of the Great Source'. A contemporary Japanese religion which combines elements of *Shinto* with fresh revelations.

Opus Dei A Roman Catholic organization for laymen and laywomen which seeks to encourage its members to play a full part in the life of the church and to increase their spiritual growth through *retreats* and a life of practical holiness and service. It was founded in 1928 by the Spanish priest Josemona Estiva de Balaguer.

oral tradition The passing down by word of mouth of teachings, stories and traditions without committing them to paper. The Bible, the life of Muhammad, most Buddhist and Hindu scriptures and the words of the early Sikh *gurus* – all of these are based on oral tradition.

Oratorian A member of the *Oratory*.

Oratory A Roman Catholic society of secular priests who live in a religious community but do not take monastic vows. It was founded by St Philip Neri in the mid-sixteenth century in Rome to bring spiritual help to young men.

order The monks, nuns or friars who follow a particular rule of monastic or mendicant life in their communities. For example, the *Benedictine* Order follows the rule of St Benedict, the *Franciscan* Order that of *St Francis of Assisi*, the *Jesuit* Order that of *St Ignatius Loyola*.

ordination The ceremony by which a person receives *holy orders*, enters an *order* or becomes a priest, monk, nun, minister or preacher in various religions. Ordination can involve a ritual which stresses that the person is going to devote his or her entire life to following the teachings of the religion: this is the case when a Buddhist is ordained and enters the *Sangha*.

In the Christian Church ordination authorizes men, and occasionally women, to celebrate the sacraments and to preach the gospel in their Church.

original sin In Christianity, the first sin. According to the *Old Testament*, it was committed by Adam and Eve in the Garden of Eden when, tempted by Satan, they broke God's law order-ing them not to eat of the Tree of Knowledge of Good and Evil, an event known as the *Fall*. Christians believe that this has caused an innate depravity in humanity, inherited from Adam and Eve; they also believe that Christ came down to earth to die as an *atonement* for all men's sins, including their original sin. The Christian sacrament of baptism enables believers to take advantage of this atonement; it removes guilt borne by the individual for imitating mankind's first sin.

Origin of Species *See*: **Darwinism**.

Orthodox Churches *See*: **Eastern Orthodox Churches**.

Orthodox Judaism. The most traditional wing of Judaism. Orthodox Jews hold firmly to the *Torah*, or Law, revealed to Moses by God of that Law contained in the *Talmud* and the *Halakah* written by Orthodox *rabbis*. They insist on keeping strictly to the letter of the Law, as well as to its spirit. Among other things, this means that they keep the rules for the *Sabbath* and the dietary laws rigorously. They do not accept marriages or conversions performed by non-Orthodox rabbis, such as *Reform* or *Liberal* rabbis. In Orthodox *synagogues* men sit separately from women, and no woman can become a rabbi. Orthodox Jews should not marry *gentiles* (that is, non-Jews) or even Jews who are not Orthodox.

Oxford Movement A nineteenth-century English *Anglican* movement which sought to revive traditional Catholic rituals in the Anglican Church, along with church ceremonials, the spiritual authority of the clergy, the use of incense and candles and the veneration of the *Virgin Mary* and other saints. It also believed that the Church of England should pay more attention to the tradition and teaching of the Church in the first eight hunted years after Christ. The modern Anglo-Catholic wing of the Anglican Church holds similar views.

p

Christians hold that God made the first man and woman to share his creation with him and gave them an idyllic garden in which to live. All nature was in harmony, as this woodcut shows, with the unicorn symbolizing innocence. Tempted by the Devil in the form of a snake, our first parents fell from grace and the sin they committed is borne by all mankind.

pacifist Anyone who believes that it is morally wrong for a human being to fight against a fellow human being and who, on these grounds, refuses to be conscripted into an army, to condone military involvement, or to take part in a military campaign. *See also*: **Jehovah's Witnesses**; **Society of Friends**; **conscientious objector**.

pagan A term of abuse used for someone not of the speaker's religion.

Pahlavi texts or books *Zoroastrian* writings, largely from the ninth century CE, composed in Pahlavi, or Middle Persian. Their origins go back at least to the sixth century and give accounts of Zoroastrian folklore and the creation myth of Zoroastrianism.

Pali The spoken language of northern India during the life of the Buddha. The oral tradition of the Buddha's teachings was in Pali, which later became the authoritative *Pali Canon*.

Palm Sunday The Sunday before the Christian festival of *Easter*. It begins *Holy Week* and commemorates Christ's ride into Jerusalem on the back of a donkey. The feast is so called because, according to the Gospels, palms were scattered on the ground before Christ's feet as he rode into the city. In Roman Catholic and many *Anglican* churches, the congregation goes in a procession around the church before the *Eucharist* on this day, holding branches of palm.

Walking in procession to proclaim their faith, these Roman Catholics in Ayacucho, Peru, are carrying palm branches to commemorate the day when palms were thrown down to line Christ's path as he entered Jerusalem on a donkey.

Panchen Lama *See*: lama.

pandit A learned and wise man in Hindu society. Ordinary Hindu families often call upon pandits to perform complex religious ceremonies on their behalf.

Panj Pyares Literally, 'the beloved five': the five original members of the *Khalsa*, or *Sikh* brotherhood, initiated into this movement by the last Sikh *guru, Gobind Singh*. He wished to form an inner group of Sikhs utterly committed to the defence of their religion and the unity of their community. Accordingly he gathered an assembly of all the Sikhs at Anandpur on *Baisakhi* Day 1699 and asked, 'Who will give me the head of a true Sikh?' Eventually five men, the Panj Pyares, went into Gobind's tent one after the other; Gobind followed each one in and came out each time with a bloodstained sword, to the horror of the crowd. At the end, however, the five men stepped out alive. The five were then initiated and became the Khalsa, receiving the name Singh, which means 'lion'. Gobind himself was also initiated and took the same additional name. Today when any Sikh is initiated into the Khalsa, five members of the brotherhood must be present, as well as the Granthi, to represent the Panj Pyares.

Pantajali Born in the second century BCE, Pantajali was the first person to commit the teaching and practices of yoga to memory and pass them on to future generations in the form of sutras, or short sayings.

Panth The Sikh community.

pantheism Any religion or philosophy that identifies God with the universe and says that God and nature are one and the same; it denies that God has any form of distinct personality, plan for the world, or moral teaching with which he might wish to guide the actions of mankind. Since all of nature is part of God and reveals God, pantheistic religions generally have no prophets and do not rely on sacred scriptures to reveal otherwise unknowable facts about God. Certain forms of Hindu philosophy have come close to pantheism.

pantheon Originally, the domed, circular temple to all the gods in Rome, built by the Emperor Hadrian in the second century CE. The term has come to refer to all the gods and heroes of a *polytheistic* religion collectively.

Pantocrator Any artistic representation of Christ as ruler of the universe, especially common in Eastern Orthodox churches on the inside of their domes.

papacy A term for the office of *Pope* with the Roman Catholic Church and for the system as its head and supreme governor. The papacy is said to have been created by Christ when he told *St Peter* that he was entrusting his church and his people to Peter and his successors.

papal authority The authority of the *Pope* as leader of the Roman Catholic Church. This Church believes that the Pope, as bishop of Rome, is the successor to *St Peter*, and has a similar authority; hence, when he speaks on doctrine or morality 'ex cathedra', that is, as head of the Catholic Church, to the Church, and for it, the Pope is *infallible* in this carefully defined type of pronouncement. Although the Pope's ordinary pronouncements and decisions are not infallible, they naturally carry great weight, and the Pope is said to have an immediate personal jurisdiction and authority over every single member of the Roman Catholic Church, clergy or laity.

papal infallibility *See*: infallibility.

parable A story told to illustrate a lesson by analogy. Jesus Christ, as recorded in the *New Testament*, revealed his teaching by means of such stories, which had a great impact on his listeners, being drawn from aspects of life they could recognize.

paradise (1) Heaven, or the final home for those who have led righteous lives. The term 'paradise' is used especially when heaven is thought of as a garden, like *Eden*. Muslims, especially, see heaven in this way. (2) An intermediate place for the souls of virtuous dead people who are awaiting resurrection at the *Day of Judgement*, according to some Christians.

Parinirvana 'Complete Nirvana', entire cessation of rebirth. The state of a Buddha who has achieved *Nirvana* on earth and who will therefore, on passing away from this life, no longer be reborn.

parish A local community of Christians living within a defined geographical area. The religious life of this community is centred on one main church, the parish church, and the people are helped and cared for in their spiritual lives by a clergyman known as a parish priest (in the Roman Catholic and Eastern Orthodox Church), a vicar or rector (in the Anglican Church) or a minister or pastor (in most Protestant Churches). Sometimes the parish is not only a unit of church organization, but also a local secular government, especially when the country has an established church.

Shiva, the Destroyer, with his necklace of skulls, is seated with his consort, Parvati. The white bull, Nandi, looks on.

parokhet An embroidered curtain which hangs in front of or just behind the doors of the *ark* in a Jewish *synagogue*. It is named after the curtain that hung in the Jerusalem Temple to screen the *Holy of Holies* from the rest of the *sanctuary*, and its colours are changed for certain festivals.

Parsis Followers of the *Zoroastrian* religion whose ancestors left Persia at the end of the ninth century CE to escape Muslim persecution and arrived in India. In spite of Westernization, most Parsis follow the religion of their fathers. Each child is initiated into the religion during the ceremony of 'naujote'.

Parsis see death as the temporary victory of evil over good and send the bodies of those who have died to *dakhmas*, or towers of silence, where they cannot pollute the community. Relatives pray from a distance and have to undergo purification once they have returned home.

Worship in a temple, where the sacred fire of Ahura Mazda burns continually, is not essential for the lay Parsi. On arriving at the temple, worshippers wash and pray to cleanse their souls and bodies and then leave an offering of wood for the fire. Temple priests supervise the fire ceremonies, but ordinary believers are expected to show devotion mainly by their every-day actions, rather than by prescribed rituals.

Parsva The major teacher in *Jainism*, an Indian teacher of the ninth century BCE, who is believed to be the twenty-third of a line of *tirthankaras*.

Parvati Literally, 'daughter of the mountain': daughter of the Himalayas and one of the names of the consort of the Hindu god *Shiva*. The goddess is represented as a beautiful, mature woman. Shiva is said to have ignored Parvati while practicing asceticism, but through her own asceticism and the help of *Kama* Parvati won Shiva's attention, and their embraces made the world tremble. Parvati had two children by Shiva, *Ganesha* and *Kartikeya*.

paschal candle Also known as *Easter candle*. A tall candle used in the Easter ritual of the Roman Catholic Church and in many Anglican churches. On the night before Easter Sunday it is blessed, lit near the altar, and kept burning at all services until the feast of the *Ascension* or *Pentecost* Sunday.

Pashupati 'Lord of animals', a title of *Shiva*.

Passion The sufferings Jesus Christ endured from the *Last Supper* to his death on the cross. They are recounted in the Gospels, and reading these Passion stories in full is a prominent feature of the *Holy Week* services in the Roman Catholic and Anglican Churches.

Passover *See*: **Pesach**.

pastor The Protestant equivalent of a parish priest or vicar; the word is used most often as a title in the *Lutheran, Baptist* and *Pentecostalist Churches*. His title comes from the Latin word for 'shepherd'.

Patanjali The traditional founder of yoga and author of the Yoga Sutras, a collection of sayings and short teachings on spiritual development. Patanjali wrote that he did not invent yoga; he just systematized the teachings and practices in his sutras. He probably lived sometime between 200BCE and CE500.

Pater Noster *See*: **Lord's Prayer**.

patriarchate (1) Any self-governing, usually national, Church within the Eastern Orthodox family of Churches that is rule over by a *patriarch*. First in honour among the patriarchates is Constantinople, the 'Ecumenical patriarchate'; others include the patriarchates of Moscow and Jerusalem. (2) Any Eastern Church not belonging to the Eastern Orthodox family but governed by a patriarch, for example, the *Jacobite Church* of Syria, ruled by the patriarch of Antioch. (3) Any of certain major *dioceses* in the Roman Catholic Church whose bishop has for centuries been known as patriarch.

Paul, St One of the major figures in the earliest period of Christianity. Originally Paul was a devout *Pharisee* and enemy of the Christians. He travelled to Damascus in order to oppose them, but on the road underwent a sudden experience of conversion and became one of the Christian *disciples*. Paul dedicated the rest of his life to founding and guiding Christian communities in Asia Minor, Greece and Italy. The letters he wrote to these communities are known as *epistles* and form a major part of the *New Testament*. He was beheaded by the Emperor Nero around CE64, about the same time as *St Peter*, with whom he shares 29 June as a feast day. Paul has deeply influenced the whole of Christian doctrine and theology since his time.

pectoral cross A cross which is worn on the breast by Christian bishops and abbots and other leading clergy to signify their position and responsibilities.

penance A sacrament, practised by the Roman Catholic, Orthodox, Anglican and Lutheran Churches and often known as *confession*, which makes it possible for individuals to confess their sins to God.

penitent (1) Someone who feels sorrow for past wrongdoings and wishes to repent, intending to live a better life in the future. (2) A person who confesses his sin to a priest in the Roman Catholic and Eastern Orthodox Churches and submits to whatever penance the priest imposes.

Pentateuch *See*: **Torah**.

Pentecost (1) The Jewish harvest festival. (2) A Christian festival coming fifty days after *Easter*. It commemorates the time when Christians believe the *Holy Spirit* descended to inspire the disciples after the Ascension of Christ to heaven. Emboldened by this experience they went out into the streets to preach the gospel. The Sunday of Pentecost is also known as *Whitsunday* or Whit Sunday. *See also*: **Weeks, Feast of**.

Pesach Also known as *Passover*. The Jewish festival that commemorates the freeing of the Hebrews from slavery in Egypt and their *Exodus*, led by Moses, towards the *Promised Land* of Canaan around 1200BCE. The event is remembered with a family meal which closely parallels the meal eaten on that first Passover night before the Exodus, when the angel of death 'passed over' the Hebrews' houses and killed the first-born children of the Egyptians. A Passover lamb is no longer sacrificed, but a roasted lamb bone is put on the plate of each as a symbol of the original meal.

A family celebrating Pesach with the traditional meal.

Pesach is also known as the *Feast of Unleavened Bread*, and on the night preceding the celebrations each household carefully searches to make sure that there is no yeast in the home. Because of their haste to leave Egypt, the Hebrews at the original Pesach meal had no time to let the bread rise: to commemorate this fact *matzah*, or unleavened bread, is the only bread eaten during the seven days of Pesach.

During the *Seder*, or Pesach meal itself, the story of deliverance from slavery is told at the table and the father of the house relates the events contained in the Book of Exodus of the *Torah* in response to questions asked by the youngest son of the family. The family leaves an empty place at the table, together with a glass of wine, in case this night should see the return of the prophet Elijah and the beginning of the Messianic age. They leave the front door open for any stranger to come in and join the feast: it might, after all, be Elijah in disguise.

Easter falls at about the same time as this festival, as it was during the seven days of Pesach that Christ was tried, crucified and raised from the dead, according to Christian beliefs.

Peter, St One of the twelve *Apostles* of Jesus Christ. His original name was Simon, but Jesus Christ nicknamed him Peter (from the Greek word for 'rock') and chose him, according to the *Gospels*, to be the rock on which the early Christian Church would be built.

Peter denied his connection with Christ before Christ's crucifixion, but later recovered his faith and courage, and set out to preach the Christian message. According to the Roman Catholic Church, the Popes, as bishops of Rome, are the successors of St Peter, who traditionally became the first bishop of Rome.

Peter is believed to have been crucified in Rome by the Emperor Nero in CE64. Two *epistles* in the *New Testament* are said to have been written by him. He shares 29 June as his feast day with *St Paul*.

Pharisees Educated Jewish laymen in ancient Judaea who often acted as teachers of the Jewish Law and as scribes. The Pharisees arose in the second century BCE at the time of the Maccabees. They were intensely nationalistic and opposed both the Greek and Roman rulers of their country; they were devout in their adherence to both the written law of Moses and the oral law later written down as the *Mishnah*. They also held several doctrines not found in the *Torah*, for example, the resurrection of the dead, the existence of hell, angels and demons and the future coming of the *Messiah*. Because they accepted the oral law and these doctrines and opposed the Romans, they disagreed with the *Sadducees*. After the destruction of Jerusalem (CE70) they were largely responsible for the reconstruction of Judaism. Essentially it is the Pharisees' interpretation of the religion which has become the *Orthodox Judaism* of today.

philosophy In its widest sense, philosophy is the love of knowledge or wisdom: in other words, the desire to learn about all things, whether practical or theoretical. In its narrower sense, philosophy is that study which deals with ultimate reality, or the most general causes or principles of things.

phylacteries *See*: **tefillin**.

Pietism A seventeenth-century German Protestant movement. The Pietists reacted against the lack of emotion in *Lutheran* religious attitudes and worship and insisted that intense prayer, purity of life and personal holiness were more important than intellectual knowledge of doctrine and the Bible. They rejected the secular, everyday world as corrupt and set up study groups to be 'churches within a church', concentrating on intimate personal prayer to Christ, good works and the development of an inner peace in intimate union with Christ. Their influence still remains in the Lutheran Churches of today, especially in the 'Inner Mission' movement in Denmark and in the Norwegian Lutheran Church.

Pilate, Pontius The Roman governor of Judaea (CE26?–36?), at the time of *Jesus Christ*. According to the Christain Gospels, Pilate was responsible for the sentence of death passed on Jesus under Roman law. Pilate is also mentioned by the first century CE Jewish writer, Josephus. A tough governor, Pilate was still capable of being thoughtful in his relationships with the Jews.

pilgrimage A journey undertaken by followers of a religion to places which are of special importance to that religion. Hindus have long regarded the rivers of India as sacred, and at the city of *Benares* pilgrims frequently enter the *Ganges*, to purify themselves by washing away their sins. Followers of *Shintoism* flock to the *shrine* of *Amaterasu* at *Ise* to show thanks whenever there is a particularly good harvest, since Amaterasu is the sun goddess upon whose generosity the crops depend. Christians make pilgrimages to Jerusalem and other sites in their Holy Land and to the Shrines of saints, particularly those of the *Virgin Mary* at Lourdes in France and Fatima in Portugal.

Many Buddhists visit the place associated with the birth, *enlightenment*, first teaching and death of the Buddha: nevertheless, pilgrimage is not that important in Buddhism. In contrast, every Muslim is duty-bound to attempt to make the pilgrimage to Mecca once in a lifetime.

plainsong An ancient system of Christian chanting, used especially for singing *psalms* and hymns in Latin in the Roman Catholic Church.

Plato One of the best-known and most influential Greek philosophers, he lived from *c.*427–347BCE, principally in Athens. A pupil of Socrates, he established an Academy to continue the teaching of philosophy, one of his own pupils being Aristotle. Many of his works, among them the *Republic* and the *Symposium*, are written in the form of dialogues or conversations and often deal with the relations between the individual and the state. The concept for which he is most celebrated is that of the Ideal: he postulated the idea that somewhere there is a world in which familiar objects exist in their true forms, thus a tree on earth is only a pale shadow of a tree in its perfect form.

Plymouth Brethren *See*: **Brethren**.

pogrom An organized persecution or massacre of a community or ethnic group, especially of Jews in eastern Europe. It was particularly widespread in the Middle Ages and continued until World War II.

polytheism Belief in many gods. Hinduism, for example, in its popular forms, is a polytheistic religion.

pontiff Another term for the *Pope*.

Pontius Pilate *See*: **Pilate, Pontius**.

Pope Also known as the pontiff, and as the Vicar of Christ (that is, Christ's earthly representative). The Pope is the bishop of Rome and head of the Roman Catholic Church; he is seen as the successor to *St Peter*, traditionally the first bishop of Rome and leader of the twelve Apostles of Christ. The papal insignia is crossed keys, symbolizing his spiritual authority, which Catholics believe was given by Christ. Each Pope is elected by the College of Cardinals. *See also*: **papal authority**.

Apart from a brief period when the papacy was situated at Avignon, the Pope has always had his seat in Rome. The Vatican City is at the heart of the Roman Catholic world and it is from the balcony overlooking Saint Peter's Square that the Pope gives his blessing and speaks to all nations.

These Buddhist monks are offering up prayers for the meal they are about to eat. Their hands are joined to indicate their concentration.

prakriti The *Samkhya* school of Hindu philosophy teaches that the physical world is made out of twenty-four different principles known as prakriti, which are divided into three groups of contrasting qualities, or *gunas*. All objects and things, including man's physical nature, are made out of prakriti. Because of the contrasting qualities, or gunas, man's physical and emotional life is a mixture of happiness, misery and delusion. When prakriti, which is always changing, is united to *Purusha*, or unchanging spiritual reality, the result is the creation of the full, conscious human being, soul and body. True happiness for a man comes, according to this philosophy, when he sees that purusha is the more important reality, which should dominate and direct prakriti: to see only prakriti in life is to deceive oneself and court unhappiness.

prana The vital, or life, force, according to Hindu *yoga* and *Vajrayana Buddhism*. The term's meaning is often restricted to the 'breath of life'. In *pranayama*, the *yogin* controls his breath in order to gain control over all his energies.

prayer Any attempt made by man to communicate with God, a god or another supernatural force that forms the object of his worship. Prayer is characteristic of most religions, and varies tremendously. It can be associated with spells, charms and magical practices and with statues or icons, etc. It can also take the form of offerings, as of food, incense or candles, and can be made privately and silently or aloud in public. Prayers can be fixed in form or composed by the worshipper himself.

Prayer Book Also known as the *Book of Common Prayer*. The authorized service book of the Anglican Church, which was first drawn up during the *Reformation*. Three versions were produced in the sixteenth century with a revision in 1662, still widely used. It has recently been modernised.

prayer mat Also known as seggadeh. A carpet on which Muslims kneel at prayer. The mat is placed so that it faces towards Mecca. Muslims often carry the mat with them in readiness for the times of prayer, since they must kneel and prostrate themselves only on clean ground.

prayer wheel A device used by Tibetan Buddhists, consisting of a cylinder around which are attached papers, all inscribed with various *mantras*. The cylinders are made in many sizes and can be turned by hand, air or water. The paper used for the inscriptions is so thin that an eight-foot wheel may contain a million repetitions of the mantra. So, when turning the wheel, one is, in a sense, repeating the mantra a million times.

preacher Anyone, who dedicates his or her life to spreading the teachings of any religion, with the aim of converting hearers to that religion. The term can also be used of anyone who delivers a sermon during a religious service.

predestination The eternal decision of God that determines in advance what will happen to individuals and to nations. Although used by St Paul, the term is especially associated with *Calvinist* theology, which makes much use of the idea. Similar concepts are also found in Jewish and Muslim thinking.

The word 'predestination' can be used in several different senses: (1) God's eternal purpose, which existed before the creation of man and the world; (2) the selection of nations or individuals to perform a task connected with this same purpose; (3) the selection of individuals to receive God's *grace* and the gift of eternal life. The ideas of (2) and (3) are also called 'election', and the people so chosen by God are often called the 'elect'. *See also*: **free will**.

prelate Anyone holding a high office within a Christian Church, especially a bishop or archbishop.

presbyter (1) An elder or leader in an early Christian community. (2) An elder or leader in a *Presbyterian* congregation other than the minister. Such elders, together with the ministers, form the local presbytery and are divided into the 'ruling elders' and 'teaching elders'.

Presbyterianism A Christian Protestant denomination which bases its beliefs and practices on the teachings of *Calvin* and maintains that the authority of the Bible is supreme, and sufficient for all aspects of Christian life and worship. Presbyterian services concentrate on scriptural readings, sermons based on the Bible, and prayers improvised by the minister. They do not contain elaborate, fixed forms of worship or ritual. The Church itself is organized in regional courts of ministers and elders, all of whom are elected by the local congregations or presbyteries for office. Their churches are normally plain and free of religious ornamentation.

presbytery A house, often beside a church, in which a priest lives.

priest An individual who has the right, or is able, to offer sacrifices or perform rituals for ordinary members of his religion. Often a priest acts as mediator between man and God or the gods.

primate (1) The highest bishop in any Anglican province, or group of dioceses, especially the archbishop of Canterbury or of York. (2) The chief Roman Catholic bishop in any predominantly Catholic country.

priory A monastery, abbey or convent governed by a prior or – in the case of a female community – a prioress, rather than by an abbot or abbess. Often a priory is subordinate to an abbey governed by an abbot or abbess.

procession Any march or walk of a ceremonial kind, usually organized on days of rejoicing. Processions have always played a great part in religious ceremonies and are still used in the major world religions on festive occasions or during services.

The congregation are leaving after the service in this Presbyterian church in Bora Bora, French Polynesia. From its base in Geneva, missionaries carried the faith all over the world.

proletariat The working class. According to Karl Marx, the proletariat really only comes into existence when society reaches the stage of capitalism. It consists of industrial workers who do not possess machinery, property or other capital and are forced to sell their labour in order to survive.

Promised Land *Canaan*, later called Israel; the land promised by God to Abraham and his Hebrew descendants in the Book of Genesis in the *Hebrew Bible* or *Old Testament*. *See also*: **Canaan, Exodus**.

Promised One Baha'u'llah. *See*: **Ridvan Festival**.

prophecy (1) The ability to foretell the future. (2) The act of declaring and interpreting the will of God to men. (3) An actual saying of a prophet.

Muhammad, often known as the Prophet, is shown outside the walls of a city, preparing to receive its submission. An angel is ministering to him.

proselyte Someone who converts from one religion to any other religion. The term originally referred specifically to a convert to Judaism.

Protestant Protestants are members of those Christian Churches which split off from the Roman Catholic Church in the sixteenth century. The name 'Protestant' was first given to followers of *Martin Luther*. Protestant churches include the Church of England and the Lutheran, Calvinist and Presbyterian Churches.

Proverbs, Book of A book of the *Old Testament* or *Torah* and a prime example of the Jewish Wisdom literature. It consists of wise sayings, maxims and discourses that attempt to give practical guidance on how to lead a pious everyday life. The book is traditionally attributed to King Solomon, but the sayings are drawn from a number of authors and were probably compiled after the sixth-century BCE exile in Babylon.

prophet A human being who has been chosen by God to act as a messenger, and to make his will known to man; a person who speaks on behalf of God. Thus the term is used of the Jewish prophets whose sayings can be found in the prophetic books of the *Old Testament* or *Hebrew Bible* and who declared God's judgment on human sin and his willingness to save and restore the fortunes of the obedient. Muhammad is said by Muslims to be Allah's final and greatest prophet, and Zoroastrians have *Zoroaster* as their prophet and founder.

Prophets, The The section of the *Hebrew Bible* containing the sixteen prophetic books and the historical narratives.

psalm A sacred hymn or poem designed for singing, especially one of the collection of 150 songs for use in Jewish worship to be found in the *Hebrew Bible*. These songs are called the Psalms of David, since he is traditionally their author. These psalms cover a wide variety of moods and subjects; some are bursts of praise to God, others are to be sung at public ceremonies such as royal coronations and solemn assemblies of the Jewish people; yet others are private confessions of sorrow for sin and grief at the human condition, or attempts to offer wise advice on life to the next generation. The Christian religion also uses these psalms extensively in its worship.

psalter A book containing the psalms of the *Old Testament* or *Hebrew Bible*, and sometimes other additional hymns, either with or without the accompanying music. Psalters are used primarily in Christian worship.

psychic An individual who claims to have supernatural powers, whether of healing, divination, precognition or interpretation of events such as omens. *See also*: **spiritualism**.

puja Worship, in Indian religions. Orthodox Hindus perform puja three times a day: in the morning before dawn, at noon and in the evening. Most homes have an area set aside as a *shrine*, where prayers can be said and flowers and offerings of food left for a god. *Jains* do puja to the *Jinas*. Buddhists perform puja to the Buddhas and *bodhisattvas*.

On a riverbank, Hindus perform puja to the goddess Durga. An image of Durga, garlanded with flowers, is at the centre of this colourful act of worship.

pulpit An enclosed stage or platform in the Christian church, from which the preacher delivers his sermon. The pulpit is raised above the level of the ground and the congregation.

Puranas A Sanskrit word meaning 'something that is old' and applied in Hinduism to the legends and stories which, along with the epics, make up the *smriti* scriptures. There are eighteen important Puranas, and, of these, the *Vishnu* Purana and the *Bhagavata* are the most widely read, being especially popular amongst members of *Vaishnavite* sects since they encourage *bhakti* or personal devotion to Vishnu and his *avatars*. The Vishnu Purana speaks of Vishnu and the supreme being who created the world and man out of a sense of playfulness, and the Bhagavata contains many legends about Vishnu's avatar, *Krishna*, and his amorous adventures with the cowgirls of Brindaban, from amongst whom came Radha, his special favourite.

Amida Buddha, who dwells in the Pure Land, in which believers aspire to be reborn.

purdah This is a corruption of the Persian term 'pardih', meaning 'veil, or curtain', and refers to the Islamic custom of Hijab, which derives from the teaching in the Qur'an that women should cover all their bodies, and are allowed to show only their faces and hands. The practice is intended to protect Muslim women's modesty and virtue, although in some parts of the Muslim world local custom dictates that women have no direct contact with men other than those of their immediate families.

Muslim women, modestly covered, outside the mosque.

Pure Land Buddhism A form of *Mahayana Buddhism* that stresses the importance of *shraddha*, or faith and confidence in the Buddha, based on intuition and experience; the dominant school of Buddhism in China and Japan.

In these countries this emotion of faith and love was directed especially to Amitabha, the symbolic, ideal Buddha of Infinite Life, and his domain, the Pure Land *Sukhavati*, a world in which everything helps you practise the Buddha's teachings and gain *enlightenment*.

The common Buddhist law of *karma* teaches that every willed action will have a result. A great *bodhisattva* constantly performs so many good, skilful actions that he or she builds up a tremendous potential for producing good results, known as his or her store of 'merit'. After his enlightenment, Amitabha used this merit, along with the supernormal powers of a Buddha, to create his Pure Land. This action has not exhausted the stock of merit. Buddhists believe that if they genuinely have faith in his power to 'save' them they will be reborn in the ideal condition of the Pure Land in their next lifetime. Amitabha has done all this because of his great compassion. Devotees worship Amitabha, reciting his name or his *mantra*, and do meditation practices that include visualizing him and his Pure Land.

This is the teaching in China and in the Jodo Shu, or Pure Land School of Japan, founded by *Honen* in 1175. But Honen's pupil *Shinran* took it a step further and in 1225 founded the Jodo Shin Shu, or True Pure Land School, also known as *Shin Buddhism*.

In Japan, Amitabha is usually called *Amida*, meaning 'the Infinite', and Shinran identified him with the *Dharmakaya*, that is, Buddhahood itself, or Absolute Reality. Similarly, the Pure Land Sukhavati is no longer another world in which one can really take birth; taking birth in Sukhavati is a synonym for gaining enlightenment itself. Release from this world is achieved by sincere faith in the compassion of Amida. This belief is expressed in the mantra 'Nembutsu' which is used to invoke the name and compassion of Amida.

purgatory A process of purification for the souls of those who have died without being completely cleansed of their sins, according to the Roman Catholic Church. Such souls must go through purgatory before entering heaven. Purgatory is often imagined as a place of purifying fire, where souls are made ready for heaven by God.

These young boys and girls in Israel are taking part in a procession to mark the feast of Purim, the feast of Lots. The giant female figure is Esther, the heroine of the story.

Purim The Jewish festival of Lots, celebrated in February or March, and based on a story in the Book of Esther in the *Torah* or *Old Testament*. A villain, Haman, wanted to destroy the Jews and, by throwing lots, chose this day for a massacre. But Esther intervened on behalf of the Jews with her husband, the Persian king. The festival commemorates this deliverance of the Jews from destruction.

The feast is celebrated in the *synagogue* by reading the Book of Esther right through from a scroll known as a *'Megillah'*. Whenever Haman's name is read out, the people stamp their feet, whistle and shake rattles to show their displeasure. The festival is a joyful one, in which children are particularly involved.

Puritans English Protestant reformers who flourished from about 1560–1660. They wanted to cleanse the English Church of what they called its 'Popish elements', that is, remnants of Roman Catholicism. The Puritans objected to wedding rings, kneeling to receive the *sacra-ments*, the sign of the cross at baptism and confirmation and all forms of religious images, pictures, statues and so forth. Most Puritans remained within the *Established Church*; others, the 'Dissenters', established meetings for worship outside it. These were such as the *Congregationalists*. Because of persecution, many Puritans fled to Holland and America.

Puritans won control over the Church from 1649–60, while England was a republic. They abolished the rank of bishop and, because they disliked fixed forms of public prayer, they published a book of general directions for the conduct of worship known as the *Directory*. The keynote to their attitude to the faith was simplicity and seriousness: simplicity in worship, in dress and in lifestyle, seriousness in their attempts to do good works as a sign of gratitude to God. Their dominance in the Church was ended by the Restoration of King Charles II to the throne in 1660 and the re-establishment of the Book of Common Prayer.

purusha (1) The unchanging spiritual reality, according to the *Samkhya* philosophers of Hinduism, that unites with the ever-changing material reality of the *prakriti* to create conscious individuals with souls, such as human beings. (2) The 'world-soul' in the *Vedas* of Hinduism. It consists of all the souls that have ever been and are still to come.

Purusha The original man of Hinduism, created by the god *Brahma*. From Purusha's body were created the different Hindu *castes*. So, from his head came the *Brahmin* or priestly caste, from his arms and trunk the *kshyatriya* or warrior caste, from his thighs the *Vaishya* or merchant caste, and from his feet the *Shudra* or peasant caste.

Purva Mimamsa A Hindu system of thought founded by *Jaimini* which teaches that the four Vedas are uncreated and eternal and that belief in the existence or otherwise of God is unimportant, since man can lead a perfectly good life simply by following the rites and duties contained in the *Vedas*. This system preaches that it is impossible to reach the truth through speculation or philosophy. Instead, correct ritual action rather than correct belief leads to liberation; the Vedas are sufficient for living a truly religious life.

q

Qadis Muslim judges who sit in the religious courts and judge in accordance with the Qur'an and the Muslim legal code known as the *Shari'a*. These courts judge private and family matters, other matters, however, which are covered by the law of the particular country, are judged in secular, or civil courts.

Qom A city in Iran: one of the holy cities of *Shi'a* Muslims and the centre of Islamic teaching in that country.

Quakerism *See*: **Society of Friends**.

quiblah Direction. When Muslims pray they face in the direction of Mecca. In a mosque the quiblah is indicated by a niche in the wall facing Mecca, known as a *mihrab*.

Quissa-i-Sanjan An epic written in 1600 which tells how the *Parsis* fled from their native Iran to escape Islamic persecution for their *Zoroastrian* faith.

Quiyas A Muslim term for the deduction made about the law on the basis of the Qur'an; the example and practice of Muhammad and the consensus of the community – the *Ijma*.

Qumran The home of an ancient Jewish community of *ascetics*, probably the *Essenes*, and the site where the *Dead Sea Scrolls* were found.

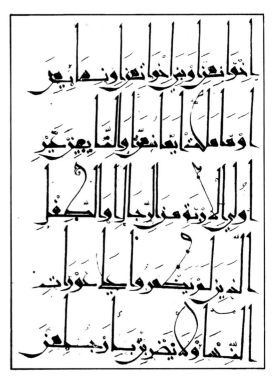

The Qur'an, since it is divine revelation, merits the most reverent handling. This surah is written in ornamental Eastern Kufic script.

Qur'an The sacred book of Islam. The Qur'an is the foundation of Islam, the word of God revealed to Muhammad and the final authority on how to lead life on this earth. Muslims believe that there is an eternal Qur'an inscribed in heaven; the earthly Qur'an is a direct copy, so they treat the book with great respect.

The Qur'an is divided into 114 *surahs*, or chapters, and its structure was finally fixed twenty years after the death of Muhammad. It is treated as *infallible*, since it was dictated to the Prophet from CE610–632 by the agent of God, the *Archangel Gabriel*. The rules and maxims of the Qur'an have become the basis of Islamic law, the *Shari'a*.

Quraysh The tribe which controlled Mecca at the time of Muhammad and to which he belonged. Many of his fellow tribesmen objected to his teachings. The Prophet's first important convert, *Abu Bakr*, also came from this tribe, which continued to be hostile and was finally defeated by Muhammad in CE630 at Mecca.

r

rabbi Literally, 'teacher': a Jewish minister, who teaches the religion and often leads worship in the synagogue. *Orthodox Jewish* rabbis are always men, but *Reform* and *Liberal* Jews now have female rabbis as well.

Rabbinic Judaism Judaism as developed by the rabbis from CE70 onwards to the present day. They compiled, interpreted and expanded on the *Talmud* in order to create a series of authoritative rulings on the law, social issues and ritual. This form of the Jewish religion exists today as *Orthodox Judaism*, and is the direct descendent of the earlier Judaism of the *Pharisees*.

Radha The wife of a cowherd who, according to the Hindu epic, the *Mahabharata*, leaves her husband to become the mistress of the god *Krishna*. The *bhakti*, or devotional, movement holds up as an ideal her love for *Krishna*, and sees their relationship as a model of love between man and God.

Radhakrishnan Twentieth-century Hindu philosopher and politician who interpreted the Hindu scriptures in the light of twentieth century needs and taught the essential, underlying unity of all the world religions.

radicalism Support for, or the implementation of, fundamental change, rather than minor reforms, in social, political, economic or religious affairs.

A study in concentration, this young Muslim inside the Mahabat Khan mosque is reading the Qur'an. The book is believed to be divine revelation which Muhammad received in Mecca and Medina.

rajas One of the three *gunas*, or qualities, which determine the characteristic of any material being, according to the *Samkhya* school of Hinduism. Rajas is the active quality of energy. *See also*: **sattva**; **tamas**.

Rajneesh, Baghwan Shri A present-day Hindu *guru* who has gained a large following amongst both Indians and Westerners.

rak'as Movements which Muslims perform during *Salat*, either in the mosque while following the prayer leader or in private prayer. The number of rak'as depends on the time of day. The worshipper begins by lifting his hands to his ears and saying in Arabic, 'God is the greatest'. After this, to the accompaniment of the opening chapter of the Qur'an and any other short chapter from it, the Muslim of the *Sunni* sect places his right hand on top of his left and covers his navel, while the *Shi'ite* Muslim lets his arms hang by his sides. Next he bows and stands upright; he repeats this movement three times while praising God. He also prostrates himself on his prayer mat, kneeling and putting his forehead on the ground. At the end of the rak'as he turns to look over both shoulders and says 'Peace be upon you and the mercy of God!'. This marks the end of the first rak'ah. *See also*: **Salat**.

The positions, or rak'as, adopted by Muslims at prayer.

rakshasas Evil spirits in Hindu mythology, one of whom was *Ravana*.

Raksha Bandhan A Hindu festival, when sisters give their brothers special coloured threads to wear on their arms as protection.

Rama The seventh *avatar*, or incarnation, of the god *Vishnu* in Hinduism. His life and words are held up as an example of morality and virtue and his story is told in the epic poem, the *Ramayana*. Rama was forced into exile with his wife *Sita* by the manipulations of his stepmother. While in exile, Sita was abducted by the *rakshasa Ravana*. Rama, with the help of his brother Lakshmana and of *Hanuman*, finally rescued Sita and returned to take over his kingdom.

Ramadan The Islamic month set aside for fasting from all food and drink every day from sunrise to sunset. Observing Ramadan is one of the *five pillars of Islam* and is obligatory to all but the pregnant, the sick and ailing, the very young or aged, and those who are travelling. During Ramadan, Muslims are encouraged to read the entire Qur'an and public readings are common. This custom arose because the Night of Power, the night when Muhammad first received revelations from the archangel Gabriel, falls in Ramadan. The day after Ramadan is celebrated as the feast of Fast-Breaking. *See also*: **Id-ul-Fitr**.

वालम्भिकंजीलोक्सःसीताजी

Sita, the heroine of the *Ramayana*, pictured here with her twins, and Guru Valmiki, the author of the saga.

Ramakrishna A nineteenth-century Hindu *guru* and mystic, who was influenced by the *bhakti* movement of Hinduism. He believed that mystical experience was the highest goal of all true religion. He stated that all religions which led to this goal were true, no matter how much their individual beliefs differed, and lived for some time as both a Christian and a Muslim. His thinking has remained influential up to the present day, and he is even worshipped by some as an *avatar*.

Ramayana A Hindu epic poem and scripture in Sanskrit, composed by Valmiki. It recounts the life of Prince *Rama*, an *avatar* or incarnation of *Vishnu*, and especially tells of the love of Rama and *Sita*, his wife, of Sita's capture by the demon *Ravana*, and of her liberation by Rama with the help of the monkey-god *Hanuman*. Their story is remembered in the feast of Diwali. The poem portrays Rama and Sita as the ideal man and woman. It has had a great influence on the *bhakti* movement and strongly emphasizes the place of *dharma*, or caste duty, in Hinduism.

Ram Das Fourth Sikh *guru*, best remembered for founding the sacred town of *Amritsar* as a meeting place for Sikhs on festive days.

Ram Mohan Roy (1772–1833) An Indian scholar, diplomat, writer and religious reformer. Steeped in Hindu culture, Roy was also strongly influenced by Western rationalism. He supported social and religious reforms, which led him to found the *Brahmo Samaj*, a *monotheistic* movement in Hinduism based on the *Upanishads*. He also admired Christian ethics, which he developed in his book, *Precepts of Jesus*.

Ranjit Singh, Maharaja Sikh military leader of the late eighteenth and early nineteenth centuries who established an independent Punjab for the Sikh community and gave his people self-government. After his death in 1839, this period of stability came to an end and the British annexed the area ten years later. The *Golden Temple* as we know it today was restored to its present form by Maharaja Ranjit Singh.

Rashi Commentator on the *Hebrew Bible* and the *Talmud* who lived in the eleventh century and whose words still form an essential part of Jewish scholarship and teachings.

Rashidun 'The rightly-guided ones' – a collective term for the first four *caliphs* of Islam, *Abu Bakr* (632–638), *'Umar* (634–644), *'Uthman* (644–656) and *Ali* (656–661). These orthodox leaders of the Muslim community, as Muhammad's immediate successors, not only led the new religion's armies, but also adopted the Islamic calendar, established the final text of the Qur'an and encouraged scholarship among the faithful. The Rashidun period spanned twenty-nine years, and was a time when religion alone dictated all personal and collective behaviour. With the founding of the *Umayyad* caliphate Islam became a more secularised religion.

Ras Tafari *See*: **Selassie, Haile**.

Maharaja Ranjit Singh, the Sikh leader, giving an audience.

The most famous Rastafarian of all, Bob Marley.

Rastafarianism A West Indian religion which sprang out of *Marcus Garvey's* Back to Africa movement, which was active in Jamaica at the turn of the century. The early Rastafarians looked to Africa for salvation and liberation from their poverty. When *Haile Selasse* became Emperor of Ethiopia and styled himself Ras Tafari, the Lion of *Judah*, these poor Jamaicans saw him as the promised *Messiah* of Judaism and Christianity, as the incarnation of the true and living God. They saw his empire, Ethiopia, and by extension the whole of Africa, as their *Promised Land*, from which they had originally come and to which they had to return to find peace and dignity; by contrast they saw themselves as being in exile in Jamaica, and they gave the name *Babylon* to the whole hostile world and culture outside Africa.

There are many different varieties of Rastafarian belief: there is no single creed or organization accepted by all. But in general, the movement believes that God is within all men, that black people are especially favoured by God, that life should be lived as close to nature as possible and that the smoking of cannabis or 'ganja' is a *sacrament*. Male Rastafarians wear their hair in 'dreadlocks' and use certain distinctive terms of speech, such as 'I and I' for 'we'. Many still hope for an eventual return to Africa, although there is a tendency to interpret 'Africa' as a spiritual state of mind rather than an actual physical place.

Rasul In Arabic, a messenger. A narrower term than *Nabi*. The Qur'an makes a distinction between those prophets to whom Allah revealed a Law, and the others. In the former group are included Moses, Jesus and Muhammad. In the Muslim confession of faith, Muhammad is described as the Rasul of God.

Rati The Hindu goddess of love, consort of Kama.

rationalism The doctrine that reason is the only source of true knowledge, since it gives us the logic and ability to argue and draw conclusions which make it possible for us to go beyond the simple knowledge supplied by our senses and reach the deeper reality of things. In theology, rationalism is an approach that rejects authority and revelation in religion and tries to establish religious truth by reason.

Ravana According to the Hindu epic, the *Ramayana*, *Ravana* the demon-king of Lanka stole *Rama's* wife, *Sita*, only to be pursued and slain by Rama with the help of the monkey-god Hanuman. At the festivals of *Diwali* and *Dussehra*, giant effigies of Ravana are burnt to celebrate Rama's victory over him.

A gigantic effigy of Ravana, the demon-king.

reactionary Someone who wants to return to a former, usually outmoded, political, social, economic or religious system or state of affairs. The word is often used abusively to refer to a conservative, someone opposed to further change or to radical change.

realism A philosophical theory that takes the opposite point of view to *idealism* and *nominalism*. In contradiction to idealism, realists state that external objects have an existence which is independent of our thoughts about them. In contradiction to nominalism, realists believe that abstract ideas and universal, general concepts, such as 'manhood' or 'goodness', do exist independently of any particular examples, as men or good actions.

real presence The doctrine in some forms of Christianity that Jesus Christ is actually present during the *Eucharist*, in his spiritual body within the consecrated bread and wine. This view is held by Roman Catholic, Eastern Orthodox and many Anglican Christians but denied by most Protestants. *See also*: **transubstantiation**.

rebirth *See*: **reincarnation**.

rector A clergyman in charge of a parish in the Anglican Church, who traditionally holds certain privileges above those of an ordinary vicar, e.g. the right to take tithes from his parishioners.

Redeemer A title of Jesus Christ, emphasizing the Christian belief that Jesus redeemed – literally, 'bought back', – the world from evil and sin by his death and resurrection.

Reformation The sixteenth-century movement, led above all by *Luther* and *Calvin*, which aimed to reform the Roman Catholic Church of the time, since they believed it had grown away from true Christian belief and practice. The refusal of the Roman Catholic authorities to accept the suggested reforms led to the formation of Protestant denominations outside the Roman Catholic Church.

Reform Judaism A nineteenth-century movement within Judaism, inspired by the philosopher Moses Mendelssohn, which states that no religion has a monopoly of the truth and that Jews merely have to accept three statements: that there is a God, that he has a plan for the world, and that the soul is immortal. Mendelssohn also preached that religions should be judged by the conduct of their followers. His disciples translated the *Torah* into German from its original Hebrew and opened the first Reform temple in Germany in 1810. They deliberately called the building a temple and not a *synagogue* to emphasize the loss of the *Temple of Jerusalem*. The Reform movement rejects Jewish nationalism and the idea that the Jews are the *Chosen People* with a personal *Messiah*. It has taken a critical attitude to the *Torah* and interpreted the dietary laws quite liberally. In its services, the movement uses the local language as well as Hebrew, and men and women sit together.

reincarnation The belief that, after death, the soul lives again on earth in another body or that the *karma* from one life is carried over to another. It is a doctrine held especially in Hinduism, Buddhism, Sikhism and Jainism. According to some of these religions, the process of rebirth may involve animals as well as human beings, and human beings can be reborn as animals. The cycle of reincarnation, and the type of body into which one is born, is governed in these religions by the concept of karma, and the cycle can only be broken when the individual has reached a state of *enlightenment* and spiritual perfection known as *Nirvana*, *moksha* or *mukti*.

The title-page of The New Testament according to Martin Luther, the architect of the Reformation.

Reiyukai A Buddhist sect, based on the *Lotus Sutra*, which stresses the need to show gratitude to the ancestors and look after the past by tending neglected tombs. Reiyukai is strong in Japan and has some three million followers, even though it was founded only as recently as 1925.

Rejoicing of the Law, Feast of Also known as Simchat Torah or Simhath Torah. A Jewish festival celebrated on the ninth day of the *Feast of Tabernacles*. During the service the final section of the *Torah*, or Law, is read, followed by the first section, for on this day the yearly cycle of reading the Law both ends and begins again. To emphasize the joyous nature of the occasion, people sing songs and carry the scrolls of the Law in procession in a sort of ritual dance. The men called to the *bimah* to read the sections of the Law are called the Bridegrooms of the Law. The whole ceremony marks the devotion of the *Chosen People*, the Jews, to their God and to the Torah he gave them.

relic Any object or part of a body that belonged to or was in contact with a saint or holy person. Such relics are said to have great power and are frequently found at pilgrimage sites, or in *shrines* or churches.

A reliquary, or casket, in which to place a sacred relic.

religion A system of beliefs about reality, existence, the universe, the supernatural or the divine and practices arising out of these beliefs. These practices usually include worship and a moral code, and often prayer, contemplation, obedience or meditation.

The term 'religion' is sometimes restricted to systems with a God or gods, that is, the *theistic* faiths. On the other hand, the sense of religion is sometimes expanded to include political beliefs such as *communism*.

remorse A sense of deep, sincere regret for an evil or harmful action or thought.

repentance Sorrow, regret and remorse for one's past wrong actions, bad deeds or sins. In Christianity, true repentance requires a sincere intention to lead a new life in obedience to God's commandments, with God's help, turning away from sin. Penitents must show repentance to God before he, or a priest in confession, can forgive them their sins.

requiem A Christian, especially Roman Catholic, *Mass* which is celebrated for the sake of the dead to help them through *purgatory* to heaven. Such Masses are held at funerals and on the anniversaries of deaths. An annual requiem Mass is said on *All Souls' Day*, 2 November, for the sake of all the dead.

response A verse, word, phrase or sentence which a congregation or gathering recites in reply to the minister's cue in a religious service or other ritual.

resurrection (1) The rising from the dead of the souls of all men, which, according to the Christian, Jewish, Islamic and Zoroastrian religions, will occur on the *Day of Judgement*. The first three religions also believe that the souls will be reunited with their bodies, now made perfect, so as to enjoy the bliss of heaven with God. (2) The bringing back to life of Jesus Christ by God the Father after Christ's death by crucifixion. The resurrection of Christ is a basic doctrine of Christianity. It is celebrated in the most important Christian festival, *Easter*.

At the very heart of the Christian faith is the belief that Christ rose again on the third day after his crucifixion. This Dürer woodcut shows Jesus emerging from the tomb in his shroud, while the guards are fast asleep. Shortly after, his disciples found the sepulchre empty.

retreat A place where people can spend time in *meditation*, prayer, reflection and religious exercises. The term can also refer to a period of time spent in this manner. It is sometimes applied to the practice among Buddhist monks of Varsava or 'Rains Residence', of observing a time of intensive study and meditation. This stems from the impossibility of travel during the monsoon season.

revelation A theological term used to describe God's disclosure of himself and his will to man. Such revelations are often contained in the sacred scriptures of a religion.

revere To look upon with respect, honour and veneration. When Christians, for example, bow or genuflect in church before the altar, they are showing their awe and respect for God, who is represented by the altar. The same is true of Sikhs who show respect for God's presence by bowing to the *Guru Granth Sahib* in the *gurdwara*. Most religions, have similar ways of expressing reverence in their sacred places.

revivalist A believer who preaches in such a way as to awaken religious zeal and enthusiasm.

revolutionary Someone who works towards the complete and often violent overthrow of an existing system, whether a political system, an intellectual approach, or traditional structures and values. Probably the best-known example of a revolutionary approach to politics is the *Marxist* doctrine, which inspired the *communist* revolution in Russia.

Ridvan Festival A *Baha'i* festival which falls on 21 April each year and lasts for twelve days. It commemorates *Baha'u'llah*'s declaration to the world that he was the 'promised one' awaited by all religions and that the message he was bringing marked a new unity between men and the beginning of a new epoch in the history of mankind. This is the most important Baha'i celebration and, during the period, spiritual assemblies and national assemblies of Baha'i are elected all over the world.

righteousness The moral and virtuous path approved by a religion. To be righteous is to act in an upright and correct manner according to one's religious or moral beliefs.

Rig Veda The first and oldest part of the *Vedas*, revered as the foundation of Hinduism. The Rig Veda is a collection of over a thousand hymns to a variety of *Aryan* gods and goddesses.

Rinzai A school of *Zen Buddhism* which was taken from China to Japan by Eisai in CE1191. It is famous for its use of *koans* in meditation.

Rishis The ancient sages who 'heard' the *Vedas* when time began, according to Hindu tradition. They also began sacrifices to the gods in imitation of cosmic events.

Risho Kosei-kai A group which separated from the *Reiyukai* and under its founder, Nikkyo Niwano, built up a large following in Japan. The Risho Kosei-kai stresses the importance of the *Lotus Sutra* and the need for group counselling. There is no clergy, for the sect is not linked to any monastic order, and the number of followers is at present somewhere in the region of a million.

ritual *or* **rite** A formal, religious ceremony or set of ceremonies which is performed according to a fixed pattern and is usually accompanied by fixed words. Church services, *Salat*, *puja* and sacrifices to the gods are all rituals, since the way in which they are carried out, and their meaning, has been laid down by tradition.

In many religions, rituals act as a link between man and God or the gods. By observing the correct procedures, believers can offer up worship, ask for protection, guard against misfortune, concentrate their thoughts, and even renew their ties with their tradition through re-enacting the history of their forefathers, as in the Sikh initiation rites of *khande-ka-amrit*.

Roman Catholicism Often known simply as Catholicism, this is the largest Christian Church or denomination. The head of this Church is the Bishop of Rome, normally known as the *Pope*, who governs the Church together with his

Pope Innocent III, the great medieval Pope, who combined masterly statesmanship with heartful spirituality.

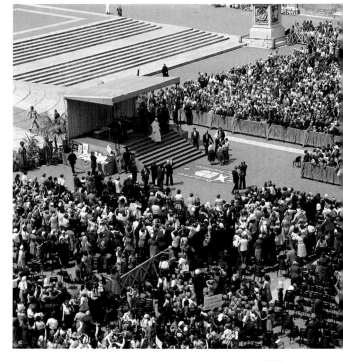

(above) An open-air Mass in Papua New Guinea, and (below) a Papal audience in Saint Peter's Square, in Rome.

advisers, cardinals, the committees known as the curia, and the bishops in their individual *dioceses*. The Catholics believe that the papacy and its authority were instituted by Jesus Christ when he appointed *St Peter* to be head of the Church. The Roman Catholic Church thus believes itself to be the direct descendant of the earliest Christian Church and to be essentially identical to that Church in its doctrines and practices. Doctrines declared since the time of Christ's original twelve *Apostles* have been formulated either by an *Ecumenical Council* of the Church or by the Pope himself. The Roman Catholic Church therefore bases its teaching both on the Bible and on the continuous tradition of the Church from the earliest times.

Some distinctive features of the practice of the Roman Catholic Church are its emphasis on the *Mass* as the central service of worship, the use of statues of saints as an aid and focus for prayer, the prominence of devotion to the saints, especially the *Virgin Mary*, the belief in *purgatory*, *transubstantiation*, *indulgences* and the use of the *rosary* in prayer.

rood An ancient term for a cross or crucifix in Christianity.

rosary A circle of beads on a string used in several religions for various purposes. Its use began in India, where some Buddhists and Hindus use it when reciting *mantras*, and was borrowed by the Muslim world: Muslims use rosaries to aid them in reciting the *Beautiful Names*. The rosary is extensively used as an aid to prayer in the Roman Catholic Church.

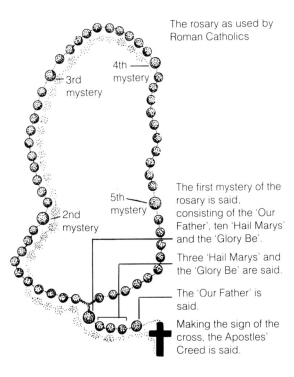

The rosary as used by Roman Catholics

4th mystery

3rd mystery

2nd mystery

5th mystery

The first mystery of the rosary is said, consisting of the 'Our Father', ten 'Hail Marys' and the 'Glory Be'.

Three 'Hail Marys' and the 'Glory Be' are said.

The 'Our Father' is said.

Making the sign of the cross, the Apostles' Creed is said.

Rosh Hashanah *See*: **Jewish New Year.**

Roshi 'Old teacher', the master of a *Zen* monastery who instructs pupils in Za-zen.

Rudra An early Hindu storm god, bringer of disease and healing. Later, most of his attributes were taken over by *Shiva*.

Russell, Charles Taze Born in 1852, Charles Taze Russell was the forerunner of the Christian movement, *Jehovah's Witnesses*. His study of Bible chronology led him to believe that the second coming of Jesus Christ was imminent. As early as 1877 he announced that the year 1914 would see the end of the 'gentile times'. He founded a magazine called *Zion's Watchtower* and gathered many like-minded thinkers around him. The name of the movement's publication was eventually changed to *The Watchtower*, the title by which it is still known.

Rutherford, Joseph Franklin Elected president of the Watch Tower Society in 1917 as successor to Charles Taze Russell after having worked as a legal representative of the Society for ten years. Under his presidency the movement became much more active in preaching, proclaiming that the Kingdom of God had been established in the heavens in the year 1914.

Rutherford's aim was to consolidate the movement into an efficient organization for spreading the message world-wide and during his term as president the Witnesses established their own printworks in many countries. In the year 1931 they officially took the name 'Jehovah's Witnesses' from the reference in Isaiah 43:12. Appointments of elders within the congregations and for special service were co-ordinated from the world headquarters in Brooklyn, New York, where they are now made by the Governing Body of Jehovah's Witnesses.

Conventions are a regular and well-known aspect of the activities of the Witnesses and their preaching from house to house readily identifies them. Following Rutherford's death in 1942, the Watch Tower Bible School of Gilead opened up foreign fields under the presidency of Nathan H. Knorr. From approximately seven thousand Witnesses active immediately after World War I, the figure has grown to well over two and a half million in over two hundred lands today.

Charles Russell, first president of the Watch Tower Society.

S

Sabbath Saturday, the seventh day of the week, which Jews observe as a day of rest in honour of God's rest on the last day of *Creation*. The Sabbath also commemorates the delivery of the Hebrews from Egypt, since this was the first commandment that they received on leaving Egypt. The day begins at dusk on Friday, and lasts till dusk on Saturday. The Sabbath is a joyful occasion, when Jews express their pleasure at the world which God has made for his people. They wear their best clothes, dressing in white to symbolize purity and hope, and light candles before the Sabbath begins to keep darkness and sorrow away. During the day much food is eaten but no work may be done; this emphasizes that it is God who controls and regulates the workings of nature – not man. At the first Sabbath meal on Friday night, people sing hymns at table and it is customary for the father of the household to bless his wife and children. *Synagogue* services are held, and the family will normally attend public worship on the Saturday morning. The end of the Sabbath is marked by the *havdalah* ritual, which involves lighting a candle to show that the holy period is over. (Jews are forbidden to light fires during the actual Sabbath itself.)

The Sabbath is a day of joyful ritual for the Jews and its ending is marked by lighting the Sabbath candles.

sacrament A major ceremony or other religious act in the Christian Church which, according to tradition, was authorized by Christ and in which God's grace is directly given to the participant, usually through some material substance, such as bread, oil or water. A sacrament is usually defined as an 'outward and visible sign of an inward and spiritual grace'. The Protestant Churches regard *baptism* and the *Eucharist* as the only sacraments. The Roman Catholic and Eastern Orthodox Churches also include *confirmation*, *penance* or *confession*, *ordination*, marriage and *extreme unction* or anointing the sick.

sacred Set apart, specially dedicated to a deity, whether by being used for a religious purpose or by association with a god or gods, or regarded with a similar reverence. Articles used in religious ceremonies, rituals that link man to God or a god, the written books of religion, and its music are all called sacred since they are set apart from everyday life and usage.

These Australian aborigines are engaged in a sacred ceremony, their bodies painted with religious symbols.

Sacred Thread Ceremony The Hindu rite of initiation, performed on boys, usually between the ages of five and twelve. It is regarded as a 'second birth' for the boy, and because only boys from the top three *castes* (*Brahmins*, *kshyatriyas* and *Vaishyas*) can undergo this ceremony, these castes are known as the 'twice born' or 'dvija' castes. Before the ceremony, the boy has to learn all the duties and responsibilities of an adult Hindu from a *guru*, as this rite marks his passage from childhood to maturity. During the rite itself, the boy and a Brahmin priest sit on opposite sides of a fire, which is sacred to *Agni*, the Vedic god of fire. Prayers and hymns are chanted: the boy has to repeat prayers after the priest, and he is clothed around the shoulders and waist with the red thread. He is also given a personal *mantra* for use during meditation. From now on he must pray three times a day, perform the ceremonies of *puja*, and study the sacred scriptures of his religion; in ancient times he also had to wander in the countryside, dependent on gifts of food and money in order to learn independence and find God in solitude. In Tibetan Buddhism, the sacred thread ceremony is performed by the great reincarnations of certain *bodhisattvas*. It bestows blessings and good *karma* on the devotee.

sacrifice An offering made to a divinity or idol, particularly one made at a *shrine* or altar. The custom is an ancient one and common to most religions. Sacrifices can be made as a means of communicating with the gods or God, of atoning for past sins, of making a gift in gratitude, or of showing reverence. Animals, food or money are often offered, but sacrifices can also take the form of prayers and worship.

sadaquat Voluntary *almsgiving* in Islam. Whereas Muslims must give *zakat*, they may also give sadaquat.

Saddharma Pundarika Sutra *See*: **Lotus Sutra**.

Sadducees A sect within the Jewish hereditary priesthood which arose in the first century BCE. The Sadducees seem to have taken their name from Zadok, the high priest who crowned Solomon as king of Israel. The only writings they regarded as sacred scriptures, revealed by God, were the five books of the *Torah*: in particular, they rejected the oral Law later written down in the *Mishnah*, as well as the *Pharisees*' interpretations of that Law. Since the Sadducees did not accept the later collections known as the Prophets and the Writings, they did not believe in the resurrection of the dead, nor in angels and demons, ideas which appear in these collections. Nor did they expect a *Messiah* to come and save them. The sect disappeared after the Romans destroyed Jerusalem and its temple in CE70.

sadhu A wandering Hindu holy man who devotes his life to becoming a saint and achieving *moksha*, or liberation.

Sahajdari Sikhs who have not yet been admitted into the *Khalsa*, or Sikh brotherhood, through the initiation rite known as *khande-ka-amrit*. They are distinguished from Khalsa Sikhs by not wearing the *Five Ks*. The term is also used for those Sikhs who, having been initiated into the Khalsa, lapse in their observance of the proper conduct for a member of the Khalsa. Such Sikhs may undergo a second or subsequent khande-ka-amrit ceremony.

Sai Baba A twentieth-century Hindu teacher who has a large following in southern India. His followers believe that he is an *avatar*, or manifestation of the god *Shiva* and his *shakti*. He preaches that all men are equal and that *enlightenment* is therefore within the grasp of anyone who looks for it, irrespective of *caste* or race.

A boy of the dvija, or twice-born, caste is being girdled by the priest with the sacred thread in this ceremony to mark his second birth, his passage from childhood to maturity.

These two young
Japanese girls are making
a sacrificial offering of
flowers in plaited baskets,
which will bc carried away
by the stream.

Wearing orange, the
colour of holiness, Sai
Baba approaches one of
his followers.

Saint Elizabeth who, late in life, gave birth to John the Baptist, the cousin of Jesus.

saint (1) A person in the Christian religion who is venerated after his or her death for great holiness and moral virtue. The Church officially recognizes that certain individuals have led such model lives that they are certain to be saints in heaven and it authorizes veneration of them by a process known as *canonization*. Roman Catholic and Eastern Orthodox Christians also pray to the saints to pray to God on their behalf. (2) A member of the *Church of Jesus Christ of Latter-day Saints*, a Mormon. (3) Any individual, such as a *bodhisattva* or *Arhat* in Buddhism, who has led a life of virtue, benevolence and holiness.

Taken from the manuscript of *The Perfection of Wisdom*, the bodhisattva Samantabhadra is shown on an elephant, according to Chinese Buddhist tradition.

St John's Gospel The last of the *Gospels* in the *New Testament* to be written. It was traditionally said to be the work of one of the twelve *Apostles* of Jesus whose name was John. It is quite different in style and structure from the other three gospels, as it meditates in a deep theological way on the meaning of Jesus's words and actions, especially his *miracles*.

St Mark's Gospel The first of the *Gospels* in the *New Testament* to be written. It is also the shortest of the four, and is very compressed and dramatic in style. It may be incomplete as we have it now, and it shows signs of having been written for Christians who were suffering persecution by the Roman empire. Traditionally it is said to have been dictated to St Mark (an unknown author) by *St Peter*, the leader of Jesus' twelve *Apostles*.

Salam 'alaikum 'Peace be upon you', the greeting used by Muslims on all occasions.

Salat The prayers which all Muslims must perform five times a day as one of the *five pillars of Islam*. The first prayer takes place before dawn, the final one after dusk. The Salat prayers are compulsory for both men and women and for all children over the age of ten, but cannot be performed if the individual is unwashed, or unaware of what he or she is doing at the time. Each set of prayers begins with ritual washing and continues with mental preparation and a certain number of *rak'a*s performed on a prayer mat. Prayers in one's own words, for one's own purposes, may be added at the end.

salvation Man's redemption from sin and his ultimate acceptance into heaven, as well as his freedom from punishments which sin deserves, namely, death and hell. This is a central concept in Christianity, Islam, Judaism and Zoroastrianism.

Salvation Army A Protestant Christian movement founded in London in 1877 by William Booth. He wanted to convert the poor and the social outcasts who seemed to be neglected by the established denominations, and organized this new *evangelical* movement on military lines, with himself as general and other members as colonels, adjutants and corporals. Within a matter of years after its founding, the Army had gathered a large following and embarked on social work both in England and elsewhere. Wherever its missionaries went, they adopted native dress and tried to gain the confidence of the poorest members of society.

In worship, the Salvation Army has pioneered mass meetings and open-air services, most of which are accompanied by its brass bands. Members of the movement have dedicated a great deal of their energies to working with released prisoners. This accords with their belief in repentance and reform. They have built and maintained homes for needy women and children and ex-prisoners out of the money raised by appeals and through selling the Army's many

The founder of the Salvation Army, General Booth.

publications. *War Cry*, the Army's magazine is frequently sold on the streets in order to finance the movement's many charitable activities.

Salvationists have always preached against the evils of alcohol and must abstain from it absolutely, as well as from smoking. In general, the Army holds to a *Puritan* type of morality.

'Why should the Devil have all the best tunes?'

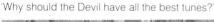

Sambhogakaya *See*: **Trikaya**.

Samkhya A school of Hindu philosophy which teaches that the world is composed of twenty-five principles. Of these, the first twenty-four are *prakriti*, the material from which material objects are made, and the twenty-fifth is purusha, the substance from which come all souls and spirits. When prakriti and purusha combine, they produce individuals. In addition the Samkha groups the prakriti into three *gunas*, forces which act upon and within the world. *See also*: **rajas, sattva, tamas**.

Samsara The world experienced as matter, thoughts and events. According to Hinduism, Buddhism and Jainism, the world, which most people experience as matter and events, actually consists of an endless cycle of arising and forming and of decay and destruction, a cycle that repeats itself over and over again through millions of aeons. Every individual follows this same pattern: birth, old age, death, rebirth. He can, however, win liberation from this cycle and from his false view of the world. The schools of Hinduism preach different ways to achieve *moksha*, or liberation from Samsara, some teaching that one should fulfil one's *caste* duty, others that one should meditate. Buddhism teaches that *enlightenment*, or liberation, depends on true insight, seeing things as they really are; this can take the form of recognizing that Samsara is really unsatisfying, impermanent and insubstantial. Jains teach that total purification leads to moksha, freedom from the cycle of Samsara.

samskaras In Hindu thought, there are sixteen samskaras, or stages, in life. If the correct observances are undertaken at each stage (such as birth) then the bad effects of *karma* can be nullified and a better rebirth sought.

sanctification *See*: **consecration**.

In an effort to achieve release from the wearisome and never-ending cycle of existence, known as Samsara, the Buddhist, Hindu and Jain seek different routes of escape. Within a temple this Jain is using a bundle of twigs to purify the statues, and is wearing a face-mask to avoid breathing in any minute form of life, since a human soul could have been reincarnated as an insect. By purification and ahimsa, non-violence, the Jain seeks to reach moksha, spiritual liberation.

sanctuary (1) (*a*) The tabernacle or tent used for worship by the ancient Hebrews during their desert wanderings. (*b*) The ancient Jewish *Temple* in Jerusalem, especially its innermost room, the *Holy of Holies*. Both the tabernacle and the Holy of Holies at some time contained the original *Ark of the Covenant*. (2) The space surrounding the altar in a Christian church, normally at the east end of the chancel. (3) Any place, such as a church, where fugitives could once ask for asylum and were granted immunity from arrest.

Sanctus A Christian hymn that is either said or sung before the prayer of *consecration* at the *Eucharist* services.

If a fugitive could reach this sanctuary knocker, he would be protected on holy ground by the church authorities.

Sanctus bell The bell which is rung during the Roman Catholic celebration of the *Mass* to draw the congregation's attention to the more solemn parts of the service, such as the *consecration* of the bread and wine.

sangat A congregation of Sikhs, especially when gathered for public worship.

Sangha The community of *bhikkhus* who followed the historical Buddha. Buddha organised them into a regular and settled community and this became the model for Buddhism. The Sangha are usually monks and nuns who uphold the Buddha's teaching – his *dharma*. The Vinaya-pitika of the *Pali Canon* is the collection of rules for these communities. The Sangha is one of the *Three Jewels* of Buddhism. In *Mahayana* groups, the term Sangha is sometimes used as a more general term for those who follow Buddhism.

Sanhedrin The supreme ruling council of Judaism consisting of seventy members, with a mixture of priests and laymen. The Sanhedrin met in Jerusalem to draw up rules for the practice of religion, and to resolve disputes, and to some extent also to judge civil and criminal cases according to Jewish Law, or *Torah*. It existed from after the time of *Judah Maccabees* until CE70, when Jerusalem and the Temple were razed to the ground by the Romans.

sannyasin A Hindu who has renounced the material world and his possessions and become an *ascetic*, giving up everything except a water pot, loincloth and alms. Through meditation and prayer he tries to achieve *moksha*, or liberation.

santi The peace which the *yogin* achieves on learning to master the body and the self by rediscovering the eternal soul within himself.

Saoshyant The saviour of the world in *Zoroastrianism*.

sat True existence or reality, as opposed to illusion, or *maya*, in Hinduism; one of the three attributes of *Brahman*, the soul of man and of the universe.

Satan The being who tempts mankind to disobey God and live a life of evil, according to Christianity, Judaism and Islam. *See*: **Lucifer, Devil**.

satori The sudden experience of *enlightenment* according to *Zen Buddhism*. To become enlightened, someone must practise and prepare, but the actual winning of enlightenment is sudden and instantaneous. Sometimes the term refers to an experience of insight that is not complete enlightenment.

Much practice and concentration are needed before the Zen Buddhist achieves sudden enlightenment. satori.

sattva One of the three *gunas*, or qualities, of the Hindu *Samkhya* system which is said to produce harmony between the other two, namely *rajas*, energy, and *tamas*, lethargy.

satyagraha Literally, 'force of the truth': the policy of non-violent but active resistance introduced into Indian politics by Mahatma *Gandhi* in 1919. Gandhi believed that this non-violent method of protest would bring India its independence from British rule, since this method alone was based on the truth about God and man. The concept was influenced by the Buddhist and Jain idea of *ahimsa* and by the moral teachings of Christianity.

From the earliest times, Christendom has seen a division between the Latin and Greek traditions. The liturgy varied, and the Byzantines grew increasingly hostile to Rome. The Crusades, which Pope Urban II hoped would unite Christendom, exacerbated the situation, and the Byzantine church almost welcomed the Turkish invasion, since the Muslims would not interfere with their liturgy or doctrine.

Saum *Also spelt* **Siyam**. The obligation upon all Muslims to fast during the month of *Ramadan*. It is one of the *five pillars of Islam*.

saviour In general, the term refers to a divine, semi-divine or human being who is believed by members of a religion to have come to earth or is expected to come to earth in the future to save believers from death, damnation, oppression and fear. Thus *Mahayaha* Buddhists believe in *bodhisattvas*, Hindus in *avatars*, Jews in the *Messiah*, Zoroastrians in the *Saoshyant* and Christians in Jesus Christ; all of these beings fulfil some or all of the functions of a saviour.

schism A division in the Christian Church. The Great Schism between the East and West occurred in 1504, when the Eastern Orthodox Church and the Roman Catholic Church split over their different interpretations of the doctrine of the *Trinity* and over their views on papal authority; the Orthodox Church refused to accept the *Pope's* demands to be recognized as supreme head of the Church.

Science and Health The textbook of the *Christian Science* movement, published in 1875 by *Mary Baker Eddy*. In the work, the authoress stresses that evil, whether sin or sickness, is really an illusion, and can be overcome through reaching God and understanding the truth of his presence. If people studied the life of Christ, she thought they would realize that goodness can banish pain and that God does not allow the enlightened to suffer.

Passages from *Science and Health* are studied at weekly meetings and healing services to this day within the Christian Science Church.

Scientology An organization founded in 1952 by L. Ron Hubbard, claiming to offer complete mental health to its adherents by releasing them from blocks which frustrate their natural powers.

scriptures The sacred writings of any religion, such as the Bible, the Qur'an, the Torah, the *Vedas* or the *Tripitaka*.

Scroll of Esther *See*: **Megillah**.

Second Adventists *See*: **Adventist**.

Second Coming The time when Christians believe Jesus Christ will return to earth in glory to judge all men, bring about the kingdom of God, and accomplish the resurrection of true believers so that they may all go to heaven.

sect A branch of a religion or group within a religion that differs from other sections or the mainstream in its practices and doctrines in certain respects, but shares the basic beliefs of the faith.

secularist Someone who rejects all forms of religion and worship and believes that public policy, particularly on education, should not give any privileged place to religious ideas or influence. Thus many secularists are opposed to the teaching of religion in schools; others prefer that pupils be taught about different religions rather than be indoctrinated in one faith.

Seder The Jewish *Passover* meal which commemorates the delivery of the Israelites from slavery in Egypt. The Seder service takes place annually in the home, on the first two nights of Passover. When the family and any guests are sitting around the table, the person conducting the service begins by breaking the three pieces of *matzah*, or unleavened bread, that are in front of him. The use of unleavened bread acts as a reminder of the haste with which the Israelites left Egypt. Next, the youngest child present asks four questions about the meaning of this meal, and in reply the father or leader recites passages from the *Torah* that retell the history of the Israelites and God's relationship with his *Chosen People*. In this way, Jewish traditions are relived and understood afresh by every Jew all over the world.

During the meal itself, each person drinks four glasses of wine to recall God's four promises to redeem Israel. In addition, *Elijah*'s cup is set on the table; this is a symbol of hospitality and a reminder that Elijah will return in the future to herald the arrival of the *Messiah*. The food served during the Seder meal is connected with the hardships and other traditions of the Israelites: bitter herbs, known as maror, charoset, symbolizing hard labour, the shank bone of the Passover lamb, a reminder of the days when it was a sacrifice to God in the *Temple* at *Jerusalem* and by every Jewish family, a roasted egg, salt water, symbolizing tears, and green vegetables.

see The centre of a bishop's diocese. The *Pope* as bishop of Rome has his see, the so-called Holy See, in the *Vatican*.

seer A wise man, or sage, who is said to possess strongly developed powers of intuition and profound moral and spiritual knowledge which helps him to foretell the future.

Sefer Torah The scrolls on which the *Torah* is written, by hand, for use in *synagogue* worship. The scrolls are of parchment and are normally covered with embroidered cloths and hung with ornaments such as crown, breastplate and bells.

These Torah rolls, richly adorned, are, from left to right, European, Indian and Persian.

Sehajdhari Sikhs who have not yet been admitted into the *Khalsa* through the initiation rite known as *khande-ka-amrit*.

Shown here in full military splendour, Haile Selassie is seen by Rastafarians as the Messiah.

Selassie, Haile (1892–1975) Emperor of Ethiopia (1930–36 and 1941–74). The *Rastafarian* religion made Haile Selassie its figurehead, since his coronation in 1930 was said to fulfill a biblical prophecy suggesting that Ethiopia would be at the centre of a movement to liberate the world from oppression. Rastafarians regard him as the *Messiah* and son of God but the believers are concerned with how to interpret his death in 1975. Many leaders of the religion argue that their saviour is not dead at all.

seminary A school for the education of young men or women who wish to become clergymen or clergywomen in their religion. Christian seminaries train people to be priests or ministers, Jewish seminaries train *rabbis*, *Sunni* Muslim seminaries train *imams*.

Sephardim The Jews who were driven out of Spain and Portugal in the fifteenth century CE and their descendants, as well as the Jews from oriental countries such as Yemen and Morocco. Sephardic theology is practically the same as that of the *Ashkenazim*, the Jews of central and eastern Europe, although there are differences in the *synagogue* services and pronunciation of biblical Hebrew.

seraphim High–ranking angels who are often represented with six wings, two above, two below and two on the sides of the head. The prophet *Isaiah* saw seraphim hovering above God's throne when he had a vision of heaven.

sermon (1) A discourse or talk preached by a religious leader to his followers, such as Christ's *Sermon on the Mount* or the Buddha's *Wheel Sermon*. (2) A speech giving instructions and explanations of the doctrines or scriptures of a religion, usually giving a service of worship. Such sermons are common to Christianity, Judaism and Islam.

Sermon on the Mount *See*: **sermon**.

service A religious ceremony, where a congregation of believers gathers together in order to worship their God or gods according to the ritual of the faith. Weddings, burials and sacrifices in any religion are all forms of service, since they follow a prescribed form of ceremonial laid down for the occasion.

Seven Precepts of the Sons of Noah Seven commandments that must be obeyed by all men and women regardless of race or religion according to Judaism: abstinence from *idolatry* or worship of images, *blasphemy*, incest, theft, murder, and eating live flesh, as well as the duty to make sure that justice is always done.

Seventh-Day Adventist *See*: **Adventist**.

shaatnez The mixing of wool and linen threads in clothing, expressly forbidden by the Jewish Law or *Torah*.

Shabouth *See*: **Weeks, Feast of**.

Shafi'ite A member of one of the four orthodox schools of law-making and legal interpretation within the *Sunni* Islamic community. Together with the Hanbalis, Malikis and Hanafis, the Shafi'ites form the *Ijma*, the consensus of the Sunni community which guides its members on law.

Shahada The first of the *Five Pillars of Islam*, this is a statement of faith in one God and Muhammad his prophet. It is also known as Ashshahada.

Shaivism The worship of the Hindu god *Shiva* as the Supreme Being. This movement is particularly strong in the south of India and includes many *ascetics*. The *lingam* is the form in which Shiva is generally worshipped, and is especially important to certain groups of Shiva worshippers known as Lingayats.

Shiva, the Destroyer in the Hindu trinity, Trimurti, delights to be worshipped under his symbol of the lingam, the phallus which promises universal creation and renewal. These Hindus have gathered before the garlanded lingam to honour the god.

Shakti The powerful or active side of the Hindu god Shiva, often portrayed as his consort or female aspect. In the Shakti cults, the consort is usually seen as being *Durga* or *Kali* rather than *Parvati*: the cults give their devotion to her, because she is active, whereas the male figure of Shiva sits still in meditation. Shiva and Shakti are often shown locked in sexual embrace, symbolizing the ultimate union of *moksha* and *Samsara*, or the going beyond the distinction between liberation and the ordinary world. Later followers of the 'left-hand' Shakti cults imitated this by using strictly controlled ritual sex, as well as drinking wine and eating meat, practices usually abhorred by Hindus.

Shakyamuni Literally, 'the sage of the Shakyas': a title of the historical Buddha, *Gautama* Siddhartha.

shaman In some so-called primitive religions, especially in north Asia, the shaman is a person who combines the roles of priest, wise man and magician. Followers believe he is able, by means of trances, frequently induced by hallucinogenic drugs or wild dancing, to communicate with the gods and act as a guide and messenger between the divine and human worlds. Shamans are often believed to become possessed by the spirit of a god, and to speak as the mouthpiece of that god.

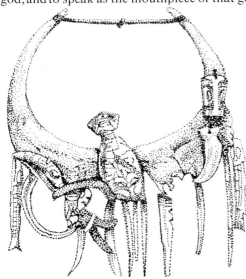

This necklace of hide and bone has magical properties and belongs to an Eskimo shaman.

Shankara A Hindu philosopher of the ninth century CE who wrote commentaries on the Brahma *Sutra* and the *Bhagavad Gita* as well as hymns and discourses on spiritual themes. Shankara developed the *advaita Vedanta* school of Hindu philosophy, which teaches that man's ideas about the reality of the world are distorted because of *maya*, or illusion. Only the insight which comes from mystical awareness can liberate man from his illusion-based existence. The liberated soul realizes that it is and always has been Brahman, God, the Absolute, the only reality, which is identical with every soul. Its qualities are *sat, chit*, anand: true being, consciousness and bliss.

Shari'a The sacred law of Islam, which is held to be based on divine revelation. The laws of the Shari'a are drawn from the Qur'an, the *sunna*, or the example of Muhammad's life and his sayings as recorded in the *Hadith*, the *Ijma*, or the consensus of the Muslim community, and *Quiyas*, which are parallels derived by looking at the first three sources. The Shari'a is not a static code, for it has evolved over the centuries to meet the challenges of a changing world, and to accommodate civil law and legislation. Saudi Arabia, Iran and Pakistan, however, are now the only major countries whose laws are almost wholly derived from the rulings of the Shari'a, for most other Islamic states have confined their use of the Shari'a to the sphere of family law, and have allowed their governments to break away from tradition when dealing with criminal, economic and civil matters.

Shatarupa In Hindu mythology, the first woman.

Shavouth *or* **Shabouth** *See*: **Weeks, Feast of.**

shechitah The ritual killing of animals for food, performed by a certified butcher in keeping with the Jewish dietary laws of *Kashrut*. The butcher must cut the animal's throat with a single stroke and ensure that all the blood drains from the meat.

Sheikh Also spelled sheik. An Arab title of respect given to chiefs and headmen, as well as to preachers and heads of *Sufi* orders and communities.

sheitel A wig which is worn by Orthodox married Jewish women, in order to obey the rabbinical rule which says that a woman must not leave her hair uncovered in the sight of any man who is not her husband.

Shekinah In Judaism, the presence of God on earth or a visible sign of his presence. The Shekinah usually takes the form of a bright cloud or a fire, sometimes with accompanying thunder and lightning. In Kabbalistic belief, the Shekinah and the *En Sof* were originally in harmony, which was disrupted by the coming of sin: when the *Messiah* comes, the two will be reunited.

Shema The Jewish prayer, also known as Shema Yisrael, beginning 'Hear O Israel, the Lord your God, the Lord is One: you shall love the Lord your God. . .' It is said in the morning and in the evening in both the synagogue and the Jewish home. Composed of extracts from the *Torah*, the Shema affirms that the Jews are the *Chosen People* of God and will act as witnesses to the splendour and power of the one true God.

Shemini Atzereth A Jewish festival, celebrated on the eighth day of *Sukkoth* and consisting of a service for the dead and prayers for rain.

Sheol In the Jewish scriptures, the underworld where the dead sleep. Often translated as 'hell'.

Shi'a *See*: **Shi'ites**.

Shi'ites Muslims who belong to the *Shi'a*, a sect within Islam, the minority groups whose separation from the majority or *Sunni* party goes back to the seventh-century CE split between the followers of *Ali* and *Husain*. Shi'ites claim that the caliphate was intended by Muhammad to remain within the family of Ali, his son-in-law, and that to gain power the Sunnis had murdered Ali's true successor, Husain, at the battle of Karbala in Iraq in CE680. Shi'ites therefore celebrate Husain's death on the tenth day of Muharram as a day of mourning for the true caliph and of vengeance on his Sunni murderers. They venerate Ali's successors as the true Muslim caliphs and call them the *imams*.

Shi'ites go on to say that at some stage the earthly Imamate came to an end, as the last imam was hidden by God somewhere, to reappear at the end of the world as the *Mahdi*, when evil will be conquered and faithful Shi'ites will receive their just rewards for being true Muslims. This hidden imam guides his followers from day to day through their spiritual leader, who is also known as an imam; he is the mouthpiece of the hidden imam.

The Shi'ites are strongest in Iran and the Yemen; their minority status and persecution by Sunnis have made them emphasize martyrdom and suffering as valuable paths to God.

Shin Buddhism The True Pure Land school of Japanese Buddhism. *See*: **Pure Land Buddhism**.

Shingon The school of *Vajrayana* Buddhism founded in Japan. It emphasizes reciting *mantras*, rituals and the practice of meditation, especially with the aid of *mandalas*.

Shinran (1173–1262) Also known as Shinran Shonin, or Shinran the Saint. The founder of the Jodo Shin Shu or True Pure Land School of Japanese Buddhism. As a young man Shinran became a *bhikshu*, or Buddhist monk, and began to study and practise Buddhism. Despite his efforts over several years and the assistance of teachers, he felt he was no closer to *enlightenment*. Then he met *Honen*, who initiated him into reciting the *mantra* of the Buddha *Amida*, the Infinite. This was the path Shinran had been seeking. He renounced his bhikshu's vows and started to teach the way of devotion to Amida, preaching to the common people of Japan. In 1225 he founded the True Pure Land School. *See also*: **Pure Land Buddhism**.

A priest of Shingon, the Japanese school of Vajrayana Buddhism.

A magnetic and anachronistic sight, these Shinto priests *(left)* are bearing a shrine through the streets of modern Japan.

The entrance to a Shinto shrine is signalled by a large symbolic gate. These torii *(below)* can be found singly or in a colonnade, as here.

Shinto The general name under which a broad spectrum of Japanese religious belief and practice is gathered and, historically speaking, the national state religion of Japan. Today Shinto no longer has a place in state education and worship is very much a personal affair, with the *shrine* and prayer at the centre of religious life. However, until the end of the last war, the Japanese Imperial Family was inevitably linked with the Shinto religion, with the emperor considered to be a deity, descended from the sun god. For this reason, Shinto has always been considered a nationalistic religion. Two of Japan's oldest literary creations – the *Kojiki* and the *Nihongi* – which mix history and legend to describe the foundations of Japanese society, are essential to the Shinto faith.

The foundations of Shinto belief maintain that a primal and supernatural force, the *Kami*, resides in all that lives, and all that is natural. Thus, all crimes against the earth strike at the heart of the force of life. Whilst the organized religious life of Shinto may have declined since Japan's defeat in the last war, the importance of Shinto in contemporary Japan should not be under-estimated. Ideas from Shinto are often combined with those of Buddhism in the religious ideas and practice of the ordinary Japanese believer. Prayer and the local shrine still remain of central importance to many Japanese families. *See also*: **Izanami, Izanagi**.

shirk The worst sin which a Muslim can commit, namely, to put anything on the same level as Allah, the supreme and only God.

Shiva Also spelled *Siva*. The Hindu god of life, death and rebirth. Shiva is an expression of the force which underlies both destruction and creation. Shiva is the object of a large following in India, whose members are called Shaivites and regard him as Mahadev, the 'great God'.

Shiva is traditionally symbolized by a *lingam*, or erect phallus, and often represented as having four hands, three eyes and a garland of skulls around his neck. His weapons include the bow, the axe, the thunderbolt and the trident. His consort, or wife, is called *Mahadevi*, the female principle and earth mother.

Shiva Ratri The main festival of *Shiva*, which is very popular in southern India.

shofar A ram's horn used by the ancient Israelites to sound orders during battle and to announce religious occasions. Nowadays the shofar is blown as a call to repentance during Jewish services at *Rosh Hashanah* and *Yom Kippur*.

shraddha The word used in Buddhism for faith in the purpose and effectiveness of Buddhism as a way to achieve *enlightenment* and *Nirvana*.

Shri A title of *Lakshmi*. More generally used by Hindus as a term of respect.

shrine Any structure or building which holds the remains or relics of a saint or holy person or is dedicated to a god or God. Some shrines are merely wayside altars, while others are large and sumptuously decorated. Shrines are visited by pilgrims and sometimes act as the focus for worship: for example, Muslims all turn towards Mecca during their daily prayers, since the *Ka'ba*, which holds the *Black Stone*, is the most sacred shrine of Islam.

shroud A cloth or sheet, nowadays usually white or off-white in colour, in which a corpse is wrapped before burial. *See also*: **Turin Shroud**.

Shrove Tuesday The last day before the Christian season of Lent. Formerly on this day, Roman Catholics were 'shriven', or absolved, from their sins by a priest. The day was characterized in medieval times by merry-making and feasting in preparation for the fasting ahead. This tradition has remained in English-speaking countries in the form of 'pancake day', since pancakes helped to use up the last of the eggs and milk which, as animal products, used to be forbidden during Lent. Although fasting is no longer required, many voluntarily deny themselves something in Lent, so this is their last day of self-indulgence. The French equivalent is *Mardi Gras*, and other Catholic countries celebrate Carnival at this time.

shruti Literally, 'hearing'. In Hinduism, shruti consists of the oldest scriptures, the *Vedas*, the eternal wisdom that was 'heard' by, or revealed to, the *Rishis*, or ancient sages. *See also*: **smriti**.

shudras The peasants and servants, the lowest of the main *caste* groups in the Hindu caste system. According to tradition, they were originally created from the feet of Purusha, the original man.

shul The *Yiddish* for synagogue.

Shulchan Aruch A book written by *Joseph Karo* that sets out how to live a Jewish life in accordance with God's teachings and blessings. The *Shulchan Aruch*, was essentially a simple summary of the Talmud, in which non-specialists as well as scholars could consult a reliable authority in their daily lives.

siddur A Jewish prayer book which contains the daily prayers, but not those which are used on holy days and festivals.

Sikhism A *monotheistic* religion founded in the Indian Punjab in the late fifteenth and early sixteenth centuries CE by *Nanak*. Nanak was a follower of the Hindu *bhakti* movement, who was also influenced by Islamic *Sufi* mysticism and by the mystical poet *Kabir*. He had a religious experience at the age of thirty which led him to become a wandering teacher and leader or *guru* of a group of like-minded disciples – the first Sikhs. He believed that both Hinduism and Islam contained something of the truth about God, but that the one truth which both were trying to express was concealed by the rituals and traditional customs of both religions. Like the Muslims, he believed in one God whom he called 'Sat Nam', the 'True Name', but thought that this God was to be discovered by looking inwards into one's heart, and by meditating on this True Name in loving devotion, not by eternal practices and ceremonies. From Hinduism he retained a belief in reincarnation, *karma* and *moksha*, or *mukti*, but he rejected all notions of *caste*, insisting that all his disciples ate together as equals, and frowned on pilgrimages, idols, fixed ritual prayers and ceremonial washing.

Before Nanak died, he appointed one of his followers to become guru of the Sikh community and so a line of gurus was instituted, each of whom contributed something to the development and consolidation of the Sikh religion. Guru *Amar Das* collected Nanak's poems and hymns together with some of Habir's and those of other Hindu and Muslim poets and thus began the formation of the Sikh sacred scripture, the *Guru Granth Sahib*. Guru *Arjan Dev* built the *Harmandir*, or Golden Temple, at *Amritsar* which became a centre of pilgrimage, contrary to Guru Nanak's ideas. Guru *Gobind Singh* instituted the brotherhood of the *Khalsa* with the amrit ceremony (*khande-ka-amrit*) to give Sikhs the chance to commit themselves more fully to their faith. He also bound members of the Khalsa to wear distinctive marks of a full Sikh, the *Five Ks*. He declared finally that after him there would be no more human gurus, but

(opposite) A rare view of the magnificent interior of the Golden Temple at Amritsar.

As well as their cartridge belts, these Sikhs *(below)* are dressed in the Five Ks, the distinctive style of the Sikh brotherhood, the Khalsa. The kara, a steel bracelet, is visible on the wrists of three of these men.

that the eleventh and final guru would be the holy book, the Guru Granth Sahib.

Sikhs believe that the spirit of Guru Nanak was passed down through the ten human gurus and lives on in the Guru Granth Sahib and in the Khalsa; they thus revere the book greatly and frequently gather as the *sangat*, or congregation, to hear it read. They have no special weekly holy day, but adopt the day most frequently left free in whichever country they live in for their *Diwan* or service. Their temple, or *gurdwara*, is essentially a house for the Guru Granth Sahib and a place of refreshment and hospitality for Sikhs and visitors; each gurdwara has a *langar*, or kitchen, where all may eat together as equals. Sikhs keep some festivals of Hindu origin, like *Divali* and *Holi Mohalla*, but now celebrate Gurpurbs in honour of the ten gurus, when an *Akand Path* is performed. They rise early each day to recite the *Japji*, a prayer by Guru Nanak, and pray again in the evening with the Sohilla prayer. They should not smoke or drink but should perform seva, loving service, for their fellow-men, in order to hasten their final union with God.

Simchat Torah *or* **Simhath Torah** *See*: **Rejoicing of the Law**.

sin Disobedience to the revealed will of God or the gods. *Monotheistic* and *polytheistic* religions have drawn up lists of actions which are seen as good, because they are approved by God or the gods, others which are condemned for being bad, because they are disapproved of by God or the gods. Anyone who fails to act according to these values is said to be a sinner, a person who has not observed the moral code of his or her religion.

Sinai, Mount *See*: **Mount Sinai**.

Sita The wife of *Rama*, an *avatar* of *Vishnu*. Sita features in the epic *Ramayana*, in which she is abducted by *Ravana*, the demon king of Lanka; she is freed by Rama, and rules at his side in triumph and justice. When Sita returns from her abduction, she is tested by Rama, who wishes to demonstrate that she remained faithful during her capture. She throws herself on a funeral pyre, but is unharmed; because of this, the word '*suttee*' is derived from her name.

Siva Another spelling of *Shiva*.

Siyam *See*: **Saum**.

skandhas A Buddhist term for the five elements which people mistake for self or 'I'. They are: (*a*) form = body (*b*) feelings (*c*) perception (*d*) mental phenomena (sankharas) (*e*) thought.

Smith, Joseph (1805–44) The founder of the Mormon Church. Born in Vermont in the United States, Joseph Smith began to have visions at the age of fifteen and, in 1827, he announced that with the guidance of the angel Moroni, who had appeared to him, he had discovered an entirely new set of scriptures written in a hitherto unknown language.

He proceeded to translate these scriptures and in 1830 published them under the title of the *Book of Mormon*. The Mormon Church was founded in the same year, with Smith as its president.

smriti Literally, 'memory', they are the Hindu scriptures which, in theory, rank below the *shruti* because they were not given to man by divine revelation, but only 'remembered' by human tradition. Smriti includes the *Ramayana and Mahabharata*; the latter also includes the very influential *Bhagavad Gita*.

Sita in the midst of the flames. She survives unhurt, protected by her purity, which had been put in doubt by her husband, Rama. In another story, she dies and Rama, distraught, carries her remains through India.

socialism A political theory which states that all members of society should jointly own, develop, produce and distribute its goods and land. Socialism rejects the idea that private individuals have the right to derive private gain from the legacy which belongs to everyone and therefore is in favour of nationalization, public owner-ship and equality of wealth and opportunity.

Society of Friends A Christian Protestant denomination founded in the mid-seventeenth century by George Fox, who wanted his followers to return to what he considered was the simple lifestyle and faith of the early Christians. He called his following the Society of Friends since he wanted them to be friends of Christ and of each other. They were dubbed 'Quakers' by a judge who, at Fox's trial in 1650, was told by Fox to 'Tremble at the voice of the Lord'. This title, although intended as an insult, was taken up by the Friends as an honour; it symbolized their submission and devotion to God.

An early engraving of a meeting of Quakers, showing the simplicity of their worship, but also their need for secrecy.

The Quakers have no priests, as they believe that God has given each man an 'inner light' which is the voice of God the *Holy Spirit* in the soul. Each man, therefore, is guided individually by God in life and in his worship, and needs no external guide. Their places of worship are known as meeting-houses, and are plain rooms with benches; the Sunday morning 'meeting for worship' is an hour of silence, broken only by the voices of those who believe the inner light has moved them to speak. These people may read from the Bible or any other book; they may pray or give a sermon to the rest of the congregation in total freedom.

There are no formal creeds or statements of doctrine in Quakerism; no sacraments are celebrated, and swearing and oath-taking are strictly forbidden. Quakers are allowed to affirm in courts of law rather than take the oath. They are complete pacifists, actively working for peace and relieving suffering; their work for the abolition of slavery, for prison reform and social justice in general is well known.

The Society is governed by a hierarchy of 'meeting' groups of Quakers who approve new members and appoint people to look after the affairs of the community. The ultimate authority in each country is the 'yearly meeting': no votes are ever taken: the clerk simply records what he feels is the 'sense' of the meeting, and this is approved by all.

The Quaker movement has spread to the Low Countries and Scandinavia, to Australia and Japan, and above all, to the United States, where William Penn founded the colony of Pennsylvania, a 'holy experiment' in Quaker living.

Society of Jesus *See*: Jesuits.

soma The fermented juice of a plant, offered to the gods in ancient India, which is personified as a deity.

Soto The oldest school of *Zen Buddhism*, brought to Japan from China by *Dogen* in 1227. Now the largest Zen school there, it stresses the constant practice of mindfulness, awareness and ethics.

soul Many religions teach that man is composed of a physical body, which does not survive death, and an eternal, invisible core which is the true self or soul. According to Christianity, Islam and Judaism, each soul will be judged at the end of the world on the basis of the individual's actions during this life on earth: it is the soul which will determine whether the individual is punished by hell or rewarded by eternal life in heaven, where it will be reunited with a transformed body. Buddhism teaches that there is no such thing as a soul or true, permanent self.

177

spell A word, phrase or formula which is believed to have magical powers. Spells may be intended for both good and evil purposes and are sometimes linked to various occult rituals. *See also*: **magic, Voodoo.**

spirit (1) See *soul*. The spirit of an individual person. (2) Any non-physical, non-material being, whether created or uncreated, good or evil. Some religions, such as Zoroastrianism, seem to worship uncreated spirits as well as their gods. Others, such as Christianity, Judaism and Islam, believe that all spirits are created by God. Good spirits, known as angels, are venerated in these last three religions, and Muslims also believe in lesser spirits, or djinns, which can affect mankind for good or ill. Jews and Christians traditionally believe also in evil spirits who carry out the will of the *Devil*, causing people to perform evil actions or to fall physically or mentally ill.

spiritual growth The developing and encouraging of the non-material side of one's nature. People who wish to lead moral lives, and achieve some understanding of the purpose of existence and man's place in the world, refuse to be tied to their bodily needs and desires and attempt to come closer to their own understanding of God and holiness.

spiritualism Any form of religious practice that attempts to communicate with the spirits of those who have died, usually by employing intermediaries known as *mediums*, to contact and speak with the dead. The Spiritualist churches developed in the nineteenth century and are now found throughout America and Europe.

Mediums use a variety of methods for contacting the dead, ranging from attempting to make the spirits materialize to receiving messages from them via the so-called 'ouija' board or through automatic writing. Most mediums have someone known as a 'guide' on the 'other side', and through this guide, while they themselves are in a trance, pass messages to and from those who contact them in our world. Mediums also give healing sessions to individuals and groups and emphasize that their power comes from God and not themselves.

sruti That which is heard. In Hinduism, the term sruti refers to the oldest scriptures, the *Vedas* and some of the *Upanishads*, which are believed to have been given to man through divine revelation. *See also*: **smriti.**

Ssu-ming-shen Also known as Tsao-shen, the Chinese Kitchen God, who is believed to return

When the time comes for the annual report to be made to heaven, Ssu-ming-shen, the Chinese Kitchen God, is given a sticky rice cake to make speech impossible, or is given sweetmeats to ensure a good report.

to heaven once a year at New Year to report on the conduct of the members of a household. The statue of Ssu-ming-shen has its face smeared with sweet things at this time so that the report will be favourable.

Star of David A six-pointed star, one of the best-known symbols of Judaism. In Hebrew it is called the 'magen David'.

Stations of the Cross (1) Fourteen pictures or other representations of scenes from Christ's journey to *Calvary* and his death, placed on the walls of most Roman Catholic Churches. (2) A popular devotional practice among Catholics, performed especially during *Lent* and *Holy Week*. Worshippers make their way from one picture to the next, kneeling at each scene and reciting appropriate prayers. This devotion is at the heart of the Good Friday service.

statue A three-dimensional figure. Religious statues usually represent a sacred being and are commonly used as a means of focusing devotion, reverence or prayer. The practice of making such figures is observed throughout the world in many religions, including Hinduism, Buddhism, non-Protestant Christianity and a wide-range of tribal religions. Jews, Muslims and most Protestants, however, reject the use of statues, as they believe that images encourage idolatry, or worship of the image itself.

Sthanakavasi A branch of the Jain *Svetambaras* who reject any form of image-worship, with the teachings of *Mahavira*, the founder of Jainism. This movement arose in the early eighteenth century CE as a result of Islamic influence on the Jain community; its members are known as 'dwellers in halls' because of the simple buildings or 'athanakas' where they hold their meetings.

sticharion A tunic, usually made of coloured silk or linen, worn by Eastern Orthodox deacons, priests and bishops. It corresponds to the alb in the Roman Catholic and Anglican Churches.

stupa A Buddhist cairn or memorial mound, often containing a relic or marking a sacred place. Stupas are common landmarks in Buddhist countries and appear in different styles.

The eyes of a Buddha, painted on all four sides of the summit of this stupa *(above)* at Bodnath, in Nepal, look out to all the corners of the earth. The gaily coloured strips of cloth are not streamers, but prayer flags.

Scenes from the Buddha's life *(below)* are carved on a gateway at the principal stupa at Sanchi.

succah *See*: **sukkah**.

Succoth *See*: **Booths, Feast of**.

Sufism An Islamic mystical movement that believes that the individual will find salvation through personal union with *Allah* and emphasizes the need for *asceticism* in everyday life. The Sufis first arose in the eighth century CE. Sometimes their views have differed considerably from the mainstream Islamic view; some, for example, taught that religious creeds are unimportant, that good and evil are unrealities, that there is no such thing as free will, and that ecstatic union with Allah is possible in this life. Much Sufi teaching and devotion is expressed in poetry of great emotional depth and intensity. *See also*: **dervish**.

Sukhavati Literally, 'the happy land': the pure land or realm created by the ideal, symbolic Buddha *Amitabha*. He was able to create Sukhavati by means of his supernormal powers and the energy of all his accumulated, skilful, good deeds, according to *Mahayana Buddhism*. Many Buddhists, especially followers of *Pure Land Buddhism*, believe that Sukhavati provides a perfect environment in which a person can gain *enlightenment*.

With the growth of Sufism within Islam came the need for Sufis to have some special building in which to live and study. The madrasas, or theological colleges, suggested themselves as suitable. The Madrasat at-Firdaws at Aleppo, shown here, is known to have had an endowed foundation for Sufis attached to it.

Celebrating Id-ul-Fitr *(below)* outside a Sufi shrine.

To re-experience their period in the wilderness, Jews yearly build a temporary structure, known as a sukkah, for the autumn festival of Sukkoth. Roofed only with branches, this flimsy shelter is, nevertheless, richly decorated for the duration of the feast.

sukkah Literally, 'a tent' or 'booth': a temporary structure, frequently made of boards and canvas and roofed with pine branches, which Jews build in or near their homes and synagogues during the Feast of Booths. The sukkah is usually used as a dining-and prayer-room during the festival, and symbolizes the tents in which the Hebrews lived during their desert wanderings after the *Exodus* from Egypt.

Sukkoth *See*: **Booths, Feast of**.

Sun Myung Moon *See*: **Unification Church**.

sunna The practice of the Muslim faith as carried out by the *Sunnis*.

Sunnis The name derived from the Arabic 'Sunnat', 'tradition', given to the majority party within Islam since the *Shi'ite* sect broke away in the late seventh century CE. Ninety per cent of Muslims belong to this party. They call themselves Sunnis because they hold that they, and not the Shi'ites, keep to the true practice, or *sunna*, of the faith laid down by Muhammad and recorded in the collections of sayings known as *Hadith*. (Shi'ites and Sunnis have differing traditions of Hadith.) The Sunnis believe that the *caliphate*, or leadership, of the religion after Muhammad should remain within the tribe from which Muhammad himself came – the Quraiph; and they hold that after the four *Rashidun* or Rightly Guided Caliphs *Abu Bakr*,

'Umar, *'Uthman* and *Ali*, the caliphate rightly passed to the *Ummayyad* and then the Abbasid dynasties and then on down to the Ottoman caliphate, which was finally abolished by the Turkish ruler Ataturk in 1923. They believe that guidance on doctrine and practice must come from the Qur'an, Hadith and *Shari'a* as interpreted by the *Ulama'* or body of scholars, not from any human authority, and here they differ from the Shi'ites, who look to their *imam* or spiritual leader for divine guidance in day-to-day Islamic living. In Sunni Islam the imam is simply an educated layman who teaches the faith and leads public prayers in the mosque.

supernatural The realm which is beyond ordinary natural human knowledge and whose presence and effects cannot be explained by the laws of science: hence it includes the spiritual world, God, the miraculous, psychic phenomena and the effects of all these on human existence.

superstition A non-rational belief or practice founded on ignorance, tradition or fear, especially of the unknown. The superstitious idea of good or bad 'luck' is often closely linked to ritual practices. In modern Western civilization, superstitions tend to be isolated beliefs divorced from any system of religion, for example, the superstitious belief that Friday the thirteenth is a day of bad luck.

Supreme Being Another term for God or the most important god within a *pantheon*.

surah Any of the 114 chapters of the Qur'an, the sacred scripture of Islam.

Surya In Hindu mythology, the Sun, an important deity in the *Vedas*.

sutra In Hinduism, this is a general term for the sayings or aphorisms which are used to guide people towards living a good moral and spiritual life. In Buddhism, sutras are discourses or talks traditionally attributed to the Buddha, such as the *Lotus Sutra*.

Now outlawed, the practice of suttee may still be found in remote country areas.

suttee A former practice among high-*caste* Hindus, illegal since 1829, by which the widow of a man whose body was being cremated would fling herself on the funeral pyre in order to show her love for him by dying in the flames. *See:* Sita.

Svetambaras The so-called 'white-clad' Jains, who emerged from the split which happened around CE80 and divided the Jain movement into distinct sects: The Svetambaras and the *Digambaras*.

Masked to prevent themselves inhaling any tiny living creature, Jains also brush the ground before them, to avoid stepping on even an ant. This belief in non-violence, or ahimsa, was adopted by Gandhi.

The Svetambaras recognize eighty-four works as scripture, passed by oral tradition since the death of *Mahavira*, the founder of Jainism. They are mainly concentrated in Gujarat and Rajasthan and are distinguished from the Digambaras in their rejection of nudity, wearing instead a white loincloth.

swami A title of honour which is given to respected Hindu religious teachers.

synagogue A Jewish building used for worship and religious instruction. When the ancient Jews were exiled to Babylon they obviously could not attend the *Temple* in *Jerusalem*, and began to form synagogues. They gathered together wherever they could praise and pray to God. After the restoration of the Temple, synagogues continued to be built for prayer. With the passing of time, synagogues were also used as courts of law and as schools. The services, which were less formal than in the Temple, were conducted by the chazzan, or reader, since the synagogues had no priests. The sacrifices of the Temple were replaced by readings from the *Torah* and Prophets and by sermons.

Synagogues today contain an ornamental cupboard called the *ark*, which holds the scrolls of the Torah and is set in the wall that faces towards Jerusalem. There is a raised platform, or *bimah*, from which the reader conducts the service. In front of the Ark is the *ner tamid*, or everlasting lamp, and a *menorah*, or seven-branched candlestick. Above the ark there are usually two tablets inscribed with the *Ten Commandments*. The *Star of David* is a common ornament. Men and women do not sit together in Orthodox synagogues and worshippers keep their heads covered as a sign of respect.

A simple and very ancient synagogue in Pekiin.

syncretism The combining of beliefs from different systems of religious thought and practice. Thus, when Buddhist teachings spread into Japan, *Shinto*, the national religion, took over many of the Buddhas and *bodhisattvas*, changed their names, and made them Shinto gods. Some contemporary movements such as the *Unification Church* and the Divine Light mission have also taken elements from Eastern philosophies and blended them with Christian traditions and their own theories on the nature of God and man. Christianity itself adapted elements from earlier religions: for example, the worship of the *Virgin Mary* was strongly influenced by cults of the Mother Goddess around the eastern Mediterranean.

t

Tabernacles, Feast of *See*: **Booths**.
Tablets of the Law *See*: **Torah**.

taboo Things, places, acts or persons which must be avoided for fear of bad luck, misfortune, punishment or death. Mankind has always surrounded things which are dangerous with taboos, many of which survive to this day, even though the reasons why they first arose have been forgotten.

Religious prohibitions, such as the sanitary and dietary laws in the Jewish Torah, are based on the need not to defile God's creation, the body, by exposing it to infection. For Muslims, the Qur'an also contains a vast body of regulations that deal with eating, cleanliness, marriage, birth and death; they are to be followed strictly for fear of divine punishment.

Tabor A mountain in Israel (Palestine), the traditional scene of the *transfiguration* of Christ.

tabot The Ark in an *Ethiopian Orthodox Church*. *See also*: **Ark of the Covenant**.

takht (1) A centre of authority on Sikh doctrine. There are four takhts, to be found at *Amritsar* (the Akal Takht), Patna Sahib, Anandpur (the Keshgar gurdwara) and Nanded (the Hazur Sahib). Each takht has its own reader or *granthi*. Together with the granthi of the *Golden Temple* at Amritsar, the takhts help the Sikh community interpret its scripture, the *Guru Granth Sahib*, whenever problems in understanding it arise. This is necessary since Sikhism has no supreme religious leader other than the Guru Granth Sahib. (2) The platform on which the Guru Granth Sahib is placed in the *gurdwara*. On it sits the granthi, or reader, and it is high enough to ensure that the holy book is above the heads of the congregation seated on the floor around it on three sides.

tallith A four-cornered Jewish prayer shawl, usually made of white wool, with black or purple stripes crossing it and eight-stringed fringes at each corner. The top of the shawl is decorated with an ornamental fringe of silver or gold thread called the 'atarah'. Jewish men wear the tallith during morning prayers at home or at the *synagogue*.

tallith katan A fringed undervest, normally made of cotton or wool, which Jewish men wear to remind themselves of God's commandments. The fringes on this garment irritate the skin and constantly make the wearer conscious of his duty to God.

Talmud A collection of rabbinical teachings compiled between the destruction of Jerusalem (CE70) and the end of the fifth century. It is regarded as the highest legal authority in Judaism after the five original books of the *Torah*. The first part of the Talmud is the *Mishnah*; the second, longer, part is the *Gemara*, or completion of the Mishnah.

The Talmud consists of interpretations of scripture, rules of hygiene and diet, legal decisions, and regulations for synagogue services. It also includes sermons, folklore and legends, and sets out how faithful Jews should lead their lives both in the family and in the world.

tamas Dullness and lifelessness; one of the three *gunas* in the Hindu *Samkhya* system. Matter, or the natural world, is made up of the three gunas, or qualities: they bond together and give form and characteristics to the material world around, including our physical and emotional selves. Thus, if someone feels listless and lethargic, tamas is uppermost in him.

tanha Literally, 'thirst': craving and greed, or strong desire for things that do not actually satisfy or are not actually necessary. According to Buddhism, tanha is the root cause of suffering and the second of the *Four Noble Truths*. If tanha is overcome, it is believed that *enlightenment* is achieved.

Tannaim A group of Jewish scholars who were active in Palestine in the first and second centuries CE, whose teachings on Jewish law and traditions have been incorporated into the *Mishrah*.

Tantra (1) Any of numerous Hindu religious books that are partly derived from the *Puranas*. Tantras usually consist of dialogues between *Shiva* and his female counterpart, *Shakti* (usually Durga or Kali). Like the Puranas, the Tantras deal with the creation and destruction of the world, with worship of the divine and with union between the worshipper and the *absolute*. The mystical and magical elements in the Tantras have been incorporated into Tantric Hinduism, or Tantrism. This branch of Hinduism uses meditation, *mantras* and *kundalini* to win *moksha*, or liberation. (2) Any of numerous texts of *Vajrayana* or Tantric Buddhism com-piled between the fifth and tenth centuries. In esoteric language they describe methods for gaining *enlightenment*.

Tantric Buddhism *See*: **Tantrism**.

Tantrism Tantric Hinduism, based on the *Tantras*, is closely associated with *Shakti* worship. It is linked with various esoteric practices which imitate the sexual union of *Shiva* and *Shakti* (*Kali*, *Mahadevi*). Tantric Buddhism flowered in the sixth century in Tibet. The movement aimed to help individuals master themselves so that they could achieve union with the cosmos and the divine. In order to get to this stage of development, followers of the movement studied under *gurus*, learning *yoga* in order to control the body and *mandalas* (symbolic diagrams) and *mantras* (words and phrases believed to have magical powers) to help themselves meditate and achieve a link with the gods and goddesses who inhabit the universe. Once the believer had managed to experience the power of the deities, this same power would then pass to that person from the gods.

Tantrism believes that the universe is divided between male and female forces, who hold it together by blending with one another. Some Tantric monks practised ritual sexual intercourse in order to become one with the structure of the universe and to absorb its strength and magical properties.

Tao *See*: **Taoism**.

Taoism Arguably, the oldest religion of China. The roots of Taoism lie in the early Shamanistic history of China c.2000BCE. It was first expounded as a religious philosophy around 500BCE. The main text of Taoism is the *Tao Te Ching*, or *Book of the Way*, attributed to a legendary figure, Lao Tzu.

The term 'Taoism' comes from the key word – Tao – which is usually translated as *The Way*. It is seen as the primal force of the universe, present in all things and yet greater than all things.

The early Taoists (c.500BCE to CE100) were ascetics and hermits, largely concerned with the philosophy of Tao and with retreat from the falsehood and disruption of life. *Chuang Tzu* – the second most important Taoist text – reflects this. This style of Taoism is called Tao Chia – translated as the School of Tao.

From the second century CE, another aspect of Taoism developed – Tao chiao – Taoist religion. This is the magic, ritualistic Taoism of the people, which is still strong today. Its origins

These Taoist priests *(above)* are assembled around a table, at the head of which is the chief priest, seated on a throne decorated with the lotus motif.

The doorway *(left)* is surrounded by prayers to the door gods to ward off ill and bless those inside.

are traced to Chang Tao-ling (*c*.106–7CE) who founded a Taoist 'church'. Through his descendents – known as the Heavenly Masters – the Tao chiao grew. Other teachers developed this aspect of Taoism. It is greatly concerned with control of the forces of yin and yang which are within each person, each place and all things. Alchemy, longevity and immortality figure amongst its concerns. Over the centuries, Taoism, Buddhism and Confucianism have emerged at a popular level to create the tapestry of present Chinese religion.

tarot cards A pack of cards used in divination and fortune-telling that is decorated with various symbolic designs and arranged in four suits of fourteen cards, showing natural elements, and twenty-two trumps, showing the signs of the zodiac and the planets. The cards are said to derive from ancient sources, but can be traced in their present form only as far back as fourteenth-century Italy.

185

Tara A *bodhisattva* in Tibetan Buddhism, the female counterpart of *Avalokitesvara*. She is particularly important in *Tantric* Buddhism.

Tat Tvam Asi 'That thou art' in Sanskrit. A basic concept in Hinduism, found in the *Vedas*, which reminds the individual of his or her identity with the universal soul or *atman*.

Tawhid 'Making one', 'asserting oneness', the unity of God, a fundamental principle of Islam.

tefillin Two black leather boxes, also known as *phylacteries*, containing tiny scrolls from the *Torah* which Jewish men strap to their left arms in line with the heart, and to their foreheads, near the mind, during weekday morning services. Wearing the tefillin is a response to and a reminder of the commandment of God in the Book of Deuteronomy of the *Hebrew Bible*, to 'bind the words of God between your eyes and upon your arm'. They are not worn on the *Sabbath* since that day, unlike working days, is devoted to nothing other than the service of God.

Tegh Bahadur The ninth *Sikh* guru, who was executed in 1675 for urging the Sikhs not to lose their faith in the face of Hindu persecution and oppression.

teleology A branch of philosophy that deals with ends or final causes, especially in relation to the evidence of design or purpose in nature.

In theology, the so-called 'teleological argument' states that the universe is not simply a haphazard collection of events and reactions, but shows signs of having been designed in a specific way and for a specific purpose; the presence of such a design means that there must be a God who designed it. Teleology is opposed to the idea that just a series of mechanical laws or the forces of nature govern life. Instead, the teleological view is that even if mechanical laws do control the processes of life, these same laws have been determined in advance by God.

Temple of Jerusalem The only authorized *sanctuary* of God in Judaism, located in Jerusalem. The first Temple, built by Solomon, contained the *Ark of the Covenant* and the tablets of the *Ten Commandments* in the innermost room, the *Holy of Holies*. The temple altar was the only place in Israel where priests could perform sacrifices. Solomon's Temple was destroyed by *Nebuchadnezzar* in 587BCE and the Ark of the Covenant was lost. A second Temple was built between 520 and 516BCE. *Herod* the Great replaced this building with a third Temple on a grand scale. The area of the former Temples was doubled in size, and the new Temple covered twenty-six acres of ground. The third Temple was burnt by the Romans in CE70. *See also*: **Western Wall**.

temporal Worldly, as opposed to spiritual. When religious teachers urge men to give up temporal concerns and joys, they mean that men should remember that nothing which is part of this earthly life will endure for ever. Thus, the pleasure we find in food, drink and sexuality will come to an end when we die.

Ten Commandments The moral commandments given by God to Moses on Mount Sinai, according to the *Old Testament* or *Torah*. God had delivered the Israelites from slavery in Egypt and wished to enter into a covenant, or agreement, with his *Chosen People*. He summoned Moses, their leader, to Mount Sinai and gave him two stone tablets on which the commandments were inscribed: these told the Israelites what God wanted them to do in exchange for his protection. Having received the commandments, Moses sacrificed an ox, splashed its blood on the altar he had built, and then sprinkled it over the Israelites. In this way, he symbolically joined the community to their God.

The first three commandments instruct the Chosen People to worship one God only, to make no image of him, and to treat his name with reverence: the fourth orders them to keep the *Sabbath* holy and the rest are concerned with social relationships, for example, forbidding killing and adultery, and encouraging respect for parents. In Islam, the Qur'an also speaks of the 'tablets of the Law' given to Moses, but without giving a number.

Ten Fetters Ten characteristics that tie a person to suffering and *Samsara*, the ordinary world of birth, death and rebirth, according to Buddhism. By breaking the Ten Fetters, a person achieves *enlightenment*. The fetters are: belief either that a separate immortal soul exists or that one's personality dies totally when the physical body dies, doubt, scepticism and indecision; dependence on external observances, such as ceremonies, for winning enlightenment; craving for pleasures of the senses; hatred; craving for existence in the world of pure form; craving for existence in the 'formless world'; conceit; restlessness; and ignorance.

Tenrikyo A *Shinto* sect which specializes in faith-healing and has a wide following.

tertiary A lay member of a Roman Catholic religious order, so-called because he or she comes third to the clerics or nuns of the order.

Pope Innocent III granted permission to Francis of Assisi to set up an order of friars who would seek to serve God, not cloistered in contemplation and prayer, but within the lay community, actively embracing humility, chastity and poverty.

Tertiaries were first formally included by *St Francis* of Assissi when he made provision for them on founding the Franciscan friars. They are expected to attend daily *Mass* and show charity to all men. They will probably meet together regularly at a monastery or friary of their order and spend time there in retreat.

testimony 'To give testimony' or 'to testify' means to make an open declaration in public of one's religion. *Evangelical* Christian Churches frequently encourage their congregations to testify to past sins and to tell how they have repented and found salvation through faith. Receiving sacraments, especially baptism, can also be seen as a testimony of commitment to the Christian religion.

theism (1) The belief in the existence of one God or Supreme Being who is involved with the universe without being part of it. Judaism, Christianity and Islam are examples of theistic religions. (2) Belief in the existence of a god or gods.

theocracy A system of government or a state which claims to be guided in its laws and constitution by the power and wisdom of God. In practice, this often means rule by priests or clergymen.

When the ancient Hebrews were governed by judges and later by kings who treated the *Torah* as state law, Israel was a theocracy. Muslim states which have elevated the *shari'a* to be the law of the land, or which are led by a *Shi'ite imam*, can also be called theocracies.

theologian A person who studies theology.

theology The systematic study of the nature of God or the gods and of how this interacts with man and the universe.

theophany (1) An appearance or manifestation of God to man. In the *Old Testament* or *Torah*, he reveals himself through thunder, fire and other symbols, and in the *New Testament* through Jesus, who is believed by Christians to be the Son of God in human form. In the Hindu *Bhagavad Gita, Krishna*, the *avatar* of the god *Vishnu*, reveals himself to Prince *Arjuna* in his full majesty as God. (2) The Christian feast of the *Epiphany* in the Eastern Orthodox Church, which celebrates the baptism of Christ, when he showed himself publicly to be one with God.

theosophy (1) Any of various teachings and religious systems that claim special knowledge of the nature of God and his relations with man, either from a revelation or mystical insight. (2) The teachings of the Theosophical Society, founded in 1875 by *Helena Blavatsky* and Colonel H. S. Olcott. This movement tries to show the universal truth of all religions by pointing to the similar mysteries and manifestations of occult and supernatural phenomena which it says can be found in all of them. Theosophy is a mixture of Buddhism, Hinduism and Christianity, with its beliefs in rebirth, *avatars* and Christian morality. A fundamental doctrine is that of *karma*: in this system, karma is a law which states that a person's future depends on events and attitudes in his or her past. Linked to this doctrine is the idea of 'World Teachers' who come down to earth in order to preach the divine message to believers and non-believers alike.

Theravada The teaching of the Elders; the form of Buddhism which prevails in Sri Lanka and South East Asia. Its teachings are based on the *Pali Canon*, its scriptures, which Theravadas believe to be the most accurate record of what the Buddha actually taught.

In Theravada countries the laity are encouraged to practise the virtues of generosity and morality. *Enlightenment* or *Nibbana* is a state almost impossible for a layman to attain: anyone really serious about striving for enlightenment becomes a *bhikku*, or monk.

Theravadas tend to describe enlightenment in terms of Absolute Wisdom, seeing things as they really are. The person who gains this wisdom is an *Arhat*. His awareness and knowledge are not as great as Buddha's, but, according to the Theravada, to become a Buddha is inconceivably difficult.

Thirteen Principles. A summary of the basic beliefs of Judaism, found in the *siddur*, or Jewish prayer book. They were drawn up in the twelfth century CE by *Maimonides*, who argued that most Jews needed clearly formulated beliefs to follow, in contrast to the feeling current to the mystics of his time.

The thirteen principles are: belief in the existence of a Creator God and providence: belief that he is one only and that he does not have physical form: belief in his eternity and that worship is due to him alone: belief in the prophets and that Moses was the greatest of them: belief in the unchangeable nature of the revelation of the *Torah*: belief that God is all-knowing and will judge men at the end of the world: belief in final punishment for the wicked, in resurrection, and belief in the coming of the *Messiah*.

Thirty-nine Articles A summary of the doctrines of the Anglican Church, drawn up during the reign of Elizabeth I (1558–1603) of England.

Three Jewels The Buddha, the *dharma* and the Sangha: the three most important and valuable things to a Buddhist. In this context, the Buddha is the ideal of enlightenment: the dharma, the path taught by the Buddha, leading to enlightenment: and the Sangha, the community of those following that path who have developed some wisdom and will one day gain enlightenment.

T'ien t'ai A Far Eastern school of Buddhism which emphasizes that meditation, devotion and the study of Buddhist texts should all be balanced and are equally important to spiritual development. The school was founded in China by Chih-i (CE538–597), who organized the vast body of Buddhist scriptures by systematically arranging them into 'five periods'. The most important text for the T'ien t'ai is the *Lotus Sutra*. The school spread to Japan in CE805, where it is known as the Tendai.

Before an image of a tirthankara is one of the Jain faithful. By his white dress he is recognizably of the Svetambara sect.

tirthankara A teacher of the *Jain* philosophy. There is said to have been a line of twenty-four tirthankaras, but only the last two, Parsva (probably the true founder) and *Mahavira* (the traditional founder), are thought to have existed in fact.

tithe A tenth part. In Mosaic law, as found in the *Torah*, the tenth of the annual produce of land was to be given to God. Because of this, some Christians now set aside a tenth of their income as a donation to their church.

Torah Literally, 'the Teaching': the sacred writings of Judaism, made up of the first five books which are attributed to Moses. They contain a traditional history of the world until the death of Moses, the law as delivered by God to Moses on Mount Sinai, and a variety of rules and regulations which deal with religious ritual, diet, justice, sexual behaviour and administration. By following the teachings of the Torah, Jews fulfill their part of the covenant which exists between them and God.

These Jews, wearing the tallith, or prayer-shawl, are reading the Torah.

Toshogu *Shinto* shrines that are found all over Japan and are dedicated to the memory of the general and dictator Ieyasu, who died in 1616.

totemism A practice found in tribal societies, such as the American Indians, by which each tribe or clan is named after an animal or plant from which it is supposed to be descended or with which it has some other close relationship. This means that all the members of the tribe or clan are also related to each other, and they worship the animal or plant as a god or guardian spirit. Such guardian animals or plants are known as 'totems' and are often represented in some way, such as a totem pole. The term 'totemism' also refers to the social structures and customs associated with these beliefs.

A carved and painted totem pole from British Columbia.

Tower of Silence *See*: **dakhma**.

trance (1) Any mental state involving greatly reduced awareness of the outside world. This state can be induced by repetitive chanting or hypnosis. (2) A mental state of extreme concentration and absorption, often produced by meditation or devotional exercises.

Transcendental Meditation Abbreviation: TM. A technique for focusing one's thoughts outside oneself, attaining self-realization, and freeing oneself from the strains and preoccupations of everyday living. Although it is not a religion, it does employ some techniques of Hindu meditation. It was first popularized by the Maharishi Mahesh Yogi in the late 1960s.

transfiguration A Christian festival celebrated on 6 August to commemorate Christ's appearance in splendour and glory before the Apostles, Peter, James and John, accompanied by Moses and Elijah. The Eastern Orthodox Church calls this the Feast of Tabor, because tradition places the event on Mount Tabor.

transubstantiation A doctrine held by certain Christians which states that during the *consecration* in the service of the *Mass* or *Eucharist*, the bread and wine, while still looking and tasting like ordinary bread and wine, change in their true invisible nature to become the body and blood of Jesus Christ. The explanation of what happens at the consecration is accepted by Roman Catholics but is rejected by most Protestants. The Eastern Orthodox Church accepts that the bread and wine become Christ's body and blood, but simply states that this is the work of the Holy Spirit, and prefers not to try to explain the change any further.

Trappist A male or female member of the Trappist branch of the Cistercians, a reformed order of Benedictine monks and nuns. The Trappists were formed in the seventeenth century at the Cistercian Abbey of La Trappe in northern France and are an austere and strict order who observe long periods of silence and rigorous fasting.

Tree of Knowledge of Good and Evil According to the *Torah* and the Qur'an, the first man and woman, Adam and Eve, were banished from Eden, as a result of eating fruit from the Tree of Knowledge. Christians believe this act of disobedience is the *original sin* which has affected the whole of mankind.

Trikaya The *Mahayana* Buddhist doctrine of the three states of existence of Buddha. (*a*) Dharma-Kaya – the essence of all Buddhas, Supreme Buddha-nature. (*b*) Sambhaga-Kaya – the special form Buddha-nature takes on when preaching to the gods or when appearing in the Paradises. (*c*) Nirmana-Kaya – the historical physical form of Buddha-nature, as in the historical Buddha, formerly Siddhartha Gautama. *See also*: **Mahayana**.

Trimurti In Hinduism, the idea that God, the Supreme Being, takes three main forms, or contains three main forces, all of them divine. *Brahma* is the creative force, *Vishnu* the preserving force and *Shiva* the destructive force. These forces all co-operate together to propel the cycle of life, death and rebirth.

Vishnu, the Preserver, one of the Hindu Trinity, the Trimurti, seated with Lakshmi.

Trinity Also known as the Holy Trinity. The union of three persons in the one God of Christianity: the Father, the Son and the Holy Spirit. Christians believe that the one God, the maker of heaven and earth, has shown himself to man in three different but undivided ways. God the Father sent his only Son, Jesus Christ, to earth to become a man at the *incarnation* and to die for the sins of the world. Before he returned to God the Father Christ promised that the Holy Spirit, the spirit of God, would enter men's hearts and minds to give strength and faith to believe in him.

Tripitaka *or* **Tipitaka** The canonical scriptures of *Theravada* Buddhists. The name means three baskets, and the Tripitaka is divided into three sections: the Vinaya Pitaka or Discipline Basket, which gives rules for the *Sangha* assembly and order, the Sutta Pitaka or Teaching Basket and the *Abhidhamma* (or Abhidarma) Pitaka.

Trotskyism The theories of *communism* developed by Leon Trotsky (1879–1940), a Russian revolutionary who helped Lenin organize the November Revolution of 1917. This revolution brought the communists to power in Russia and Trotsky became a leading member of the government. When Lenin died (1924) and Stalin came to power, Trotsky was exiled (1927) and finally murdered in Mexico.

In his writings, Trotsky developed Marx's ideas of the 'permanent revolution', that is, the spread of communist revolution from one country to another until the whole world is communist. He also severely attacked Stalin and his policies.

Leon Trotsky, here seen addressing Red Army troops, was commissar for war in Russia from 1918 to 1925, and it was he who created and led the Red Army to victory in the civil war between the Bolsheviks and the anti-communists.

tulku *See:* **lama.**

Tulsi Das A sixteenth-century CE Hindu poet who popularized the *Ramayana* by retelling that poem in the Hindi language. He adapted it from the original Sanskrit, which few could understand.

turban A piece of cloth that is wound around the head to cover the hair. Men in many different societies wear turbans, but male Sikhs are obliged to wear them once they are capable of tying the material without help. There are various reasons for this rule, but it was insisted upon by the Sikh *gurus*. The turban is not only an outward sign that a man is following in the gurus' footsteps, but also symbolizes his attempt to live up to their example. Turbans can be of any colour and, of course, they are practical since they make it easier for Sikhs to keep their uncut hair in place.

The consort of Shiva is Shakti, the female principle. Her name means 'power', and she has many forms, some benign, like Parvati, some terrifying, like the bloodthirsty goddess Kali, and some gentle, like Uma. Shakti represents the dynamic force which causes the universe to function and her union with Shiva is life-giving. She is shown seated composedly on a seat decorated with carved lotuses.

Turin Shroud A piece of linen which appears to be stamped with an outline of a man who was beaten with whips, fell while carrying a heavy object, and was crucified. Many Christians believe that Jesus Christ was wrapped in this cloth after he was crucified. It has been extensively tested by scientists over the years, but the evidence revealed has been interpreted in different ways.

Twelvers A *Shi'ite* Muslim sect also known as the *imamis*, that believes that the twelfth *imam*, Muhammad al-Muntazar, disappeared in CE878 into the cave of the Great Mosque at Samarra when he was five years old. This 'hidden imam' is said to be waiting for the end of the world, when he will return as the *Mahdi*, the divinely guided one; his coming will bring peace to earth and will hasten the Last Day, when *Allah* will judge all men. The imam is believed to appoint his own representatives, also known as imams, to guide his followers on earth.

twelve tribes of Israel According to the Book of Genesis in the *Torah* or *Old Testament*, Jacob, one of the three *patriarchs* or founding fathers of the Israelites, had twelve sons. Each son proceeded to found a tribe which was known by that son's name.

twice-born In Hinduism, a name applied to those who have undergone the *Sacred Thread Ceremony*.

typology The study of 'types' in literature, especially the sacred scriptures of Judaism and Christianity. Types are symbols, often symbolic people, used in the scriptures.

u

uji gami A Shinto term for the family or ancestral spirit.

Ulama' The teachers and experts of Islamic law, who are responsible for guiding the *Umma*, or Muslim community, along the correct Islamic path.

Uma *Shiva*'s consort. As 'light', Uma is a gracious and kind being, in contrast with some of the other aspects of *Mahadevi*.

'Umar The second *caliph* after the death of Muhammad, best remembered for his stern manner and rigid rule. During his time, Islam spread as far as Egypt in the west and western Persia in the east. He was murdered in 644 in the mosque at Medina.

Umayyad A clan based in Mecca at the time of Muhammad. From its ranks came the third *caliph, 'Uthman*. After the assassination of the fourth caliph, *Ali*, an Umayyad dynasty was established in Damascus and proceeded to rule from there until it was overthrown by the Abbasids in the eighth century.

Umma A collective term meaning 'nation', for the Islamic community.

unconscious That part of the mind which affects our actions without our being aware of its influence. Many people believe that it contains our deepest instincts and desires, including some which might disturb us too much if we were aware of them. Therefore we repress these into the unconscious. The healing science of psychoanalysis attempts to help psychologically and mentally disturbed people by plumbing the depths of the unconscious.

unction *See*: **extreme unction**.

underworld In many religions, the place where *souls* go after life has left the physical body. Many mythologies describe this as a region to be found under the surface of the earth, presided over by a god of the dead.

Unification Church Founded by the Korean *Sun Myung Moon* in 1954, this Church has taken Christian and Taoist ideas and blended them into one doctrine. The Church teaches a dualistic faith, seeing history as a struggle between Good and Evil. It looks to the appearance of a coming Messiah, though some see Sun Myung Moon as that person. Members sell their magazine, *One World*, on the street and are keen to convert people to their faith.

The movement is strongly anti-communist, probably in reaction to the division of Korea into two states, a capitalist south and a communist north.

Unitarians Members of the *Unitarian Church*, a church dating from the eighteenth century and associated with Christianity. It is wide-spread in England and North America. Unitarians believe in one God, but deny the doctrine of the *Trinity*. They believe that all religions are different paths to the same truth, and so will sometimes read from the sacred books of religions other than Christianity as well as from the Bible in their services. They believe in a liberal approach to religious faith and morality, and in using reason to criticize traditional approaches where necessary. Each congregation has complete control over its own affairs.

United Reformed Church A Protestant denomination of England and Wales, formed by a merger between *Congregationalists* and *Presbyterians*. Like other reformed Churches, it emphasises Bible readings and the singing of hymns and sermons in its worship. Its organization is similar to that of the Presbyterians.

Universal Black Improvement Society Also known as the Universal Negro Improvement Society. Founded by the Jamaican preacher *Marcus Garvey* in 1914, it urged black people to come together and work for God and self-improvement.

Universal House of Justice The supreme ruling council of the *Baha'i* sect, founded by the prophet *Baha'u'llah* and based on the teachings of the *Bab* (Sayyad Ali Muhammed).

Unleavened Bread, Feast of In Judaism, an alternative title for the feast of *Pesach* or *Passover*. The title comes from the rule that for eight days the Jews must eat only *matzah*, unleavened bread, to remember their hasty departure from slavery in Egypt. *See also*: **Passover, Pesach.**

Matzah, unleavened bread eaten during the Passover.

Untouchables The communities and groups at the bottom of the Hindu *caste* system. Traditionally, according to Hindu law, physical contact with an Untouchable would pollute a high-caste Hindu, who had to ritually purify himself if that happened. Untouchables were greatly restricted because of the prohibitions on contact with them. Only after India's independence in 1947 was the practice of Untouchability outlawed, but it is still widespread in the countryside where most people live. This has caused many Untouchables to convert to Buddhism or Islam, which do not have caste systems. *Gandhi* gave the name Harijans (children of God) to the Untouchables.

These are Untouchables, praying before Gandhi's memorial stone. He renamed them Harijans, children of God, and bitterly opposed the caste system which demeaned and debased them.

Upanishads The second oldest group of Hindu scriptures, often regarded as the last section of the *Vedas* and therefore often called the *Vedanta*. The Upanishads are concerned with the nature of human awareness, the reality (*Brahman*) which produces and includes all other forms of existence, and the relationship between *atman*, the human soul, and the cosmic reality that is Brahman. Many of the Upanishads are made up of parables and speculate about the meaning of human existence rather than lay down teachings to be accepted. 'Upanishad' means 'to sit down beside' and refers to the form of many passages where a pupil sitting near his teacher asks him questions and receives wise answers.

'Uthman The third *caliph* and Muhammad's son-in-law, who succeeded to the caliphate in 644. He supervised the compilation of the authoritative version of the Qur'an and was murdered while at prayer in his own home in 656.

utilitarianism An ethical doctrine which states that the goodness of an action depends on its 'utility' or capacity to increase happiness, and that an individual's conduct should therefore aim to promote the greatest happiness of the greatest number of people.

Utopia Originally an imaginary continent described in Sir Thomas More's book *Utopia* (1516), where the people enjoy a perfect system of government. More invented the word 'utopia' itself, which means 'no place'. Nowadays the word usually describes a perfect world or society without any problems, or it can suggest impractical schemes to make our world a better place.

V

Vairochana In Hindu mythology, a title of the Sun. In *Mahayana* Buddhism one of the jinas. Vairochana is regarded as the supreme Buddha in Java and by the Shingon school in Japan.

Vaisheshika A school of Hindu philosophy founded by Kanda and close in many ways to the *Nyaya* school. It teaches that the external world can be studied by the application of logic. According to this system, the world is constructed of nine 'atoms' which have all existed eternally but which are forever combining under the influence of a personal God. Four of these 'atoms' are material, namely earth, water, fire and air. The other five are non-physical: they include soul, spirit and mind.

Vaishnavism The worship of the Hindu god *Vishnu*: one of the major *bhakti* groups within Hinduism. Followers preach that Vishnu is the Supreme Being and usually worship him in the form of his *avatar*, *Krishna*. Most Vaishnavites are in northern India. Their major scripture is the *Bhagavad Gita*. Vaishnavites mark themselves with the *naman*, usually just on the forehead, but sometimes over the whole body.

(opposite) The god Vishnu, decked with garlands beside his consort, is worshipped by Vaishnavites.

Vaishyas The merchants, traders and businessmen, or third of the main *caste* groups in Hinduism, coming below the *Brahmins* and *Kshyatriyas*. Like them, Vaishyas are permitted to study the *Vedas*. According to tradition they were originally created from the thighs of *Purusha*, the original man.

vajra A diamond-thunderbolt, one of the most important symbols of *Vajrayana* or *Tantric Buddhism*. The vajra is pictured as a double-headed sceptre. The sceptre is a symbol of kings, and the sceptre of the king of the gods is a thunderbolt. This symbol is taken over from pre-Buddhist mythology and used to stand for *enlightenment* or reality itself.

Vajrayana Literally, 'Diamond Vehicle': also known as *Tantric Buddhism*. The Vajrayana is a school of *Mahayana* Buddhism that puts a tremendous emphasis on practice, especially through *mantras*, rituals and meditation. It seeks to use every possible type of action to involve the entire person in striving for *enlightenment*. It started to develop in India around CE500, where it built up a complex mythology and so cosmology, involving *chakras*, *mandalas*, the five *Jinas*, or symbolic Buddhas, and other symbols. One of the most important symbols is the *vajra*, or diamond-thunderbolt, after which the school is named.

The Vajrayana is the dominant form of Buddhism in Tibet, Mongolia and the Himalayas, and is found in Japan as the *Shingon* school.

Valmiki The traditional author of the Hindu epic, the *Ramayana*.

Varanasi *See*: **Benares**.

Vardhamana Another name for *Mahavira*, the traditional founder of the *Jain* religion.

Varuna In ancient Indian mythology, god of the sky and king of the universe, Varuna later lost much of his importance, and in the *Bhagavad Gita* is regarded as king of the water-creatures.

Vatican The palace which is the chief residence of the *Pope* in Vatican City, an independent state within the city of Rome.

Vatican Councils The last two *Ecumenical Councils* of the Roman Catholic Church, that is, the gathering of bishops under the leadership of the *Pope*, called to settle administrative and doctrinal matters.

The first Vatican Council was held in 1869 by Pope Pius IX, to interpret and lay down the dogma of *papal infallibility* and to define the exact nature of papal authority. The second Vatican Council under Pope John XXIII was summoned in 1962 to renew the Church's life, liturgy and structures. At this conference, the *Mass* and other services were reformed to make room for local languages, and the Roman Catholic Church resolved to open a wider dialogue with other Christian bodies and other religions.

The Grand Procession of the Ecumenical Council at Saint Peter's, Rome, convened in 1869 so that the bishops of the Church could discuss articles of faith and dogma.

Vedanta (1) Another name for the *Upanishads*, which are often regarded as the end of the *Vedas*, hence the name. (2) The school of Hindu philosophy that developed the teachings of the Upanishads and has become the most influential of all Hindu schools. The greatest teacher of Vedanta was *Shankara*, who taught that only *Brahman*, the Absolute, is ultimately real, and that Vedanta can be identified with the *atman*, the soul or self of each person.

Vedanta Sutra A collection of aphorisms attributed to the *Rishi*, or Hindu sage, Badarayana. It sets out to combine the teachings of the *Upanishads* into a consistent philosophical system. The interpretation of the *sutra* was already a matter of controversy shortly after its origin, since the sayings were not only difficult in themselves, but were accompanied by an equally unclear commentary.

Vedas The ancient scriptures of India. They are regarded as the chief scriptures of Hinduism and said to be *sruti*, 'heard' by the *Rishis*, or ancient sages. The Vedas are divided into four sections. The first is the *Rig Veda*, which consists of chants and hymns to Indo-European gods, especially Indra, king of the gods, and nature gods such as Dyaus, heaven. The Yajur and Sama Vedas, which follow, consist largely of the same chants but arranged so that they can be

Indra, the god of war and king of the gods, is praised and glorified in the Rig Veda.

used for rituals during sacrifices. The last Veda, the Athara Veda, is made up of spells and incantations.

The Vedas all open with chants, continue with Brahmanas, instructions on how to conduct sacrifices and rituals, and conclude with Upanishads, philosophical passages, and speculations on the nature of life and the universe.

vegan A strict *vegetarian*, who excludes not only meat from his or her diet, but also fish and all animal products such as eggs, milk, cheese and butter. Most vegans also refuse to buy or wear leather, and often wool too.

vegetarian Anyone who, either because of moral principles or on account of nutritional theories, refuses to eat meat. Vegetarians may also exclude fish or products which derive from animals such as eggs, milk and cheese. All *Jains* and many Buddhists and Hindus are vegetarians. *See also*: vegan.

veneration The expression of reverence and respect, particularly towards some sacred object or person. Veneration is often accompanied by some physical motion, such as bowing or kneeling.

vestments Ecclesiastical garments worn by members of the clergy when they are conducting Christian services.

vestry The room or building in which vestments used in Christian church services, and liturgical objects, are kept. Vestries can also be used for prayer meetings and Sunday Schools.

vicar (1) In the Anglican Church of England, the vicar is the priest in charge of a parish. Some vicars are also known as rectors. (2) The local representative or deputy of a higher authority, for example, a *patriarch*'s representative in a foreign country (the Vicar Patriarchal).

Vicar of Christ One of the titles of the *Pope*, the head of the Roman Catholic Church. This title emphasizes the Roman Catholic belief that, as head of this church, the Pope acts as Christ's representative on earth, as Christ is seen as the head of the whole Christian Church, ruling it from heaven.

vidya Knowledge, especially spiritual wisdom and philosophy. In both Hinduism and Buddhism, if a person develops vidya in its most specialised, spiritual sense, he or she wins liberation from *Samsara*.

vihara A Buddhist monastery, community centre, or place of meditation or worship.

vinaya The Buddhist code of discipline and practical life in Buddhist monasteries.

Borne up by exulting angels, the Virgin Mary, alone among humankind, was without sin and could thus enter paradise immediately, as Masolino, the medieval artist believed.

Virgin Mary The mother of Jesus Christ. Mary was engaged to Joseph, a carpenter of Nazareth, when the archangel Gabriel appeared to her and told her that she was soon to become the mother of the *Messiah* by a process that has come to be known as the 'virgin birth'. Mary then travelled to Bethlehem with Joseph and gave birth to the infant Jesus in a stable. When Jesus started preaching Mary accompanied him to Cana and Capernaum and witnessed one of the *miracles* he is said to have performed. She was also present on Calvary, when Jesus was crucified.

Roman Catholic and Eastern Orthodox Christians celebrate the feast of the Assumption, on 15 August, believing that Mary rejoined her son in heaven as soon as she had died. They pray to her for intercession with God, call her Mother of God, carry her statue or icon in processions, and dedicate altars and shrines to her honour. In addition, Catholics assert that Mary was kept free from *original sin* by God so that she might be perfectly prepared to receive his son into her womb, and bring him up in the most devout Jewish home possible; this dogma is known as the *Immaculate Conception*.

virtue Moral goodness, or acts which are termed 'virtuous' according to the world view of a particular society. Whatever differences may exist between each religion's views on what is good and what is evil, most faiths nevertheless divide human activity into these two categories: the virtuous and the corrupt. Religious people who wish to lead upright lives are guided in their choices by the sacred scriptures of their faith and, in this way, can learn how to pursue the virtuous path. Other people may look to the ethical writings of moral philosophy for guidance.

Vishnu The Hindu god who preserves and maintains life. Along with *Shiva* and *Brahma* he is one of the most important Hindu deities. He descends to earth periodically in the form of an *avatar* to reveal the truth to the world. *Krishna* and *Rama* are the best-known of the avatars. Generally, the number of avatars who have already appeared is put at nine, with one, *Kalki*, still to come. The Vaishnavites, or worshippers and devotees of Vishnu, regard him as God, the Supreme Being.

Vivekananda A nineteenth-century Hindu religious leader and disciple of *Ramakrishna*, who is best remembered for his pronouncement that all religions are true.

voluntarism A philosophical theory which states that will is the fundamental principle in the individual or the universe.

Voodoo The folk religion of Haiti. It is of African origin, and contains both a belief in a supreme deity and also rituals which are intended to influence the 'loa', that is, the spirit or gods which inhabit the invisible world and represent natural forces such as fertility, death, sea and fire. These loa take over the bodies of the devotees during the rituals, causing the possessed person to act in a way characteristic of the loa inside him.

A night-time ritual dance *(right)* on a pit of flames is part of this Voodoo ceremony.

vow A binding promise made to God, another deity, a saint, or an individual, to perform an act or enter some condition. Thus, when individuals make this form of pledge, they commit themselves to a particular act or series of acts which they then have to fulfil. 'Taking vows' is a phrase used especially of those who enter a religious order or community.

Vrindavana Also known as Brindaban. The Indian town traditionally associated with *Krishna*, since he reputedly came here to live among the cowherds. Worshippers come to Vrindavana to pay him homage, and the town contains over a thousand temples.

Vulgate The Latin translation of the Bible prepared by St Jerome in the fourth century CE and used as an official translation of the book by the Roman Catholic Church.

vyasa A legendary editor of Hindu scriptures. According to tradition, a succession of vyasas has been sent down to earth over the centuries to share the form of the scriptures. All these individuals are manifestations of one divine being. The epic poem, the *Mahabharata*, is said to have been composed by a man called Vyasa, but nothing is known of the author.

W

wafer A thin disc of unleavened bread used in the Roman Catholic and Protestant services of the *Eucharist*. It is usually stamped with a cross.

Waheguru Wonderful Lord: a Sikh name for God, first arising at the time of *Guru Arjan*. Sikhs use the term frequently.

Wahhabis A *Sunni* Muslim sect founded by Muhammad ibn Abd al-Wahhab in the eighteenth century. The Wahhabis view the worship of saints as decadence and demand a return to the practices of the earliest Muslims. With their puritanism and extreme orthodox fervour, they began the wave of reaction which was to sweep through Islam in the nineteenth century, condemning all concessions to modernization, westernization and *Sufi* mysticism. The majority of the population of Saudi Arabia are still Wahhabis, and they control Mecca and Medina, the holiest cities in Islam.

wat A collection of Buddhist buildings in Thailand, including the bot, halls containing Buddha images, monasteries, *dagobas* and out-buildings.

Weeks, Feast of Also known as *Shavouth* or *Pentecost*. The Jewish summer festival which is linked with harvest time in the *Holy Land* and

The Feast of Weeks, Shavouth, is a Jewish harvest festival. Here the synagogue is being decked with flowers.

commemorates the occasion when Moses received the *Ten Commandments* on *Mount Sinai*. In ancient times, to celebrate the wheat harvest, two loaves of bread were brought to the Temple. Nowadays, the celebration of the giving of the Commandments takes precedence over this aspect of the feast and many Jews stay up for the whole of the previous night, studying the *Torah*.

The hall of the synagogue is decorated with flowers, fruit and greenery, as a reminder that the normally barren Mount Sinai burst into fruit in preparation for the giving of the Torah, and to recall the harvest-time origins of the feast. During the service on this day, the account of how Moses received the Commandments is read aloud, as are passages from the Book of Ruth from the *Hebrew Bible*, which tells how Ruth converted to Judaism after helping with the gleaning at harvest time.

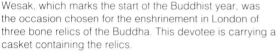

Wesak, which marks the start of the Buddhist year, was the occasion chosen for the enshrinement in London of three bone relics of the Buddha. This devotee is carrying a casket containing the relics.

Wesak A Buddhist festival celebrating the *enlightenment* of the Buddha and, in some countries, also his birth and death. It is held on the full-moon day of May when processions are held and various ceremonies performed.

Wesley, John (1703–91) The English preacher who founded *Methodism*. John Wesley first received the nickname 'Methodist' while studying at Oxford, because of the methodical way in which he read and studied the Bible. He was ordained as a minister in the *Church of England* and had a spiritual experience in his mid-thirties that made him feel that Christ had taken away his sins and that he was marked out for *salvation*. Bolstered by his new-found certainty, Wesley set out across England to preach, to pass on the message of Christ's forgiveness of repentant sinners and of the damnation which would come to those who did not turn to the light of faith. Within a matter of years, Wesley had made many converts and began to establish a

John Wesley founded Methodism, which has attracted converts all over the world. The Methodist minister *(above)* is preaching to a congregation in Boston in 1826.

separate organization within which to work. The Church of England disapproved of the emotional nature of his sermons and banned Wesley from speaking in its pulpits. By the time of his death, the Methodist movement had established its own preachers and congregations.

Western Wall Sometimes referred to as the Wailing Wall, a remnant of the foundation wall of the Temple at Jerusalem: it is all that now remains of that temple, which the Romans destroyed in CE70. Since that time, Jews have come there to pray and to recite from the *Torah*, bewailing the loss of their national home and the scattering of their people throughout the world. After the Arab–Israeli war of 1967, the Western Wall passed into the control of the Jewish State of Israel.

Whitsunday The Christian festival of *Pentecost*. The name itself derives from the ancient tradition that people baptized and confirmed at *Easter* would wear the white or 'whit' garment received at that service until Pentecost Sunday.

Wilderness A desolate remote area in Judaea where, according to the *New Testament*, *Satan* tempted Christ to alter the course of his ministry but was rejected. The wilderness is important in early Jewish history: *Elijah* fled into the wilderness, where he was fed by ravens; it was into the wilderness that the scapegoat was released, and in the wilderness that the Israelites wandered for forty years.

The Western Wall, or Wailing Wall, is of central significance to the Jews, since it links them to the days before the *diaspora*. These Orthodox Jews *(above)* are praying and reading holy scripture and *(below)* a festival is taking place, with the Torah rolls being carried to the wall.

Eliphas Lévi's engraving from his *Transcendental Magic* of 1896 is charged with symbols which would be known to 'initiates of the occult', including the pentagram on the forehead and the goat's head and cloven hooves.

God to men, commandments, for example, or doctrines. Often these revelations are given to specially chosen and inspired people, known as prophets. The term is also used for the written record of such revelations in the sacred scriptures of a religion. Thus the *Hebrew Bible* is the word of God for Jews, the whole Bible for Christians, the Qur'an for Muslims, and in Hinduism the *Upanishads* and *Vedas* are regarded as revelations inspired by God. The Sikh *Guru Granth Sahib* and the Zoroastrian *Avesta* are also considered as the word of God to their respective communities. (2) In Christianity, Jesus Christ is often termed the Word of God (in Greek, the Logos) as he is considered by Christians to be God's supreme revelation and self-expression to mankind through his *incarnation*.

world civilization An idea which occurs in many belief-systems, but which is a specific goal for members of the Baha'i faith. In order to break down the divisions which exist between nations and men, the Baha'i urge mankind to eliminate the extremes of poverty and wealth which divide and trap human beings and to adopt international language, and a federal world government. The exploitation and competitiveness of the contemporary world will be replaced by a united brotherhood of peoples, whose resources and knowledge will be shared equally for the good of all.

This Australian witchdoctor is using his powers to drive out any harm a witch may have caused.

witchcraft Believed to stem from the Anglo-Saxon 'wicca', meaning wise. The term is often used to describe the practice of magic, especially in a pejorative sense. In medieval Europe, and in the Salem witch trials, many people were accused of witchcraft, which appears to have been identified by their accusers with worship of the *Devil*. The word has been used more recently by followers of a religion which claims to be a revival of the 'Old Religion' of Europe and which is centred on the worship of a Mother Goddess and her consort, the Horned God.

witchdoctor A medicine man in so-called primitive religions, whose duties can include those of healer, priest, diviner and herbalist.

Witnesses *See*: **Jehovah's Witnesses**.

word of God (1) In many religions, this term is used for any message or revelation given by

World Council of Churches An organization set up by Protestant Churches after World War II to encourage the union of the different Christian denominations and sects in one universal Church and to enable the Churches to speak with one voice on the problems facing mankind, whether spiritual, moral or political. The Eastern Orthodox Churches have joined the council, but the Roman Catholic Church, has not yet joined. Nevertheless, it supports the general aims of the council and many of its documents on religious and secular problems.

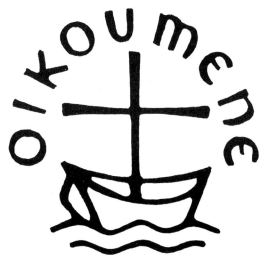

The symbol of the World Council of Churches.

World Fellowship of Buddhists Founded in 1950, this organization was set up to unite all Buddhists across the world in the common goal of spreading the Buddhist faith.

worship To pay reverence and homage to God, a god, a sacred person or any object which is regarded as sacred or worthy of respect. Worship may be given by means of prayer, sacrifice, hymns, chants or other rituals.

Writings The third of the three divisions of the *Hebrew Bible*. The others are the *Torah* and the *Prophets*. The Writings incorporates the psalms, the Wisdom literature, and the later histories such as the Books of Ezra and Nehemiah.

Wu-wei Literally, 'without action'. This term is frequently used both by *Confucius* and in *Taoist* teachings to emphasize the need to allow nature and all that is natural to evolve without human interference. For example, Chinese Taoist scholars urged the emperor to concentrate on cleansing his own soul and to refrain from becoming involved in government affairs.

y

yad A silver pointer used in Jewish *synagogues* to guide the eye of the reader of the *Torah* during services. This allows the reader to proceed without having to touch the sacred words with his finger.

Yahna valkya A legendary Hindu sage, said to have composed the Brihadaranyaka *Upanishad*, and often credited with founding the system of *yoga*.

Yahweh The most likely approximation of the name given to God in Judaism. The name is always written simply as the four consonants YHWH, hence its Greek name, the 'tetra-grammaton': the vowels are never inserted. When Jews read the scriptures, they never say the word out loud because of its sacredness: they say 'Adonai' instead, which means 'Lord'. Only once a year was the name pronounced out loud, by the High Priest in the Temple at Jerusalem on *Yom Kippur*. This ceremony was no longer performed after the Romans destroyed the Temple in CE70, and the correct pronunciation was forgotten. For a long time, Christians pronounced the name wrongly as *Jehovah*, using an adaptation of the vowels of 'Adonai' between the four consonants.

Yama (1) In Hinduism, the god of the dead and of the underworld. He is the god who sits in judgement on men's souls, awarding them punishment or purification before their rebirth in this world. (2) In the Hindu philosophy of yoga, yama means the moral duty to restrain and control one's desires. It is one of the eight angas or limbs of yoga which help the practitioner to attain complete concentration.

yantra Any artistic object which helps man to develop spiritually. The philosophy of yoga distinguishes between essential art, which aids spiritual growth by acting as a focus for contemplation, and non-essential art, which is just a product of skill and expertise. *Mandalas* are examples of yantra, but abstract paintings exemplify non-essential art.

Yards *Rastafarian* communities.

yarmulka A skull cap worn by Jewish men. It is also known as a kipah, and it is a sign that man is always in the presence of God

Yasna The main rite of temple worship in ancient *Zoroastrianism*. The words of this rite form part of the sacred book, the *Avesta*, and stress the fact that the divine spirit is present in all things in this world.

Yasukuni shrine A *Shinto* shrine built to commemorate the souls of those who died for Japan on the battlefield up until the end of World War II. Many critics of Japan's war-like past and the sufferings it caused fear that the presence of this shrine could encourage nationalism, and they urge a separation between the state and religion.

Yazatas Worshipful beings, somewhat like angels, in Zoroastrianism. The Yazatas can grant favours and will intercede with *Ahura Mazda* if individuals ask them to. They are venerated as saint-like figures whose role is to guide and assist the faithful.

Yazid The sixth Islamic *caliph*, best known for crushing the rebellion led by *Husain*, son of *Ali*, in CE680, and beheading Husain himself at the battle of *Karbala* in present-day Iraq.

Yeshivah A *Talmudic* academy that promotes religious scholarship.

Yiddish A German dialect developed by the *Ashkenazim* Jews.

Yin-Yang The Chinese theory of opposites. The universe is said to be composed of two opposite and complementary principles, the active posi-

In the centre of the diagram is the classical symbol of the two modes of being, the darker Yin and the lighter Yang, each having within itself the germ of the other and opposite quality. They are surrounded by eight trigrams, *pa kua*, each a permutation of broken and unbroken lines.

tive male Yang and the passive negative female Yin. All events depend on how the two forces are combined. *Taoism* teaches that the person who follows the Tao can overcome the opposition between the two and reconcile them.

The Yasukuni shrine with the Divine Gate bearing the imperial crest of the chrysanthemum. The shrine is framed by the distinctive form of the torii gate.

yoga (1) One of the six orthodox schools of Hindu philosophy. According to tradition, it was first set out in a systematic form in the *yoga sutras* of *Patanjali*. The yoga philosophy was originally quite close to that of the *Samkhya* school: the yogin, or follower of yoga, sought *moksha*, or liberation, in the total unification and isolation of the individual soul in itself. But today yoga is similar to the Vedanta, striving for the unification of the soul with *Brahman*, the *absolute*.

Patanjali developed the system known as the Eight Limbs of Yoga: social morality, personal morality, posture or physical position, breath control, control of the senses, concentration, meditation, and samadhi, the yogin's goal. In the West, the term 'yoga' is often used just for the third limb, that is, *asana* or posture, also known as Hatha Yoga. It is the practice of physical postures and exercises that have a strong influence on the mind. But the yogin may choose to adopt other means: Bhakti Yoga, or devotion to God; Karma Yoga, or work and performing one's duties; Jnana Yoga, or the development of wisdom. (2) Any technique or system used for spiritual growth in Buddhism and Indian religions. Thus, yoga can simply mean 'meditation' in *Mahayana* and *Vajrayana* Buddhism.

yogi *or* **yogin** A person who practices any form of *yoga*.

Yom Kippur Also known as the *Day of Atonement*. The holiest day in the Jewish year. Yom Kippur ends the 'Ten Days of Return' begun at *Rosh Hashanah* and is devoted entirely to prayer, to the worship of God, and, above all, to repentance for all the sins of the past year. Jews do no work on this day and fast for twenty-five hours from the previous evening until nightfall on Yom Kippur itself. During one of the services, a passage is read which tells how the high priest of ancient Israel went into the *Holy of Holies* in the *Temple* of *Jerusalem* to atone for his sins and those of the community. The final service on this day comes at sunset and is called 'Neilah'. Everyone stands throughout the service, the *ark* is kept open, and at the end the *shofar* is blown, followed by the response, 'Next year in Jerusalem'.

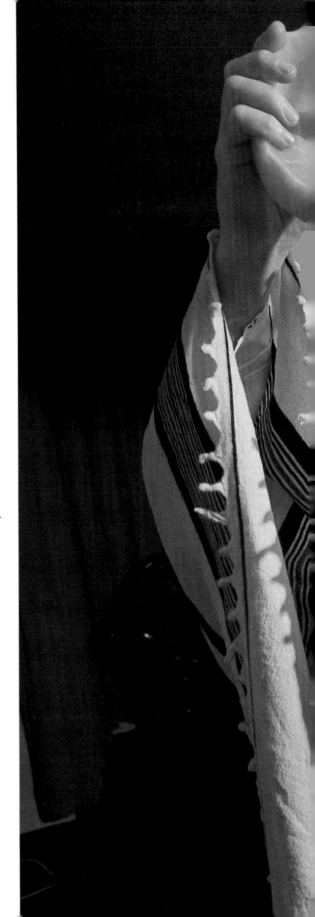

The shofar, or ram's horn, is blown on certain occasions in the Jewish religious calendar, notably at the beginning of Rosh Hashanah and on Yom Kippur, the final day of this period of atonement, to signal the end of the fasting.

yoni The female reproductive organs, used as a symbol in Hinduism. The yoni and the *lingam*, or erect phallus, together represent all of nature and existence and are associated with the god *Shiva* and his *Shakti*.

Young, Brigham (1801–77) The successor to *Joseph Smith* as leader of the Mormons. Young led the Mormons on a famous 1300-mile journey from the Mississippi River to their present centre, Utah, where he founded Salt Lake City in 1847.

Yudhishthira The eldest brother of the Panadava family features in the Hindu epic, the *Mahabharata*. Yudhishthira is heroic but also thoughtful, compassionate and truthful, and is known as the 'king of *dharma*'.

Yuga In Hinduism, an age of the world, of which there are four, the last being the Kali-Yuga. The four together make up a Maha-Yuga, or 'great age'.

Yu Huang The *Taoist* sky god, also called the Jade Emperor. He rules the present and is the symbol of heaven.

Z

zaddik A spiritual teacher and leader of a community of *Chasidic* Jews.

Zaidis A subdivision of the *Ismaili* sect of *Shi'ite* Islam, found in the highlands of the Yemen. The Zaidis have their own *imam*, or religious and secular leader, and they regard him as the earthly representative of the *Mahdi*.

zakat The giving of *alms*. This is one of the *five pillars of Islam* and is repeatedly stressed in the Qur'an as the duty of every Muslim. In some Islamic countries it is collected as a tax by the state and then distributed to the needy; in others the local mosques organize the collection, but the amount is fixed at two and a half per cent of the believer's savings. Voluntary alms, known as *sadaquat*, can always be given and are highly esteemed by Muslims.

Zawiya A community house, often very large, inhabited by *Sufi sheikhs* and their disciples; it may also refer to other places where a Sufi may seek seclusion.

zazen Meditation in the traditional, cross-legged, sitting posture of Zen. The term also refers to the Buddhist practice of continuous awareness and mindfulness throughout the day.

Seated on the tatami, or straw matting, the monk meditates, while he who is in charge walks with a stick, a keisaku with which he may deliver a blow to the inattentive.

The spirit of Zen Buddhism has informed not only its followers but the sensibility of the Japanese people in even the simple everyday act of drinking tea. In accordance with a desire to reflect the chance and asymmetric nature of the world, the ceremony is held in a small room, itself irregular, in a wooden building designed for this purpose. The person who will make the tea enters the room by a particular route and the physical actions he or she performs will be flowing and spontaneous, but, at the same time, entirely disciplined.

Zen Known as *Ch'an* in China. The school of *Mahayana Buddhism* in the Far East that emphasizes meditation as the means of gain enlightenment. Ch'an comes from the Sanskrit word 'dhyana', which means meditation. Ch'an began in China in the fifth century CE and grew into a separate school in the eighth century, though its roots can be traced back to the Buddha himself. Around 1200 *Eisei* brought Ch'an to Japan, where the word was pronounced 'Zen'.

Throughout China and Japan, Zen has had a strong impact on painting, poetry and all aspects of culture. It has attracted small circles of followers throughout Europe and America.

Zen urges people not to waste time in philosophy or even study of Buddhism. It is concerned with what it sees as the living spirit of Buddhism, an urgency to gain enlightenment at any price: nothing may stand in the way. Disciples are urged to depend on their mind only, since mind

provides a contact with Absolute Reality. With meditation as the tool, one can see into one's own true nature and become enlightened. This is not a process of reasoning. Zen masters, often with the aid of *koan*, try to bring pupils beyond the limits of reason, when they will experience and understand reality by intuition. When this happens, it happens suddenly: this is known as *satori*, the Zen word for the experience of enlightenment.

Zinzendorf, Count Nikolaus Ludwig von (1700–60) The founder of the Moravian Brethren. Zinzendorf united the descendants of persecuted German Protestants from present-day Czechoslovakia with *Lutheran* sympathizers into a new movement that hoped to unify all Protestant Christians. He was also very active as a missionary, travelling throughout Europe and to America, and encouraged missionary work among non-Christians.

Zionism The political movement to establish and develop a national homeland for Jewish people. The Zionist movement was founded in the nineteenth century by Theodor Herzl, a Hungarian Jew, as a response to the oppression and persecution of Jews in eastern Europe and to the rise in anti-Semitism. In 1917 the British government, which was theoretically supervising the administration of Palestine, agreed in principle to the need for a Jewish state. The persecution and slaughter suffered by the Jews during World War II increased the pressure to create such a country, and the modern State of Israel was proclaimed in 1948. Although it is basically a secular and not a religious movement, Zionism nevertheless echoes many of the promises made by God through the prophets in the *Torah* that the Jews would recover the *Promised Land*, and many in the movement have linked the creation of a Jewish state with the beginning of Israel's mission to found the *kingdom of God* on earth.

Zohar An important part of the Jewish *Kabbalah* that explains the hidden, mystical meaning of the *Torah*. Tradition attributes it to Rabbi Simeon bar Yohai, a second-century Hebrew scholar. In fact, the Zohar was probably composed in Spain in the thirteen century CE and came to northern Europe when the Jews were expelled from that country. It deals with many occult subjects such as *astrology*, and is written largely in allegorical language. Today it is still studied, especially by *Chasidic* Jews.

Zoroaster The founder of *Zoroastrianism*, who is believed to have lived around 1500BCE in Iran. Zoroaster came from a family of priests and, until his thirtieth birthday, lived a settled family life. Then he had a series of visions of God, on the basis of which he began to preach. Rejected by his own clan, he fled and chanced upon a rival king, Vishtaspa, whom he converted to his message. Zoroaster's teachings conflicted with the *polytheism* of the old religion, since he stated that the only good God was *Ahura Mazda* and that he would judge each individual soul after death. Tradition has it that Zoroaster was murdered by a priest from the old religion while performing the fire ceremony of his own faith, at the age of seventy-seven.

Zoroaster, the founder of a small but influential religion in which fire ceremonies and fire temples are important.

This is the famous stone garden from the Ryoanji temple and aptly illustrates Zen acceptance of the natural order of things. The sand is raked in the traditional way and the abstract, seemingly random disposition of the stones induces a sense of tranquillity and stimulates awareness. Satori, or enlightenment, is achieved by an intuitive response, rather than a painful accretion of knowledge.

Zoroastrianism The ancient religion of Persia, founded by a Persian priest named Zoroaster, who lived around 1500BCE. He modified the existing religion, which was very close to the Hinduism of the *Vedas*, and transformed it into a faith which is neither *monotheistic*, nor *polytheistic*, but *dualist*: it believes in two divine forces, one good, one evil, which are continually at war with each other. The good god is known as *Ohrmazd* or *Ahura Mazda*, the evil one as *Ahriman* or *Angra Mainyu*. Zoroaster taught that man can help tip the balance so as to enable Ahura Mazda to win finally.

The sequence of events which will usher in the Last Judgement is as follows. Just before the final battle between Ahriman and Ahura Mazda takes place, the *Saoshyant*, or saviour of the world, will be born from the miraculously preserved seed of Zoroaster. When the battle between good and evil has finally been won by Ahura Mazda, helped by the thoughts, words and deeds of good men, the Saoshyant will raise the dead and prepare them for judgment. Souls will be reunited with their bodies and will have to cross the narrow 'Accountants' Bridge'. If they are not ready for heaven, they will fall off into *purgatory*, where they will be purified, so as to enter heaven at a later stage. Finally, all the dead will share in the eternal *Kingdom of God*.

Besides Ahura Mazda, Zoroastrians also venerate *Amshaspentans* or *Holy Immortals*. They also worship fire (atash or atar) as sacred to Ahura Mazda, and in all their temples a sacred fire is kept burning by the *dastur* or priest; thus fire plays a central part in their daily rite of worship, the *Yasna*. They are bound to pray five times a day and to keep seven high feasts during the year, one of which is in honour of fire. When a boy is ready to undertake these reponsibilities, the dastur clothes him with a thread or *kusti*, which he wears continually. Since Zoroastrians venerate the elements of earth, air, fire and water as holy, they cannot allow them to be polluted by the corpses of their dead; they thus expose their dead in *dakhmas* or towers of silence. The beliefs of the Zoroastrians can be found in their sacred book, the *Avesta*.

Zurvanism A *heresy* within *Zoroastrianism* which teaches that Zurvan, the Absolute, was the creator of both *Ahura Mazda* and *Ahriman*, and so was the source of all that is good and evil on this earth.

Appendices

IN THIS SECTION of the book are included appendices: a map, charts and statistics, all of which have been designed to expand upon the information already in the dictionary. They also add new elements which will complement and further clarify the picture of the world's beliefs, ancient as well as modern.

The calendar of religious festivals describes the different feasts which may be celebrated at any one time by members of faiths all over the world. Where possible, exact dates have been indicated, and separate charts of the Jewish and Islamic calendars have been compiled.

A further appendix presents a digest of the most important gods and goddesses of the ancient world, together with information about forms of worship in societies such as those of the ancient Egyptians, the Aztecs and the Celts. There is, moreover, a section which deals with the gods worshipped by preliterate and tribal societies, although, clearly, this cannot claim to be an exhaustive list; rather it is there to stimulate interest and to recognise that very many peoples worship gods known only to those living within their restricted community.

A major section is made up of chronological tables indicating the dates of significant events and the countries where they took place. They have been so designed that the reader can compare the movements and developments of religion throughout the world over the centuries. What it has not been possible to do, clearly, is to give a precise date for very many events of the greatest importance, either because no records exist to indicate a date even approximately, or because such events were, by their nature, less events than long-evolved movements and developments. Their omission is by no means a denial of their profound significance and it should be borne in mind by the reader that the very foundations of all that we are today were laid in the ages before recorded history.

There follows a number of extracts from the sacred scriptures of some of the major religions, extracts which should reveal the true spirit of a particular faith and how it expresses itself.

This is followed by a map which gives a graphic representation of where the various religions have their greatest following and this is accompanied by a statistical breakdown of the numbers of people in the world who profess the different religions.

Finally, there is a bibliography which aims to encourage the interested layman to read further on a subject which has captured his interest.

All the family join together in this joyful celebration of the Chinese New Year. Offerings of fruit and cakes are made, and candles in large quantities are burned by the jostling crowd of celebrants.

A calendar of religious festivals

January

1st **New Year:** the festival according to the Gregorian Calendar.
Ganjitsu: the Japanese New Year Festival.

6th **The Epiphany:** the Christian festival which commemorates the coming of the three wise men to offer gifts to the infant Jesus.

6th and 7th **Christmas Eve** and **Christmas Day:** Christians who follow the Russian Orthodox calendar celebrate the birth of the infant Jesus in Bethlehem.

19th **The Epiphany:** the festival according to the Russian Orthodox Calendar.

— **Birthday of Swami Vivekananda:** the feast of the nineteenth-century Hindu leader.

A young man, seated on a white bull, enacts the role of Shiva.

21st Jan. to 19th Feb. **Yuan Tan:** the Chinese New Year Festival. Yuan Tan is the Mandarin version, Hsin Nien the Cantonese version of its name.

February

2nd **Candlemas:** a Christian festival commemorating the presentation of Jesus in the temple at Jerusalem. Candles are carried to symbolize Christ as the light of the world.

15th **Parinirvana:** a Mahayana Buddhist festival celebrating the Buddha's final passing from this world.

— **Shiva Ratri:** a Hindu festival of the Dance of Shiva. Shiva is portrayed dancing within a ring of fire, on the back of the demon which is ignorance.

— **Magha Puja (Full moon day):** a Theravada Buddhist festival marking the day that the Buddha ordained 1,250 of his disciples.

— **Birthday of Sri Rama Krishna:** Born a Brahman, he became chief priest at the Kali temple in Calcutta. He postulated that there is Universal Truth in all religions and lived for a time as a Muslim and as a Christian. His birthday is celebrated by Hindus.

FEBRUARY/MARCH

— **Shrove Tuesday (Mardi Gras):** the Christian day of feasting before the season of Lent.

— **Ash Wednesday:** the day after Shrove Tuesday, marking the beginning of Lent.

— **Lent:** the period of forty days of prayer and penance observed by Christians, ending on Easter Sunday.

— **Purim:** the Jewish festival of Lots. It commemorates the saving of the Jews from a massacre, as described in the Torah.

— **Lantern Festival (Teng Chieh):** the end of the Chinese New Year.

— **Mahashivaratri:** the Hindu festival in honour of Shiva, one of the three principal gods.

March

11th to 20th **Farvardegan Days:** the period when the Parsis think of fravashis, the spirits of the dead who have returned to God (Ahura Mazda) to help in the fight against evil. This date is celebrated by the Fasli sect. (During leap years the date varies slightly).

21st **New Year:** the celebration at the Spring equinox of the New Year, according to the Fasli sect of Zoroastrianism.

— **Jamshedi Naoroze:** the Zoroastrian New Year celebration when the men dress in white and women wear coloured clothes. All try to wear something new. Ritual bathing, worship and the exchange of gifts occur.

— **Khordad Sal:** the birthday of Zarathustra, celebrated by the Parsis.

— **Naw Ruz:** the Baha'is New Year, which follows one Baha'i month (nineteen days) of fasting.

25th **Lady Day:** the day chosen by Christians to celebrate the annunciation to the Blessed Virgin Mary that she would bear the Messiah.

— **Ramanavmi:** the birthday of Lord Rama, celebrated by Hindus.

MARCH/APRIL

— **Holi (Spring Festival):** the Hindu festival commemorating the love of Krishna and Radha.

— **Hola-Mohalla (Spring Festival):** the Sikh festival which is identified with Holi, featuring sporting competitions.

— **Palm Sunday:** the Sunday before Easter, commemorating Christ's entry into Jerusalem on a donkey.

— **Holy Week:** the week from Palm Sunday to Easter Sunday when Christians contemplate Christ's sufferings and death on the cross.

— **Maundy Thursday:** on this day Christians commemorate the Last Supper of Christ and his Apostles.

— **Good Friday:** the Friday of Holy Week, the day commemorating Christ's crucifixion.

— **Holy Saturday:** the day before Easter Sunday when Christ's body lay in the tomb.

— **Pesach (Passover):** a Jewish festival celebrating the freeing of the Hebrews from slavery in Egypt and their exodus, led by Moses. When the angel of death passed over their houses the Hebrews escaped by painting the lintels with the blood of a lamb, as instructed by God.

April

4th or 5th **Ch'ing Ming (Festival of Pure Brightness):** a Chinese feast when the spirits of the ancestors are honoured and their graves are tended.

8th **Buddha Sakyamuni's Birthday:** Mahayana Buddhists celebrate the birth of the first Buddha, Siddhartha Gautama.

13th **Baisakhi:** a Sikh and Hindu festival marking the religious New Year in April and, for Sikhs, the formation of the Khalsa.

21st **First Day of Ridvan:** a Baha'i festival lasting for twelve days, commemorating Baha'u'llah's declaration that he was the promised one.

25th **Sekiten:** a festival celebrated by the Japanese, acknowledging the debt owed to the contributions Confucius made to culture.

30th **Zarthastno Diso:** the day chosen by the Fasli sect of Parsis to commemorate the death of Zarathustra, also called Zoroaster.

— **Mahavir Jayanti:** Jains celebrate the birth of Mahavira, the last of the twenty-four tirthankaras.

APRIL/MAY

— **Ascension Day:** the celebration of Christ's ascension into Heaven, held forty days after Easter.

May

2nd **Twelfth Day of Ridvan:** the end of Ridvan, when no work is done. On this day administrative bodies of the Baha'i assemblies are elected.

15th **Hollyhock Festival:** hollyhocks are offered to the gods at two Shinto shrines in Kyoto, Japan.

29th **Declaration of the Bab:** a Baha'i festival celebrated in honour of the day when Siyyid 'Ali-

Muhammad announced that he was the Bab, the Gate of God.

29th **Ascension of Baha'u'llah:** Baha'is honour the death of Baha'u'llah in 1892.

— **Zarthostno Diso:** the day chosen by the Kadmi sect of Parsis to honour the death of Zarathustra.

— **Wesak (Full Moon Day):** a Theravada Buddhist festival celebrating the birth, enlightenment and death of the Buddha.

MAY/JUNE

— **Shinran-Shonin Day:** the festival to celebrate two Japanese Buddhists who were the founders of Pure Land Amida Buddhism.

— **Whit Sunday:** the Christian festival of Pentecost, seven weeks after Easter, to commemorate the descent of the Holy Spirit upon the disciples of Christ.

— **Trinity Sunday:** the Sunday after Whit Sunday, when Christians celebrate the unity of the Father, the Son and the Holy Spirit.

— **Corpus Christi:** the Thursday after Trinity, on which Roman Catholics celebrate Christ's real presence still among them.

— **Shavuoth (Pentecost):** a Jewish summer festival, commemorating the time that Moses received the Ten Commandments on Mount Sinai.

— **Martyrdom of Guru Arjan Dev:** a Sikh festival commemorating the death of the fifth guru, who was killed when the Emperor Jehangir began persecuting the Sikhs.

— **Ratha Yatra:** the Hindu festival at Puri to honour Jagannatha, the Lord of the Universe. Images are pulled through the street on huge chariots, or rathas, and the word juggernaut derives from this feast.

June

1st **Zarthostno Diso:** the death of Zoroaster, or Zarathustra as he is often known, commemorated by the Shahenshai sect of Parsis.

21st **Summer Solstice:** the longest day.

24th **Poson (Dhamma Vijaya), Full moon day:** Theravada Buddhists in Sri Lanka commemorate the fact that Asoka, the great ruler, sent his son to teach the Buddhist path to the Sinhalese people.

July

9th **Martyrdom of the Bab:** a Baha'i festival marking the day in 1850 when the Bab was executed by a firing squad in Tabriz.

13th **Obon:** a Japanese Shinto/Buddhist festival in which twenty-seven lanterns are lit to guide the spirits of ancestors to the family home for an annual visit. There is much celebration and a folk dance marks the end of the day.

— **Farvardegan Days:** a Zoroastrian festival celebrated by the Kadmi sect. (*See* 11th to 20th March.)

— **New Year Day:** the Zoroastrian New Year for the Kadmi sect.

— **Khordad Sal:** the birth of Zarathustra is celebrated by the Kadmi Sect.

— **Asala Puja (Full moon day):** Theravada Buddhists celebrate the feast known as Dhammacakka Day.

JULY/AUGUST

— **Tisha b'Av (Fast of the 9th Ab):** a Jewish fast, commemorating the destruction of the first and second temples in Jerusalem

— **Festival of Maidens:** young Chinese girls ask the gods to grant that they become wives of loving husbands.

August

1st **Lammas Day:** the name derives from Hlaf-Masse (loaf mass). This Christian festival celebrates the harvest. The loaf made from the first grain was taken to the church.

15th **Assumption of Blessed Virgin Mary:** a Christian festival in honour of the Blessed Virgin's ascending directly into heaven.

— **Farvardegan Days:** the Shahenshai sect of Parsis celebrate the feast at this time.

— **New Year:** the feast celebrated by the Shahenshai sect of Parsis.

— **Khordad Sal:** the birth of Zarathustra is celebrated by the Shahenshai sect of Parsis.

— **Raksha Bandhan:** a Hindu family festival in which sisters present brothers with a rakhi, a red and gold thread, to protect them from harm or evil. In return brothers promise to look after sisters.

— **The Anniversary of Guru Granth Sahib:** the Sikh festival to honour the sacred scripture which is now the final guru.

— **Yue Lan:** the Feast of Hungry Ghosts celebrated by Chinese Taoists. Food, fruit and money are left for wandering ghosts.

— **Chung Yuan (All Souls' Day):** a Chinese Buddhist festival to honour the souls of the departed.

AUGUST/SEPTEMBER

— **Janmashtami (Janan Ashtami):** the Hindu feast to celebrate the birthday of Krishna.

— **Ganesh Chaturthi:** a temple festival to Ganesha, the elephant-headed Hindu God.

— **Paryushan (Penance):** The Jain year ends in August/September. The last eight days of the old year are Paryushan—days of penance, the final day being a day of fasting.

At Suwa, in Japan, an autumn festival is held to venerate the god Okuninushi no mikoto, descended from Amaterasu; he passes half the year in the spring shrine and half the year in the autumn shrine.

September

29th **Michaelmas:** the Christian feast to honour the archangel Michael.

— **Farvadin:** a Zoroastrian ten-day festival during which the dead are said to visit the homes of their descendants.

SEPTEMBER/OCTOBER

— **Rosh Hashanah:** the Jewish New Year beginning with the Ten Days of Return which end on Yom Kippur.

— **Yom Kippur:** the holiest day in the Jewish year, devoted to prayer, worship and repentance of sins.

— **Sukkoth (also known as Booths):** a Jewish festival at the end of the harvest, lasting for seven days. It commemorates God's protection of his 'Chosen People'.

— **Simchath Torah (Rejoicing of The Law):** a Jewish festival during which the final section of the Torah is read, followed by the first section, since on this day the yearly cycle of reading the law begins and ends.

— **Chung Ch'iu (Mid-Autumn Festival):** the feast of the Moon Goddess. It is sometimes called the Mooncake festival, since special cakes are made. Some are offered to the gods and some are eaten by the Chinese celebrants.

— **Birthday of Confucius:** the Chinese celebrate in honour of the birth of the philosopher.

— **Durga Puja:** the main Hindu festival in honour of the goddess Durga, lasting nine nights. Images of the goddess are at the centre of festivities.

— **Navaratra:** the ninth night of Durga Puja, when images of the goddess are washed.

— **Ch'ung Yeung (Double Ninth):** the day set aside by the Chinese for honouring ancestors. Their graves are tended and the feast recalls how, warned by a soothsayer, a man escaped doom by climbing on to high ground. People imitate this by kite flying and climbing on to high places.

October

20th **Birth of the Bab:** the Baha'i faithful celebrate the birth of the Bab, the 'Gate to God'.

31st **Hallowe'en:** a Christian festival originally signalling the end of the summer and the eve of the Celtic New Year. A time, traditionally, for warning off evil spirits.

OCTOBER/NOVEMBER

— **Diwali:** the Indian New Year feast celebrated by Hindus and Sikhs. Hindus celebrate the return of Rama and his reunion with Sita. Bonfires are lit and images of the evil Ravana burnt. People light lamps to welcome Lakshmi, goddess of wealth, into their homes. The Sikhs celebrate the laying of the foundation stone of the Golden Temple by Guru Ram Das.

November

1st **All Saints' Day:** a Christian feast to commemorate the known and unknown martyrs and saints of the Christian church.

2nd **All Souls' Day:** many Christian denominations pray on this day for all souls who are believed to be in Purgatory.

12th **Birth of Baha'u'llah:** the Baha'is celebrate the birth of the 'Promised One'.

15th **Shichi-go-san:** in Japanese this means seven, five, three. Parents take girls aged seven, boys of five and all children of three years of age to the temple in thanksgiving that they have lived so long and to pray that they will grow in health and happiness.

30th **Birthday of Guru Nanak:** the Sikhs rejoice in commemoration of the birth of the founder of their religion.

— **Time of Sending Winter Clothes to Ancestors:** for fear the ancestor spirits of the Chinese may grow cold in winter, clothes made from paper are created and then burned so that the spirits may receive them and so keep warm.

NOVEMBER/DECEMBER

— **Advent Sunday:** this day begins the Christian Church's year and lasts for four weeks until Christmas. It is a time for preparing for Christ's second coming.

— **Chanukah:** the Jewish festival of lights, celebrating the recapture and rededication of the temple at Jerusalem in 164BCE.

December

8th **Immaculate Conception of the Blessed Virgin Mary:** a Roman Catholic celebration of their belief that the Virgin Mary was born without original sin.

8th **Bodhi Day:** Mahayana Buddhists celebrate this as the day of the Buddha's enlightenment. Siddhartha Gautama became Buddha Sakyamuni—the first Buddha. His image is covered with pink flowers and tea made with hydrangea leaves is poured over the head of the statue.

A ceremonial drummer at the Temple of the Tooth in Kandy, Sri Lanka. At the feast of Perahera, the summer festival, the sacred relic of the Buddha is venerated.

24th **Christmas Eve:** the Christian feast of preparation for the birth of Jesus.

25th **Christmas Day:** together with Easter, the most important day of the Christian calendar, a festival celebrating the birth of Christ. It is a time for giving and receiving gifts, the singing of carols and feasting.

DECEMBER/JANUARY

— **Birthday of Guru Gobind Singh:** a Sikh festival honouring the tenth guru who introduced the khande-ka-amrit ceremony and who chose as his successor the Adi Granth, the sacred scripture.

Islamic festivals

THESE festivals fall about eleven to twelve days earlier each year. The Muslim day begins in the evening and is dependent upon the actual sighting of the new moon.

The months of the year are as follows: Muharram (30 days), Safar (29 days), Rabi I (30 days), Rabi II (29 days), Jumad I (30 days), Jumad II (29 days), Rajab (30 days), Shaban (29 days), Ramadan (30 days), Shawwal (29 days), Dhual-Aa'dah (30 days), Dhu al-Hijja (29 or 30 days).

The dates of the chief festivals are indicated according to the Muslim calendar, which is dated AH, meaning After Hijra.

Day of Hijra: 1st Muharram: This feast, commemorates the journey of Muhammad and his followers from Mecca to Medina. The date was originally not exactly the present date, but 1st Muharram was chosen by 'Umar, the caliph.

10th Muharram: A day of fasting, it marks the overthrow of the Egyptians, when Moses led his people, the Israelites, out of slavery. Muhammad himself kept the day as a fast and wished all Muslims to do so. On this day also, Shi'ite Muslims observe the death of Husain, the grandson of Muhammad, who died in battle. Mourning continues for forty days. On the tenth day there is a mourning procession and no public entertainments or television broadcasts are allowed on that day.

Mawlid ul-Nabi: 12th Rabi ul-Awwal: known as Prophet's Day this marks the birthday of Muhammad which is celebrated with readings and prayers. The whole month of Rabi ul-Awwal is 'birth month'.

Lailat ul-Isra: 27th Rajab: The Night Journey. This feast commemorates the journey that Muhammad made to Jerusalem, from where he was taken to Heaven and then returned to earth.

Ramadan: Muslims spend Ramadan fasting from one new moon to the next. Neither food nor drink may be taken from sunrise to sunset.

Id ul-Fitr: The feast to mark the end of Ramadan, signalled by the new moon. There is much rejoicing, and people greet each other with the words 'Id Mubaraq'—'Happy Id'. The day begins with bathing, followed by prayer, then a visit to the mosque. People wear new clothes, and samosas (potato and meat dumplings) are cooked.

Id ul-Adha: 10th Dhu al-Hijja: A four-day festival when sacrifices are made, after a visit to the mosque. Those who cannot, because of the culture in which they live, personally sacrifice a cow, goat, sheep or camel, send money to relatives who will do it on their behalf. Any meat not eaten by the family is given to the needy, and gifts are given to the poor.

Hajj: Dhu al-Hijja: Pilgrimage. Every Muslim aspires to go to Mecca, the most sacred place in the Islamic faith. The pilgrim wears special clothing and goes to Bayt ul-haram, the mosque where the Ka'ba is found. It is to be circled seven times, the pilgrim trying to kiss the Black Stone, if possible. Then he or she must run seven times between Safa and Marwa and then go to Mina. On the ninth day there are prayers on Mount Arafat after which forty-nine pebbles are collected for Jamrat, the ceremony of stoning the Devil, at Mina. Then the pilgrims return to Mecca and circle the Ka'ba again, at which point the pilgrimage is over. Pilgrims can take the name al-hajji and they select some presents to take home with them—dates or holy water from zam zam, the holy well.

Lailat ul–Bara'h, the Night of Forgiveness: This is the feast when, in preparation for Ramadan, old quarrels are settled and special prayers are offered that the coming year will be holy. The feast takes place on the night of the full moon two weeks before the commencement of Ramadan.

The Jewish calendar

THE INDIVIDUAL FEASTS of Judaism have been incorporated into the main calendar, but the names of the Jewish months are listed below, showing their relation to the months of the Gregorian calendar:

January/February	Shevat
February/March	Adar
March/April	Nisan
April/May	Iyar
May/June	Sivan
June/July	Tamuz
July/August	Av
August/September	Ellul
September/October	Tishri
October/November	Cheshvan
November/December	Kislev
December/January	Teveth

Ancient deities and worship in primal societies

Aztec worship

THE AZTECS, who lived in Mexico, were worshippers of gods who, they believed, demanded human sacrifices. The priests would offer up the hearts of many victims to placate the deities.

Chicomecoatl: the goddess of maize, and one of the most popular of the gods.

Coatlicue: the mother of Quetzalcoatl, she was a moon goddess who gave birth to the sun.

Huitzilopochtli: his name means 'hummingbird wizard', or 'blue hummingbird on the left', and he was the god of the sun and war, in conflict with darkness and night.

Nezahualcoyotl: an Aztec ruler who lived from CE1418 until CE1472. He was disturbed at the huge numbers of human sacrifices and he tried to halt the practice, urging, instead, worship of Tloque Nahuaque who was the sole god from whom all others derived their being.

Quetzalcoatl: his name is derived from the sacred Quetzal bird, though some interpretations give it as 'precious twin', and he is a major figure in both the Mayan and Aztec religions. It is possible that he was a king of a pre-Aztec civilization. Myth has it that he was the god of air who descended to earth to bring civilization to human beings. This, together with his opposition to human sacrifice, aroused the wrath of the other gods and he was forced to flee in a boat made of snakeskin. He is often represented by his symbol of a plumed serpent. The high priests of the Aztec religion were given his name as a token of their high office.

Tezcatlipoca: the god of the night, he was a magician whose symbol is the jaguar. His name means 'that which cause the Black Mirror to shine', or 'mirror that smokes'.

Tlaloc: 'he who makes things grow', the god of rain and plants. For the festival to honour him, priests sacrificed babies and young children.

Tloque Nahuaque: Nezahualcoyotl, the Aztec king, worshipped him as the supreme god, and attempted to lead his people to venerate him as 'the cause of all causes, the unknown god'.

Tonatiuh: the god of the sun who was ever thirsty for human blood.

Xipe Totec: the god of agriculture, he was usually represented by a mask of a flayed human face, which linked him with the maize which was also skinned alive. His name means 'the flayed one' and sacrifices to him were outstandingly cruel.

XIUHTECUHTLI

COATLICUE

Xiuhtecuhtli: the 'turquoise lord', he was the ancient Mexican god of fire, and in every home and temple there burned a fire in his name.

Celtic worship

Belenos: the Celtic god of spring and of healing, he may have been associated with the sun. His name means 'bright' or 'shining'.

Beltane: the spring festival from which the modern May Day celebrations have derived. The name, 'shining fire', suggests that fires were lit to induce the sun to come forth to imitate them.

Bran: a hero god associated with the raven, and celebrated in the *Mabinogion*, the Welsh book of legend.

Brighid: the goddess of prophecy and of healing and learning. Her equivalent in Gaul was linked by the Romans with Minerva. Her feast day is held on the same day as Beltane.

Cernunnos: 'the horned one', a god associated with fertility. He was seen as the protector of the animal kingdom, and was frequently portrayed with a stag or a horned serpent or a bull.

Dagda: the king of the Tuatha de Danaan, the people of Danu, he was the 'good one', the god of wisdom and knowledge and the patron of the druids.

Danu: sometimes known as Anu, her name means 'plenty'. She was the Celtic goddess of the earth and the mother of all Irish gods.

Donn: 'the dark one', the Irish god of the dead. The god of storms and ship wrecks, he was thought to live on Tech Duinn, off the south-west coast of Ireland. He was also a protector of cattle and flocks.

CERNUNNOS

Lugh: known as Lleu by the Welsh, this god of war was also venerated for his influence over trade and money-making. He is often portrayed as a young traveller, and Julius Caesar compared this most honoured of Celtic gods with Mercury, the messenger of the gods in the Roman pantheon. He has given his name to Lyon, Loudun and Carlisle.

Manannan: the Irish sea god, who rode the waves and who granted eternal life to the other gods. He is symbolised by three armour-clad legs joined to form a wheel, which is the emblem of the Isle of Man. The symbol is explained by the phrase 'whichever way you throw me, I stand'.

Morrighan: the goddess of battle, she is the dark queen of Celtic myth who haunts the battlefields, often disguised as a crow. Whenever she appears, often accompanied by two other crows, it is a sign of impending doom and destruction.

Nuadha: a Celtic deity, who lost his arm in battle and had a silver arm fitted. He is associated with healing, and the sick and barren would go on pilgrimage to his temple.

Tuatha de Danaan: the 'tribes of the goddess Danu', they ruled Ireland after a series of battles established them as the principal Irish gods.

Ancient Egyptian worship

Amun: the king of the gods, whose name means 'hidden' deity of the pharaohs. In a later age he became identified with the sun god, Amun-Re.

Anubis: the god of the dead, often portrayed with the head of a jackal. It was he who conducted the souls of the dead to judgement, where they were weighed in the balance against a feather, which represented truth. He was also the guardian of tombs and cemeteries and helped Isis to restore and embalm the dismembered body of Osiris, thus creating the first mummy.

Aten: Aten was the sun. For a brief period he was the only god worshipped by decree of the Pharaoh Akhenaten.

Hathor: originally a sky goddess, she later became mistress of the stars and goddess of love and of the dance, as well as of the underworld. She is depicted as a cow, or as a woman with cow's horns, between which is a solar disc.

Horus: one of the best known gods; he was the sky god of lower Egypt and the hawk-headed god of the sun. He formed a triad of gods with his parents Isis and Osiris.

Isis: queen of the gods, she was the great mother goddess whose particular charges were fertility and corn growing. She was the ideal woman and mother.

Khnum: often depicted with a ram's head, he was the god of the upper Nile, dating from the Old Egyptian period. He was the creator of mankind.

Maat: goddess of justice, she was the daughter of Re and wife of Thoth.

Osiris: first venerated as a god of fertility and plant life, he later became the supreme god of Egypt, together with Re, and the king of the dead.

Ptah: seen by his priests as the god of creation and fertility, he was also the god of the dead. One version of the creation story has Ptah shaping the world, in the form of an egg, on the potter's wheel.

Re: the sun-god, the mighty god recognized by the dynastic line of ancient Egypt. The king of the gods, he was the father of human beings and the especial protector of kings.

Sebek: the god of water who was sometimes identified with evil and death. He was manifest in the form of a crocodile.

Seth: this god was perceived as evil and dangerous. He was the god of storms and it was he who was responsible for the death of Osiris. Often shown with the head of a pig.

Thoth: the moon-god, he was later associated with wisdom, learning and magic, and he invented writing. As early as 400BCE Greek travellers to Egypt associated him with Hermes.

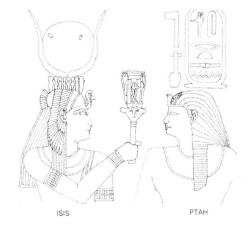

ISIS   PTAH

Ancient Greece and Rome

THE ANCIENT CIVILIZATION of Greece was much admired by the Romans, and very many of the Greek deities were adopted and adapted to their own fashion by the Roman people.

Ares *(Greek),* **Mars** *(Roman)*: the god of war.

Aphrodite *(Greek),* **Venus or Cytherea** *(Roman)*: the goddess of beauty, love and of fertilty.

Apollo *(Greek and Roman)*: the beautiful young god associated with the sun, who was the god of prophecy, music and medicine.

Artemis *(Greek),* **Diana** *(Roman)*: the goddess of hunting, who also influenced fertility and was the goddess of childbirth.

Asclepios *(Greek),* **Aesculapius** *(Roman)*: the god of healing and medicine, his symbol was a staff around which two snakes are intertwined, a symbol still used in modern times.

Athene *(Greek)*: a warrior-goddess who was the protectress of Athens and is depicted with helmet and shield.

Demeter *(Greek),* **Ceres** *(Roman)*: the goddess of agriculture, in particular the ripening of corn.

Dionysus *(Greek),* **Bacchus** *(Roman)*: the god of fruit, crops and, especially, the grape. Feasts which followers held to celebrate the turning of the grape into wine often degenerated into drunken orgies, and the adjective Bacchanal is used in a pejorative sense today. He was also believed to be the god of the underworld.

Hephaestus *(Greek),* **Vulcan** *(Roman)*: the mighty god of fire and volcanoes.

Herakles *(Greek),* **Hercules** *(Roman)*: the powerful hero who rescued the Greeks from many dangers, among them the Lernaean Hydra.

HERAKLES or HERCULES

Hera *(Greek),* **Juno** *(Roman)*: the Greek goddess, the wife of Zeus, was associated with the moon, while Juno was the wife of Jupiter and was seen as the patroness of marriage, women and childbirth.

Hermes *(Greek),* **Mercury** *(Roman)*: the wing-heeled messenger of the gods.

Hestia *(Greek),* **Vesta** *(Roman)*: the goddess of the hearth, the home and family life. Vesta was the goddess of Rome.

Persephone *(Greek),* **Proserpina** *(Roman)*: the goddess of vegetation who must spend half the year in Hades with Pluto. Her six months of absence correspond with winter.

Pan *(Greek)*: a bearded god with the horns and lower limbs of a goat, who embodied male sexuality and who was patron of herds and herdsmen.

Poseidon *(Greek),* **Neptune** *(Roman)*: originally, he was the 'earthshaker', the sender of earthquakes. Subsequently he became the god of the sea, in which rôle, with the trident as his symbol, he is most familiar to us today.

Zeus *(Greek),* **Jupiter** or **Jove** *(Roman)*: the father of the gods and of mortals, and the god of the sky and the weather.

DIONYSUS

Inca worship

Chasca: 'the long-haired star', the personification of the planet Venus, thought of by the Incas as patron of princesses, girls and flowers.

Huaca: any one of a host of divinities that the Incas worshipped. It is also the name of a shrine.

Inca: the divine king who was sovereign of the Incas.

Inti: the sun god of the Incas.

Mama Quilla: the goddess of the moon, who was both wife and sister of the sun.

Pachacamac: the leader of the gods. A shrine was erected by the followers of his cult near the city of Lima, Peru.

Pachacutec: the ninth Inca, or king, who was born in CE 1438. He rebuilt the city of Cuzco and he proclaimed Viracocha to be the supreme god.

Tiuhuanaco: at the centre of a mighty South American civilization, which existed around CE 1000 to CE 1300, was this city, 'the city of the dead'. The god venerated by the people of this city was a weeping god, but when the Incas came they linked him with their own sun-god and the city was dedicated to Viracocha.

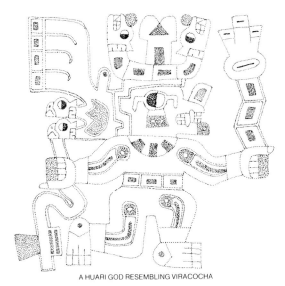

A HUARI GOD RESEMBLING VIRACOCHA

Viracocha: also known as Huiracocha. The god who created, but who was not, himself, created. His holy city was Tiuhuanaco.

Virgins of the Sun: the 'Chosen Women', or Aclla Cuna. At the age of ten, young girls were taken to the sun temple. Some were chosen as wives of the Inca, others became sacrificial victims. They were ruled by a chief priestess, Coya Pacsa, who was thought to be the human consort of the sun god.

Norse worship

THE ANCIENT PEOPLES of Scandinavia worshipped the Aesir and the Vanir. The former were the great gods, who dwelt in Asgard, while the latter were lesser gods who had been, at one time, in conflict with the Aesir, but who had subsequently become reconciled with them.

THE AESIR

Balder: the most beautiful of the gods, the son of Odin and Freja. His name means 'the bright one' and he was thought invincible until he was slain by Loki's mischief.

Loki: the father of monsters, a mischievous god who brought ill luck to Asgard. It was through Loki that Balder died.

Odin: also known as Wotan or Woden, he was the father of all the gods. He was worshipped by chiefs and warriors in his rôle as the god of war and 'father of the slain.' The day of the week known as Wednesday was named after him.

Thor: 'the thunderer.' He is portrayed as a mighty god with a hammer. The strongest of the gods, he was the patron of fertility.

THE VANIR

Frey: the ruler of the sun and the rain. He was the son of Njord and was the god of fertility.

Freyja: also known as Frigg, she was the sister of Frey, the consort of Odin and the goddess of love and fertility.

Heimdall: the watchman of the gods, he was known as 'the white god'.

Njord: the ruler of the winds and of the seas and oceans.

In the Norse pantheon, there were also figures who were less than the gods, but who were also significant.

The Valkyries: these were Odin's war-maidens who selected warriors who had died in battle for entry into Valhalla, the favourite home of Odin.

ODIN

Other religions

Astarte: the Phoenician and Canaanite fertility goddess who was extremely popular.

Baal: the name means 'master'. The chief god of fertility of the Canaanites and Phoenicians.

Baiame: in Australian aboriginal creation stories, he is the all-father, whose name means 'to make, to build'.

Chac: the rain god of the Mayan civilization. This benevolent god was depicted as an old man, weeping, with a face directed to the four corners of the earth. He was called upon to bring fertility when new seeds were being sown.

Chi: also known as Chineke, he is the supreme god of the Ibo people in Nigeria.

Dagon: a god associated with the Philistines. It was in his temple that the captured Ark of the Covenant was placed.

Dreamtime: *See* Ungud.

Enlil: the ancient Sumerian god of wind, who persuaded the other gods to send a flood to the earth.

Great Rainbow Snake: a mighty Australian totemic god of the Ungud, or Australian Dreamtime. He gives life, by sending the rain, and in the days of creation laid down the waters and regenerated the earth. To some he was the all-father, to others a great mother. He controls life and death.

Gilgamesh: a hero of Babylonian myth, he fought and was victorious against monsters.

Hadad: worshipped by the Assyrians and Babylonians as a storm god. His symbol was a lightning flash and the bull was his sacred animal.

Hecate: the earth goddess worshipped in Asia Minor, who held sway over the practice of magic and over death. She was depicted with three faces and was accompanied by torches and hounds.

Hinenuiotepo: the Maori god of the underworld.

Itzamara: chief of the Mayan gods, he was god of the sky and a patron of learning and healing. It was he who discovered writing.

Kaitiaki: a guardian spirit in the Maori religious belief.

Kalunga: the Bantu-speaking peoples name for the underworld.

Kukailimoku: the god of war in the Hawaiian pantheon.

Kwoth: the god of the Nuer people in East Africa.

Laima: the Latvian goddess of fate and birth.

Mana: the word used by Polynesians to express the invisible spiritual power which flows through all creation.

Manabusch: the hero of the Algonquin and other North American Indian tribes, he was believed to have brought life back to the earth after a great flood and to have introduced medicine and crafts to mankind.

Managan Tengri: the god of wild game of the Mongols.

Marduk: the god of the Babylonians who succeeded Enlil. He was worshipped as Bel, the Supreme Lord.

Maui: the great hero god of Polynesia. He was full of tricks and used them to help mankind.

Mawu: a name, common to many West African peoples, for the supreme god, the creator of gods who gives mankind its souls.

Mimi: shy, gentle nature spirits in northern Australia.

Mithra: also known as Mithras, he was the sun god of the ancient Persians. From the mythology which was built around him developed the precepts of Zoroastrianism, which is the religion of the Parsis. The symbolic representation of Ahura Mazda incorporates an eye, which is Mithra.

Molk (Molloch): a god to whom human sacrifices were offered, most particularly near Jerusalem in the Valley of Hinnom.

Mulungu: variations of this name are Murungu and Mungu, and it is a word common to several East African languages, signifying the supreme god.

Namandi: unlike *mimi*, they are malevolent nature spirits in northern Australia, who attack solitary travellers.

Ngai: the name for god in several East African languages.

Ngewo: the supreme god of the Mende people in Sierra Leone.

Nkulukulu: 'the Old, Old One', the Zulu name for god.

Nyame: 'the Shining One', the name for the supreme god in Ghana.

Patagaliwabe: the supreme god of southern Papua New Guinea. He punishes wrongdoers with sickness, war or death.

Perun: also known as Perkunas, the supreme god of ancient Russia, who ruled thunder and lightning.

Rarohenga: the underworld of the Maoris.

Rongo: the Maori god of agriculture.

Shango: the storm god of the Yoruba people, his symbol is an axe, and his sacred animal, a ram. His cult has been found in Haiti and South America.

Sol Invictus: an alternative name for *Mithra*, his cult was the official Roman imperial cult until Constantine embraced Christianity.

Tangaroa: the Polynesian god of creation, and the sea and sea creatures.

Tengri: the supreme god of the Mongols, sometimes known as the Eternal Tengri.

Thunderbird: in North American Indian religions he was the bird who watched over the eastern gateway to the world. The figure of the bird, as an eagle, is frequently seen at the top of the totem pole.

Topileta: a hermaphrodite god of the Trobriand islanders, gate keeper of their heaven, Tuma, an island of spirits. The Trobriand islanders live in the Massim of Papua New Guinea.

Uguns Mate: the Latvian fire goddess.

Ungud: the Australian Dreamtime, also known as Wongar, the age when the totemic ancestors shaped the earth and life came to be. Dreamtime ancestors usually produced human and animal ancestors.

Wovoka: a Paiute North American Indian mystic, who lived from CE 1856 to CE 1932. He encouraged his people to fight against their white invaders through the ghost dance.

Yum Kaax: the corn god of the Mayan people, portrayed as a young man holding a flowering plant.

Zemes Dievs: the Latvian god of the farm, who may be associated with *Perun*.

Zemes Mate: The Latvian earth goddess.

KUKAILIMOKU

A chronology of beliefs in historical context

	WESTERN EUROPE	EASTERN EUROPE, THE NEAR EAST & AFRICA	
2000 BCE		2000 Abraham, the prophet	**2000 BCE**
	1600–1500 Height of Cretan civilization	*c.*1600 Hebrews enter Egypt	
1500		1580–1100 'New' Kingdom, or Egyptian empire *c.*1360 Atenism in Egypt 1360–1350 Tutankhamun, pharaoh of Egypt 1200 The siege of Troy *c.*1200 The Exodus from Egypt led by Moses	**1500**
1000	753 Rome is founded 683 Kingship abolished in Athens	1012–972 King David 970–931 King Solomon; construction of the Temple of Jerusalem *c.*900 Period of writing of Homer's *Epics* 931–721 The Kingdom of Israel 931–587 The Kingdom of Judah 586 Capture of Jerusalem: Judah deported to Babylon	**1000**
500	447 Building of Parthenon begun 427–347 Plato, philosopher 321 Death of Aristotle, philosopher 280 Translation of *Pentateuch* into Greek 44 Julius Caesar assassinated 31 Augustus becomes Emperor of Rome	538 Babylon taken by Persians 336 Rise of Alexander the Great 331 Death of Darius and end of Persian empire 164 Recapture and rededication of Temple at Jerusalem 63 Palestine ruled by the Romans 39–4 King Herod	**500**
CE	18 Death of Ovid	4–30 Jesus 25–30 Pontius Pilate, procurator of Judaea 28–9 Preaching of John the Baptist	**CE**
50		51–7 Missionary travels of St Paul	**50**

	THE AMERICAS	THE FAR EAST AND AUSTRALASIA	
2000 BCE		*c.*2000 Early roots of Taoism *c.*2000 Australian aboriginals long established in Australia with distinct religious culture 1750–1112 Shang dynasty in China	**2000 BCE**
1500		*c.*1500 Aryan warriors invasion of the Indus valley 1500–500 The Vedic Period	**1500**
	1200–1400 Chavin cult, Peru. Worship of a feline animal known as 'The Smiling God' or 'Staff God'	*c.*1200 The *Riga Veda* *c.*1122–256 Chou dynasty	
1000	1000–500 Early civilization in Yucatan, Mexico	*c.*900 Approximate time of the founding of Jainism *c.*700 The earlier Upanishads 604 Traditional date of Lao Tsu's birth 588 Traditional date of Zoroaster's revelation	**1000**
500	*c.*200 Early Mayan temples built at Tikal and Vaxactum	*c.*500 Tao religious philosophy expounded 540 Mahavira, founder of Jainism, is born *c.*563–483 Siddhartha Gautama—the Buddha 551–479 Confucius, philosopher 327–325 Alexander the Great in India 300 The *Bhagavad Gita* 251 First Buddhist mission into Sri Lanka 250 Ashoka establishes a Buddhist kingdom 268–231 The reign of Ashoka 221–206 Ch'in dynasty	**500**
CE			**CE**
50			**50**

WESTERN EUROPE		EASTERN EUROPE, THE NEAR EAST & AFRICA	
		64 St Paul beheaded	
		70 The fall of the Temple of Jerusalem	
		70–100 Gospels of St Mark, St Matthew and St Luke	
		c.80–90 Council of Yavneh. Judaism redefines itself after the fall of Jerusalem	
100	100–250 Worship of Mithra, or Mithras, and Christianity spread throughout the Roman empire	100 Gospel of St John	**100**
	117 Roman Empire at its greatest extent		
		135 The destruction of Jerusalem	
150			**150**
200			**200**
	216–77 Mani, the founder of Manichaeanism		
250		250 Persecution of Christians by Decius Pope Fabian martyred	**250**
		268 Synod of Antioch condemns heresy of Paul of Samosata	
		280 Armenia Christianized	
		285 Beginning of monastic life in Egypt	
300			**300**
	312–37 Constantine, Emperor of Rome		
	313 Milan Edict recognizes Christianity		
		325 Council of Nicaea called by Emperor Constantine	
350			**350**

	THE AMERICAS	THE FAR EAST AND AUSTRALASIA	
		61 Legendary dream of Emperor Ming about the Buddha. Reputed beginning of Chinese Buddhism 78–103 Reign of Kanishka, India 97 Chinese expedition penetrates to Persian Gulf	
100		c.100 Tao Chias—Taoist religion formed. Chang Tao Ling, the Taoist leader	**100**
150		80–150 Asvaghosha, the disciple of the Buddha	**150**
200	200–500 City of Tuiahuanaco, Lake Titicaca, Bolivia	200 The *Lotus Sutra*	**200**
250		220 End of Han dynasty, China 230 Emperor Sujin of Japan	**250**
300	300 Zapotec culture established		**300**
350	300–900 Maya culture and religion developed	320 Gupta dynasty reunites India	**350**

	WESTERN EUROPE	EASTERN EUROPE, THE NEAR EAST & AFRICA	
400	379–95 Reign of Theodosius the Great		**400**
450	354–430 St Augustine, theologian 432–61 St Patrick's mission in Ireland 451 Council of Chalcedon 451–3 Europe overrun by Attila the Hun		**450**

500	476 End of the Western Roman empire
	480 Benedict founds the Benedictine order
	484–519 First schism between Western and
	     Eastern Churches
	496 Clovis, King of the Franks, converted to
	     Christianity
		484–519 First schism between Western and
		     Eastern Churches
		491 Armenia secedes from Byzantium and Rome
			500

550			**550**
600	590 Gregory the Great becomes Pope 597 St Augustine lands in Britain	570 Birth of Muhammad	**600**
650	634 Battle of Heavenfield, England. Oswald becomes king and introduces Celtic Christianity	610 Muhammad's vision on Mount Hira 622 The Hijra. Muhammad goes to Medina 630 Muhammad takes Mecca 632 Death of Muhammad 623–4 Abu Bakr, caliph 636 Arab conquest of Iran 637 Conquest of Palestine 634–44 'Umar, caliph 644–56 'Uthman, caliph	**650**

	THE AMERICAS	THE FAR EAST AND AUSTRALASIA	
400	*c.*400 Temple of the Sun at Pachacamac: centre of pilgrimage up to the Spanish conquest	*c.*400 Asanga and Vasubandhu—two brothers who opposed teachings of Nagarjuna Buddhist philosophy *c.*400 Buddhaghosa, Buddhist philosopher wrote Theravadin commentary on scripture, in Sri Lanka	**400**
450			**450**
500			**500**
550		520 Bodhidharma founds Ch'an Buddhist tradition in China 538–97 Chih-i; founded T'ien t'ai school of Buddhism 538 *or* 552 Official introduction of Buddhism into Japan	**550**
600	600–1000 Spread of Tiahuanaco religion and the Huari empire in Peru	581–618 Sui dynasty in China 581–604 Reign of Wen Ti	**600**
650		606–48 Reign of Harsha in northern India 618–907 T'ang dynasty, China 574–622 Prince Shotoku, Japan 635 Alopen, a Nestorian bishop takes Christianity to China 645 Downfall of Soga clan in Japan, who had established Buddhism	**650**

	WESTERN EUROPE	EASTERN EUROPE, THE NEAR EAST & AFRICA	
	663 Synod of Whitby, England. Roman Christianity triumphs over Celtic Christianity	656–61 Ali, caliph 661–750 Ummayad dynasty in Damascus 678–711 Islamic conquest of North Africa 680 Death of Husain 680–1 Sixth council of Constantinople condemns monophysitism and monotheletism	
700			**700**
	718 Pelayo founds Christian kingdom in Spain 726 Pope Gregory II opposes Iconoclast movement 732 Conquest of France by Muslims halted at Poitiers 734 Muslims conquer western Switzerland 750 Beginning of Abbasid caliphate	705–15 Conquest of Central Asia, Sind, Spain, by Islam 726 Byzantine Emperor Leo III begins Iconoclast movement	
750	754 Beginning of temporal power of the Papacy		**750**
800	800 Coronation of Charlemagne		**800**
	827 Muslims invasion of Sicily 840 Muslims occupy southern Italy		
850			**850**
900	899 Death of Alfred the Great	c.900 onwards, Islam penetrates East Africa	**900**
	910 Cluny Abbey founded 928 Henry the Fowler, first Saxon Holy Roman Emperor captures Brandenburg	909–1171 Caliphate of the Fatimids in Tunisia and, from 969, Egypt 873–935 al-Ashari, theologian 852–942 Saadiah Gasn, Jewish theologian 942 Bishop of Passau Christianizes Hungary	
950			**950**

	THE AMERICAS	THE FAR EAST AND AUSTRALASIA	
700	*c.*700 Mexican city of Testihuacan falls to invaders *c.*700 Pueblos first constructed in American south- west, especially in New Mexico and Arizona		**700**
750		710–94 Nara period, Japan 712 Muhammad ibn Kasim establishes Muslim state in Sind	**750**
800	*c.*800 Cajamarca culture widespread in Peru	760–1142 The Pala dynasty in Bengal and Bihar 794–1192 Heian period, Japan *c.*800 Sankara, Vedanta philosopher	**800**
850			**850**
900	*after* 900 Influence of Mixtec people, Mexico, at its height	866 Fujiwara period begins, Japan 900–1279 Islam penetrates into China and wins over many western Chinese tribes	**900**
950		907–57 Five dynasties in China divide 936 Zoroastrians (Parsis) arrive in India	**950**

A chronology of beliefs

WESTERN EUROPE	EASTERN EUROPE, THE NEAR EAST & AFRICA
965 King of Denmark accepts Christianity	966 King of Poland accepts Christianity 968 Fatimids established in Egypt
1000	**1000**

1054 Schism between Eastern and Western
        Christianity
1050
	1054 Schism between Eastern and Western
	        Christianity
	1050

1066 Norman conquest of England 1073–85 Pope Gregory VII 1084 Carthusians founded at Chartreuse, France by St Bruno 1084 Normans sack Rome 1096 The First Crusade 1098 Cistercians founded at Charteaux, France **1100** by St Robert	1096–1270 The Crusades **1100**
1122 Concordat of Worms **1150** 1150 Carmelites founded	1058–1111 al Ghazzali, theologian and mystic **1150**

1170 Murder of Thomas à Becket in Canterbury
        Cathedral, England
 	
1200 1198–1216 Pope Innocent III
	1169–93 Saladin, ruler of Egypt, resists
	        the Crusaders
	
	1136–1204 Maimonides, Jewish philosopher **1200**

1209–29 Albigensian wars against heresy 1170–1221 St Dominic, founder of the Dominican order 1181–1226 St Francis, founder of the Franciscan order 1167–1227 Genghis Khan, the great Mongol ruler 1233 Inquisition established by Pope Gregory IX **1250**	1209 Jews expelled from England 1167–1227 Genghis Khan, the great Mongol ruler **1250**

	THE AMERICAS	THE FAR EAST AND AUSTRALASIA	
		960–1279 Sung dynasty	
1000	985–1200 Second Mayan empire in Yucatan c.1000 Leif Ericsson landed in America c.1000 Huari empire disintegrated in Peru c.1000 Serpent mounds in Ohio and upper 　　　　Mississippi valleys	999–1030 Reign of Mahmud the Great of Ghazni	**1000**
1050	*after* 1000 Mississippi culture pattern influences 　　　　most of south-east United States. Links 　　　　with Mexican traditions		**1050**
1100	1100　Height of Inca civilization in Mexico		**1100**
1150			**1150**
1200	1200–c.1460 Chimu empire, Peru c.1200 Incas settle in the Cuzco area	1160–1206 Reign of Muhammad of Ghur 1175　Jodo Shu or Pure Land School founded 1192–1333 Kamakura period, Japan; a feudal era 1130–1200 Chuttsi, Neo-Confucian philosopher 1200　Eisei brought Ch'an (Zen) Buddhism to Japan	**1200**
1250		1206–1526 Sultanate of Delhi 1133–1212 Honen, founder of the Jodo sect 1141–1215 Eisei—Japanese Zen master 1225　　Jodo Shin Shu or True Pure Land School 　　　　founded 1167–1227 Genghis Khan, the great Mongol ruler 1200–53 Dogen, founder of the Soto school	**1250**

A chronology of beliefs

	WESTERN EUROPE	EASTERN EUROPE, THE NEAR EAST & AFRICA	
	1244–74 Aquinas, theologian		
1300		1301 Beginning of the Ottoman empire	**1300**
	1309–77 Avignon papacy		
1350	1353 Statute of Praemunire prevents papal intervention in England		**1350**
	1378–1417 papal schism 1320–84 John Wycliff, reformer	1394 Jews expelled from France	
1400	1401 The burning of heretics made legal in England		**1400**
	1415 Council of Constance ends Great Schism		
1450	1453 The fall of Constantinople 1454 Papal indulgence printed		**1450**
		1472 Portuguese arrive in East Africa	
	1481 Inquisition of Castile 1492 Jews expelled from Spain		
1500			**1500**
	1517 Luther posted Ninety-five Theses on church door at Wittenberg 1484–1531 Zwingli, reformer 1534 Henry VIII takes control of English Church 1540 Jesuit order approved by Pope 1541 Reformation in Geneva 1483–1546 Martin Luther, reformer	1526–1858 The Mughal empire	
1550	1545–63 The Council of Trent		**1550**

	THE AMERICAS	THE FAR EAST AND AUSTRALASIA	
1300		1173–1262 Shinran Shonin, founder of True Pure Land School, Japan 1279–1368 Yuan (Mongol) dynasty 1222–82 Nichiren, founder of the Nichiren sect 1216–94 Kubla Khan, Mongol leader	**1300**
1350		1336 Ashikaga period, Japan; great feudal lords, semi-independent of Sho-gun's authority	**1350**
1400	c.1370 Aztec city of Tenochtitlan founded	1368–1644 Ming dynasty, China	**1400**
1450	1438–1532 The Inca empire		**1450**
1500	1464 Chimu kingdom overthrown by the Incas c.1470 Height of Inca empire in Peru 1492 Columbus discovered America	1498 Vasco da Gama sails to India round the Cape	**1500**
1550	1519 Cortes begins conquest of Mexico 1532 Pissarro begins conquest of Peru	1510 Portuguese established at Goa 1440–1518 Kabir, founder of the Hindu sect 1526–1858 The Mughal empire 1479–1531 Vallabharaya, founder of the Vaishnawa sect 1469–1539 Nanak, founder of Sikhism 1549 The first Christian mission to Japan 1504–52 Angad successor to Nanak	**1550**

237

A chronology of beliefs

	WESTERN EUROPE	EASTERN EUROPE, THE NEAR EAST & AFRICA	
1600	1506–52 Francis Xavier, Jesuit missionary 1491–1555 Ignatius Loyola, founder of the Jesuits 1509–64 John Calvin, reformer 1505–72 John Knox, reformer 1562–98 Wars of Religion in France 1598 Edict of Nantes. French Protestants free to worship		**1600**
1650	1611 The Authorized version of the Bible published 1620 The Pilgrim Fathers sail to the New World 1628 French Protestants lose political powers 1641 Massacre of Protestants in Ireland		**1650**
1700	1688 Act of Toleration, England 1624–91 George Fox, founder of the Quakers	1700–60 Israel Baal Shem Tov founds the Chasidic movement of Judaism in Poland	**1700**
1750	1729 Methodist movement begins at Oxford, England		**1750**

1800	1773 Pope suppresses Society of Jesus
	
	1729–86 Moses Mendelssohn, founder of modern
	      Reform Judaism
	1790 Civil constitution of the clergy, France
	1703–91 John Wesley, founder of Methodism
		1791 Establishment of the Jewish pale in Russia
		1703–92 al-Wahhabi, founder of the Wahhabi
		      movement
			1800

1850	1806 End of the Holy Roman Empire
	1809 Birth of Charles Darwin, scientist, whose
	      work led to the theory of evolution
	
	1827 Plymouth Brethren founded
	1829 Catholic emancipation in Britain
	1770–1831 Georg Hegel, philosopher
	1883 Beginning of Oxford Movement, England
		1810 First Reform Temple opened in Germany
		      by Moses Mendelssohn
		1818 Birth of Karl Marx, the architect of Marxist
		      philosophy which gave rise to communism
		
		1849 *The Communist Manifesto*
		1819–50 Bab Sayyid Ali Mohammed, founder
		      of Babism
			1850

	THE AMERICAS	THE FAR EAST AND AUSTRALASIA	
		1556–1605 Reign of Akbar 1573 End of the Ashikaga Shogunate 1479–1574 Amar Das, third Sikh guru	
	1580 Inca rule disintegrates		
1600		1600 Adi Granth compiled by Guru Arjan	**1600**
		1563–1606 Arjan, fifth Sikh guru 1552–1610 Matteo Ricci, first Jesuit missionary to China	
	1620 Pilgrim Fathers settle in New England		
		1639 British settlement in Madras 1644–1912 Ch'ing (Manchu) dynasty	
1650			**1650**
		1658–1707 Reign of Aurangzeb	
		1680 Death of Sivaji, Maratha war leader	
1700		1699 Khalsa (Sikh castless brotherhood) formed	**1700**
		1666–1708 Gobind Singh, tenth Sikh guru	
		1734 Dasam Granth, a holy book in Sikhism 1735–96 Reign of Ch'ien Lung	
		1750–92 China extended influence over Tibet, Burma and Nepal	
1750			**1750**
	1776 American Declaration of Independence 1783 American Revolution ends in Treaty of Paris 1789 Constitution of the United States	1778 First British settlement in Australia	
1800			**1800**
	1830 Church of Jesus Christ of Latter-day Saints founded 1805–44 Joseph Smith, founder of the Church of Jesus Christ of Latter-day Saints 1847 Salt Lake City founded by Brigham Young	1828 Foundation of the Brahmo Samaj, India 1829 Suttee declared a crime 1780–1839 Ranjit Singh, Sikh leader	
1850	1848 Christadelphians established by John Thomas	1850–64 T'ai P'ing rebellion, China	**1850**

239

A chronology of beliefs

	WESTERN EUROPE	EASTERN EUROPE, THE NEAR EAST & AFRICA	
	1859 Darwin publishes *The Origin of Species* 1867 Marx publishes *Das Kapital* 1869–70 The First Vatican Council 1877 Salvation Army founded by William Booth 1884 Fabian Society founded 1801–90 Cardinal Newman, the Oxford Movement 1892 Death of Charles Darwin, scientist 1897 Zionist Congress founded	1861 Emancipation of serfs in Russia 1867 Baha'i faith founded by Baha'u'llah 1867 *Das Kapital*, Marx's book, is published 1883 Death of Karl Marx 1892 Baha'u'llah dies in Akka	
1900			**1900**

	1910 World Missionary Conference, Edinburgh
	1914–18 First World War
	
	1928 Opus Dei founded by Spanish priest
	1933 Hitler's rise to power
	1934 Barmen Declaration voices Christian
	        opposition to Nazis
	1939–45 Second World War
	1948 The World Council of Churches is established
		1912 Israelites formed in South Africa
		1914–18 First World War
		1917 The Balfour Declaration favours the establishment
		        of a Jewish 'National Home' in Palestine
		1917 Bolshevik Revolution in Russia
		1870–1924 Vladimir Ilich Lenin, Russian leader
		1934 God's Kingdom Society, established in Nigeria
		1879–1940 Leon Trotsky, Russian leader
		1939–45 Second World War
		1948 Establishment of the State of Israel	

1950			**1950**

	1958–63 Pope John XXIII
	1962 The Second Vatican Council
		1957 Baha'i Shoghi Effendi dies
		
		1973 International Teaching Centre of the
		        Baha'i Faith founded
		1892–1975 Haile Selassie, Emperor of Ethiopia,
		        and Ras Tafari	

1980			**1980**

	THE AMERICAS	THE FAR EAST AND AUSTRALASIA	
	1860 Emancipation of slaves in the United States 1861–5 American Civil War 1875 *Science & Health* by Mary Baker Eddy, published 1801–77 Brigham Young, leader of the Mormons 1879 Jehovah's Witnesses movement founded	 1875 Foundaton of Arya Samaj, India 1798–1887 Nakayama Miki, founder of Tenri-Kyo	
1900		1862–1902 Ramakrishna, Vedantist mystic	**1900**

	1821–1910 Mary Baker Eddy, founder of Christian
	  Science
	1911 Mexican Revolution
	1914–18 First World War
	
	1939–45 Second World War
	1941 President Roosevelt makes 'four freedoms'
	  speech to the United States Congress
	1946 First meeting of the United Nations
		1839–1908 Mirza Ghularu Ahmad, founder of
		  Ahmadiyya sect in Islam
		
		1914–18 First World War
		c.1920 Vietnamese religion Cao-Dai founded
		1939–45 Second World War
		1939 Hoa Hoa sect founded in Vietnam
		1947 India becomes independent
		1869–1948 Mohandas K. Gandhi, Indian reformer	

1950		1949 China becomes communist	**1950**
		1952 Japanese sovereignty restored 1954 Unification Church founded by Sun Myung Moon 1900–58 Toda Josei, co-founder of Soka Gakkai	
1980			**1980**

241

Readings from sacred scriptures

The following extracts are taken from the holy scriptures of some of the major religions. It is hoped that the reader will gain a greater appreciation of the prime concerns, and of the nature and disposition of a religion by reading from the original texts.

The Old Testament or Torah

Exodus: Chapter 20, verses 1–22

These verses relate how God gave ten commandments to Moses, so that Israelites should know how to serve him.

1. And God spake all these words, saying,
2. I *am* the LORD thy God, which have brought thee out of the land of Egypt, out of the house of bondage.
3. Thou shalt have no other gods before me.
4. Thou shalt not make unto thee any graven image, or any likeness *of anything* that *is* in heaven above, or that *is* in the earth beneath, or that *is* in the water under the earth:
5. Thou shalt not bow down thyself to them, nor serve them: for I the LORD thy God *am* a jealous God, visiting the iniquity of the fathers upon the children unto the third and fourth *generation* of them that hate me;
6. And shewing mercy unto thousands of them that love me, and keep my commandments.
7. Thou shalt not take the name of the LORD thy God in vain; for the LORD will not hold him guiltless that taketh his name in vain.
8. Remember the sabbath day, to keep it holy.
9. Six days shalt thou labour, and do all thy work:
10. But the seventh day *is* the sabbath of the LORD thy God: *in it* thou shalt not do any work, thou, nor thy son, nor thy daughter, thy manservant, nor thy maidservant, nor thy cattle, nor thy stranger that *is* within thy gates:
11. For *in* six days the LORD made heaven and earth, the sea, and all that in them *is*, and rested the seventh day: wherefore the LORD blessed the sabbath day, and hallowed it.
12. Honour thy father and thy mother: that thy days may be long upon the land which the LORD thy God giveth thee.
13. Thou shalt not kill.
14. Thou shalt not commit adultery.
15. Thou shalt not steal.
16. Thou shalt not bear false witness against thy neighbour.
17. Thou shalt not covet thy neighbour's house, thou shalt not covet thy neighbour's wife, nor his manservant, nor his maidservant, nor his ox, nor his ass, nor any thing that *is* thy neighbour's.
18. And all the people saw the thunderings, and the lightnings, and the noise of the trumpet, and the mountain smoking: and when the people saw *it*, they removed, and stood afar off.
19. And they said unto Moses, Speak thou with us, and we will hear: but let not God speak with us, lest we die.
20. And Moses said unto the people, Fear not: for God is come to prove you, and that his fear may be before your faces, that ye sin not.
21. And the people stood afar off, and Moses drew near unto the thick darkness where God *was*.
22. And the LORD said unto Moses, Thus thou shalt say unto the children of Israel, Ye have seen that I have talked with you from heaven.

I Kings: Chapter 6, verses 1 and 9–13

The account is given of how Solomon built a mighty temple in Jerusalem in God's name.

1. And it came to pass in the four hundred and eightieth year after the children of Israel were come out of the land of Egypt, in the fourth year of Solomon's reign over Israel, in the month Zif, which *is* the second month, that he began to build the house of the LORD.
9. So he built the house, and finished it; and covered the house with beams and boards of cedar.
10. And *then* he built chambers against all the house, five cubits high: and they rested on the house with timber of cedar.
11. And the word of the LORD came to Solomon, saying,
12. *Concerning* this house which thou art in building, if thou wilt walk in my statues, and execute my judgments, and keep all my commandments to walk in them; then will I perform my word with thee, which I spake unto David thy father:
13. And I will dwell among the children of Israel, and will not forsake my people Israel.

Psalms: Psalm 23

Perhaps the best loved of all the psalms of David.

1. The LORD is my shepherd; I shall not want.
2. He maketh me to lie down in green pastures: he leadeth me beside the still waters.
3. He restoreth my soul: he leadeth me in the paths of righteousness for his name's sake.

4. Yea, though I walk through the valley of the shadow of death, I will fear no evil: for thou *art* with me; thy rod and thy staff they comfort me.

5. Thou preparest a table before me in the presence of mine enemies: thou anointest my head with oil; my cup runneth over.

6. Surely goodness and mercy shall follow me all the days of my life: and I will dwell in the house of the LORD for ever.

The New Testament

St Matthew: Chapter 5, verses 1–19 and Chapter 6, verses 24–34

These are taken from the Sermon on the Mount, Jesus's most famous sermon, teaching that love is all-important.

1. And seeing the multitudes, he went up into a mountain: and when he was set, his disciples came unto him:

2. And he opened his mouth, and taught them, saying,

3. Blessed *are* the poor in spirit: for their's is the kingdom of heaven.

4. Blessed *are* they that mourn: for they shall be comforted.

5. Blessed *are* the meek: for they shall inherit the earth.

6. Blessed *are* they which do hunger and thirst after righteousness: for they shall be filled.

7. Blessed *are* the merciful: for they shall obtain mercy.

8. Blessed *are* the pure in heart: for they shall see God.

9. Blessed *are* the peacemakers: for they shall be called the children of God.

10. Blessed *are* they which are persecuted for righteousness' sake: for their's is the kingdom of heaven.

11. Blessed are ye, when *men* shall revile you, and persecute *you*, and shall say all manner of evil against you falsely, for my sake.

12. Rejoice, and be exceeding glad: for great *is* your reward in heaven: for so persecuted they the prophets which were before you.

13. Ye are the salt of the earth: but if the salt have lost his savour, wherewith shall it be salted? it is thenceforth good for nothing, but to be cast out, and to be trodden under foot of men.

14. Ye are the light of the world. A city that is set on an hill cannot be hid.

15. Neither do men light a candle, and put it under a bushel, but on a candlestick; and it giveth light unto all that are in the house.

16. Let your light so shine before men, that they may see your good works, and glorify your Father which is in heaven.

17. Think not that I am come to destroy the law, or the prophets: I am not come to destroy, but to fulfil.

18. For verily I say unto you, Till heaven and earth pass, one jot or one tittle shall in no wise pass from the law, till all be fulfilled.

19. Whosoever therefore shall break one of these least commandments, and shall teach men so, he shall be called the least in the kingdom of heaven: but whosoever shall do and teach *them*, the same shall be called great in the kingdom of heaven.

St Matthew: Chapter 6, verses 24–34

24. No man can serve two masters: for either he will hate the one, and love the other; or else he will hold to the one, and despise the other. Ye cannot serve God and mammon.

25. Therefore I say unto you, Take no thought for your life, what ye shall eat, or what ye shall drink; nor yet for your body, what ye shall put on. Is not the life more than meat, and the body than raiment?

26. Behold the fowls of the air: for they sow not, neither do they reap, nor gather into barns; yet your heavenly Father feedeth them. Are ye not much better than they?

27. Which of you by taking thought can add one cubit unto his stature?

28. And why take ye thought for raiment? Consider the lilies of the field, how they grow; they toil not, neither do they spin:

29. And yet I say unto you, That even Solomon in all his glory was not arrayed like one of these.

30. Wherefore, if God so clothe the grass of the field, which to day is, and to morrow is cast into the oven, *shall he* not much more *clothe* you, O ye of little faith?

31. Therefore take no thought, saying, What shall we eat? or, What shall we drink? or, Wherewithal shall we be clothed?

32. (For after all these things do the Gentiles seek:) for your heavenly Father knoweth that ye have need of all these things.

33. But seek ye first the kingdom of God, and his righteousness; and all these things shall be added unto you.

34. Take therefore no thought for the morrow: for the morrow shall take thought for the things of itself. Sufficient unto the day *is* the evil thereof.

St Matthew: Chapter 6, verses 9–14

During the Sermon on the Mount, Jesus taught this prayer to his disciples, and it is said throughout Christianity.

9. After this manner therefore pray ye: Our Father which art in heaven, Hallowed be thy name.

10. Thy kingdom come. Thy will be done in earth, as *it is* in heaven.

11. Give us this day our daily bread.

12. And forgive us our debts, as we forgive our debtors.
13. And lead us not into temptation, but deliver us from evil: For thine is the kingdom, and the power, and the glory, for ever. Amen.
14. For if ye forgive men their trespasses, your heavenly Father will also forgive you:

The Bhagavad Gita

Chapter 2: verses 17–25

Krishna teaches that the soul is immutable and concern for the body is misguided, since the concerns of the material world are a delusion.

17. That which pervades the entire body is indestructible. No one is able to destroy the imperishable soul.
18. Only the material body of the indestructible, immeasurable and eternal living entity is subject to destruction; therefore, fight, O descendant of Bharata.
19. He who thinks that the living entity is the slayer, or that the entity is slain, does not understand. One who is in knowledge knows that the self slays not nor is slain.
20. For the soul there is never birth nor death. Nor, having once been, does he ever cease to be. He is unborn, eternal, ever-existing, undying and primeval. He is not slain when the body is slain.
21. O Pārtha, how can a person who knows that the soul is indestructible, unborn, eternal and immutable kill anyone or cause anyone to kill?
22. As a person puts on new garments, giving up old ones, similarly, the soul accepts new material bodies, giving up the old and useless ones.
23. The soul can never be cut into pieces by any weapon, nor can he be burned by fire, nor moistened by water, nor withered by the wind.
24. This individual soul is unbreakable and insoluble, and can be neither burned nor dried. He is everlasting, all-pervading, unchangeable, immovable and eternally the same.
25. It is said that the soul is invisible, inconceivable, immutable and unchangeable. Knowing this, you should not grieve for the body.

Chapter 2, verses 55–72

Krishna describes how detachment from wordly passions and desires is the true path to peace and contentment.

55. The Supreme Personality of Godhead said: O Pārtha, when a man gives up all varieties of sense desire which arise of invention, and when his mind finds satisfaction in the self alone, then he is said to be in pure transcendental consciousness.

56. One who is not disturbed in spite of the threefold miseries, who is not elated when there is happiness, and who is free from attachment, fear and anger, is called a sage of steady mind.
57. He who is without affection either for good or evil is firmly fixed in perfect knowledge.
58. One who is able to withdraw his senses from sense objects, as the tortoise draws his limbs within the shell, is to be understood as truly situated in knowledge.
59. The embodied soul may be restricted from sense enjoyment, though the taste for sense objects remains. But, ceasing such engagements by experiencing a higher taste, he is fixed in consciouness.
60. The senses are so strong and impetuous, O Arjuna, that they forcibly carry away the mind even of a man of discrimination who is endeavouring to control them.
61. One who restrains his senses and fixes his consciousness upon Me is known as a man of steady intelligence.
62. While contemplating the objects of the senses, a person develops attachment for them, and from such attachment lust develops, and from lust anger arises.
63. From anger, delusion arises, and from delusion bewilderment of memory. When memory is bewildered, intelligence is lost, and when intelligence is lost, one falls down again into the material pool.
64. One who can control his senses by regulated principles, and who is free from attachment and aversion, can obtain the mercy of God.
65. For one who is so situated, the threefold miseries of material life exist no longer; in such a happy state, one's intelligence is steady.
66. One who is not in transcendental consciousness can have neither a controlled mind nor steady intelligence, without which there is no possibility of peace. And how can there be any happiness without peace?
67. As a boat on the water is swept away by a strong wind, even one of the senses in which the mind becomes fixed can carry away a man's intelligence.
68. Therefore, O mighty-armed, one whose senses are restrained from their objects is certainly of steady intelligence.
69. What is night for all beings is the time of awakening for the self-controlled; and the time of awakening for all beings is night for the introspective sage.
70. A person who is not disturbed by the incessant flow of desires—that enter like rivers into the ocean which is ever being filled but is always still—can alone achieve peace, and not the man who strives to satisfy such desires.
71. A person who has given up all desires for sense gratification, who lives free from desires, who has given up all sense of proprietorship, and is devoid of false ego—he alone can attain real peace.

72. That is the way of the spiritual and godly life, after attaining which a man is not bewildered. Being so situated, even at the hour of death, one can enter into the kingdom of God.

Chapter 8, verses 3–10

The nature of Brahman is revealed and the inconceivable power of the Supreme Godhead is described.

3. The Supreme Personality of Godhead replies: The indestructible, transcendental living entity is called Brahman, and his eternal nature is called the self. And action pertaining to the development of these material bodies is called *karma*, or fruitive activities.
4. The physical nature is known to be endlessly mutable. The universe is the cosmic form of the Supreme Lord, and I am that Lord represented as the Supersoul, dwelling in the heart of every embodied being.
5. Anyone who, at the end of life, quits his body remembering Me, attains immediately to My nature, and there is no doubt of this.
6. In whatever condition one quits his present body, in his next life he will attain to that state of being without fail.
7. Therefore, Arjuna you should always think of Me, and at the same time you should continue your prescribed duty and fight. With your mind and activities always fixed on Me, and everything engaged in Me, you will attain to Me without doubt.
8. By practising this remembrance without being deviated, thinking ever of the Supreme Godhead, one is sure to achieve the planet of the divine, the Supreme Personality, O son of Kuntī.
9. Think of the Supreme Person as one who knows everything, who is the oldest, who is the controller, who is smaller than the smallest, who is the maintainer of everything, who is beyond any material conception, who is inconceivable, and who is always a person. He is luminous like the sun, beyond this material nature, transcendental.
10. One who, at the time of death, fixes his life air between the eyebrows and in full devotion engages himself in remembering the Supreme Lord will certainly attain to the Supreme Personality of Godhead:

Chapter 18, verses 51–54

The follower of Krishna is fulfilled once transcendental consciousness of him is achieved.

51–53. Being purified by his intelligence and controlling the mind with determination, giving up the objects of sense gratification, being freed from attachment and hatred, one who lives in a secluded place, who eats a small quantity of food, who controls the body and the speaking power, who is always in trance, detached and free from false ego, false strength, false pride, lust, anger and acceptance of material things—such a person is certainly elevated to the position of self-realization.

54. One who is thus transcendentally situated at once realizes the Supreme Brahman and becomes fully joyful. He never laments nor desires to have anything; he is equally disposed toward every living entity. In that state he achieves pure devotional service unto Me.

The Qur'an

Every surah is prefaced by the following verse: 'In the Name of Allah, the Compassionate, the Merciful'.

33:41 *God, Allah proclaims Muhammad as his prophet.*

Prophet, We have sent you forth as a witness, a bearer of good news, and a warner; one who shall call men to Allah by His leave and guide them like a shining light.

Tell the faithful that Allah has bounteous blessings in store for them. Do not yield to the unbelievers and the hypocrites: disregard their insolence. Put your trust in Allah; Allah is your all-sufficient guardian.

35:8–18 *Allah reveals how he is the Lord of Creation.*

Allah created you from dust, then from a little germ. Into two sexes He divided you. No female conceives or is delivered without His knowledge. No man grows old or has his life cut short but in accordance with His decree. All this is easy for Him.

The two seas are not alike. The one is fresh, sweet, and pleasant to drink from, while the other is salt and bitter. From both you eat fresh fish and bring up ornaments to deck yourselves with. See how the ships plough their course through them as you sail away to seek His bounty. Perchance you will give thanks.

He causes the night to pass into the day and the day into the night. He has forced the sun and the moon into His service, each running for an appointed term. Such is Allah, your Lord. His is the sovereignty. The idols whom you invoke besides Him have power over nothing. If you pray to them they cannot hear you, and even if they hear you they cannot answer. None can guide you like the One who is all-knowing.

Men, it is you who stand in need of Allah. He is all-sufficient and glorious. He can destroy you if He will and replace you with a new creation; this is no impossible thing for Allah.

35:27–32 *The prime importance of the Book, the Qur'an, is confirmed.*

Those who recite the Book of Allah and attend to their prayers and give alms in private and in public may hope for imperishable gain. Allah will give them their rewards and enrich them from His own abundance. He is forgiving and bountiful in His rewards.

What We have revealed to you in the Book is the truth confirming previous scriptures. Allah knows and observes His servants.

We have bestowed the Book on those of Our servants whom We have chosen. Some of them sin against their souls, some follow a middle course, and some, by Allah's leave, vie with each other in charitable works: this is the supreme virtue.

97:1–5 *A poetic surah, which relates how the Qur'an was given to mortals on the Night of Qadr, Night of Glory.*

WE revealed the Koran on the Night of Qadr.
Would that you knew what the Night of Qadr is like!
Better is the Night of Qadr than a thousand months.
On that night the angels and the Spirit by their Lord's leave come down with His decrees.
That night is peace, till break of dawn.

Tao Te Ching

Chapter I

The very attempt to define the undefinable is doomed to failure. The Tao is unknowable.

The Tao that can be expressed is not the eternal Tao;
The name that can be defined is not the unchanging name.
Non-existence is called the antecedent of heaven and earth;
Existence is the mother of all things.
From eternal non-existence, therefore, we serenely observe the mysterous beginning of the Universe;
From eternal existence we clearly see the apparent distinctions.
These two are the same in source and become different when manifested.
This sameness is called profundity. Infinite profundity is the gate whence comes the beginning of all parts of the Universe.

Chapter XXII

The apparent paradox of these words is resolved within the higher understanding that Taoism brings.

'Be humble, and you will remain entire.'
Be bent, and you will remain straight.
Be vacant, and you will remain full.
Be worn, and you will remain new.
He who has little will receive.
He who has much will be embarrassed.
Therefore the Sage keeps to One and becomes the standard for the world.
He does not display himself; therefore he shines.
He does not approve himself; therefore he is noted.
He does not praise himself; therefore he has merit.

He does not glory in himself; therefore he excels.
And because he does not compete; therefore no one in the world can compete with him.
The ancient saying 'Be humble and you will remain entire'—
Can this be regarded as mere empty words?
Indeed he shall return home entire.

Chapter XLI

The contradictions that may appear within Tao are recognised and accepted.

When the superior scholar is told of Tao,
He works hard to practise it.
When the middling scholar is told of Tao,
It seems that sometimes he keeps it and sometimes he loses it.
When the inferior scholar is told of Tao,
He laughs aloud at it.
If it were not laughed at, it would not be sufficient to be Tao.
Therefore the proverb says:
'The greatest square has no angles;
The largest vessel is never complete;
The loudest sound can scarcely be heard;
The biggest form cannot be visualized.
Tao, while hidden, is nameless.'
Yet it is Tao alone that is good at imparting and completing.

Adi Granth

The Japji

This is the morning prayer of Sikhs, composed by Guru Nanak, and consists of a meditation followed by hymns.

No. 4 *Guru Nanak teaches the importance of loving and honouring the holy Name.*

The Lord is the Truth Absolute,
True is His Name.
His language is love infinite;
His creatures ever cry to Him;
'Give us more, O Lord, give more';
The Bounteous One gives unwearyingly.

What then should we offer
That we might see His Kingdom?
With what language
Might we His love attain?

In the ambrosial hours of fragrant dawn
Think upon and glorify
His Name and greatness.
Our own past actions
Have put this garment on us,
But salvation comes only through His Grace.

O Nanak, this alone need we know,
That God, being Truth, is the one Light of all.

No. 38, *In a sustained metaphor, the process of coming to the truth is likened to minting a golden coin.*

In the forge of continence,
Let patience be the goldsmith,
On the anvil of understanding
Let him strike with the hammer of knowledge;

Let the fear of God be the bellows,
Let austerities be the fire,
Let the love of God be the crucible,
Let the nectar of life be melted in it;

Thus in the mint of Truth,
A man may coin the Word,
This is the practice of those
On whom God looks with favour.
Nanak, our gracious Lord
With a glance makes us happy.

No. 44, *A revelation of the need to lose oneself in the godhead.*

Where Self exists,
God is not;
Where God exists,
There is no Self.
Sage, probe this mystery,
Of the immanence of the Lord in all that is,
Without the grace of the Guru
We could not know this essence of truth.

When we encounter the True Teacher,
And when the little Self dies,
Doubt and fear die with it,
And the pains of birth, death and rebirth,
The Guru's teaching is the highest wisdom
Since it shows us where our Liberator is.
Nanak repeats: 'I am that. That is I.'
The three worlds are included in that formula.

Writings of Baha'u'llah

XLI *Baha'u'llah reveals how he was inspired by God to bring people to a knowledge of his perfect love.*

GOD IS MY WITNESS, O people! I was asleep on My couch, when lo, the Breeze of God wafting over Me roused Me from My slumber. His quickening Spirit revived Me, and My tongue was unloosed to voice His Call. Accuse Me not of having transgressed against God. Behold Me, not with your eyes but with Mine. Thus admonisheth you He Who is the Gracious, the All-Knowing. Think ye, O people, that I hold within My grasp the control of God's ultimate Will and Purpose? Far be it from Me to advance such claim. To this I testify before God, the Almighty, the Exalted, the All-Knowing, the All-Wise. Had the ultimate destiny of God's Faith been in Mine hands, I would have never consented, even though for one moment, to manifest Myself unto you, nor would I have allowed one word to fall from My lips. Of this God Himself is, verily, a witness.

LXXXI *The people are assured that the soul will pass into the presence of God, once the life of the body has passed away.*

AND NOW concerning thy question regarding the soul of man and its survival after death. Know thou of a truth that the soul, after its separation from the body, will continue to progress until it attaineth the presence of God, in a state and condition which neither the revolution of ages and centuries, nor the changes and chances of this world, can alter. It will endure as long as the Kingdom of God, His sovereignty, His dominion and power will endure. It will manifest the signs of God and His attributes, and will reveal His loving kindness and bounty. The movement of My Pen is stilled when it attempteth to befittingly describe the loftiness and glory of so exalted a station. The honour with which the Hand of Mercy will invest the soul is such as no tongue can adequately reveal, nor any other earthly agency describe. Blessed is the soul which, at the hour of its separation from the body, is sanctified from the vain imaginings of the peoples of the world. Such a soul liveth and moveth in accordance with the Will of its Creator, and entereth the all-highest Paradise. The Maids of Heaven, inmates of the loftiest mansions, will circle around it, and the Prophets of God and His chosen ones will seek its companionship.

CXIX *The rulers and potentates are warned that they should govern with humility and justice, and not use their powers unjustly.*

O YE RULERS of the earth! Wherefore have ye clouded the radiance of the Sun, and caused it to cease from shining? Hearken unto the counsel given you by the Pen of the Most High, that haply both ye and the poor may attain unto tranquillity and peace. We beseech God to assist the kings of the earth to establish peace on earth. He, verily, doth what He willeth.

O kings of the earth! We see you increasing every year your expenditures, and laying the burden thereof on your subjects. This, verily, is wholly and grossly unjust. Fear the sighs and tears of this Wronged One, and lay not excessive burdens on your peoples. Do not rob them to rear palaces for yourselves; nay rather choose for them that which ye choose for yourselves. Thus We unfold to your eyes that which profiteth you, if ye but perceive. Your people are your treasures.

The Dhammapada

Maggavaggo: The Path, verses 1–3

The Dhammapada, or 'path of virtue', communicates the spirit of the teachings of Siddhartha Gautama, the Buddha. He tells of the noble eightfold path.

1. Of paths the eightfold is the best; of truths the (best are) four sayings (truths); of virtues freedom from attachment is the best; of men (literally two-footed beings) he who is possessed of sight.
2. This is the path; there is none other that leads to the purifying of insight. You follow this (path). This will be to confuse (escape from) Māra (death, sin).
3. Going on this path, you will end your suffering. This path was preached by me when I became aware of the removal of the thorns (in the flesh).

verses 5–6 *He preaches the necessity of realising that all is impermanent and unsatisfactory in the material world that loss of a sense of 'self' is 'the path of purity'.*

5. 'All created things are impermanent (transitory).' When one by wisdom realizes (this), he heeds not (is superior to) (this world of) sorrow; this is the path to purity.
6. 'All created things are sorrowful.' When one by wisdom realizes (this) he heeds not (is superior to) (this world of) sorrow; this is the path to purity.

Nagavaggo: The Elephant, verses 1–2 *In Buddhism the elephant symbolises strength and restraint, and it is a title given to the Buddha.*

1. I shall endure hard words even as the elephant in battle endures the arrow shot from the bow; the majority of people are, indeed, ill natured.
2. They lead a tamed elephant into battle; the king mounts a tamed elephant. The tamed is the best among men, he who endures patiently hard words.

Buddhavaggo: The Buddha, verse 1 *'The awakened' refers to any Buddha, not Gautama only.*

1. He whose conquest is not conquered again, into whose conquest no one in this world enters, by what track can you lead him, the awakened, of infinite perception, the trackless?

verses 4–5 *It will not be easy to follow the teachings of the Buddha.*

4. Difficult is it to obtain birth as a human being; difficult is the life of mortals, difficult is the hearing of the true law, difficult is the rise of buddhahood (or enlightenment).
5. The eschewing of all evil, the perfecting of good deeds, the purifying of one's mind, this is the teaching of the Buddhas (the awakened).

Science and Health

Christian Science Practice

It must be clear to you that sickness is no more the reality of being than is sin. This mortal dream of sickness, sin, and death should cease through Christian Science. Then one disease would be as readily destroyed as another. Truth is affirmative and confers harmony. All metaphysical logic is inspired by this simple rule of Truth . . . By the truthful arguments you employ, and especially by the spirit of Truth and Love which you entertain, you will heal the sick.

The Book of Mormon

Chapter 7

And now I, Moroni, write a few of the words of my father, Mormon, which he spake concerning faith, hope and charity, for after this manner did he speak unto the people, as he taught them in the synagogue which they had built for the place of worship.

And now I, Mormon, speak unto you, my beloved brethren: and it is by the grace of God the Father and Our Lord Jesus Christ and his holy will, because of the gift of his calling unto me, that I am permitted to speak unto you at this time.

Chapter 10

24. And now I speak unto all the ends of the earth—that if the day cometh that the power and gifts of God shall be done away among you it shall be because of unbelief . . .
26. And wo unto them who shall do these things away and die, for they die in their sins and they cannot be saved in the Kingdom of God; and I speak it according to the words of Christ; and I lie not. And I exhort you to remember these things for the time speedily cometh that ye shall know that I lie not for ye shall see me at the bar of God and the Lord God will say unto you: Did I not declare my words unto you which were written by this man, like as one crying from the dead, yea even as one speaking out of the dust?

The major religions and their distribution

THE FOLLOWING STATISTICS have been compiled from the most up-to-date information available when going to press.

Christianity	*995 million followers*
Roman Catholicism	*580 million followers*
Eastern Orthodox Churches	*75 million followers*
Protestantism	*340 million followers*
Islam	*600 million followers*
Hinduism	*480 million followers*
Buddhism	*255 million followers*
Confucianism	*155 million followers*
Shinto	*57 million followers*
Taoism	*31 million followers*
Judaism	*14.3 million followers*
Sikhism	*16 million followers*

The map on the following pages indicates the geographic distribution of the major world faiths. Areas of low density of population have been left blank, although this by no means implies that no religious life exists in such places. Similarly, in countries where one religious group predominates, no inference should be drawn that followers of other religions are few in number. Finally, countries where a religion is not recognized by the state have, nevertheless, been included, since there is evidence of religious practice continuing, despite official discouragement.

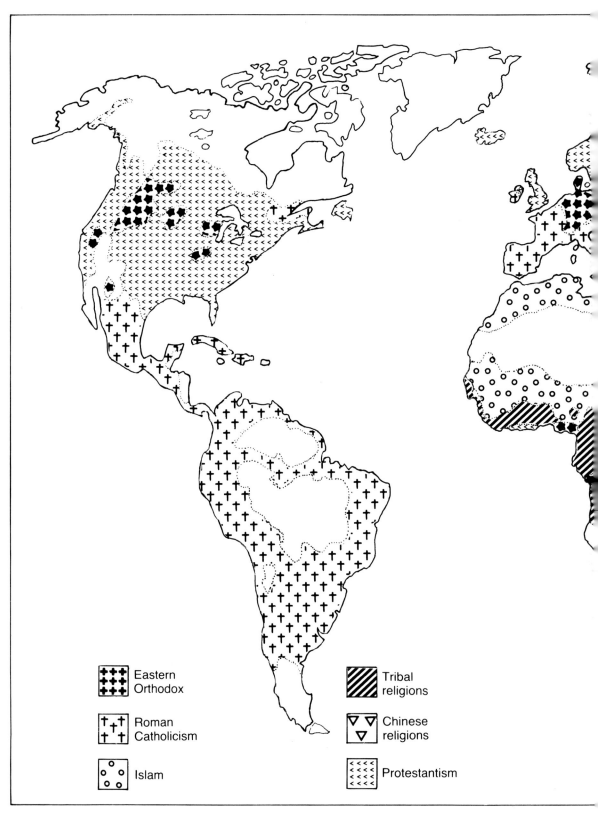

Eastern Orthodox

Roman Catholicism

Islam

Tribal religions

Chinese religions

Protestantism

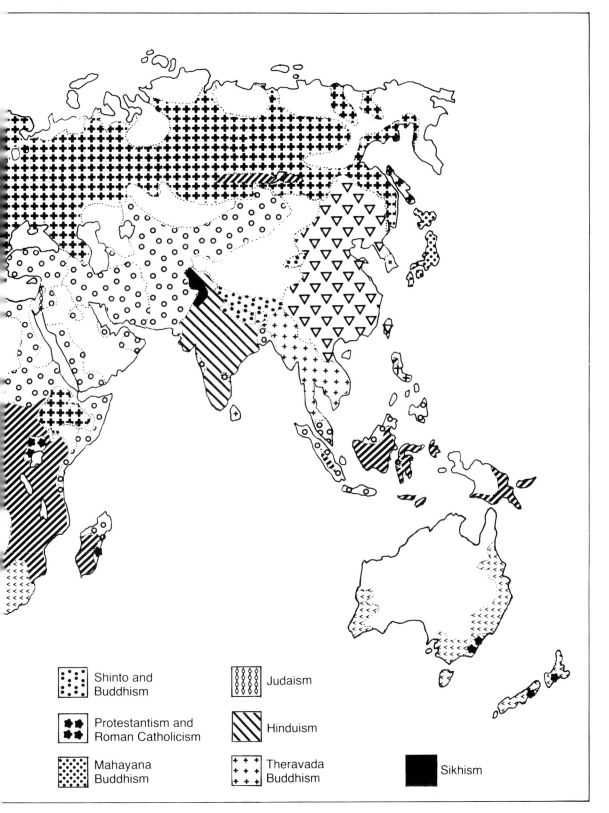

Shinto and Buddhism

Protestantism and Roman Catholicism

Mahayana Buddhism

Judaism

Hinduism

Theravada Buddhism

Sikhism

Bibliography

GENERAL

S. G. F. BRANDON: *A Dictionary of Contemporary Religion* Weidenfeld (London); Scribner's (New York) 1970

S. G. F. BRANDON: *Man and His Destiny in the Great Religions* Manchester University Press (Manchester) 1962

M. ELIADE *(ed.): From Primitives to Zen: A Thematic Sourcebook of the History of Religions* Collins (London) 1967; Harper and Row (New York) 1978; Fount Books (London) 1978

J. R. HINNELLS *(ed.): A Handbook of Living Religions* Penguin (Harmondsworth; New York) 1984

T. LING: *A History of Religion East and West* Macmillan (London; New York) 1968

R. OTTO: *The idea of the Holy* Oxford University Press 1950

N. SMART: *The Religious Experience of Mankind* Scribner's (New York) 1969; Collins (London) 1971

H. SMITH: *The Religions of Man* Harper and Row (New York) 1965

D. SOPHER *and* I. RAGI AL FARUQI *(eds.): A Historical Atlas of the Religions of the World* Collier Macmillan (London); Macmillan (New York) 1974

R. C. ZAEHNER: *A Concise Encyclopedia of Living Faiths* Hawthorn Books (New York) 1959

R. C. ZAEHNER: *Mysticism, Sacred and Profound* Oxford University Press 1957

BUDDHISM

D. R. BHANDARKAR: *Aśoka* University of Calcutta (Calcutta) 1969

BUDDHAGHOSA: *Path of Purification (tr.* by Nanamoli) Semage (Colombo) 1964; 2 vols., Shambhala (Berkeley, Calif.) 1976

E. CONZE: *Buddhist Scriptures* Penguin Books (Harmondsworth; Baltimore, Md.) 1979

E. CONZE: *A Short History of Buddhism* Allen and Unwin (London) 1979

F. FREMANTLE *and* C. TRINGPA *(trs.): The Tibetan Book of the Dead: The Great Liberation through Hearing in the Bardo* Shambhala (Berkeley, Calif.; London) 1975

H. V. GUENTHER: *Philosophy and Psychology in the Abidharma* Shambhala (Berkeley, Calif.) 1976; Motilal Banarsidass (Delhi) 1974

C. HUMPHREYS: *Exploring Buddhism* Allen and Unwin (London) 1974

K. N. JAYATILLEKE: *The Message of Buddha* Allen and Unwin (London); Free Press (New York) 1975

T. LING: *The Buddha: Buddhist Civilisation in India and Ceylon* M. T. Smith (London); Scribner's (New York) 1973

T. R. V. MURTI: *The Central Philosophy of Buddhism* Allen and Unwin (London) 1980

M. PYE: *Skilful Means: A Concept in Mahayana Buddhism* Duckworth (London) 1978

S. RADHAKRISHNAN: *The Dhammapada* Oxford University Press (London) 1950; (Bombay) 1969

M. E. SPIRO: *Buddhism and Society* Allen and Unwin (London) 1971; Harper and Row (New York) copyr. 1970

E. J. THOMAS: *The Life of the Buddha: As Legend and History* Routledge (London) 1975

G. TUCCI: *The Religions of Tibet* Routledge (London); University of California (Berkeley, Calif.) 1980

CHINESE WORSHIP

J. BREDON *and* I. MITROPHANOW: *The Moon Year: A Record of Chinese Customs and Festivals* Ch'eng Wen (Taipei); Chinese Materials Center (San Francisco, Calif.) 1972

W. T. CHAN *(tr.)* HUI NENG: *The Platform Scripture* St. John's University Press (New York) 1963

K. CH'EN: *Buddhism in China* Princeton University Press (Princeton, N.J.) 1974

A. CHRISTIE: *Chinese Mythology* Hamlyn (London; New York) 1968

H. G. CREEL: *Chinese Thought from Confucius to Mao Tsê Tung* University of Chicago Press (Chicago, Ill.) 1953; Methuen (London) 1962

R. DAWSON: *Imperial China* Hutchinson (London) 1972

W. EBERHARD: *A History of China* Routledge (London); University of California Press (Berkeley, Calif.) 1977

M. GRANET: *The Religion of the Chinese People* Blackwell (Oxford); Harper and Row (New York) 1975

D. C. LAU *(tr)* LAO TZU: *Tao Te Ching* Penguin Books (Harmondsworth; Baltimore Md.)

J. RAWSON: *Ancient China* Book Club Associates (London); British Museum (London); Harper and Row (New York) 1980

D. H. SMITH: *Chinese Religions* Weidenfeld (London); Holt, Rinehart (New York) 1968

A. WALEY *(tr.)* CONFUCIUS: *The Analects* Allen and Unwin (London) 1938; Random House (New York) 1966

H. WELCH: *Taoism: The Parting of the Way* Beacon Press (Boston, Mass.) 1966; Methuen (London) 1958

CHRISTIANITY

S. E. AHLSTROM: *A Religious History of the American People* Yale University Press (New Haven, Conn.; London) 1972; 2 vols., Doubleday (Garden City, N.Y.) 1975

T. J. ALTIZER *and* W. HAMILTON: *Radical Theology and the Death of God* Penguin Books (Harmondsworth) 1968

A. S. ATIYA: *A History of Eastern Christianity* University of Notre Dame Press (Notre Dame, Ind.) 1968; Methuen (London) 1968; Kraus (New York) 1980

D. ATTWATER: *The Penguin Dictionary of Saints* Penguin Books (Harmondsworth; Baltimore, Md.) repr. 1979

R. H. BAINTON: *The Horizon History of Christianity* American Heritage 1964; pubd. in Britain as *The Penguin History of Christianity* 2 vols. (Harmondsworth) 1967

W. O. CHADWICK: *From Bossuet to Newman* Cambridge Press (Cambridge) 1957

L. W. COWIE *and* J. SELWYN GUMMER: *The Christian Calendar* Weidenfeld and Nicolson (London) 1974

F. L. CROSS *and* E. A. LIVINGSTONE *(eds.):* The Oxford Dictionary of the Christian Church* Oxford University Press (London; New York) 1974

C. H. DODD: *The Founder of Christianity* Macmillan (New York) 1970; Collins (London) 1971

H. C. GRAEF: *Mary: A History of Doctrine and Devotion* 2 vols., Sheed and Ward (New York; London) 1963–65

R. T. HANDY: *A History of the Churches in the United States and Canada* Clarendon Press (Oxford; New York) 1979

J. HICK: *The Existence of God* Macmillan (New York); Collier-Macmillan (London) 1964

H. KAMEN: *The Rise of Toleration* Weidenfeld (London); McGraw-Hill (New York) 1967

H. KÜNG: *Does God Exist? An Answer for Today* Collins (London); Doubleday (Garden City, N.Y.) 1980

J. T. MCNEILL: *The Celtic Churches: A History, A.D. 200 to 1200* University of Chicago Press (Chicago, Ill.) 1974

J. MEYENDORFF: *Byzantine Theology* Fordham University Press (New York) 1974; Mowbray (London) 1975

B. MITCHELL: *The Justification of Religious Belief* Macmillan (London; New York) 1973

C. F. D. MOULE: *The Holy Spirit* Mowbray (London) 1978; Eerdmans (Grand Rapids, Mich.) 1979

C. H. ROBERTS: *Manuscript, Society and Belief in Early Christian Egypt* Oxford University Press (London; New York) 1979

D. E. ROBERTS: *Existentialism and Religious Belief* Oxford University Press (New York) 1957

A. SCHMEMANN: *The Historical Road of Eastern Orthodoxy* Harvill Press (London); Holt, Rinehart (New York) 1963

K. THOMAS: *Religion and the Decline of Magic* Penguin Books (Harmondsworth) 1973; Scribner's (New York) 1971

G. VERNES *(ed. and tr.):* The Dead Sea Scrolls in English* Penguin Books (Harmondsworth; Baltimore, Md.) 1970

M. WARNER: *Alone of All Her Sex: The Myth and the Cult of the Virgin Mary* Weidenfeld (London) 1976

HINDUISM

A. L. BASHAM: *The Wonder that was India* Sidgwick (London) 1967; Taplinger (New York) 1968; Fontana (London) 1971

S. M. BHARDWAJ: *Hindu Places of Pilgrimage in India* University of California Press (Berkeley, Calif.) 1973

A. DANIÉLOU: *Hindu Polytheism* Routledge (London); Princeton University Press (Princeton, N.J.) 1964

S. N. DASGUPTA: *A History of Indian Philosophy* 5 vols. Cambridge University Press (Cambridge) 1955; Motilal Banarsidass (Delhi) 1975; Orient Book Distributors (Livingston, N.J.); Humanities (Atlantic Highlands, N.J.)

J. DOWSON: *A Classical Dictionary of Hindu Mythology and Religion, Geography, History and Literature* Routledge (London) 1968

E. FRAUWALLNER: *History of Indian Philosophy* 2 vols., Motilal Banarsidass (Delhi); Orient Book Distributors (Livingston, N.J.) 1973; Humanities (New York) 1974

D. D. KOSAMBI: *The Culture and Civilization of Ancient India* Routledge (London) 1965; Vikas (Delhi) 1975

R. LANNOY: *The Speaking Tree: A Study of Indian Culture and Society* Oxford University Press (London; New York) 1974; (Bombay) 1968

G. J. LARSON: *Classical Samkhya* Motilal Banarsidass (Delhi) 1969

T. O. LING: *A History of Religion East and West* Macmillan (London) 1969; St Martin's (New York) 1968

W. D. O'FLAHERTY: *Asceticism and Eroticism in the Mythology of Śiva* Oxford University Press (London; New York) 1973

SIR S. RADHAKRISHNAN *(trs)* BADARAYANA: *The Brahma Sutra* Allen and Unwin (London) 1960

L. RENOU *(ed.):* Hinduism* Braziller (London; New York) 1963; Taraporevala (Bombay) 1969

R. C. ZAEHNER: *The Bhagavad-Gita* Clarendon Press (Oxford) 1969; Oxford University Press (New York) 1973

R. C. ZAEHNER: *Hinduism* Oxford University Press (London; New York) 1966

INDIGENOUS RELIGIONS

L. E. BARRETT: *The Rastafarians: The Dreadlocks of Jamaica* Heinemann (London) 1977

E. BEST: *Maori Religion and Mythology* Government Printer (Wellington); AMS (New York) 1976

M. DEREN: *Divine Horsemen: The Voodoo Gods of Haiti* Thames and Hudson (London) 1953

M. ELIADE: *Australian Religions: An Introduction* Cornell University Press (Ithaca, N.Y.; London) 1973

M. ELIADE: *Shamanism* Pantheon (New York); Routledge/Princeton University Press (London) 1965

C. GEERTZ: *The Religion of Java* Free Press (Glencoe, Ill.) 1960; University of Chicago (Chicago, Ill.) 1976

W. HERBERT: *The Eskimos* Collins (London) 1978; Franklin Watt (New York) 1978

W. HOWELLS: *The Heathens: Primitive Man and his Religions* Doubleday (New York) 1962

A. HULTKRANTZ: *The Religions of the American Indians* University of California Press (Berkeley, Calif.) 1979

E. B. IDOWN: *African Traditional Religion* SCM (London) 1973

B. MALINOWSKI: *Argonauts of the Western Pacific* Routledge (London) 1978; Dutton (New York) 1961

B. MALINOWSKI: *Magic, Science and Religion* Doubleday (New York) 1955

J. S. MBITI: *African Religion and Philosophy* Heinemann (London) 1969

J. S. MBITI: *Concepts of God in Africa* SPCK (London) 1975; Praeger (New York) 1970

A. METRAUX: *Voodoo in Haiti* Deutsch (London) 1958; Schocken (New York) 1972

V. S. NAIPAUL: *The Middle Passage* Deutsch (London) 1962

R. POIGNANT: *Oceanic Mythology: The Myths of Polynesia, Micronesia, Melanesia, Australia* Hamlyn (London) 1967

E. G. PARRINDER: *African Traditional Religion* Sheldon Press (London) 1974

G. E. SIMPSON: *Black Religions in the New World* Columbia University Press (New York) 1978

J. V. TAYLOR: *The Primal Vision* SCM (London) 1963

R. W. WILLIAMSON: *Religion and Social Organization in Central Polynesia* Cambridge University Press (Cambridge) 1937; AMS (New York) 1977

ISLAM

A. J. ARBERRY: *Sufism* Allen and Unwin (London) 1950

A. J. ARBERRY: *The Koran Interpreted* Allen and Unwin (London); Macmillan (New York) 1955

N. A. DANIEL: *Islam and the West: The Making of an Image* Edinburgh University Press (Edinburgh) 1960

H. GÄTJE: *The Qur'an and Its Exegesis: Selected Texts with Classical and Modern Muslim Interpretations (tr. and ed. by A. T. Welch)* Routledge (London); University of California Press (Berkeley, Calif.) 1976

SIR HAMILTON A. R. GIBB: *Modern Trends in Islam* University of Chicago Press (Chicago Ill.) 1947; Octagon (New York) 1971

A. GUILLAUME: *Islam* Penguin Books (Harmondsworth; New York) 1956

P. K. HITTI: *A Short History of the Arabs* Princeton University Press (Princeton) 1943

M. PERKINS *and* P. HAINSWORTH: *The Baha'i Faith* Ward Lock Educational (London) 1980

F. RAHMAN: *Islam* Weidenfeld and Nicolson (London) 1966

M. RODISON: *Mohammed* Allen Lane (London) 1971; Pantheon (New York) 1980

J. S. TRIMINGHAM: *The Influence of Islam upon Africa* 2nd edn. Longman (London); Librairie du Liban (Beirut) 1980

W. MONTGOMERY WATT: *Muhammad, Prophet and Statesman* Oxford University Press (Oxford) 1961

J. A. WILLIAMS: *Themes of Islamic Civilization* University of California Press (Berkeley, Calif.; London) 1965

JAINISM

P. S. JAINI: *The Jaina Path of Purification* University of California Press (Berkeley, Calif.) 1979

T. LING: *Jainism* in *The Encyclopedia of Ancient Civilizations (ed. A. Cotterell)* (New York) 1980

JAPANESE WORSHIP

M. ANESAKI: *A History of Japanese Religion* Routledge (London) 1963

M. ANESAKI: *Nichiren, the Buddhist Prophet* Harvard University Press (Cambridge, Mass.); Oxford University Press (London) 1916

A. BLOOM: *Shinran's Gospel of Pure Peace* University of Arizona Press (Tucson, Ariz.) 1965

W. K. BUNCE *(ed.)*: *Religions in Japan: Buddhism, Shinto, Christianity* Tuttle (Rutland, Vt.; Tokyo) 1959; Greenwood (London) 1978

H. B. EARHART: *Japanese Religion: Unity and Diversity* Dickenson (Encino, Calif.) 1974

SIR C. ELIOT: *Japanese Buddhism* Routledge (London); Barnes and Noble (New York) 1959

J. HERBERT: *Shinto: At the Fountainhead of Japan* Stein and Day (New York); Allen and Unwin (London) 1967

I. HORI: *Folk Religion in Japan: Continuity and Change* University of Chicago Press; University of Tokyo Press 1968

J. M. KITAGAWA: *Religion in Japanese History* Columbia University Press (New York) 1966

M. PYE: *Zen and Modern Japanese Religions* Ward Lock Educational (London) 1977

H. VAN STRAELEN: *The Religion of Divine Wisdom; Japan's Most Powerful Religious Movement* Veritas Shoin (Kyoto) 1957

D. T. SUZUKI: *Zen Buddhism* Doubleday (New York) 1956

JUDAISM

W. F. ALBRIGHT: *From the Stone Age to Christianity* Johns Hopkins Press (Baltimore, Md.) 1957

S. W. BARON: *A Social and Religious History of the Jews* Columbia University Press (New York; London) 1952–76

H. DANBY *(tr.): The Mishnah* Oxford University Press (London) 1954

D. L. EDWARDS: *A Key to the Old Testament* Oxford University Press (Oxford) 1967

I. EPSTEIN: *Judaism* Penguin Books (Harmondsworth; New York) 1959

J. GUTTMAN: *Philosophies of Judaism: The History of Jewish Philosophy from Biblical Times to Franz Rosenzweig* Routledge (London); Holt, Rinehart (New York) 1964

L. JACOBS: *A Jewish Theology* Darton (London); Behrman (New York) 1973

M. MARGOLIS *and* A. MARX: *A History of the Jewish People* Harper Torchbooks (New York) 1965

C. ROTH: *A Short History of the Jewish People* East and West Library (London) 1969; Hartmore (Hartford, Conn.) 1970

D. S. RUSSELL: *The Jews from Alexander to Herod* Oxford University Press (Oxford) 1967

A. UNTERMAN: *Jews: Their Religious Beliefs and Practices* Routledge (London; Boston, Mass.) 1981

H. J. ZIMMELS: *Askenazim and Sephardim* Oxford University Press (London) 1958

SIKHISM

W. O. COLE *and* PIARA SINGH SAMBHI: *The Sikhs: Their Religious Beliefs and Practices* Routledge (London; Boston, Mass.) 1978

HARBANS SINGH: *Guru Nanak and Origins of the Sikh Faith* Asia Publishing House (Bombay; New York) 1969

KHUSHWANT SINGH: *A History of the Sikhs* Princeton University Press (Princeton, N.J.); Oxford University Press (London) 1963–66 Oxford University Press (Bombay) 1967

W. H. MCLEOD: *Guru Nanak and the Sikh Religion* Clarendon Press (Oxford) 1968; Oxford University Press 1968

ZOROASTRIANISM

M. BOYCE: *Zoroastrians: Their Religious Beliefs and Practices* Routledge (London; Boston, Mass) 1979

J. DUCHESNE-GUILLEMIN: *The Hymns of Zarathustra* Murray (London) 1952

W. B. HENNING: *Zoroaster: Politician or Witchdoctor?* Oxford University Press (London) 1951

J. R. HINNELLS: *Zoroastrianism and the Parsis* Ward Lock Educational (London) 1981

R. C. ZAEHNER: *Zurvan: A Zoroastrian Dilemma* Clarendon Press (Oxford) 1955; Biblo (New York) 1973

R. C. ZAEHNER: *The Dawn and Twilight of Zoroastrianiam* Weidenfeld (London) 1975; Putnam (New York) 1961

PHILOSOPHY AND POLITICAL PHILOSOPHY

SAINT THOMAS AQUINAS: *Basic Writings (ed. A.C.Pegis)* 3 vols. Burns and Oates (London)

ARISTOTLE: *Nichomachaean Ethics* Penguin (Harmondsworth) 1959

ARISTOTLE: *Physics* 2 vols. Heinemann (London) 1960

ARISTOTLE: *Metaphysics* Dent (London) 1961

SAINT AUGUSTINE: *City of God* Oxford University Press (Oxford) 1963

SAINT AUGUSTINE: *Confessions* Penguin (Harmondsworth) 1961

A. J. AYER: *Language, Truth and Logic* Gollancz (London) 1946; Penguin Books (Harmondsworth) 1971

S. I. BENN *and* R. S. PETERS: *Social Principles and the Democratic State* Allen and Unwin (London) 1959

G. BERKELEY: *Three Dialogues between Hylas and Philonous* Collins (London) 1962

M. BLACK: *Critical Thinking* Prentice-Hall (London) 1952

H. J. BLACKHAM: *Six Existentialist Thinkers* Routledge (London) 1952

B. BLANSHARD: *The Nature of Thought* 2 vols. Allen and Unwin (London) 1939

I. CAMERON *and* D. EDGE: *Scientific Images and Their Social Uses: An Introduction to Scientism* Butterworth (London; Boston, Mass.) 1979

I. COPI: *An Introduction to Logic* Collier-Macmillan (London) 1961

R. DESCARTES: *A Discourse on Method* Dent (London) 1937

R. DESCARTES: *Meditations on Great Philosophers* Dent (London) 1953

R. HARE: *The Language of Morals* Oxford University Press (London) 1952

G. HEGEL: *The Philosophy of History* Dorer (London) 1956

T. HOBBES: *The Leviathan* Penguin (Harmondsworth) 1968

D. HUME: *Dialogues Concerning Natural Religion* Clarendon Press (Oxford) 1935; Bobbs-Merrill (Indianapolis Ind.) 1947

W. JAMES: *The Varieties of Religious Experience* Fontana (London) 1960

I. KANT: *A Critique of Practical Reason* Longmans (London) 1959

Bibliography

I. KANT: *A Critique of Pure Reason* Dent (London) 1934

I. KANT: *Prolegomena to any Future Metaphysics* Manchester University Press (Manchester) 1953

S. KIERKEGAARD: *Philosophical Fragments* Princeton University Press (Princeton, N.J.) 1962

S. KIERKEGAARD: *Training in Christianity* Oxford University Press (London) 1941

N. MACHIAVELLI: *The Prince* Penguin (Harmondsworth) 1961

K. MARX: *Capital* Penguin (Harmondsworth) 1978

K. MARX: *Selected Writings in Sociology and Social Philosophy* Penguin (Harmondsworth) 1970; McGraw-Hill (New York) 1963

J. S. MILL: *Essential Works* Bantam (New York) 1961

J. S. MILL: *Essay on Liberty* Oxford University Press (London) 1954

W. MONTAGUE: *The Ways of Knowing* Allen and Unwin (London) 1925

G. E. MOORE: *Philosophical Studies* Routledge (London) 1922

THOMAS MORE: *The Complete Works* Yale University Press (New Haven) 1976

F. NIETZCHE: *The Philosophy of Nietzche* New English Library (London) 1966

B. PASCAL: *Pensées* Penguin (Harmondsworth) 1966

PLATO: *The Republic* Penguin (Harmondsworth) 1966

K. POPPER: *The Open Society and Its Enemies* 2 vols. Routledge (London) 1962; Routledge/Princeton University Press 1966

J.-J. ROUSSEAU: *Social Contract* Dent (London) 1968

B. RUSSELL: *Human Society in Ethics and Politics* Allen and Unwin (London) 1954; Simon and Schuster (New York) 1955

B. RUSSELL: *A History of Western Philosophy* Allen and Unwin (London) 1939

B. RUSSELL: *The Problems of Philosophy* Oxford University Press (London) 1967

G. RYLE: *The Concept of Mind* Hutchinson (London) 1967

G. SABINE: *A History of Political Thought* Harrap (London) 1963

J.-P. SARTRE: *Being and Nothingness* Methuen (London) 1957

J.-P. SARTRE: *Existentialism and Humanism* Methuen (London) 1948

B. F. SKINNER: *Beyond Freedom and Dignity* Penguin (Harmondsworth) 1973; Knopf (New York) 1971; Bantam (New York) 1972

B. SPINOZA: *Ethics* Dent (London) 1959

F. VOLTAIRE: *Candide* Penguin (London) 1968

M. WARNOCK: *Ethics since 1900* Oxford University Press (London) 1966